# THE GUODIAN *LAOZI*

*Proceedings of the International Conference, Dartmouth College, May 1998*

EARLY CHINA SPECIAL MONOGRAPH SERIES NO. 5

# THE GUODIAN *LAOZI*

## *Proceedings of the International Conference, Dartmouth College, May 1998*

## Edited by Sarah Allan and Crispin Williams

THE SOCIETY FOR THE STUDY OF EARLY CHINA

AND

THE INSTITUTE OF EAST ASIAN STUDIES, UNIVERSITY OF CALIFORNIA, BERKELEY

2000

Display typeface is ITC Galliard; body is Adobe Minion. Designed and produced by
Multilingual Design 東版 , Seattle, Washington (hgoodman@nwlink.com).

Printed and bound in the United States of America.

Library of Congress Cataloging-in-Publication Data

International Conference on the Guodian Laozi (1998 : Dartmouth College)
    The Guodian Laozi : proceedings of the international conference, Dartmouth
College, May 1998 / edited by Sarah Allan and Crispin Williams.
        p. cm. — (Early China special monograph series ; no. 5)
    Includes bibliographical references and index.
    ISBN 1-55729-069-5 (alk. paper)
    1. Lao-tzu, Tao te ching—Congresses. 2. Manuscripts, Chinese—China—Ching-
men shih—Congresses. 3. Philosophy, Taoist—Congresses. I. Allan, Sarah. II. Williams,
Crispin. III. Lao-tzu, Tao te ching Selections. IV. Title. V. Series.

BL1900.L35 I58 1998
299′.51482—dc21                                                                00-021567

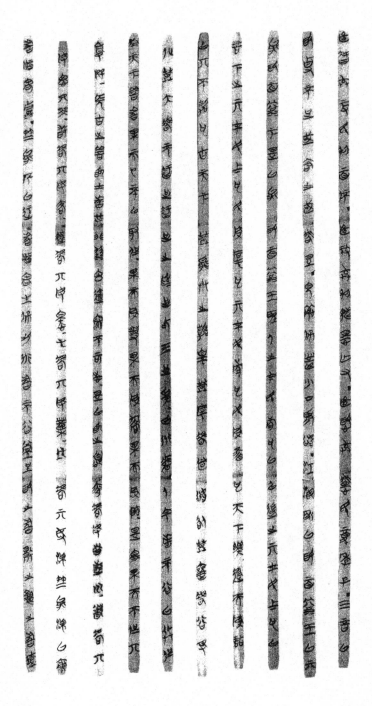

*Laozi* A, slips 1–10.
After *Guodian Chu Mu Zhujian* (Beijing, 1998). Courtesy of Wenwu Press.

Dedicated to Wing-tsit Chan (1901–1994)


Professor at Dartmouth College, 1942–1966

# THE GUODIAN *LAOZI*

## TABLE OF CONTENTS

PARTICIPANTS:   Sarah Allan, Roger Ames, William G. Boltz, Cai Min
蔡敏, Carine Defoort, Chen Guying 陳鼓應, Gao Ming 高明,
Donald Harper, Robert Henricks, Ikeda Tomohisa 池田知久, Marc
Kalinowski, Li Boqian 李伯謙, Li Jinyun 李縉纭, Li Ling 李零, Li
Xueqin 李學勤, Liu Zuxin 劉祖信, Andrew Meyer, Peng Hao 彭浩,
Qiu Xigui 裘錫圭, Isabelle Robinet, Harold Roth, Edmund Ryden,
Paul M. Thompson, Rudolf Wagner, Wang Bo 王博, Wang Tao 汪濤,
Susan R. Weld, Crispin Williams, Xing Wen 邢文, Xu Aixian 許愛仙,
Xu Kangsheng 許抗生, Xu Shaohua 徐少華, and Robin Yates

# THE GUODIAN *LAOZI*

## TABLE OF CONTENTS

PARTICIPANTS:    Sarah Allan, Roger Ames, William G. Boltz, Cai Min 蔡敏, Carine Defoort, Chen Guying 陳鼓應, Gao Ming 高明, Donald Harper, Robert Henricks, Ikeda Tomohisa 池田知久, Marc Kalinowski, Li Boqian 李伯謙, Li Jinyun 李縉紜, Li Ling 李零, Li Xueqin 李學勤, Liu Zuxin 劉祖信, Andrew Meyer, Peng Hao 彭浩, Qiu Xigui 裘錫圭, Isabelle Robinet, Harold Roth, Edmund Ryden, Paul M. Thompson, Rudolf Wagner, Wang Bo 王博, Wang Tao 汪濤, Susan R. Weld, Crispin Williams, Xing Wen 邢文, Xu Aixian 許愛仙, Xu Kangsheng 許抗生, Xu Shaohua 徐少華, and Robin Yates

# TABLE OF CONTENTS

# Introduction

## SARAH ALLAN

In October, 1993, a tomb of the Warring States period (475–221 BC) was excavated at Guodian — near Jingmen, Hubei province. Soon thereafter, rumors began circulating about the existence of a bamboo-slip version of the *Laozi* that was substantially different from the received text. In August, 1997, Robert Henricks and I attended the International Conference on Daoism in Beijing, where a brief report on the find was made. This report included the tantalizing information that bamboo slips with material corresponding to that in the *Laozi Daodejing* had, indeed, been discovered, and that the bamboo-slip material had substantial differences from the received text. Moreover, this was one of a number of philosophical texts found in this tomb that were being prepared for imminent publication by Wenwu Publishing House. Our interest thus piqued, we began planning the conference of which this volume is the proceedings.

The idea of the conference was to bring together some twenty to thirty scholars, both Chinese and Western, with different fields of expertise. We would simply read through the newly discovered *Laozi* together. Our aim was not to establish a definitive reading but to clarify the points of contention and thus establish a basis for future research. Classical Chinese texts that have been transmitted from this period come to us with about two thousand years of careful analysis, commentaries, and debate. Excavated texts, on the other hand, especially those written before the standardization of the script in the Qin dynasty, present numerous problems that no single individual can deal with adequately.

Several factors severely limited the number of scholars that we could invite, most importantly an early decision to conduct the conference as a small seminar in order to encourage free and intense discussion. We nevertheless tried to cover a number of different viewpoints and specializations. These included archeology, history, epigraphy, text criticism, Chinese philosophy, comparative philosophy, Daoism, excavated texts, the *Laozi*, and related Daoist works, especially the so-called "Huang-Lao" texts. About half the participants were Chinese; a quarter came from the U.S., the others from Japan, Canada, Great Britain, France, Germany, and Belgium. Since the subject was a Chinese text and Chinese was the common language of the group, we decided to conduct the discussion in Chinese. We did not offer systematic translation, but called upon several younger scholars with good language skills to assist in translating, when that became necessary.

The participants included:

Sarah Allan (Dept. of Asian and Middle Eastern Languages and Literatures, Dartmouth College)

Roger Ames (Dept. of Philosophy, Univ. of Hawaii)

William G. Boltz (Dept. of Asian Studies, University of Washington, Seattle)

Cai Min 蔡敏 (Wenwu Publishing House, Beijing)

Chen Guying 陳鼓應 (Dept. of Philosophy, Taiwan University)

Carine Defoort (Dept. Orientalistiek, Katholiek Universiteit, Leuven)

Gao Ming 高明 (Dept. of Archaeology, Beijing University)

Donald Harper (Dept. of East Asian Languages, University of Chicago)

Robert Henricks (Dept. of Religion, Dartmouth College)

Ikeda Tomohisa 池田知久 (Dept. of Chinese Philosophy, Tokyo University)

Marc Kalinowski (Sect. Sciences Religieuses, École Pratique des Hautes Études, Sorbonne)

Li Boqian 李伯謙 (Dept. of Archaeology, Beijing University)

Li Jinyun 李縉紜 (Wenwu Publishing House)

Li Ling 李零 (Dept. of Chinese, Beijing University)

Li Xueqin 李學勤 (Institute of History, Chinese Academy of Social Sciences)

Liu Zuxin 劉祖信 (Jingmen City Museum, Hubei Province)

Andrew Meyer (East Asian Languages and Literatures, Harvard University)

Peng Hao 彭浩 (Jingzhou Museum, Hubei Province)

Qiu Xigui 裘錫圭 (Dept. of Chinese, Beijing University)

Isabelle Robinet (Dept. of Chinese Studies, Provence University)

Harold D. Roth (Dept. of Religious Studies, Brown University)

Edmund Ryden (John Paul II Peace Institute, Furen Catholic University, Taiwan)

Paul M. Thompson (Dept. of East Asian Studies, School of Oriental and African Studies, University of London)

Rudolf Wagner (Institute of Chinese Studies, Heidelberg University)

Wang Bo 王博 (Dept. of Philosophy, Beijing University)

Wang Tao 汪濤 (Dept. of Art and Archaeology, School of Oriental and African Studies, University of London)

Susan R. Weld (East Asian Legal Studies, Harvard University)

Crispin Williams (Dept. of East Asian Studies, School of Oriental and African Studies, University of London)

Xing Wen 邢文 (Dept. of Archaeology, Beijing University)

Xu Aixian 許愛仙 (Wenwu Publishing House)

Xu Kangsheng 許抗生 (Dept. of Philosophy, Beijing University)
Xu Shaohua 徐少華 (Dept. of History, Wuhan University)
Robin Yates (Centre for East Asian Studies, McGill University)

*Guodian Chu Mu Zhujian*[1] 郭店楚墓竹簡 was published as planned in the spring of 1998, and our conference was held May 22 to 26, 1998, at Dartmouth College. The texts, which more than lived up to our expectations, included three bamboo-slip texts with material corresponding to that now found in the *Laozi* but in a different order and containing many variations. One of these texts was originally bound together with previously unknown material, given the title *Tai Yi Sheng Shui* 太一生水 in the *Guodian Chu Mu Zhujian*. The latter isolated some sixteen other bamboo-slip texts. With the exception of the *Zi Yi* 緇衣 (transmitted as a chapter of the *Liji* 禮記 ) and the *Wu Xing* 五行 (found at Changsha Mawangdui), these texts were previously entirely unknown.

Our conference focused on the *Laozi* and *Tai Yi Sheng Shui*. The first day of the conference was devoted to background talks. Since the date of the tomb was an important issue, we first asked Li Boqian to discuss Chu archeology more generally and to place the Guodian tomb within this context. We next asked Liu Zuxin, who had participated in the excavation and post-excavation work, to discuss the circumstances of the excavation and the tomb itself. Peng Hao, who had also participated in the excavation and taken the major responsibility for the transcriptions and annotations published in *Guodian Chu Mu Zhujian*, described the post-excavation work and the problems encountered in preparing the publication. Qiu Xigui, who acted as reader for Wenwu Publishing House and contributed to the annotations, described his own role and some of the methods of analyzing the Chu script. Furthermore, since Chinese scholars are often unacquainted with the methods of Western text criticism, we asked William G. Boltz and Harold Roth to present papers on methodological issues as a background for the subsequent discussion.

After the background papers, we began reading the *Laozi* materials and *Tai Yi Sheng Shui*, section by section (according to the divisions in the Guodian slip-texts) in the order presented in *Guodian Chu Mu Zhujian*. A few people were assigned to do background research and lead the discussion for each section. We did not read all texts to the same level of detail, but Li Xueqin was also asked to summarize the textual materials as a whole within the context of the tomb; and we devoted one session to the *Wu Xing* text and one to a general discussion of all of the texts found within the tomb. Xu Aixian, Cai Min, and Li Jinyun concluded this part of the conference with a summary of the plans for future publication of excavated texts by Wenwu Publishing

---

[1] Jingmen Shi Bowuguan 荊門市博物館, *Guodian Chu Mu Zhujian* 郭店楚墓竹簡 (Beijing: Wenwu Press, 1998).

House and *Wenwu* journal.

Since our format had limited the number of attendees, the last day, which included a summing up and general discussion, was open to the general public. A number of other scholars in the region attended this session and a few of their comments are included in our summary of the discussion.

Revised versions of talks given by Li Boqian, Liu Zuxin, Peng Hao, William G. Boltz, Qiu Xigui, Harold Roth, and Li Xueqin are all published here in Section One. We have also included a paper by Gao Ming, who had been specially asked to present alternative epigraphic analyses to those published in *Guodian Chu Mu Zhujian*. During the discussion, Paul Thompson proposed a color-coded layout as part of a methodology for the formal treatment of the textual witnesses. A grey-scale version of his proposal for the section corresponding to chapter 66 in the received text, together with his explanatory notes, is included in Section One.

Section Two is a summary (by Sarah Allan and Crispin Williams) of the discussion that accompanied our reading, edited and arranged by topic rather than in chronological order. It is divided into three parts: (I) *The Tomb and Its Contents*. This section includes questions to the archeologists about the prior robbery of the tomb and the conservation and ordering of the slips as well as dating, the status of the occupant, etc. (II) *The Laozi*. This includes discussion of methodological issues in transcribing the text, the scribes, punctuation and division of the text, the sequence of material, etc., as well as discussion of philosophical questions, including themes and particular concepts, the philosophical stance of the slip-texts, etc. (III) *Other Texts and the Question of Philosophical Schools*. Here we include detailed discussion of the *Tai Yi Sheng Shui* and *Wu Xing*, as well as more general discussion of the other texts, the significance of the corpus as a whole, and the question of philosophical schools.

Section Three is a revised version of an edition of the Guodian bamboo-slip *Laozi* A, B, and C and *Tai Yi Sheng Shui* texts that Edmund Ryden prepared for use at the conference. All references to these texts herein use the format established by Ryden (text, slip number: character number) and are readily matched with the photographs in *Guodian Chu Mu Zhujian*. Suggested readings of individual characters given during the course of the conference, as well as those in *Guodian Chu Mu Zhujian*, have been keyed into his apparatus. Philological issues are also included in his notes, rather than in the summary of the discussion in Section Three.

Section Four includes material gathered after the conference. All of the participants have had the opportunity to read a draft of our account of the discussion (Section Two) and to correct or clarify their own statements where they felt that they had not been properly understood, or had not expressed themselves with sufficient clarity in Chinese, and we have incorporated these comments in Section Two. However, ideas not presented at the conference and revised opinions, including additions to Edmund

Ryden's edition of the texts, are placed in Section Four, under "Additional Textual Notes and Afterthoughts." These include a rethinking by Qiu Xigui of his analysis of two characters presented in his paper in Section One. Section Four also includes a review article by Xing Wen of the Chinese publications in the year following the conference with a bibliography.

At the Dartmouth conference, each participant had a preliminary version of the edition by Edmund Ryden that we are publishing here (Section Three), a copy of *Guodian Chu Mu Zhujian*, and a comparative edition of the Guodian *Laozi* material and the Mawangdui silk manuscript prepared by Robert Henricks.[2] In order to follow the papers and discussion with greater ease, we suggest that readers first turn to Section Three and acquaint themselves briefly with the text and the format of Ryden's edition (see especially the *sigla*, p. 192), before reading the individual papers and discussion in the previous sections.

This volume is a presentation of academic process rather than of mature research. It is "proceedings," the record of an actual discussion by some thirty people with different viewpoints and backgrounds and scholarly conventions. Thus, although we have done some editing, and added some material and translations where necessary to follow the discussion — and the participants have sometimes edited their own comments and added translations, we have not translated Chinese terms and passages where we did not feel it was essential and might falsely project an unintended sense upon the speaker. For similar reasons, we have not provided detailed textual references to particular editions in many cases.

There are no simple answers to the problems presented by the Guodian bamboo-slip texts. As the reader will discover, we ended up with as many different viewpoints as scholarly participants. Even the fundamental issue of what this material is and how it relates to the transmitted editions of the *Laozi Daodejing* cannot be easily decided. Just as our purpose in this conference was not to come to conclusions about the newly discovered texts — clearly, this will take years, probably generations — but to clarify points of controversy and learn other methodologies, in presenting our materials for publication, we have concentrated as much on the questions raised as the answers given. Many of the answers are, in any case, preliminary conjectures, but they should alert others to possibilities and to possible problems for future research.

Readers may wonder why we chose to devote our attention to the *Laozi* material and *Tai Yi Sheng Shui* rather than to the other texts found in Guodian Tomb Number One. As mentioned, above, the excitement of the possibility of a new version of the *Laozi* inspired us to begin planning with those texts in mind. Since the other texts

---

[2] Robert G. Henricks, "Lao Tzu's *Tao Te Ching*: A Translation of the Startling New Documents Found at Guodian" (New York: Columbia University Press), forthcoming.

were previously unknown, it was only after publication that their importance could be understood. Some of them are of startling significance, seminal texts of the Confucian school that were entirely unknown before the discovery of this tomb. These texts are no less worthy of study than the *Laozi* material, perhaps even more so, and we expect that this first conference will lead to further cooperative conferences in which the other materials can be considered in more detail.

We are grateful to Dartmouth College for the immediate support that allowed us to proceed with our plans and to the Henry Luce Foundation for funding that allowed us to plan a more extensive project for the study of excavated manuscripts. We were also very fortunate in achieving cooperation from Wenwu Publishing House, who set a definite date for publication so that we could plan to meet soon after the release of the text.

We would also like to express our thanks to the many people who have helped us in compiling these *Proceedings*. We would especially like to thank Xing Wen, who is preparing a Chinese version of this book for publication, and has contributed substantially to this one, with numerous corrections and suggestions, as well as providing the brush-written Chu-form characters used herein. We also owe a great deal to Howard Goodman of Multilingual Design, in Seattle, for his advice in the editing process and for his creative contribution to various typesetting problems. We are grateful to Ikeda Tomohisa for providing a bibliography of research on the Guodian texts. Unfortunately, we have not been able to use this in full, but it served as a basis for the bibliography to Xing Wen's review of Chinese scholarship. Janice Foong Kam compiled the index to this work. We would also like to thank Susan Blader for reading proofs, and for helping us during the conference on which this volume is based.

Finally, we would like to express particular thanks to the Chinese archeologists, especially the local archeologists from the Jingzhou and Jingmen City Museums, upon whose careful work during and after the excavation all subsequent scholarly work depends. We would also like to acknowledge the fine work of the editors and readers of *Guodian Chu Mu Zhujian* and to express our gratitude to Wenwu Publishing House for their exemplary publication.

*Sarah Allan*
*Dartmouth College, June 1, 1999*

# SECTION ONE:

# BACKGROUND PAPERS

# A Brief Account of the Origins
# and Development of Chu Culture

## LI BOQIAN

### THE ORIGINS OF CHU CULTURE

Chu was both an ancient state and a clan. The genealogy of the Chu ancestors is recorded in detail in pre-Qin texts and in the "Chu Shijia 楚世家" section of the Shiji 史記. These texts all agree that the Chu were direct descendants of Jilian 季連, who was himself a descendant of Zhuan Xu 顓項, one of the five mythical emperors. Later scholars have had different theories concerning the origins of the Chu: that they originally came from the Central Plains region; that they came from the east; and even that they migrated to the Yangzi River Valley from somewhere beyond the western regions.

Archeological evidence for the origins of the Chu may be found in the early-Zhou oracle bones excavated at Zhouyuan 周原, Shaanxi. These include an inscription that refers to a Chu prince's coming to report the death of his father.[1] So, at least as early as the start of the Western Zhou period (ca. 1050–771 BC), the Chu tribe were in contact with the Western Zhou court. However, archeologists have not, as yet, been able to distinguish Chu cultural remains from the early Western Zhou period on the basis of material evidence.

The earliest material remains that scholars generally recognize as belonging to the Chu cultural complex are from the middle of the Western Zhou period. These consist mainly of sandy red-brown pottery li 鬲 vessels that have tapered legs, a mouth that is smaller than the body, and the cord marks polished smooth at the neck. Sites where these have been found include Shangzhou 商州, Shaanxi;[2] Dangyang Mopanshan 當陽磨盤山, Hubei;[3] and Lixian Wenjiashan 澧縣文家山, Hunan.[4] Analysis

---

[1] See Chen Quanfang 陳全方, Zhou Yuan yu Zhou Wenhua 周原與周文化 (Shanghai: Shanghai Renmin Press, 1988), section two, p. 71, number 4.

[2] See Yang Yachang 楊亞長, Wang Changfu 王昌富, "Shangzhou Donglongshan Yizhi Kaogu Huo Zhongyao Chengguo 商州東龍山遺址考古獲重要成果," Zhongguo Wenwu Bao, November 25, 1998.

[3] Yichang Diqu Bowuguan 宜昌地區博物館, "Dangyang Mopanshan Xi Zhou Yizhi Shijue Jianbao 當陽磨盤山西周遺址試掘簡報," Jiang Han Kaogu 1984.2.

[4] Hunansheng Wenwu Kaogu Yanjiusuo 湖南省文物考古研究所 (He Jiejun 何介鈞, et al.), "Hunan Lixian Shang Zhou Shiqi Gu Yizhi Diaocha yu Tanjue 湖南澧縣商周時期古遺址調查與探掘," Hunan

of their forms indicates that all such *li* vessels had evolved gradually from a Zhou-style *li*. By the Eastern Zhou, this had become one of the representative pottery types of Chu culture. Indeed, it may be possible to see the traces of the origin, formation, and spread of Chu culture during the middle Western Zhou from the distribution of this type of *li*.

## THE RISE AND FALL OF CHU CULTURE AS SEEN FROM THE MOVEMENT OF THE CAPITAL OF THE CHU STATE

According to textual records, Chu's first capital was Danyang 丹陽. At the beginning of the Spring and Autumn period (770–476 BC), the capital was moved to Ying 郢 (present-day Jiangling Ji'nancheng 江陵紀南城, Hubei), and, at the end of the Spring and Autumn period, to Ruo 鄀 (present-day Yichengxian 宜城縣, Hubei), after which it was returned to Ying. In 278 BC, the Qin general Baiqi 白起 seized Ying, and the Chu moved their capital to Chen 陳 (present-day Huaiyang 淮陽, Henan). In 253 BC the capital moved to Juyang 鉅陽 (Taihe 太和, Anhui); in 241 BC to Shouchun 壽春 (Shouxian 壽縣, Anhui); and, in 223 BC, Chu was destroyed by Qin. (See figure 1.)

Scholars have identified various places as the location of the first capital, Danyang. These include sites in present-day Zhijiang 枝江 and Zigui 秭歸, both in Hubei, and at the conflu-ence of the Dan 丹 and Xi 淅 Rivers (He-nan). Accord-ing to our anal-sis of the evi-dence, from the relation-ship between, on the one hand, Chu and the Zhou ro-yal court in the Western Zhou and, on the other, the

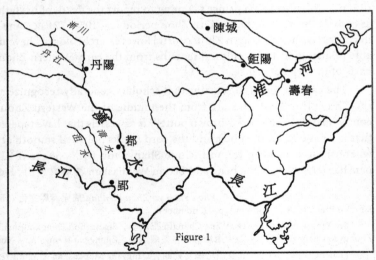

Figure 1

excavations of middle-period Spring and Autumn tombs of Chu nobility at Xichuan Xiasi 淅川下寺, Henan, the Dan-Xi confluence is the correct location.

*Kaogu Jikan* 4 (1987), pp. 1–10.

We can see from the movement of their capitals, that the Chu most likely arose in the region where the present-day borders of southeast Shaanxi, southwest Henan, and northwest Hubei meet. Once they moved into western Hubei and made Ying their capital, they flourished rapidly and conducted successful military expeditions to the north and east, greatly increasing the power of their state. After the middle Warring States period, under pressure from Qin, they were gradually driven eastward. Their power declined and, not long after, they were destroyed by Qin.

## CHARACTERISTICS OF CHU CULTURE

An overview of the course of the development of Chu culture suggests that, at its inception, it gradually emerged from and then separated from Zhou culture. Chu material culture only began to emerge distinctly during and after the middle of the Spring and Autumn. Since excavated habitation sites are relatively few, we will compare Chu tombs with contemporary tombs from the Central Plains and surrounding areas in order to provide a general description of Chu culture. Characteristics of Chu culture include the following four features.

*1) Construction of head and side compartments as part of the grave furniture*

In the tombs of the Central Plains region during the Eastern Zhou, we customarily find inner and outer coffins, but we do not find additional head and side compartments inside of the outer coffin. However, in tombs from the Chu state beginning in the middle of the Spring and Autumn, we customarily find compartments used to hold burial goods constructed on the inside of the outer coffin, at the head or sides of the inner coffin.

*2) Customary assemblages of grave goods*

The most popular set of pottery vessel types in Central Plains-area Eastern Zhou tombs in which the vessels imitate bronze forms are *ding* 鼎, *dou* 豆, and *hu* 壺. Later, the *he* 盒 replaced *dou* among the three. In Chu, however, the customary set was *ding, fu* 簠, and *hu*, for which later we see that *dui* 敦 supplanted *fu*. For tombs with bronze vessels, assemblages of *ding, gui* 簋, *dui, fou* 缶, *pan* 盤, and *yi* 匜 are relatively common.

*3) Characteristic artifacts*

The pottery vessel types that are most significant as indicators in identifying Chu tombs include: the narrow-mouthed *li*; the long-necked *guan* 罐, also referred to as a *hu*, and the high conical-legged *gui*. Among bronzes, the flat-bottomed *sheng ding* 牪鼎 is the most distinctive. Lacquer or wooden guardian creatures are also characteristic Chu burial objects. None of these artifacts is found in other early cultures (at best they are very infrequent).

*4) Lacquer ware, silk manuscripts and paintings, bamboo and wooden slips and tablets*

The above are frequently found in Chu tombs and are a major characteristic of

Chu burials. Their frequency may also be related to the advantageous conditions in this wet region contributing to their preservation.

## PERIODIZATION OF CHU CULTURE

The earliest Chu culture sites, as determined by the presence of pottery *li* vessels of the characteristic Chu type, are sites dating to the middle Western Zhou and found in such areas as southern Shaanxi and western Hubei. However, although the *li* is found, the associated assemblage of vessels from within its cultural layer cannot be clearly determined.

The particular features of Chu culture are best represented by tombs. The development of Chu culture can be divided into the following periods on the basis of the changes in the assemblages and the formal evolution of vessel types. These periods are summarized below:

### Period 1: Late Western Zhou

Only vessels made of pottery have been found in tombs from the late-Western Zhou period. The customary assemblage of vessels is *li*, *yu* 盂, and *guan*, sometimes with additional *dou*. The mortuary pottery is usually red-brown in color, the same as that found in the habitation remains. Examples include the pottery vessels excavated from the tombs ZM6, ZM13, and ZM18 at Dangyang Zhaojiahu 當陽趙家湖 .[5] (See figure 2a.) However, we know from the inscriptions on the Duke Ni of Chu 楚逆公 bells excavated from the tomb of Marquis Mu of Jin 晉穆侯 at Quwo Beizhao 曲沃北趙 , Shanxi,[6] that Chu was already powerful by late in the Western Zhou.

### Period 2: Early Spring and Autumn

For the early Spring and Autumn, some tombs have yielded bronze vessels and some only pottery vessels. The typical pottery vessel assemblage continued to be *li*, *yu*, and *guan*, sometimes with additional *dou*, yet we see slight changes in the vessel forms. The vessels from the ZHM6 tomb at Dangyang Zhaojiahu are one such example (see figure 2b). An example of a tomb with bronze vessels is ZHM2 at Dangyang Zhaojiahu, in which were placed bronze *ding* and *gui* vessels, as well as pottery vessels, including *ding* that imitate bronze forms and *li*, *dou*, *gui*, and *guan*. The shapes of the bronze *ding* and *gui* vessels are the same as those found in the Central Plains area of this period (see figure 2c).[7]

---

[5] Hubeisheng Yichang Diqu Bowuguan 湖北省宜昌地區博物館 , Beijing Daxue Kaoguxi 北京大學考古系 , *Dangyang Zhaojiahu Chu Mu* 當陽趙家湖楚墓 (Beijing: Wenwu Press, 1992), p. 200, fig. 157.

[6] Li Boqian 李伯謙 , "Cong Jin Hou Mudi Kan Xi Zhou Gong Mu Mudi Zhidu de Jige Wenti 從晉侯墓地看西周公墓墓地制度的幾個問題," *Kaogu* 1997.11.

[7] See note 5, *Dangyang Zhaojiahu Chu Mu*, p. 186, fig. 130; p. 175; p. 117.

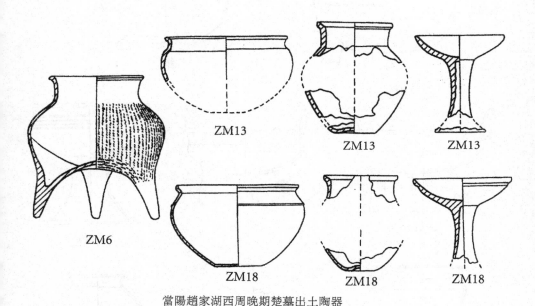

ZM13

ZM13

ZM13

ZM6

ZM18

ZM18

ZM18

當陽趙家湖西周晚期楚墓出土陶器

Figure 2a. Chu Culture: Period 1 (Pottery from late Western Zhou tombs at Dangyang Zhaojiahu).

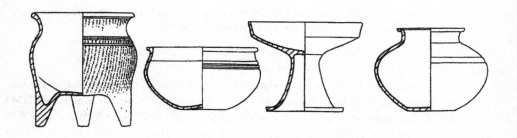

當陽趙家湖春秋早期楚墓 ZHM6 陶器

Figure 2b. Chu Culture: Period 2 (Pottery from an early Spring and Autumn
tomb at Dangyang Zhaojiahu).

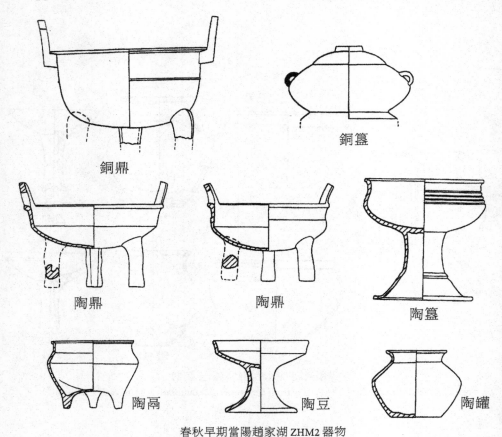

銅鼎

銅簋

陶鼎

陶鼎

陶簋

陶鬲

陶豆

陶罐

春秋早期當陽趙家湖 ZHM2 器物

Figure 2c.  Chu Culture: Period 2 (Bronzes and pottery from an early Spring and Autum
tomb at Dangyang Zhaojiahu).

*Period 3: Middle Spring and Autumn*

The bronze vessel sets and designs gradually developed their own characteristics,
distinguishing them from those of the Central Plains. Representative tombs are ZHM4
and ZHM8 at Dangyang Zhaojiahu and tombs M7, M8, and M36 at Xichuan Xiasi 淅川
下寺. ZHM4 and ZHM8 still had vessel sets centered around the *ding* and *gui*, whereas
the Xiasi tombs had sets that primarily featured such vessels as the *ding, gui, yu fou* 浴
缶, *pan*, and *yi*, in the manner that became popular in Chu tombs (see figure 3).[8]

---

[8] *Dangyang Zhaojiahu Chu Mu*, pp. 176–77, figs. 119, 120; Henansheng Wenwu Yanjiusuo 河南省
文物研究所 , et al., *Xichuan Xiasi Chunqiu Chu Mu* 淅川下寺春秋楚墓 (Beijing: Wenwu Press, 1991),
pp. 4–49.

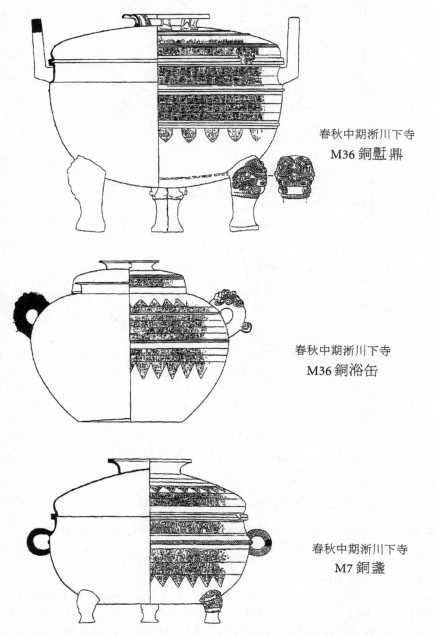

春秋中期淅川下寺
**M36 銅𧶛鼎**

春秋中期淅川下寺
**M36 銅浴缶**

春秋中期淅川下寺
**M7 銅盞**

Figure 3.  Chu Culture: Period 3 (Bronzes from middle Spring and Autumn tombs at Xichuan Xiasi).

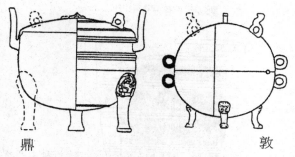

鼎　　　　　　　敦

春秋晚期當陽趙家湖 YM6 銅器

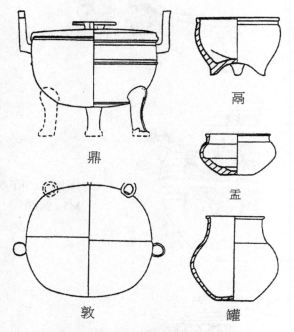

鼎　　　　　　　鬲

敦　　　　　　　孟

　　　　　　　　罐

春秋晚期當陽趙家湖 JM235 銅器陶器

Figure 4.　Chu Culture: Period 4 (Bronzes and pottery from late Spring and Autumn tombs at Dangyang Zhaojiahu).

## Period 4: Late Spring and Autumn

In this period, the particular characteristics of Chu culture are fully evident. Representative tombs are JM235 and YM6 at Dangyang Zhaojiahu (see figure 4), and M1, M2, M3, and M4 at Xiasi (see figure 5). The vessel sets in JM235 and YM6 at Dangyang Zhaojiahu are centered around *ding* and *dui*, while the Xiasi M1 to M4 sets are centered around such vessels as *ding, gui, yu fou, zun fou* 尊缶 , *pan, yi, zhan* 盞 , and *he* 盍 .[9]

*Period 5: Early Warring States*

A representative tomb with only pottery vessels is JM229 at Dangyang Zhaojiahu. The main burial goods in this tomb were ceremonial bronze-style pottery vessels, such as *ding, gui, dui, hu, yu fou,* and *pan* (see figure 6). Representative tombs with bronze vessels within the Chu cultural sphere for this period are the tomb of Zeng Hou Yi 曾侯乙 in Suixian 隨縣, Hubei,[10] and Tomb Number One at Changsha Liuchengqiao 長沙瀏城橋, Hunan.[11]

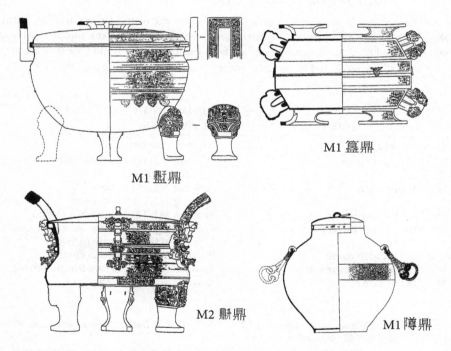

M1 盥鼎

M1 簋鼎

M2 䰞鼎

M1 障鼎

Figure 5. Chu Culture: Period 5 (Bronzes from late Spring and Autumn tombs from Xichuan Xiasi).

[9] *Dangyang Zhaojiahu Chu Mu*, p. 187, figs. 135, 136; *Xichuan Xiasi Chunqiu Chu Mu*, pp. 50–246.

[10] Hubeisheng Bowuguan 湖北省博物館, *Zeng Hou Yi Mu* 曾侯乙墓 (Beijing: Wenwu Press, 1989).

[11] Hubeisheng Bowuguan 湖北省博物館, "Changsha Liuchengqiao Yihao Mu 長沙瀏城橋一號墓," *Kaogu Xuebao* 1972.1, pp. 59–72.

*Period 6: Middle Warring States*

Representative tombs of this period include Tombs One and Two at Jiangling Wangshan 江陵望山, Hubei,[12] Tombs One and Two at Jiangling Baoshan 江陵包山,[13] Hubei, and the Chu tombs at Xinyang 信陽, Henan[14] (see figure 7).

*Period 7: Late Warring States*

A representative tomb is that of King You of Chu 楚幽王 at Shouxian Zhujiaji 壽縣朱家集, Anhui.[15]

## THE DATE AND STATE AFFILIATION OF GUODIAN TOMB NUMBER ONE JUDGING FROM THE EXCAVATED ARTIFACTS

The pottery, bronzes, lacquer ware, and jades excavated from Guodian Tomb Number One are all in styles frequently seen in Chu burials of the middle Warring States (Period 6).[16] Some examples of artifacts from Guodian Tomb One that are very similar to those excavated from Chu tombs include the following (see figure 8):

| Guodian Tomb Artifact | Similar Artifact from Period 6 Chu Tomb Site |
|---|---|
| (inventory number) | (inventory number) |
| M1(T1) pottery *ding* | Baoshan M1(12) round-bodied pottery *ding* with lid |
| M1(B4) pottery *he* | Baoshan M1(28) pottery *he* |
| | Xinyang M2(216) pottery *he* |
| M1(B26) lacquer box (*lian*) | Baoshan M1(17) lacquer box (*he*) |
| M1(B10) lacquer ear-cup | Baoshan M1(14) lacquer ear-cup |
| | Xinyang M1(531) lacquer ear-cup |
| M1(T22) wooden comb | Baoshan M1(15) wooden comb |
| M1(T24) square bronze mirror | Baoshan M2(432) square bronze mirror |
| M1(B28) bronze *pan* | Xinyang M1(739) bronze *pan* |

[12] Hubeisheng Wenwu Kaogu Yanjiusuo 湖北省文物考古研究所, *Jiangling Wangshan Shazhong Chu Mu* 江陵望山沙冢楚墓 (Beijing: Wenwu Press, 1996), pp. 5–162.

[13] Hubeisheng Jingsha Tielu Kaogudui 湖北省荊沙鐵路考古隊, *Baoshan Chu Mu* 包山楚墓 (Beijing: Wenwu Press, 1991), pp. 8–277.

[14] Henansheng Wenwu Yanjiusuo 河南省文物研究所, *Xinyang Chu Mu* 信陽楚墓 (Beijing: Wenwu Press, 1986).

[15] Anhuisheng Bowuguan Choubeichu 安徽省博物館籌備處, *Anhuisheng Bowuguan Suocang Chu Qi Tulu* 安徽省博物館所藏楚器圖錄 (1953); Liu Jie 劉節, *Chu Qi Tushi* 楚器圖釋 (Beijing: Beiping Tushuguan, 1935).

[16] Hubeisheng Jingmenshi Bowuguan 湖北省荊門市博物館, "Jingmen Guodian Yihao Chu Mu 荊門郭店一號楚墓," *Wenwu* 1997.7, pp. 35–48.

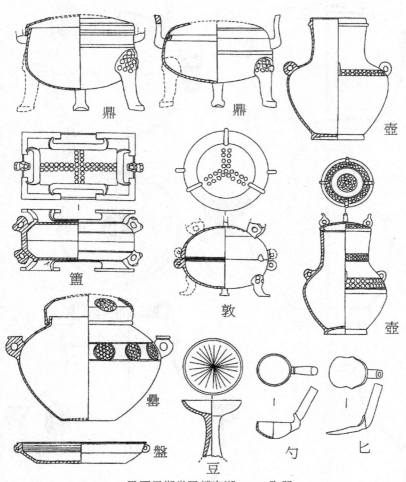

鼎　鼎　壺

簠　敦　壺

罍　盤　豆　勺　匕

戰國早期當陽趙家湖 JM229 陶器

Figure 6. Chu Culture: Period 5 (Pottery from an early Warring States tomb from Dangyang Zhaojiahu).

The style in which the characters are written on the bamboo slips is also found on other bamboo slips excavated from middle Warring States Chu tombs. Moreover, the tomb is close to the remains of Ying, the capital of the state of Chu in the Spring and Autumn and middle Warring States periods, and among other tombs considered to be those of Chu nobles. Thus, we can conclude with assurance that Guodian Tomb Number One is a Chu tomb of the middle Warring States period.

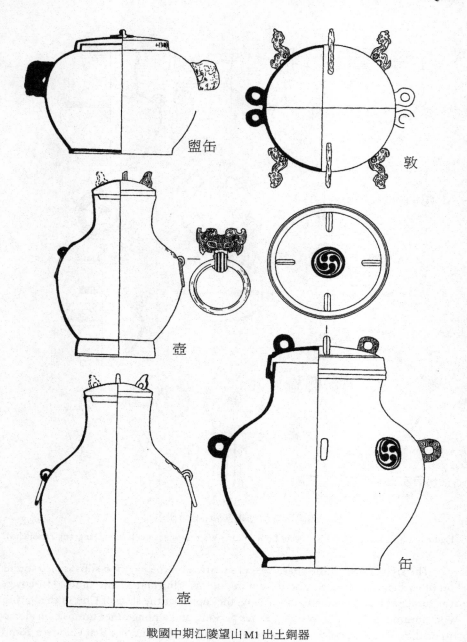

盥缶

敦

壺

壺

缶

戰國中期江陵望山M1出土銅器

Figure 7.  Chu Culture: Period 6 (Bronzes from a middle Warring States tomb at Jiangling Wangshan).

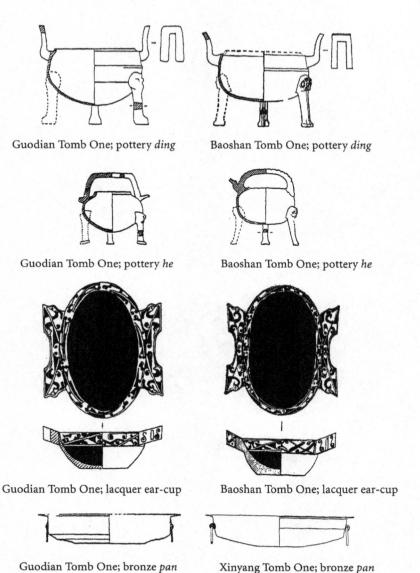

Guodian Tomb One; pottery *ding*        Baoshan Tomb One; pottery *ding*

Guodian Tomb One; pottery *he*        Baoshan Tomb One; pottery *he*

Guodian Tomb One; lacquer ear-cup        Baoshan Tomb One; lacquer ear-cup

Guodian Tomb One; bronze *pan*        Xinyang Tomb One; bronze *pan*

Figure 8. Comparison of artifacts from Guodian Tomb One with artifacts from the middle Warring States tombs Baoshan Tomb One and Xinyang Tomb One.

# An Overview of Tomb
# Number One at Jingmen Guodian

## *LIU ZUXIN*

I n the village of Fangpu 方鋪, in the Shayang 沙洋 area of Jingmen City 荊門市, Hubei, there is a famous area of low hills called Jishan 紀山 — hundreds of large and small "earthen mounds," as the local people call these hills, made from earth piled up over tombs. The mounds are densely distributed over a vast area whose natural topography places some on higher ground and others in low-lying areas. Normally, a large tomb is placed in the center, with other tombs arranged around it in a specific order. Archeologists call these groups cemeteries (*mudi* 墓地 ), and refer to the burial area formed by a number of such cemeteries as a burial complex (*muqun* 墓群 ).

The complex of ancient tombs at Jishan is made up of more than twenty cemeteries. According to surveys, the complex includes more than 300 tombs with extant earthen mounds; tombs whose mounds have already been flattened number in the thousands. It is located nine kilometers north of the ancient Chu capital of Ying 郢 . Because the site is south of the Jishan mountains, people call it Ji'nancheng ("City South of Ji 紀南城 "). The complex of ancient tombs is closely related to the ancient Chu capital of Ying, and it was most probably a burial site for the capital during the Warring States period.

According to current archeological evidence, the ancient tombs in the Jishan area are essentially all Chu tombs and almost all from the Warring States period. Furthermore, the arrangement of the tombs within each cemetery suggests that all of the burials in this area had characteristics associated with clan cemeteries. The tomb from which the bamboo slips with the *Laozi* material were excavated is a small tomb in the Guodian 郭店 cemetery in the Jishan tomb complex (see figure 9). It was designated "Guodian Tomb Number One" by the excavators and is in the southern part of the Guodian cemetery. Its earthen mound had been leveled at some time in the past. Prior to excavation, the land was used by the villagers to grow dry crops. In October, 1993, the tomb was robbed and the robbers' tunnel broke through to the head compartment of the outer coffin. As soon as archeologists from the Jingmen City Museum heard about the robbery, they organized an excavation of the tomb to salvage its contents. Thus, they discovered the bamboo slips and a number of other artifacts. A brief description of the tomb and its contents follows.

## THE STRUCTURE OF THE TOMB

Guodian Tomb Number One was a rectangular earth-built shaft tomb with a wooden outer coffin. That is to say, the horizontal cross-section of the tomb was rectangular in shape; the tomb wall and fill-in material were all earth; a vertical cross section of the tomb forms a shaft-like shape; and the coffin chamber was made of wood. Since the burial mound no longer existed when the tomb was excavated, it was necessary to remove only 50 centimeters of agricultural topsoil to uncover the opening of the tomb and tomb ramp.

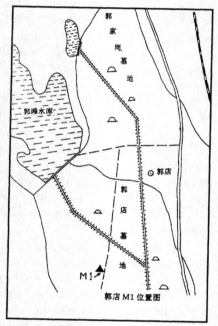

The shape of the earthen pit from the tomb opening to the coffin chamber can be described as that of an inverted ladle — larger on top and smaller at the bottom. The opening of the pit was 6 meters long, running west to east, and 4.6 meters wide; the coffin chamber was 3.4 meters long and 2 meters wide; the pit was a total of 6.92 meters in depth; a sloping tomb ramp at the east side of the pit was 9 meters long, 2 to 2.3 meters wide. The direction of the tomb was 100 degrees east of north (figure 10).

The top layer of the fill-in earth was yellow soil intermixed with red (i.e., soil which had been removed to make the pit, then put back in to fill it after the burial), 3.7 meters thick; the middle layer was 0.6 meters of brownish grey soil; the lower layer was 1.2 meters of dark grey kaolin mud (*gao ni* 膏泥).[1] The wooden outer coffin was 1.3 meters high; and under the coffin chamber were two wooden planks, 0.12 meters thick.

Figure 9. Village of Guodian and Tomb Number One (M1). After *Wenwu* 1997.7, p. 35.

---

[1] [Translators' Note: Liu Zuxin and Peng Hao explained on May 25, 1999, in response to the translators' enquiry, that the grey color is a discoloration of soil with chemical content similar to kaolin (as used in ceramics). For details about this phenomenon, see *Kaogu Xuebao* 1959.1, p. 43.]

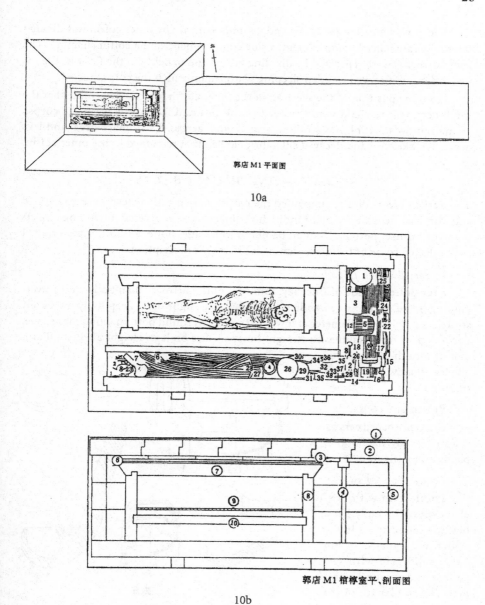

郭店 M1 平面图

10a

郭店 M1 棺椁室平、剖面图

10b

Figure 10.　Guodian Tomb Number One. After *Wenwu* 1997.7, pp. 36–37.

The grave had an outer coffin and an inner coffin. The outer coffin was divided internally into a head compartment, a side compartment, and a coffin chamber. The compartments were separated by dividing beams and panels. On the floor of the inner coffin was a carved wooden sleeping platform on which the corpse rested.

From the position of the skeleton in the inner coffin, we can determine that the tomb occupant was laid with the head to the east and feet to the west; the corpse facing upwards, with limbs straight, arms folded across the stomach area, and legs apart. The skeleton and decayed silk fabrics are all that remained in the inner coffin.

## ACCOMPANYING BURIAL OBJECTS

The burial objects that accompanied the corpse were mostly placed in the head and side compartments. Fifty-eight individual objects were recovered, including objects made of bronze, pottery, lacquer, bamboo, iron, jade, bone, and other materials. I have selected some of the more significant items for description.

*Pottery* ding 鼎 *tripod:*

Grey pottery made of fine clay. Rim of mouth narrower than body (to fit overlapping lid); flat rim; side handles, vertical with a slight flare; deep body; relatively straight sides; largest diameter at lower part of body; round bottom; hoof-shaped feet decorated with animal masks; straight inner surface on legs. Height 30.4 cm; diameter of mouth 25.4 cm; diameter of body 30.5 cm (see figure 11.1).

*Bronze ear-cups:*

Crescent-shaped ears on sides; oval body; flat bottom; plain surface (figure 12.2).

*Bronze* jian 劍 *sword:*

Pointed tip with beveled edges. The body has a blade, a raised spine in the center, and a guard; the hilt has a solid grip with two collars and a round pommel. The full length of the sword is 75.4 cm. The scabbard is formed of two thin rectangular boards joined together, the surface coated with black lacquer (figure 12.5).

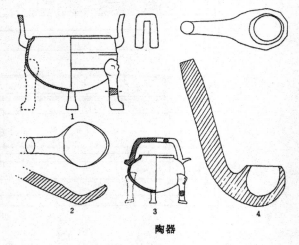

陶器

Figure 11.  Pottery artifacts from Guodian Tomb Number One.
After *Wenwu* 1997.7, p. 38.

*Bronze* ge 戈 *halberd:*

Long blade with wide beard (*hu* 胡); three holes on inner edge of beard; one hole in tang (*nei* 內); stylized bird design on end of tang (figure 12.6).

*Bronze* pi 鈹 *pike or "sword-shaped spear":*

The head of the pike is shaped like the tip of a sword and has an exquisitely made sheath. The shaft (now mostly decayed) was originally made of bamboo and had a bronze finial (figures 12.9, 13.7).

The sheath was made by joining two thin rectangular boards. It was encased in silk and leather. The edges of both faces of the sheath are ornamented with six pairs of spiral designs inlaid in gold. Both faces are decorated with corresponding patterns, each divided into three sections. The upper section has a curled double-phoenix design beneath a swirling cloud pattern on one face and a curled single-

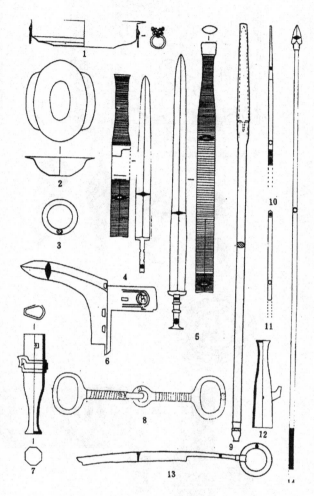

Figure 12.　Bronze artifacts from Guodian Tomb Number One.
After *Wenwu* 1997.7, p. 40.

dragon design on the other; the middle section is damaged on one face and has an open-work design of stylized curled double phoenixes on the other; the lower section is decorated with animal-head designs in relief on both faces.

The remains of the bamboo shaft have an oblate oval cross-section. The top of the (bronze) finial has an oval cross-section; the lower part is waisted and hexagonal. The bronze head of the pike was originally inserted into the hollow inside of the bam-

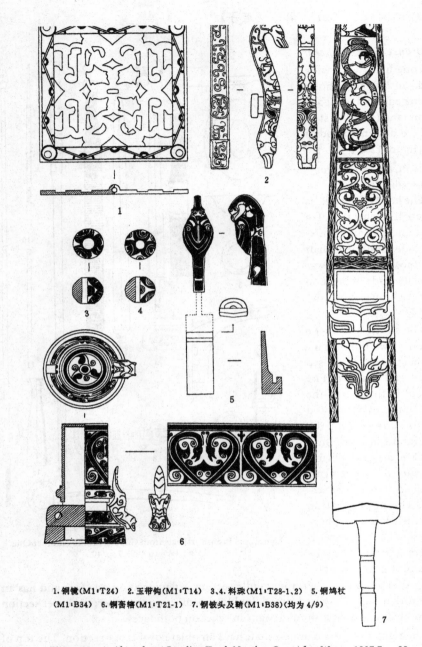

1. 铜镜(M1·T24)　2. 玉带钩(M1·T14)　3、4. 料珠(M1·T28-1、2)　5. 铜鸠杖
(M1·B34)　6. 铜害辖(M1·T21-1)　7. 铜铍头及鞘(M1·B38)(均为 4/9)

Figure 13. Artifacts from Guodian Tomb Number One. After *Wenwu* 1997.7, p. 39.

boo shaft and the bottom of the shaft fitted into the finial. The total length of the pike is 170 cm; the length of the sheath is 39 cm, the width 3.4 to 5 cm.

*Bronze bird-headed walking staffs:*

The heads of the walking staffs are in the shape of recumbent doves: the dove has round eyes, a hooked beak, and the head turned round with its beak on its back. Its entire body is decorated with inlaid gold and silver in feather and swirling cloud patterns. The wooden staffs had already decayed, but their cross-sections would have been oblate. The bronze staff-ends are rectangular with oval indentions running from top to bottom for the secure encasement of the lower end of the wooden staff (figure 13.5).

*Lacquer-painted bronze mirror:*

Square with a bridge-shaped knob. The base of the knob is decorated with a calyx pattern, surrounded by four open-work phoenixes in a red lacquer design on a black lacquer background. The border is decorated with a geometrical swirling-cloud pattern. The entire mirror is the product of two bronze castings. One casting produced the face of the mirror which was then polished to make the reflective surface. The other casting produced the back of the mirror with its exquisite decoration. A piece of silk fabric was placed between the front and the back pieces of the mirror and then they were mortised together with studs at the four corners. The side length is 11 cm, the width 0.3 cm (figure 13.1).

*Jade belt hook:*

The hook is rectangular. Dragon heads, joined with one body, are carved on both ends of the hook. The entire body of the dragon is ornamented with entwined designs of dragon and phoenix, all with a phoenix head, dragon body. On the back is an oval shaped knob. The belt hook is 11.5 cm long, 1.2 to 1.5 cm wide, and 1.1 to 1.3 cm thick (figure 13.2).

*Lacquer square-ear cup:*

Squared raised ears, with a concave hollow in the mid-section; oval body shape; flat base. The cups are entirely coated with black lacquer on the outside, red on the inside. The ears are ornamented with symmetrical bird-head designs and swirling cloud designs. Interlinked cloud patterns decorate the outside of the cup rim; abstracted phoenix and swirling cloud designs decorate the inner rim. On the bottom of the cup there are four inscribed characters, 東宮之師 .[2] The mouth of the cup measures 12 cm to 18.5 cm across; the base, 6 cm to 11.4 cm (figure 14).

---

[2] In the original excavation report (*Wenwu* 1997.7, p. 42), the last character of this inscription was read as *bei* 杯 ("cup").

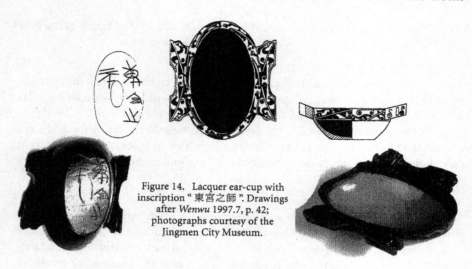

Figure 14. Lacquer ear-cup with
inscription " 東宮之師 ". Drawings
after *Wenwu* 1997.7, p. 42;
photographs courtesy of the
Jingmen City Museum.

*Wooden* qin 琴 *instrument:*

Made from two pieces of carved and interlocking wood. The head section is relatively long and more or less rectangular, with a curved surface. The bridge is inserted into a groove made in the surface of the *qin*. The face of the bridge is arched, 10.5 cm long, 0.8 cm thick, and there are seven string holes in the outer edge, 1.5 to 1.7 cm apart. The inner cavity of the instrument is hollowed into a T-shape, forming a resonance box. Total length, 83 cm; height, 7.1 cm; width, 12.6 cm.

*Bamboo slips:*

804 slips, found in the head compartment. The original binding strings had rotted, so the sequence of the slips was muddled. The total number of characters is about 13,000. The majority of slips were preserved whole; only a minority were damaged or broken.

## CULTURAL CHARACTERISTICS AND THE DATE OF THE BURIAL

### List of Chu Characteristics Evident in Tomb Structure and Excavated Artifacts

1. The tomb pit is a rectangular earth-built shaft tomb, with an opening that is larger than the bottom, forming an inverted ladle shape. The coffin chamber was sealed over with dark grey kaolin mud. There was a rectangular, sloping tomb ramp. These are all common construction methods for Chu tombs.

2. The wooden chamber of the outer coffin was divided into a head compartment, side compartment and inner compartment. The chamber of the inner coffin was rectangular with a separate carved wooden sleeping platform on which the corpse was laid. These are burial customs unique to Chu culture.

3. The contents of the tomb:

(a) the shapes and decoration of pottery ceremonial vessels, bronze ceremonial vessels, chariot parts, weapons, and so on, are all in styles characteristic of burial artifacts that accompanied the dead in Chu tombs;

(b) the form and style of the characters on the bamboo slips are similar to those of the Jingmen Baoshan 荊門包山 slips and are standard Chu script;

(c) the bird-shaped walking staff heads are similar in form and decoration to examples excavated from the Chu tombs 163 and 277 at Jiangling Yutaishan 江陵雨台山 and Tomb Number One at Jingmen Baoshan. The only differences are that some of the staff heads have a dragon rather than a bird design and variation in the length of the staff;

(d) bronze mirrors were articles of daily use in ancient China and are commonly found, but only the Chu people coated bronze mirrors with lacquer and painted them;

(e) the square lacquered bronze mirror from Guodian Tomb Number One is so similar in design, casting, and decoration to the mirror excavated from Baoshan Tomb Number Two that it looks like it came from the same mold;

(f) lacquer square-ear cups are relatively common in Chu tombs. This tomb itself had 16 pieces, piled together in sets, their color and luster as if new. The shape of the cups from this tomb are identical to those from Tomb Number 245 at Jiangling Yutaishan and Tomb Number One at Jingmen Baoshan, and their patterning and decoration are nearly the same. Also the characters 東宮之師 ("teacher of the prince") on one of these cups are written in Chu-style script.

*Burial Dated to the Middle of the Warring States Period*

The lacquer ear cups from this tomb are essentially the same as those from Tomb 245 at Jiangling Yutaishan (a tomb which dates to the fourth period of that site) and Tomb 1 at Jingmen Baoshan. The pottery *ding* vessel is essentially the same as those from Tomb Numbers 176 and 179 at Jiangling Yutaishan (fifth period of that site) and similar to the same vessel types excavated from Tomb Number One at Jingmen Baoshan, as well as to those of the the sixth period, eleventh division, of the Chu tomb site excavated at Dangyang Zhaojiahu 當陽趙家湖. The bronze mirror is identical in shape, patterning, and decoration to the one excavated from Tomb Number Two at Jingmen Baoshan (figure 15).

The Chu tombs at Jingmen Baoshan are mid-Warring States period. The fourth- and fifth-period Chu tombs from Jiangling Yutaishan are also mid-Warring States period. The eleventh division of the sixth period of the Chu tomb site at Dangyang Zhaojiahu is at the end of the mid-Warring States period. On the basis of these comparisons, Tomb 1 at Guodian has the characteristics of a late mid-Warring States tomb, and the burial ought to have taken place sometime between the mid-fourth and early-third century BC.

Figure 15. Rubbings of the bronze mirrors from Guodian Tomb One and Baoshan Tomb Two. After *Wenwu* 1997.7, p. 40; and *Baoshan Chu Mu*, p. 195.

*Tomb Occupant's Status as Knight* shi 士

We may conjecture about the rank of the tomb occupant on the basis of the tomb structure, excavated artifacts, and textual records of the pre-Qin burial system, as follows. The grave furnishing consisted of one outer and one inner coffin and there was a tomb ramp. The "Tangong" section of the *Liji* says, "The inner coffin of the Son of Heaven has four layers," to which the Zheng Xuan commentary adds, "Dukes, three layers; lords, two layers; nobles, one; knights, not layered."[3] According to this classification, a tomb furnished with one outer and one inner coffin is that of a knight 士. However, because the artifacts from this tomb are especially exquisite — of a quality seldom seen in this type of Chu tomb, we may conjecture that the status of the tomb occupant's family was relatively high.

## BIBLIOGRAPHY OF EXCAVATION REPORTS

For the original excavation report of Guodian Tomb Number One, see:

Hubeisheng Jingmenshi Bowuguan 湖北省荊門市博物館 . "Guodian Yihao Chu Mu 郭店一號楚墓 ." *Wenwu* 1997.7, pp. 35–48.

The excavation reports of related sites include, for Jingmen Baoshan:

Hubeisheng Jingsha Tielu Kaogudui 湖北省荊沙鐵路考古隊 . *Baoshan Chu Mu* 包山 楚墓 . Beijing: Wenwu Press, 1991.

For Dangyang Zhaojiahu:

Hubeisheng Yichang Diqu Bowuguan 湖北省宜昌地區博物館, Beijing Daxue Kaoguxi 北京大學考古系. *Dangyang Zhaojiahu Chu Mu* 當陽趙家湖楚墓. Beijing: Wenwu Press, 1992.

For Jiangling Yutaishan:

Hubeisheng Jingzhou Diqu Bowuguan 湖北省荊州地區博物館 . *Jiangling Yutaishan Chu Mu* 江陵雨台山楚墓. Beijing: Wenwu Press, 1984.

---

[3] *Liji Jijie* 禮記集解 , "Tangong 檀弓 , *shang* 上 " (Beijing: Zhonghua Shuju, 1989), p. 235.

# Post-Excavation Work on the Guodian Bamboo-Slip
## *Laozi*: A Few Points of Explanation

## *PENG HAO*

he bamboo slips were removed from Tomb Number One at Guodian still encased in mud, and the cleaning process began once they had been transported from the site to the Jingmen Museum. The main steps in this process were:

1) removal of surface mud;
2) making of drawings of the top and side views of the clump of bamboo slips;
3) photographing the clump of slips;
4) separation of the bamboo slips (diagrams were made at this stage and the slips were assigned excavation numbers);
5) preliminary cleaning; at this stage the slips were black and the characters were not legible;
6) conservation and treatment to reveal the characters on the slips;
7) formal photography of the writing on the slips; and
8) preservation of the slips in test tubes of distilled water.

This work was done by specialist conservators, and the whole process took about three months, from October to December, 1993.

The first stage in the process of ordering bamboo slips is to separate the slips into a number of different texts on the basis of clearly defined criteria. Only in the next stage do we reconstruct the order and sequence of the slips within each text. The final stage is transcription and annotation. In the following, I will report briefly on the division of the *Laozi* material into groups; the manner in which marks are used in the bamboo-slip *Laozi* to divide chapters and sentences; and the methods used to join broken slips and arrange them in sequence.

### DIVISION INTO GROUPS

The bamboo slips with *Laozi* material (Guodian *Laozi*) were divided into three groups on the basis of the different shapes of the slips and the distance between the binding marks. The first group contained 39 slips — each 32.3 cm long, with both ends beveled; and each with a distance of 13 cm between the upper and lower bindings. This group was given the title "Slip-text A." The 18 slips in the second group, "Slip-text B," were each 30.6 cm in length, with flat ends, and the gap between the bindings, 13 cm. The third group, "Slip-text C," comprised 14 slips, 26.5 cm in length, with flat ends and a gap between bindings of 10.8 cm.

Normally, bamboo slips from the same copy of a work are the same length and shape, and their binding gaps are the same. In explaining the character *deng* 等 ("equal"), the *Shuowen* 説文 says: "even bamboo slips 齊簡也." That bamboo slips were indeed grouped as bundles of even length has been corroborated by the discoveries of bamboo-slip texts of recent years. Of the groups above, Slip-text A and B have the same distance between bindings, but their overall lengths are different and the shape of the slips is not the same. At the same time, the characters of the first group are relatively small and close together, while those in the second group are relatively large and spaced more widely apart. For these reasons, we judged that these two groups of slips were separately copied and independently bound.

There are other examples of two or more copies of the same work excavated from a single tomb. The *Laozi* text is itself one such example: the Changsha Mawangdui silk-manuscript *Laozi* texts (Mawangdui Copies A and B), made at different times (A earlier than B, judging from the taboos observed by the scribes) were found in a single tomb. Another example is the three *Yili* 儀禮 texts on wood and bamboo slips discovered in 1959 in a Wang Mang-period (9–23 AD) tomb, Tomb Number Six at Wuwei Mozuizi 武威磨嘴子, Gansu.[1] Texts A and B each included a version of "Fu Zhuan 服傳," section 8, whereas Text C only included one section, "Sang Fu 喪服." These copies had also been made at different times.

## SYMBOLS MARKING CHAPTER AND SENTENCE DIVISIONS

The Guodian *Laozi* material includes three types of mark: a short stroke ——; a small black square ◢; and a tadpole-shaped mark ᒪ. It is difficult to determine their function because of scribal inconsistency in their usage. Clearly, not all the bamboo-slip material is divided into sentences or chapters by these marks. Moreover, the usage of the short stroke and the small black square is not standardized. The different circumstances in which these marks occur are summarized below:

*a) Symbols used as punctuation: usually at the end of a sentence and used consistently within a continuous section of text*

The following are two examples of black squares or short strokes used as sentence ending punctuation: (1) the section of continuous text on the first two slips of *Laozi* A corresponding to chapter 19 of the received text, that is A 1:1 to 2:18, 凶 (絕)

[1] Gansusheng Bowuguan 甘肅省博物館, Zhongguo Kexueyuan Kaogu Yanjiusuo 中國科學考古研究所 , *Wuwei Hanjian* 武威漢簡 (Beijing: Wenwu Press, 1964).

智（知）弃（棄）卞（辯）... 少厶（私）須（寡）欲 (see p. 195 for Ryden's edition with black squares marked). Here, the squares act as sentence or clause markers. (2) A 8:3 to 10:21（長古之善為士者 ..., see p. 199). This section corresponds to chapter 15 in the received text. Here short strokes function similarly.

### b) Symbols used to mark chapter divisions

The bamboo-slip *Laozi* preserves most of the chapter divisions. In the majority of cases these are indicated with a small black square; in a minority of cases, they are indicated by a short stroke. In most cases, the last character is separated from the next one by a space the size of one or more characters, although there are also cases where no extra space is left between the characters. For example, after 天下皆智（知）美之為美也...是以弗去也 (A 15:8 to 18:8; received *Laozi*, chapter 2), there is a small black square at the bottom right — at the end of the sentence (i.e., after the 也 ) — and a space of about two characters between this and the following words, making the division between chapters extremely clear.

Another example is 為亡為，事亡事 ... 古（故）終亡難 (A 14:13 to 15:7), before and after which there are small black squares indicating that this is an independent chapter, although no space is left above or below. When the small black square appears in such a situation, it always indicates a chapter division.

The A slips include a section 辠（罪）莫厚虖（乎）甚欲 ... 知足之為足、此互（恆）足矣 (A 5:14 to 6:16) which corresponds to chapter 46 of the received *Laozi*. In the Mawangdui silk-manuscript Copy A the section corresponding to chapter 46 is divided into two chapters by round dots placed at the beginning and in the middle of the section. The round dot in the middle, just before 罪莫大乎可欲 ..., can serve as evidence that the following section is an independent chapter. In the bamboo-slip text, the beginning of this section is not divided from the previous section, but the last sentence is separated from the following text by a short stroke. On the basis of Mawangdui Copy A, we know that this is the end of a chapter and the bamboo slips are using the short stroke to mark a chapter division.

There is another, rather special usage of the short stroke mark. In the Guodian *Laozi* slips, there is a short stroke separating the lines 是胃（謂）果而不強. 其事好 (A 7:25 to 8:2; received chapter 30) from the following text. Judging from the parallel examples in Mawangdui and the received text, the Guodian *Laozi* has omitted the character 還 after 其事好. Qiu Xigui has suggested that the short stroke after the character 好 is a mark made by someone checking the text for mistakes to indicate this omission. Since this mark functions to divide sections in the bamboo-slip text in some examples, it can also be regarded as a chapter marker here.

### c) The tadpole-shaped mark

The shape of this mark is like that of the Eastern Zhou character 以 and its meaning is similar to that of 止 ("stop"). This mark is also seen in the Baoshan 包山 bamboo slips (slip number 214). It appears twice in the Guodian *Laozi* material; once after the lines 攻（功）述（遂）身退，天之道也 (end of the slip, A 39:2–9); and once after 我谷（欲）不谷（欲），民自樸 (end of slip, A 32:15–22). In both cases, it is placed on the right, at the end of the sentence, and marks the end of large sections of text made up of several received-text chapter divisions. In the first case, the punctuation sets off four such chapters; and in the second, three. However, the longest block of text in the A slips is that from 㱃（絕）智（知）弃（棄）卞（辯）to 猶少浴（谷）之與江海 (A 1:1 to 20:28), which includes about ten received-text chapter divisions written continuously on 20 bamboo slips, but there is no tadpole-shaped mark to be found. This suggests that perhaps there were originally more chapters marked off by each such symbol than those found in the Guodian slip-texts.

## THE SEQUENCE OF THE GUODIAN LAOZI BAMBOO SLIPS AND THE DETERMINATION OF THE TRANSCRIPTION

Slip sequences were determined by reference to the sequence of the lines in the Mawangdui copies, and where these copies were damaged, to the Wang Bi, Heshang Gong, and other editions. Slip order was reconstructed by comparing the order of the characters to the corresponding lines of received text. For example, for slips 1 to 20 of *Laozi* A, the order was fixed by the character order in the corresponding received text. Slips 21 to 23 are an independent section. It is impossible to determine whether or not this section is linked to the section of slips 1 to 20. For this reason, when we composed the text for publication, we left a one-line space between this section and the preceding and following ones. Other such sections are arranged in the same manner.

As we explain in the legend to *Guodian Chu Mu Zhujian*, for variant characters, modern readings are placed in parentheses: ( ), following a transcription of the original. Words written with phonetic loans are treated similarly — the original loan character is followed by the bracketed modern character form for the word denoted. Variant character forms were relatively easy to identify. In the case of phonetic loans, there was sometimes a choice in deciding what the original word was. In most cases, the silk manuscript and received texts could be used as a guide. In other cases, where it was not obvious that the Guodian bamboo-slip character was a loan for a character found in the received editions or Mawangdui silk manuscripts, the pronunciation of the character, the analysis of its meaning, the context, and so on, were considered in determining whether the character was a phonetic loan and, if so, what word was denoted by it. Below are three examples to illustrate these points.

Example 1: 𧸐惻亡又 (A 1:13–16; received chapter 19) is read as 盜賊亡有 based on the Mawangdui and received editions. And in the same way, in Guodian *Laozi*: 音聖之相和也 (A 16:19–24; received chapter 2), 聖 is read as 聲 .

Example 2: 三言以為貞不足 (A 1:25 to 2:4; received chapter 19): 貞 is taken as a variant form for 弁, to be read in this context as 辨, meaning "to distinguish, differentiate." 三言 presumably refers to the phrases in the previous lines: 絕智棄辯, 絕巧棄利, and 絕偽(偽)棄慮(詐)(following Gao Heng's 高亨 commentary). The meaning of this line is that the methods enumerated in these three phrases are still insufficient to make a differentiation; therefore, the text continues, it is sometimes necessary to 命(令)之 or 屬(乎)豆(屬), 見索(素)保僕(樸)、少厶(私)須(寡)欲 (A 2:5 to 2:18). In the equivalent section of both Mawangdui and Wang Bi, we find 文 for 貞, usually explained as 文飾 ("literary polish"). Reading the Guodian *Laozi* character 貞 as 辨 gives the line a more precise meaning.

Example 3: 咎莫僉屬(乎)谷(欲)得 (A 5:20–25; received chapter 46): 僉 can be read as 險, meaning 危 ("dangerous"). 僉 can also be read as 憯, based on Mawangdui Copy A, meaning 痛 ("painful"). The two are not entirely equivalent in meaning, and the reading 險 seems to fit the context better.

Bamboo slips during conservation process, with legible characters.
Photograph by Zhou Guangshu, Jingmen City Museum.

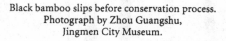

Black bamboo slips before conservation process.
Photograph by Zhou Guangshu,
Jingmen City Museum.

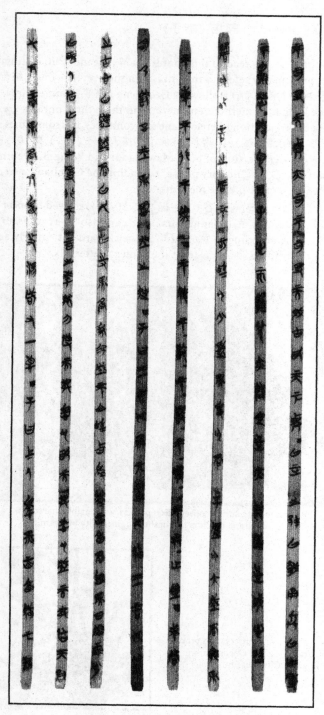

Unsorted bamboo slips of the *Laozi* and *Zi Yi*.

# The Study of Early Chinese Manuscripts: Methodological Preliminaries

## WILLIAM G. BOLTZ

The Guodian manuscripts in the aggregate include two kinds of texts, those for which there are no extant transmitted counterparts and that are therefore unknown apart from the manuscript at hand and those that are already known from transmitted versions. This makes a difference in how one deals with certain kinds of textual problems, and yet it makes no difference in regard to certain underlying methodological principles. I will try to make these differences and "no-differences" clear in the course of these comments.

There are in general three main methodological considerations that bear on the study of early manuscripts. The first is the business of *transcribing the manuscript*, the second is *reading the manuscript*, that is, deciding what words the characters of the manuscript stand for. And the third is *affiliating the manuscript*, i.e., determining what relation the manuscript in question has to other known versions of the same text. Here I shall deal only with the first two of these three, leaving the matter of methods of determining textual affiliation aside.

## TRANSCRIBING THE MANUSCRIPT

We are fortunate in the case of the Guodian mss.to have available for our inspection high quality photographs of the original bamboo slips, showing the script as clearly and as legibly as anyone could ask. We cannot assume that originals will always be so conveniently and so legibly available. Most of the time many of us will have to rely on published transcriptions of the originals, making the question of an accurate transcription crucially important. For the purpose of setting out guidelines governing transcriptions, we need to recognize two distinct situations: type (i), where the manuscript passage is intact and legible, and type (ii), where the passage is defective or to some degree illegible.

### Type (i): Intact and Legible Passages

For the first type the general rule is this: manuscripts should be transcribed so as to reveal the exact form of what is written as precisely and unambiguously as possible without introducing any interpolations, alterations or other extraneous material based on assumptions, biases or subjective decisions of the scholar-transcriber or of anyone else. In a nutshell, this means that the transcription should reflect exactly what is written and nothing more.[1] The transcription itself is not the place to include decisions as to what the editor thinks the "intended" character or word might be for a non-standard, rare, or anomalous character, or what the "correct" character or word is for those characters that the transcriber deems "wrong." At this stage there is no such thing as a "wrong" character; there is only what is written and that is what must be transcribed. To decide a character is "wrong" depends on deciding what word the character is intended to stand for, because the only sense in which the notion of "right and wrong" applies to what is written is in regard to the match between character and word, and that question does not bear on the exact transcription of the manuscript per se. All such decisions, corrections, and judgments should be recorded as part of the critical apparatus either in notes separate from the transcription itself or inserted within the transcription, clearly indicated by the proper kind of bracket or other diacritic mark. To include such decisions in the transcription proper, that is, by changing the characters from what the manuscript actually has to what an editor thinks the manuscript intends, especially if these changes are unmarked as departures from the manuscript itself, deprives every other reader and scholar of the chance to decide for himself what the manuscript actually says. It is crucial that the transcriptions be as accurate, unambiguous, and objectively rendered as possible, reflecting what is actually written in the manuscript, as opposed to what an editor or textual critic has decided is the intended text of what is written. We can phrase this somewhat formally as:

*Transcription Rule I: Characters that are wholly visible and legible must be transcribed exactly as written, without either abbreviation or elaboration of their constituent graphic structure.*

The principle upon which this rule rests is that the *structural constituency* of the graph must be preserved in the transcription exactly as it exists in the manuscript, and transcriptions therefore should not deviate from the actual structural form of the graph in the manuscript. Transcriptions that differ only in adventitious calligraphic respects are not precluded by this rule, as long as the transcriptional variation does not obscure the graph's constituent structure as it is originally written.

Examples:

1. the first character of the first slip of the *Laozi jia* 老子甲 (A 1:1) manuscript is transcribed in *Guodian Chu Mu Zhujian* 郭店楚墓竹簡 as 㐱, matching exactly its manuscript form;

---

[1] Please note that when I say "what is written" I mean the graphs (=characters), i.e., what is physically present in graphic form on the mansucript. I do not mean "what is meant" by what is written, not in other words, the words behind the graphs.

2. the fourth character on the same slip (A 1:4) is transcribed as 下 , a form that does not match the manuscript graph in that it does not include the element 又 clearly visible as a part of the bottom of the character. The transcription according to the principle suggested in Rule I here ought to be 支.

*Type (ii): Defective or Partially Illegible Passages*

When a character or passage is defective, no matter to what extent, its transcription becomes, apart from the option of simply leaving a blank, inevitably a matter of conjecturing what the original, undamaged character or passage was, and of indicating in the transcription what is known from the direct evidence of the manuscript and what is conjecturally restored. Here the range can be between 0% (wholly conjecture) to 100% (full confidence), for those cases where even though a character is defective, its original form is a virtual certainty, to those that are entirely obliterated or missing, and no conjectural restoration is feasible.

Marking the various kinds of conjectural emendations and proposals that the text critic would like to lay out becomes a matter of using an established and clear set of brackets and diacritic signs to indicate unambiguously what the nature of the proposal is. The set of such marks and brackets that the editors of the *Guodian Chu Mu Zhujian* have used, and that is familiar to us from past publications, works well and need not be revisited here. The important point is simply that whatever kind of markings are used, the fundamental requirement here is the same as it was for type (i) passages, viz., to present a transcription that shows as precisely and unambiguously as possible what the manuscript has, while still allowing the editor or textual critic to insert conjectures about readings or graphic equivalents in an efficient and useful way. The most important consideration is that what is conjecturally added by the editor is unambiguously distinguishable from what the manuscript writes. We might phrase this second main principle formally as:

*Transcription Rule II: The transcription must rigorously distinguish what the manuscript writes from what the editor adds, subtracts, or emends by way of conjecture.*

## READING THE MANUSCRIPT

"Reading the manuscript" means simply deciding what words the characters written in the manuscript stand for. This is not as trivial as it may at first sound. To the extent that the writing system is standardized and the use of characters follows an established convention, knowing what word to associate with a given character is a straightforward and unproblematic matter. But as is well known, the writing system of the preimperial age was not as formally or fully standardized as it became from the Han on, and the manuscripts extant from that time present numerous orthographic differences from what would become the norm after the third or second century BC.

Even so, the script was not entirely capricious and devoid of conventional usages; no writing system can be called a "system" and used effectively anywhere by anyone if it is not strongly grounded in an established conventional association of graph with word. It is just that the degree of this established conventional association is not as great for the period prior to the Han dynasty as it is later.

There are two types of variation from what we recognize as later conventional orthographic practice: first, the use of familiar characters to stand for words that according to later recognized conventions they do not typically stand for; and, second, the use of unfamiliar or anomalous characters, which, given their unfamiliarity, have by definition no conventional, established lexical associations at all in the post-Han standardized form of the script. (The two types are examined more thoroughly in the following subsections of this article.) In the case of familiar characters, the problem for the reader is to decide whether the character in the particular occurrence in question stands for the same word that it conventionally stands for, or whether it is in that occurrence standing for a different word. In the case of unfamiliar characters, the problem is simply to determine what word is intended. In both cases the problem reduces itself to one of identifying what word is intended by a given written character. In effect these kinds of orthographic variability are what the Qing philologists and their predecessors called by the terms *jia jie zi* 假借字 'loan characters' and *yi ti zi* 異體字 'orthographic variants' in their studies of early transmitted texts.

The Qing philologists recognized that loan character usages had to conform to two phonological criteria: the rhyming part of the word *customarily* written with the character in question had to belong to the same *Shijing* rhyme class as the final of the word that the character is suspected of standing for in its loan usage; and the initials of the same two words (what we might call the "customary word" and the "suspect word") must be homorganic.[2] Neither of these two criteria is absolute; each allows for some latitude when other indications are sufficiently compelling. The second especially is often relaxed in certain respects for the simple reason that even now we understand the overall system of the initials of the pre-Han language much less fully than we do that of the finals. But in general the further a proposal deviates from these two criteria the more speculative its status becomes.

The orthography of the Guodian manuscripts varies substantially enough from what we think of as normal based on the post-Han standardized script that we must constantly be on guard not to assume uncritically that such-and-such a character in the manuscripts "naturally" stands for such-and-such a word just because it does so conventionally in the later writing system with which we are familiar. We must always

---

[2] "Homorganic" means simply that two sounds are made in the same position in the mouth. Typically this means that /p, b, m/ are homorganic "bilabials," i.e., they are all produced with the lips; that /t, d, n/ are homorganic "dentals"; and /k, g, ng/ are homorganic "velars."

explicitly ask what word does the character in question stand for, and we must be prepared for the possibility that the answer will be different from what it would be for the same character in a transmitted text, or even elsewhere in another (or the same) manuscript. The problem tends to be more acute for unconventional or anomalous characters than for standard ones, even though standard characters can, and often are, of course, used to write words different from the ones they customarily write.

An unconventional or anomalous character can occur in a manuscript passage that has a transmitted counterpart, in which case it constitutes a *textual variant* relative to the transmitted, received version of the text, or it can occur in an otherwise unknown passage, in which case it is an orthographic anomaly, perhaps a *hapax graphomenon* (that is, a character of which the instance in question is the only known occurrence.) In the former case the transmitted variant constitutes one possible answer to the question of what word is intended by the non-standard character. In the latter case the textual analyst must try to determine what word is intended without the help of a transmitted version, that is, without an accepted traditional opinion, as a starting point. In both cases the goal is to determine as best one can what word the unusual character stands for, but the starting points and subsequent methods and reasoning for determining this are different.

*Characters with Variants in Transmitted Versions*

Textual variation occurs anytime two or more versions ("witnesses") of the same text vary in what is written at the same place in that text. For example, when Hamlet speaks in one version of his "too, too solid flesh" and in another version of his "too, too sullied flesh" we have a clear case of textual variation (*Hamlet* I,2,129). This variation we immediately recognize as one between the two different words *solid* and *sullied*. This is called *lexical variation*. By contrast when we find in Clarence's dream in *Richard III* (I,4,46) the phrase "that sour ferry-man" in one version and "that sowre Ferry-man" in another, we know, of course, that the variation between *sour* and *sowre* is not a difference of words, but merely of "spelling," i.e., of the writing system. This kind of variation we call *orthographic*, or simply *graphic variation*. Anytime we are confronted with a case of textual variation, we must decide whether it is variation between *different words* (lexical variation) or just variation between *different ways of writing the same word* (graphic variation). This is the fundamental problem for the textual critic at this stage of reading the manuscript.

Deciding which is which in Shakespeare is usually fairly easy because different spellings, as we find in the variation between *sour* and *sowre*, do not often make different words, and thus constitute variation at an orthographic level "below" that of the whole word. But since Chinese is written in a script where every character has the capacity to stand for a word, any difference in how a character is written has the potential to constitute a difference in intended word, i.e., to be lexical variation. This is the *sullied/solid* type. In Chinese writing, in other words, textual variation cannot in principle occur at a level lower than that of the word, so *all* textual variation is potentially of the *sullied/solid* type, i.e., lexical variation. The consequence of this is that deciding whether a variant is graphic or lexical in a Chinese text is a much less trivial matter than it is for a text written alphabetically. The goal proper to analyzing instances of textual variation is *not* to explain the unfamiliar or anomalous variant "away," leaving the traditional reading of the received text standing alone, unchallenged, but to determine whether the variation is one between different graphs for the same word or one between different words.

In his work on the Mawangdui *Laozi*, D. C. Lau has given a good example of the non-trivial nature of the problem.[3] The traditional, received text (Heshang Gong 河上公 version) of the first line of chapter 41 is: "上士聞道勤而行之，中士聞道若存若亡，下士聞道大笑." This Lau translates as:

When the best student hears about the way,

He practises it assiduously;

When the average student hears about the way,

It seems to him one moment there and gone the next;

When the worst student hears about the way,

He laughs out loud at it.

The second (Copy B) of the two Mawangdui manuscripts of the *Laozi* has the first sentence of this line written as 上□□道堇能行之. The remaining part of the line is identical with the received version of the text save for the occurrence of a direct object pronoun *zhi* 之 at the end of the last sentence, i.e., 大笑之. The other (Copy A) *Laozi* manuscript from Mawangdui is defective at this point and this line is entirely missing from it. Thus, we have the variants Heshang Gong : 勤而行之 : : Mawangdui Copy B : 堇能行之, and we must decide what to make of them. It would be perfectly reasonable to suppose that the alternation 勤 : : 堇 is no more than graphic variation, both characters standing for the word *qin* < *$g\grave{a}n$ 'assiduous', where the Mawangdui Copy B silk manuscript writes the word without the classifier 019, 力, component, reflecting a prevalent inconsistency in the use of semantic classifiers ("radicals") in pre-Han manuscripts. Similarly, it would be easy to recognize the variation 而 : : 能 as lexical, since the two different common characters normally stand for two different common words, *er* < *$zn\grave{\partial}g$ 'then', and *neng* < *$zn\acute{\partial}ng$ 'able'. Taking the line in this way would require us to understand it as "he is assiduously able to practise it," slightly different from Lau's translation of the received text line.

But Lau goes on to point out that both the graphs 而 and 能 can stand for the word *er* < *$zn\grave{\partial}g$ 'then', that is to say, the character 能 is well known as a loan graph for

---

[3] D. C. Lau, *Chinese Classics: Tao Te Ching* (Hong Kong: Chinese University Press, 1982), p. 172.

而 in early texts.[4] This means that we are obliged to consider the possibility that the 而 :: 能 variation is graphic rather than lexical, in which case the line would have to be understood as equivalent to the Heshang Gong version.

Finally, just as we recognize that the variation 而 :: 能 can be interpreted either as lexical or graphic, so we must also recognize the same thing for the variation 勤 :: 堇. It is only the later tradition, as reflected in the received, transmitted version of the line, that suggests to us that the graph 堇 ought to stand for the word *qin* 'assiduous', normally written 勤 . We may decide that another interpretation is preferable, and consider what other words could just as plausibly be written with the graph 堇 . Lau suggests that it might stand for the word *jin* < \**gⁱən̉* < 'barely', a word normally written 僅 , i.e., the 堇 of the manuscript with the addition of classifier 009, 人 . This interpretation, coupled with taking 能 as *neng* 'able', leads Lau to translate "he is barely able to practise it," a considerable difference in overall meaning from the traditional "he practises it assiduously."

There is no formal difference between proposing to take 堇 as 僅 and proposing to take it as 勤; both proposals entail no more than a recognition that classifiers were often not written as intrinsic parts of the characters in early manuscripts. The fact that the received version of the text has 勤 , not 僅 , intending, presumably, to write the word *qin* 'assiduous' not *jin* 'barely', is no more than one opinion, one interpretation, that has become sanctified by default, so to speak, as a consequence of the fact that it is the interpretation that became standard in the transmitted version of the text. This is important, of course, to take note of, but it is not in itself decisive.

At this point we have four possible interpretations of the line in the Mawangdui Copy B manuscript, relative to the line of the received version:

1. where both instances of textual variation are taken as graphic, making the line identical in wording with Heshang Gong, *qin er xing zhi* 勤而行之 'he assiduously practises it';

2. where the first instance is taken as lexical, the second as graphic, *jin er xing zhi* 僅而行之 'he barely practises it';

3. where the first is taken as graphic, the second lexical, *qin neng xing zhi* 勤能行之 'he is assiduously able to practise it';

4. where both are taken as lexical, which is Lau's final suggestion, *jin neng xing zhi* 僅能行之 'he is barely able to practise it'.

---

[4] The character 能 often rhymes with words ending in \*-*ə̌g* 之部 and has *xiesheng* 諧聲 derivatives with the same final, thus indicating that it is in the same rhyme class as 而. At the same time, the initials of 而 and 能 are phonemically the same. Therefore both phonological criteria for loan graph usage are satisfied. See Bernhard Karlgren, "Grammata serica recensa," *Bulletin of the Museum of Far Eastern Antiquities* 29 (1957), pp. 1–332 (series 885, item *a*).

While some of these four possibilities may be stylistically better than others, none is grammatically or meaningfully impossible. The problem for the textual critic is here, as it often is, to choose a preferred version among several possibilities, where "preferred" means not just subjectively satisfying the idiosyncratic predispositions of the critic vis-à-vis the text, but also objectively accounting as far as possible for all of the textual and linguistic evidence that impinges on the variation. In this case there is little objective evidence to turn to.[5] Lau's suggestion of *jin* 'barely' for Mawangdui Copy B's 董 is entirely speculative, yet in this context it seems to me exceedingly attractive, and is in my view very likely to be correct. This is an excellent example of what is often called *emendation by divination* because it is based on an insight or inspiration rather than on documentary textual evidence, and it shows at once both the inevitable subjectivity of the textual critic's procedures and the importance of his conclusions.

If our interest is in establishing a version of the text that is as close to the form of the original as possible, we will have to decide which of the lexical variants is likeliest to represent that original, explaining as best we can how the other variants might have arisen. Even if we are prepared to set aside the question of an "original," trying to see how two or more lexical variants in a particular passage came about, that is, trying to see what the semantic, phonetic or other relation between the variants is such that one might have given rise to the other, can be a very useful exercise for coming to a good understanding of all versions of the passage, quite apart from providing an answer to the question of which one might have been the original reading. This is a problem that inevitably relies heavily on the subjective judgment of the textual critic, what A. E. Housman called 'common sense'.[6] But it is also a problem that requires assembling as much pertinent data as we can find and considering a few basic "rules" (really just statements of probabilities) that might apply. The most general, and therefore most useful, of these "rules" states that when you have two (or more) possible variants, the more (or most) obscure or difficult to understand is the probable original. The rationale is that difficult readings are likelier to be changed by editors, copyists, etc., into something easier to understand than the reverse.

One example, again from chapter 41 of the *Laozi*, may be cited briefly to illustrate this principle.

---

[5] The Guodian manuscript version of this line varies from both Heshang Gong and Mawangdui Copy B and would seem to suggest still further complications in understanding the passage. That, of course, was not known to Lau when he made his study a decade or more ago.

[6] See A. E. Housman, "The Application of Thought to Textual Criticism," *Proceedings of the Classical Association* 18 (1921), pp. 67–84.

Mawangdui Copy B:　　　　　　明道如費，進道如退，夷道如類．

Heshang Gong:　　　　　　　　明道若昧，進道若退，夷道若類．

Guodian B 10:14 to 11:3:　　　明道女孛，迀道女繢，□道若退．(乙, str. 10–11)[7]

The variant that I would like to examine briefly is the Mawangdui Copy B : 費 [*fei* < *$p^h\partial ts$* 'extravagant'] : : Heshang Gong : 昧 *mei* < *$m\partial ts$* 'dim' : : Guodian : 孛 [*bei* < *$b\partial ts$* 'comet', 'sprouting plant' < 'burst forth', 'exuberant'] set. By putting the pronunciations and meanings of the Mawangdui Copy B and Guodian variants in brackets I am conceding as a starting point what I would take to be the "default" position, viz., that both of these are graphic variants for *mei* 昧 'dim'. The editors of the Mawangdui silk manuscript have taken the Mawangdui Copy B variant that way, explaining that the 費 may be a "mistake" for a rare character written 暳, known only lexicographically, starting with the *Shuowen*, where it is said to mean 目不明也 (*Shuowen Gulin* 1461).

Notice that in taking the position that these three variants all stand for the word *mei* < *$m\partial ts$* 'dim' (conventionally written 昧 ) we are not just excluding the possibility of lexical variation, i.e., that either the Mawangdui Copy B 費 or the Guodian 孛 (or both) stand for a word different from *mei* 'dim', we are also deciding that of the three lexical possibilities identified so far, 費 *fei* 'extravagant', 昧 *mei* 'dim', and 孛 *bei* 'exuberant', the 昧 *mei* 'dim' of the received text is the preferred choice. In traditional terms this means that we are implying, or claiming, that 費 and 孛 are 'loan characters' for 昧, and that the "right" word here (by implication the word in the "original" version of the text) was 昧 *mei* 'dim'.

If we examine the reasons why we have chosen 昧 *mei* 'dim' instead of one of the other two possibilities as the preferred reading, they come down to two:

1. given that the senses of sentences two and three of the line as expressed in both the Mawangdui Copy B and Heshang Gong versions clearly suggest an "ironic opposition" in their respective meanings: "the advancing Dao seems as if withdrawing," and "the smooth-surfaced Dao seems as if marred by rough spots," the expected parallel reflection of that opposition in the first sentence with 明道 seems to be more keenly apparent in 昧 *mei* 'dim' than it is in either 費 *fei* 'extravagant' or 孛 *bei* 'exuberant'; and

2. 昧 *mei* 'dim' is the word to which we are inexorably drawn by our familiarity with the transmitted version of the line and the bias that that imparts.

---

[7] Li Jiahao has identified a two-character fragment among the residual pieces of these strips that seems to fit both physically and contextually at the end of strip 10 of the 乙 ms. here, containing the characters 女繢 . See Li Jiahao 李家浩 , "Guanyu Guodian *Laozi* Yizu Yizhi Canjian de Pinjie 關于郭店《老子》乙組一支殘簡的拼接," *Zhongguo Wenwu Bao*, October 28, 1998, p. 3. I am grateful to Professor Li Ling of Peking University for bringing Li Jiahao's article to my attention.

In other words, no one would think of suggesting that the word represented by all three variants was, for example, *fei* 'extravagant' and that 昧 and 孛 are loan characters for 費 (or *mutatis mutandis* all three stood for the word *bei* 'exuberant').

Of the two reasons for choosing 昧 *mei* 'dim', the second is no more than one early anonymous editor's decision that has become ratified, if not sanctified, by tradition. It deserves to be considered, but it does not intrinsically carry any more authority than any other opinion, and it certainly is not in and of itself decisive. The first of the two reasons arises from the structure of the passage proper. It is a logical inference, given the apparent syntactic and semantic parallelism of the three sentences with one another in the other versions of the text. But before concluding that 昧 *mei* 'dim' is the preferred reading, and that the variants are merely graphic, we must consider the alternatives. The main alternative is, of course, that the variation is lexical, not graphic, and that the *meanings* of the three versions vary according to what is written. This would give us as a starting point the three variants:

Mawangdui Copy B:    明道如費 "the brilliant Dao seems as if *extravagant*";

Heshang Gong:         明道若昧 "the brilliant Dao seems as if *dim*";

Guodian:              明道女孛 "the brilliant Dao seems as if *exuberant*."

Lexicologically the two words 費 *fei* < \**pʰəts* 'extravagant' and 孛 *bei* < \**bə́ts* 'exuberant' are likely to be cognate to each other, but not to 昧 *mei* < \**məts* 'dim'. Phonetically they are closer to each other than either is to 昧 *mei*, and semantically they both belong to a root sense of √ EMERGENT, BURST(ING) FORTH, which does not seem to apply to 昧 *mei* 'dim'.[8] This means that in effect the Mawangdui Copy B version and the Guodian version are lexical variants of each other, and constitute a single semantic alternative to 昧 *mei* 'dim' of the Heshang Gong text.

The fact that the 費 of Mawangdui Copy B and the 孛 of the Guodian slips are cognates intuitively militates against taking them both as mere loan characters for the Heshang Gong 昧 ; that would seem an unlikely coincidence. By the same token we now have a two-way lexical choice rather than a three-way choice: 'extravagant/exuberant' vs. 'dim', and we must consider the possibility that the line in its original form had either 費 *fei* < \**pʰəts* or 孛 *bei* < \**bə́ts*, and meant something like "the brilliant Dao seems as if radiantly-exuberant." The word 費 *fei* occurs in the *Zhao Hun* 招魂 poem of the *Chuci* in a similar usage: 晉制犀比 , 費白日些 "the Jin-made *xibi* buttons — radiating candescent and sun-like... ."[9] Beyond this, we must also reckon with the

---

[8] This set of cognate words could easily be expanded by looking no further than the 弗 and 孛 *xiesheng* series. The common sense of 費 as 'waste(ful)' is just a semantic specialization of 'bursting forth'; cf. Eng. *profligate*, literally 'to burst or dash forward'.

[9] I am indebted to Professor Ding Xiang Warner for drawing my attention to this line and for suggesting its possible pertinence to the question here.

possibility that the graphs 費 and 孛 could in their different versions of the text stand for words other than *fei* < \**pʰəts* 'extravagant' and *bei* < \**bəts* 'exuberant', respectively, but that still were at least phonetically and perhaps also semantically compatible with that orthographic representation. One of the best such possibilities is the word *fei* < \**pʰəts*, phonetically identical with 費 *fei* < \**pʰəts* 'extravagant', but meaning 'first light of the new moon' and conventionally written 朏. This word is likely a member of the √ EMERGENT, BURST(ING) FORTH word-family identified above, which has come to have a specialized, somewhat technical meaning. As a counterpart to *ming* 明 in the line in question, still preserving some aspect of the "ironic opposition" of the other lines, 朏 *fei* < \**pʰəts* 'first light of the new moon' seems a satisfactory possibility. At the same time, that very "ironic opposition" that is apparent in the Heshang Gong version of the text is much less a factor when the Guodian version is looked at independently. The Guodian word corresponding to Mawangdui Copy B and Heshang Gong 進 is missing altogether, leaving us unable to know from the evidence of the Guodian manuscript itself what kind of Dao might have been mentioned here as "like withdrawing," and the Guodian manuscript character that corresponds to the Mawangdui Copy B and Heshang Gong 夷 is a somewhat unfamilar graph 辿, given in the *Shuowen* as an alternate graph for *chi* 遲 'to move slowly, tarry' (*SWGL* 0764). If we take this at face-value, then the word *chi* 'slow-moving' as an adjunct to a Dao that is then described as "as if marred by bumps" seems not to evoke the same "ironic opposition" identifiable in the other versions. In the final analysis, then, the argument from semantic parallelism does not support the decision to see the Guodian manuscript 孛 as a graphic variant of 昧 standing for the word *mei* 'dim' in any particularly compelling way.

By contrast, it is comparatively easy to see how an original line that said either "the brilliant Dao seems as if *radiantly-extravagant/exuberant*" or "the full-shining Dao seems as if *newly luminous*" (in both cases writing either 費 *fei* < \**pʰəts* or 孛 *bei* < \**bəts*) could have been altered to "the brilliant Dao seems as if *dim*" (with 昧 *mei* < \**məts*) to bring out the contrastive sense of the line more sharply, making it a closer match to the "ironic opposition" of the second and third sentences as they came to appear in the Mawangdui Copy B and Heshang Gong texts than it was originally. The phonetic compatibility of 昧 *mei* < \**məts* with 費 *fei* < \**pʰəts* / 孛 *bei* < \**bəts* would have constituted a strong secondary factor reinforcing the shift. It is less easy to see how an original line with 昧 *mei* 'dim' would have come to be altered to one with either 費 *fei* or 孛 *bei* 'radiant/exuberant, newly emergent'. The reasoning is that we are able to identify a motivating factor in the first case, viz., the appeal of achieving a sharply expressed semantic parallelism between at least the first two sentences of the passage, if not among all three. For the alternative hypothesis, a shift from 昧 *mei* 'dim' to 費 *fei* or 孛 *bei*, the phonetic compatibility remains but there is no longer any clear semantic or stylistic motivation. This reasoning is a form of the application of the general rule that says that the "more difficult" reading is likely to be original. The sense of "more difficult" often includes, as in this case, an element of both "lexically less common" and "more idiosyncratic" relative to the content and style of the passage.

### Characters in Passages with No Known Transmitted Counterparts

When confronted with an unfamiliar or otherwise unattested and unknown character in a passage that has no transmitted, received counterpart, the problem becomes one of identifying a pronunciation and an associated meaning from a given but unfamiliar graphic form. This means in effect identifying the unknown graph with a known word. Pronunciation of unattested characters is best determined from *xiesheng* 諧聲 evidence; meaning from word-family evidence. I shall illustrate this briefly with one example from the first line of the *Tai Yi Sheng Shui* 大一生水 manuscript, a text that has no known transmitted, received counterpart.

The first line of this text is written as 大一生水二反楠大一是以成天二反楠大一是以成垟. The character 楠 occurs twice, clearly in parallel contexts. Its graphic structure is transparent: it consists of the "phonetic component" (more accurately called a *phonophoric*) 甫 *fu* < \**pà?* and the semantic classifier ("radical") 木 'wood, tree'. When we examine the set of characters based on 甫 *fu* < \**pà?* as a phonophoric, i.e., the 甫 *fu xiesheng* 諧聲 series, we find among others the following characters and words:

1. 輔 *fu* < \**bà?* 'to assist or support through some kind of reciprocity or complementarity';
2. 輔 *fu* < \**bà?* 'human jawbone; supporting struts at the sides of a carriage';
3. 浦 *puu* < \**pʰá?* 'river bank';
4. 酺 *pwu* < \**báh* 'drinking match';
5. 匍 *pwu* < \**báh* / *fwu* < \**bàh* 'to crawl';
6. 黼 *fuu* < \**pà?* 'complementary black and white matching decorative figures (often axe figures)';
7. 補 *buu* < \**pá?* 'mend, repair, shore up, fill in'.

Except for the last item of this list, each word can be seen to include a sense of reciprocity or complementarity in its meaning. This bears significantly on correctly identifying the word intended by the character 楠 and on understanding its precise meaning in this passage. The approach is to extract that element of meaning that seems to run through the whole set of words (or at least through most of them), and then to combine that with the meaning of whichever one of the words seems to fit the context best. Among the set of words above, clearly numbers 2–6 are too specific and concrete to make any sense in the line in question; that leaves 1 and 7. Given the apparent context of the line, 1 is a more suitable choice than 7, especially since it already can be seen to incorporate in its semantic plasma, so to speak, the common sense of "reciprocity /complementarity." Our conclusion then is that 楠 is best understood as a heretofore unattested allograph for 輔 *fu* 'to act reciprocally, to act in complementary concert with'. The whole line I would translate, tentatively, as:

Tai Yi ("The Grand Solitary One") begat the Waters; the Waters reciprocated in turn with Tai Yi, bringing forth thus Heaven. Heaven reciprocated in turn with Tai Yi, bringing forth thus Earth.

# On the Analysis and Transcription of Early Chinese Characters: Examples from the Guodian *Laozi*

## QIU XIGUI

The analysis and transcription of early Chinese characters are based primarily on their graphic forms and on the semantic context in which they occur. The Guodian bamboo slips are a collection of philosophical texts. Among them, the *Laozi* 老子 and *Zi Yi* 緇衣 can be collated with traditionally transmitted texts, while the *Wu Xing* 五行 can be collated with the silk-manuscript copy excavated at Changsha Mawangdui. Thus, the contents of the Guodian slips provide a more familiar context than many other types of paleographic material, and this greatly facilitates our analysis.

This paper will use examples from the bamboo-slip *Laozi* to discuss the methodology of analysis and transcription of early Chinese characters.[1] Some Guodian *Laozi* graphs have generally accepted transcriptions and these do not require analysis here.[2] For those graphs that do need analysis, our method of approach differs according to their particular attributes. These attributes are categorized below, with examples of the appropriate analytic technique for each category.

*A. Where textual evidence provides a direct basis for the interpretation of graphic form and semantic context, the interpretation will be relatively easier and more readily accepted.* Examples:

---

[1] The reader is also referred to Qiu Xigui, *Chinese Writing*, trans. Gilbert L. Mattos and Jerry Norman, Early China Special Monograph Series 4 (Berkeley: The Society for the Study of Early China and The Institute of East Asian Studies, University of California, 2000).

[2] [Translators' note: For the sake of clarity of exposition, we have sometimes translated *zi* 字 as "graph" and sometimes as "character." "Graph" is used specifically to refer to a Chu-script character before analysis, i.e., as it appears on the bamboo slip, before it has been interpreted as any known ancient or modern character. Otherwise, we translate *zi* as "character." We would also like to thank Gilbert Mattos for providing us with a number of the translations for technical terms used in Qiu Xigui, *Chinese Writing*, ibid., which we have followed in many cases here. All English translations of original text have been provided by the translators of this article.]

*#1.* 亙 （恆）

| Guodian Laozi | Received Text |
|---|---|
| A 6:8–16 | ch. 46 |
| 智（知）足之為足，此亙足矣． | 故知足之足，常足矣． |

In the text of Mawangdui Copy A, the character corresponding to 常 is 恆 (in Mawang-dui Copy B this character is damaged). Since 恆 was changed to 常 to respect the taboo on the name of Liu Heng 劉恆, the Han emperor Wen (r. 179–157 BC), 恆 ought to be the character originally used in the *Laozi*. The *Shuowen* (13 下，二部 ) says: 恆，常也．…亙, 古文恆从月．"詩"：如月之恆．[3] The form of the graph 亙 in the Guodian *Laozi* matches the old-script (*guwen*) 古文 form of 恆 found in the *Shuowen*. In bamboo slips from Chu, 恆 is usually written in this form.[4] Strictly speaking, this graph should be transcribed as 亙 and interpreted as 恆. Chu slips with examples of 恆 with the added 心 component further support this reading.[5]

*#2.* 𪾀 （道）

| Guodian Laozi | Received Text |
|---|---|
| A 6:17 to 7:3 | ch. 30 |
| 已（以）𪾀差（佐）人宔（主）者， | 以道佐人主者，不以兵強天下． |
| 不谷（欲）已（以）兵弜（強）於天下． | |

The graph 𪾀 also occurs at Guodian *Laozi* A 10:16 and A 13:3, for which the corre-sponding characters in the received text (chapters 15 and 37) are both 道 (elsewhere in the Guodian *Laozi* A, B, and C the other occurrences of 道 use the character form with the component 首 , i.e., 道 ). The *Han Jian* 汗簡 records that 道 was sometimes written 𪾀, with an example attributed to the *Guwen* ("old-script") *Shangshu* 古文尚書.[6] The *Guwen Si Sheng Yun* 古文四聲韻 also lists this variant form under the entry for 道 , attributing it to an "old" *Shangshu* 古尚書. Moreover, it gives an example at-tributed to an "old" *Laozi* 古老子, written as 𪾀.[7] All of these correspond to the graph 𪾀 in the bamboo slips.

    *B. Where the appropriate character is clear from the textual context, but its graphic form requires additional explanation. Examples:*

---

  [3] *Shuowen Jiezi* 說文解字 (Beijing: Zhonghua Shuju, 1972), 13 *xia*, p. 286.

  [4] See Teng Rensheng 縢壬生 , *Chuxi Jian Bo Wenzi Bian* 楚系簡帛文字編 (Wuhan: Hubei Jiaoyu Press, 1995), pp. 959–61.

  [5] Ibid.

  [6] *Han Jian, Guwen Si Sheng Yun* 汗簡．古文四聲韻 (Beijing: Zhonghua Shuju, 1983), p. 5.

  [7] Ibid., p. 44.

*#3.* 迻　（絕）

This graph appears three times on slip 1 of the Guodian *Laozi*: A 1:1, 9, 17; the corresponding characters in chapter 19 of the received text are in each case 絕 . For example, 迻巧弃利 in slip 1 is read in the received text as 絕巧弃利. The *Shuowen* entry for 絕 says: 絕，斷絲也，从糸，从刀，从卩. 𢇍古文絕，象不連體絕二絲 (" 絕 is cut silk, derived from 糸 , from 刀, from 卩. 𢇍 is the old-script form of 絕 ; it resembles two pieces of silk that are cut and not joined to one another").[8] The character 絕 is written as 𢇍 in the inscription on the *Zhongshan Wang Cuo Hu* 中山王䤿壺 bronze vessel.[9] From this, we can see that the graph was a representation of a knife cutting silk. The old-script form in the *Shuowen* entry mistakenly splits the 刀 component in two. The entry in the *Shuowen* for 繼 is also mistaken when it says 反𢇍為繼 (" 繼 is a reversed 𢇍").[10] In fact, apart from a small number of characters, such as ナ (左) ("left") and 又 ( 右 ) ("right"), the right-left orientation of a graph does not have semantic significance in early Chinese writing; the old-script form of 絕 should not be regarded as an exception.

In the Baoshan 包山 bamboo slips, one of the spirits to whom sacrifice was made is called 迻無後者 .[11] In both *Baoshan Chu Jian* 包山楚簡 and *Chuxi Jian Bo Wenzi Bian*, this is transcribed as: 繼無後者. However, as other scholars have already pointed out, this graph should be transcribed as 絕 rather than 繼; 絕無後者 means 絕子絕孫 的人 ("one who cuts off descendants"). For the 絕 in the first sentence of chapter 20 of the received text, Guodian *Laozi* actually has the form 迻 (B 4:8). When used as a component in early Chinese characters, the single and double 幺 are usually equivalent; for example, in Chu bamboo slips 幾 is usually simplified and written with one 幺 (�).[12] There is no difficulty, then, in concluding that the graph 迻 on slip 1 of Guodian *Laozi* A is a simplified form of 絕. 絕 is also written in this form on the burial inventory slips from the Chu Tomb Number Two at Wangshan 望山 ; however, both the *Wangshan Chu Jian* 望山楚簡 and *Chuxi Jian Bo Wenzi Bian* mistakenly transcribe the graph as 䌉 ( 繼 ).

*#4.* 攷　（考）

The graph 攷 in the line 絕攷弃利 (Guodian *Laozi* A 1:9–12) is a commonly seen character and appears in the *Shuowen*. However, the corresponding character in the received text is not 攷 but 巧 . We must thus explain, from the standpoint of graphic

---

[8] *Shuowen Jiezi*, 13 *shang*, p. 271.

[9] *Jinwenbian* 金文編 (Beijing: Zhonghua Shuju, 1985), p. 858.

[10] *Shuowen Jiezi*, 13 *shang*, p. 272.

[11] See *Baoshan Chu Jian* 包山楚簡 (Beijing: Wenwu, 1991), slips 249, 250.

[12] *Chuxi Jian Bo Wenzi Bian*, p. 328; Guodian *Laozi* A 25:21 also has this form of 幾 .

form, how 攷 can be read as 巧 . The archaic pronunciation of these two characters was very similar; and they share the phonetic signifier 丂, the *Shuowen* entry for which says: 古文以為丂(于)字，又以為巧字 .[13]

From early times on, the characters 考 and 攷 have been used interchangeably when the meaning denoted is 考察 ("investigate," "inspect"). For example, where the "Shundian 舜典" section of the *Shangshu* 尚書 has: 三載考績, the *Shangshu Dazhuan* 尚書大傳 has: 三載攷績 . Where the *Zhou Li* 周禮 has: 攷乃職事 , in the same phrase in the *Yi Zhoushu* 逸周書, 攷 is written 考 .[14] Moreover, in this period, the characters 考 and 巧 were also used interchangeably. For example, in the "Jinteng 金縢" section of the *Shangshu* we find: 予仁若考, whereas in the same phrase in the "Lu Shijia 魯世家" section of the *Shiji* 史記, 考 is written 巧 . In the *Yijing* 易經 we find the sentences 視履考祥 and 有子考, while in the Mawangdui silk-manuscript edition both 考 are written as 巧 .[15] Clearly, then, there is no difficulty with reading 攷 as 巧 . In such cases, where the interchangeable relationship between characters is clear, such supporting evidence is generally omitted in concise annotations.

*C. Where there is no clear textual evidence to support an interpretation of a graph, it is necessary to employ direct analysis of its form.* Examples:

#5. 見 （視）

| Guodian Laozi | Received Text |
| --- | --- |
| B 3:1–7 | ch. 59 |
| 長生舊 ( 久 )見之道也 | 長生久視之道 |
| | |
| C 5:7–11 | ch. 35 |
| 見之不足見（見） | 視之不足見 |

The scholars who transcribed and annotated the Guodian bamboo-slip texts observed correctly that the bottom component of 見 is usually in the form of a kneeling human figure: ㇌; but that, in cases where the bottom component is a standing human figure: ㇏, then the character is 視 .[16] Thus, the graph 見 is a semantographic protoform of 視 ("to look").

In previously excavated Chu-script materials, the bottom component of the character which represents the word 見 is always the kneeling figure. In the Baoshan bam-

---

[13] *Shuowen Jiezi*, 5 *shang*, 丂 *bu*, p. 101.

[14] *Zhou Li* 周禮, 夏官, 職方氏 ; *Yi Zhoushu* 逸周書, 職方 .

[15] Mawangdui silk-manuscript *Yijing* 易經 : "Lü, top nine," "Gu, first six" ( 履, 上九 ; 蠱, 初六 ). See *Mawangdui Han Mu Wenwu* 馬王堆漢墓文物 (Changsha: Hunan Press, 1992), pp. 107, 108.

[16] *Guodian Chu Mu Zhujian*, p. 114, note 6.

boo slips, an official title, written 𢇛日 , was initially transcribed as 見日 , but in fact should be transcribed as 視日. In the "Chen She Shijia 陳涉世家" section of the *Shiji*, we find: 周文 , 陳之賢人也 , 嘗為項燕軍視日 .[17] The last two characters are also the title of a Chu office, which might be related to the 視日 in the bamboo slips.

Having clarified the difference between 見 and 𢇛 in the Chu bamboo slips, we now turn to earlier paleographic materials. We find that the distinction also holds true in the Yinxu oracle-bone inscriptions, the Zhouyuan oracle-bone inscriptions, and Western Zhou bronze inscriptions. In these materials, if any graph previously transcribed as 見 has a standing human figure for the bottom component, the transcription should be changed to 視 .[18]

It is noteworthy that among the occurrences of the graph which represents 見 in the Guodian *Wu Xing* 五行 text are examples where the bottom component is a standing human figure 𠆢; in these cases, 見 is not differentiated from 視.[19] This indicates that the tendency to abandon the use of the human figure component under the 目 component to differentiate between the two words had already begun at this time. In fact, the graph 睍, which combines semantic and phonetic signifiers to denote 視 , appears earlier than this in the He Zun 何尊 inscription.[20]

#6. 𣊒 ; 尋 *(A 31:12 has 㝈 )*

| Guodian Laozi | Received Text |
|---|---|
| A 1:15–18 | ch. 19 |
| 𣊒尋亡又 | 盜賊無有 |

| A 31:11–14 | ch. 57 |
| 𣊒㝈多又 | 盜賊多有 |

The use of 亡 for 無 and 又 for 有 is common in early texts and excavated paleographic materials. However, the bamboo-slip characters 𣊒尋, corresponding to 盜 and 賊 in the received text of the *Laozi*, are very particular and require specific explanation.

The former of the two is best classified as a character with both semantic and phonetic signifiers. Its right-hand component is 兆 , which ought to be the phonetic

---

[17] *Shiji, juan* 48 (Beijing: Zhonghua Shuju, 1959), p. 1954. [This line is ambiguous and may be read as "Zhou Wen was a worthy man of Chen; he once divined days for Xiang Yan's army" or "he was once the *shiri* for Xiang Yan's army." Ed.]

[18] For a detailed discussion of 視 and 見 in oracle-bone inscriptions, see Qiu Xigui, "Jiaguwen zhong zhi Jian yu Shi 甲骨文中之見與視," in *Jiaguwen Faxian Yibai Zhounian Xueshu Yantaohui Lunwenji* 甲骨文發現一百週年學術研討會論文集 (Taibei: Wenshizhe, 1998).

[19] See slips 23 and 29.

[20] See *Jinwen Bian*, p. 619.

signifier.[21] The left-hand component is the semantographic protoform that represents 視 (𥄎); when used as a semantic signifier, it is equivalent to 見. Thus, 𥄎 can be transcribed as 覜, a character that appears in the *Shuowen*. The accepted reconstruction of its initial consonant in archaic Chinese falls in the 透 category of initials and the 宵 rhyme group. Its pronunciation would have been very close to that of 盜, whose initial is in the 定 group and whose rhyme group is the same. Thus, we can conclude that in the Guodian bamboo slips, the character 覜 has been borrowed to represent 盜.

The graph 悥 also has both a semantic and a phonetic signifier. The semantic component is 心. As for the phonetic component, in the Guodian slips, the character 則, originally written 𢧵, 𢧵, 𠞆, etc.,[22] is often written in a simplified form as 𤕟, 𤕝, 𤕓, and 𢆶.[23] We can surmise, then, that 悥 is the character 惻, composed of the semantic signifier 心 and the phonetic signifier 則. The character 賊 was originally written 𧵥, composed of the semantic signifier 戈 and the phonetic signifier 則.[24] Since both 惻 and 賊 have the phonetic element 則, their pronunciation in archaic Chinese would have been very close. Thus, the bamboo slips use 惻 as a phonetic loan for 賊.

*D. Where it is possible to determine an interpretation based on the textual context, but not possible to explain the form of the graph. Examples:*

#7. 逄    (失)

| Guodian Laozi | Received Text |
|---|---|
| C 11:6–10 | ch. 64 |
| 執之者逄之 | 執者失之 |
| | |
| A 11:11–15 | ch. 64 |
| 亡（無）執古（故）亡（無）逄 | 無執故無失 |
| | |
| B 6:6–13 | ch. 13 |
| 得之若纓（驚），逄之若纓（驚） | 得之若驚，失之若驚 |

The graph in this example also occurs in the Chu silk manuscript and the Baoshan bamboo slips and can be represented in a modern form as 遊. Until recently the character was usually interpreted as 達 or 逆, but with these readings the passages in which

---

[21] Compare the character 逃, *Chuxi Jian Bo Wenzi Bian*, pp. 145–46. Also Guodian *Laozi* A 25:9; the 兆 component of 菲 (used as a loan for 兆), is written in this way.

[22] The first two of these three graphs are from the *Chuxi Jian Bo Wenzi Bian*, p. 350; the third is from Guodian *Laozi* C 12:5.

[23] Sources for the previous four graphs: 1) Guodian *Xing Zi Ming Chu* 性自命出, slips 2, 19, 20, etc.; 2) ibid., slip 25; 3) Guodian *Zi Yi* 緇衣, slips 2, 4, 5, etc.; and 4) Guodian *Laozi* A 35:12; *Laozi* B 2:5; *Zi Yi*, slip 31; etc.

[24] See *Shuowen Jiezi*, 12 *xia*, 戈 *bu*, p. 266.

the character occurs are difficult to understand. Scholars have now realized, on the basis of as yet unpublished Chu slips, that this character should be read as 失 and that all instances of this character in the Chu silk manuscript from Zidan and bamboo slips from Baoshan should be read in this way (in some cases 逤 should be read as 佚, equivalent to 逸).[25] The Guodian slips provide further evidence for this reading. Nevertheless, from the point of view of graphic form, we are still not clear why this character can be read as 失.

E. *Cases in which, unlike the above examples, the bamboo-slip texts contain characters which do not match the corresponding characters in the received text.*

In such cases, if we find it impossible to make sense of a character in the sentence in which it occurs, then we must consider the possibility that the graph was written incorrectly. But if we can make sense of the sentence, then we may conjecture that the characters in the Guodian *Laozi* bamboo-slip text and the received text simply are different.

When the Guodian *Laozi* and received text characters differ, those of the Guodian *Laozi* slips are all the more valuable in understanding the history of the text. For example, the received text, chapter 19, states: 見素抱樸, whereas Guodian *Laozi* A 2:11–14 has: 夕 (視, to be read as 示 here) 素保樸. The phrase 示素 ("exhibit plainness") is more appropriate than 見素 ("see plainness"). Moreover, although the meanings of 保 and 抱 are similar and the two could be interchanged as loans, 保樸 ("preserve simplicity") is more understandable than 抱樸 ("embrace simplicity"). Thus, the Guodian *Laozi* version makes better sense than the received text, and it is very likely that this was what originally appeared in the *Laozi*. Below are a few further examples:

#8. 㚓 (辯)

| Guodian Laozi | Received Text |
|---|---|
| A 1:1–4 | ch. 19 |
| 絕智弃㚓 | 絕聖棄智 |

The scholars who annotated the *Guodian Chu Mu Zhujian* correctly read 㚓 as 辯. C 8:16 to 9:3 has: 是已(以)㚓牆(將)軍居左; according to the corresponding received text in chapter 31, the character 㚓 should be read as 偏. The Guodian slip-text of *Cheng Zhi Wen Zhi* 成之聞之, slips 31–32, has: 分為夫婦之㚓, the last character of which is undoubtedly a variant form of 㚓; their transcription reads this as 辨. The Guodian slip-text *Zun De Yi* 尊得義, slips 13–14, has: 善(教)已(以)㚓兌 ... ; the annotators' transcription reads the two characters after 已 as 辯說. The Guodian *Wu*

[25] For the Chu silk manuscript, see Rao Zongyi 饒宗頤, *Chu Di Chutu Wenxian San Zhong Yanjiu* 楚地出土文獻三種研究 (Beijing: Zhonghua Shuju, 1993). For the Baoshan slips, see Hubei Sheng Jingsha Tielu Kaogudui 湖北省荊沙鐵路考古隊, *Baoshan Chu Jian* 包山楚簡 (Beijing: Wenwu Press, 1991).

*Xing*, slips 33–34, has: 甲（中）心𧨼然而正行之. The graph 𧨼 is clearly composed of the semantic signifier 言 and the phonetic signifier 弁. The Mawangdui silk-manuscript *Wu Xing* has 辯焉 for the phrase 𧨼然.

The archaic Chinese pronunciations for 偏, 辨, and 辯 are very close, and this supports the above readings. However, the *Guodian Chu Mu Zhujian* transcription 下 given for 弁 is not convincing. The character 弁 also occurs on slip 2, slip 12, etc., of the bamboo slips from Tomb Number Two at Wangshan, and the following annotation is given in *Wangshan Chu Jian*: "The old-script form of 鞭 in the *Shuowen* is 𠓥; the graph here is 弁 — the graphic form is slightly different. Here this character apparently ought to be read as 縺 ."[26] We can adopt their analysis. The Guodian *Laozi* form of 弁 is even closer to the old-script form of 鞭 in the *Shuowen*. The archaic pronunciation of 鞭 is also very close to that of 偏, 辨, and 辯 . In the Mawangdui *Laozi* Copy A, 偏 is written as 便 in the phrase 偏將軍 . In Western Zhou bronze inscriptions, 便 has the form 偁,[27] a representation of a whip being used to beat a person, which originally indicated the verbal use of 鞭 . This can be considered as supporting evidence for our analysis of 弁 as the old-script form of 鞭 .

Thus, the Guodian line 絕智棄辯 ("cut off wisdom and discard disputation") is most probably the line as it occurred in the original *Laozi*, and the corresponding line in the received text 絕聖棄智 ("cut off sageliness and discard wisdom"), a change made by someone at a later period. This question is further discussed below.

#9.

| *Guodian Laozi* | *Received Text* |
|---|---|
| A 1:17–24 | ch. 19 |
| 絕𢚩弃𢝺, 民復季＜孝＞子（慈） | 絕仁弃義, 民復孝慈 |

The Guodian *Laozi* phrase comes after: 絕巧棄利, 盜賊無有, whereas in the received text it comes before. Mawangdui Copies A and B are basically the same as that in the received text. Both 𢚩 and 𢝺 are characters with semantic and phonetic signifiers and in both cases the semantic signifier is 心 .

The graph 𢚩 has the phonetic signifier 為 ; this component is written with the same form as the character 為 in the Guodian *Laozi* A, slips 2, 3, 10, 11, 17, 25, 29, etc. The phonetic signifier of 𢝺 is 虐, and its form is the same as that of the 虐 component in the Chu bamboo-slip characters 襦 and 虐.[28] In the character 虐, 且 acts as the pho-

[26] Hubei Sheng Wenwu Kaogu Yanjiusuo, Beijing Daxue Zhongwen Xi 湖北省文物考古研究所, 北京大學中文系, ed., *Wangshan Chu Jian* 望山楚簡 (Beijing: Zhonghua Shuju, 1995), p. 116, note 16.

[27] *Jinwen Bian*, p. 566.

[28] *Chuxi Jian Bo Wenzi Bian*, pp. 22, 69.

netic signifier. When used as phonetic signifiers, 且 and 虍 can be interchanged with one another. Examples in early texts, where 櫨 is written as 柤, and 嫭 written as 姐, all illustrate this point. Therefore the Chu bamboo-slip character 蒩 is equivalent to 苴 and 裭 is equivalent to 詛 (for example, the phrase 盟詛 is written in Chu slips as 盟裭). The *Hanshu* 漢書 has variant forms of the character 詛: 諎 and 裭;[29] the latter example is identical in form to that of the Chu slip.

The phonetic signifier 且 is also interchangeable with the phonetic signifier 乍. The old-script form of 殂 in the *Shuowen* is 虘. The poem "Gufeng 谷風" in the "Beifeng 邶風" section of the *Shijing* contains the line: 既阻我德, but the *Taiping Yulan* 太平御覽 (*juan* 835) quotes this line from the *Hanshi* 韓詩 with 阻 written as 詐. The ode "Dang 蕩," from the "Daya 大雅" section of the *Shijing* contains: 侯作侯祝 ; and the *Jingdian Shiwen* 經典釋文 says: "for 作 some editions have 詛." When this line is quoted in the *Zhengyi* 正義 commentary to the "Wuyi 無逸" section of the *Shangshu*, it actually uses 詛 .

The character 作 was also interchangeable with 詐 in early texts. The "Yueling 月令" chapter of the *Liji* ("Jichun zhi yue 季春之月" section) has the line: 毋或作為淫巧, about which the commentary of Zheng Xuan 鄭玄 explains: "In the current *Yueling*, 作為 is written as 詐偽 ." Thus, without doubt, the Guodian *Laozi* A 1:17–20: 絕惡棄慮, should be read 絕偽棄詐 ("cut off artifice and discard deceit"). This is most probably the original form of the text. Someone later changed 偽 and 詐 to 仁 and 義; and then, because the latter two were considered to be more significant than 巧 and 利 , the line 絕仁棄義 was moved in front of 絕巧棄利 .

Examples 8 and 9 both come from text in the Guodian slips that corresponds to text of the received text chapter 19. According to the analysis above, the ideas contained in this chapter originally did not include one that espouses opposition to 聖 ("sageliness"), 仁 ("humaneness"), or 義 ("rightness"). The 絕聖 and 絕仁棄義 in the received text are a reaction to the Confucianist and Mohist emphasis on those very same qualities. Clearly, then, the date of this chapter in the received text is relatively late. In comparison, what the Guodian *Laozi* bamboo slips oppose is 智 ("wisdom"), 辯 ("disputation"), 巧 ("cleverness"), 利 ("profit"), 偽 ("artifice"), and 詐 ("deceit"). Since the thought expressed is relatively less sophisticated, the Guodian version ought to be judged as earlier than that of the received text. This is of the greatest importance for research on the development of Daoist thought and the origin and development of the *Laozi*. That the Mawangdui silk-manuscript edition had already undergone change and is basically the same as the received text further demonstrates the value of the bamboo-slip edition.[30]

---

[29] See the *Hanshu* 漢書: for the first example, *juan* 60 ("Wai Qi Zhuan 外戚傳"); for the second, *juan* 15 ("Wang Zi Hou Biao 王子侯表") and *juan* 27 ("Wuxing Zhi 五行志").

[30] [Editors' note: Qiu later revised his analysis of these two graphs; see pp. 236–37.]

*#10.* 埶 （設）

| Guodian Laozi | Received Text | Mawangdui |
|---------------|---------------|-----------|
| C 4:1–6 | ch. 35 | Copies A and B |
| 埶大象 | 執大象 | 執大象 |

I have already suggested in an earlier paper, "On the Analysis of the Yinxu Oracle Bone Script 遠, 狱(邇) and Related Characters," that in archaic Chinese, the characters 埶 and 設 were very close phonetically, such that the former could be used as a phonetic loan for the latter.[31] In the bamboo-slip edition of the *Yi Li* 儀禮 that was found at Wuwei 武威, 埶 usually denotes 設; and such examples also occur in Yinxu oracle-bone divinations. In an unpublished paper, "Examples of the Use of 埶 as a Loan for 設 and Its Confusion with 執 in Early Texts," I give further early examples where the former should be read as the latter, also pointing out that 埶 is sometimes mistakenly written as the graphically similar 執. Such evidence supports the reading of 埶 as 設 in this example.

The meaning of 設 in the phrase 設大象 is nearly the same as that in the phrase 設卦觀象 from the "Xici 繫辭 " (*shang* 上 ) section of the *Yijing*: 聖人設卦觀象 , 繫辭焉而明吉凶... ("the sage set out the hexagram and looked at the image; appending a statement there, he clarified the auspicious and inauspicious...").[32] The 執 given in the received *Laozi* is most likely a mistake for the graphically similar 埶.

*#11.* 眉 （狀）

| Guodian Laozi | Received Text | Mawangdui |
|---------------|---------------|-----------|
| A 21:1–8 | ch. 25 | Copies A and B |
| 又 ( 有)眉蟲 <蟲> 成 ， | 有物混成 ， | 有物昆成 ， |
| 先天墬(地)生 | 先天地生 | 先天地生 |

An English translation of the received text's phrase would be: "There is a thing from murk formed, born before heaven and earth." The authors of *Guodian Chu Mu Zhujian* state that: "眉 has the semantic signifier 爿 and phonetic 百 (百 and 首 are variant forms of the same character); we suspect it should be read as 道. The 物 of the Mawangdui copies is a reference to 道. Also, 蟲 is the original form of 昆 (as in 昆蟲) and can be read as 混."[33] However, if the first sentence reads 有道混成 ("There is *a way* from murk formed"), and we take the language of the subsequent lines into account, then the sense of the passage is not clear. Here the Guodian *Laozi* reads: 未智 ( 知 ) 元 ( 其 ) 名 ，

---

[31] Qiu Xigui, *Guwenzi Lunji* 古文字論集 (Beijing: Zhonghua Shuju 1992), p. 7.

[32] *Yijing*, sect. "Xici 繫辭 " (*shang* 上 ).

[33] *Guodian Chu Mu Zhujian*, p. 116, note 51.

芽 ( 字 ) 之曰道 ("Not yet knowing its name, I give it the honorific 'way'"). The corre-sponding reading in the received text is: 吾不知其名 , 字之曰道 ("I do not know its name, I give it the honorific 'way'"). Evidently 頒 ought not be read as 道 .

The Guodian *Wu Xing*, slip 36, also has the character 頒 in the line that reads: 已 ( 以 ) 亓 ( 其 ) 外心與人交 , 遠也 , 遠而頒之 , 敬也 . The annotators note that: "in the Mawangdui *Wu Xing*, the character in question is written 奘 , and in the commentary section of the *Wu Xing*, the character used is 莊 . 頒 has the phonetic signifier 爿 and can be interchanged with 莊 ."[34] This explanation is correct.

The graph 頒 (*Laozi* A 21:2) should, without doubt, also be analyzed as having the semantic signifier 百 ( 首 ) and phonetic signifier 爿 , and should be read as a loan for 狀 on the basis of its context, noting that the latter also uses 爿 as phonetic signi-fier. In chapter 14 of the received text we find: 視之不見名曰夷 , 聽之不聞名曰希 , 搏之不得名曰微 . 此三者不可致詰 , 故混而為一 . [Mawangdui Copies A and B have 一者 here] 其上不皦 , 其下不昧 , 繩繩不可名 , 復歸於無物 . 是謂無狀之狀 , 無物之象 , 是謂惚恍 . ...

What cannot be seen is called nebulous; what cannot be heard is called rarefied; what cannot be felt is called minute. These three cannot be reckoned. And so they are mixed up and looked upon as one. [As for the One,] Its upper part is not dazzling; its lower part is not obscure. Endless, it cannot be named, and returns to being nothing. This is called the shape that has no shape, the image that is no thing. This is called indistinct and shadowy. ...

The 頒 ( 狀 ) of A 21:2 is that of 無狀之狀 ("the shape that has no shape "), so it is more logical to read this character as 狀 ("shape") than 物 ("thing").

These are only a few examples of our analysis of graphs in the Guodian bamboo-slip *Laozi*. However, there are still many graphs in the Guodian texts which cannot be interpreted accurately at present, and these await further study.

[34] Ibid., p. 153, note 47.

# Some Observations concerning the Transcription and Punctuation of the Guodian *Laozi*

## *GAO MING*

The Guodian bamboo-slip *Laozi* 老子 is comprised of three different groups of slips, each with different contents. The scholars who sorted and arranged the slips divided them into three groups: A, B, and C. This was done on the basis of the shape of the slips and the style of the writing. None of the groups is divided into a *Dejing* 德經 and *Daojing* 道經 , as are both the received text and the silk-manuscript copies from Changsha Mawangdui. The three Guodian groups internally mix material from both the *Dejing* and *Daojing*. Group A begins with a section corresponding to the received text, chapter 19, and comprises twenty such chapters. Group B starts with chapter 59 and comprises eight chapters. Group C starts from chapter 17 and is made up of five chapters.

The second half of chapter 64 appears in both A and C, the only case of a repeated section of text. In total, the three groups have 32 chapters, equivalent to approximately two-fifths of the complete text of the received *Laozi*. Apart from a different chapter order and a few differences in characters, the majority of the contents of the Guodian bamboo-slip *Laozi* is essentially the same as, or similar to, the Han silk-manuscript from Mawangdui. We should acknowledge the difficulty of the task accomplished by the Guodian compilers, who ordered materials that were originally a jumble of slips containing various ancient texts, and which were excavated from a previously disturbed tomb. This work is truly a great contribution to scholarship.

Scholars have different views concerning the manner of composition and the nature of the Guodian *Laozi*; and there is stil no consensus of opinion. I believe that none of its three *Laozi* groups represents the original form of the *Laozi* and, furthermore, that they are not complete texts in themselves, but constitute copied selections from the classic text of the *Laozi*. They cannot take the place of the silk-manuscript or received *Laozi*. Time constraints have made it impossible to undertake a complete study of the whole of the Guodian bamboo-slip *Laozi*, so I am unable as yet to express an overall opinion concerning the text and will simply make some observations on a few transcriptions and points of punctuation.

*#1. A 1:17-24*

| *Guodian Laozi* A 1:17–24 | *Mawangdui* Copies A and B | *Received Text* ch. 19 |
|---|---|---|
| 絕[illegible]棄[illegible], | 絕仁棄義, | 絕仁棄義, |
| 民復季子. | 民復孝慈. | 民復孝慈. |

Of the eight Guodian *Laozi* characters, three are phonetic loans and one is miswritten. Based on a collation with Mawangdui silk-manuscript Copies A and B, the second clause ought to read 民復孝慈; the character 子 (A 1:24) is a phonetic loan for 慈; and the 季 is clearly an incorrectly written 孝. It is the four characters previous to these that are worthy of closer study. From the Mawangdui manuscript copies, we can see that the transcription of the two characters as 絕 and 棄 is correct. However, in *Guodian Chu Mu Zhujian*, [illegible] is transcribed as 㥶 and explained as a phonetic loan for 偽; [illegible] is transcribed as [illegible] and read as a phonetic loan for 詐, yielding the line 絕偽棄詐 ("cut off artifice and discard deceit"). Compared with the corresponding text of both the Mawangdui and received text ("cut off humaneness and discard righteousness"), we get an entirely different meaning. With regard to how this difference should be understood, some scholars believe that the Guodian version was the original form of the *Laozi* and that the characters in the Mawangdui manuscripts are an alteration made by someone at a later stage.

Although we cannot rule out the possibility of alteration by a later hand, we should not take the argument that these two characters are being used as loans in this manner as conclusive. For example, let us first consider the character 㥶, not found in lexicons. Its form is made up of a 心 component used as semantic signifier and a 為 as phonetic signifier. Thus, it ought to be a variant form of the character 譌, since 心 and 言 could be interchanged in ancient Chinese script when used as semantic signifiers. For example, 訓 could also be written with a 心 component, yielding [illegible]; 警 could be written 憼; and 慕 could be written as 謨. These examples are evidence that the characters 㥶 and 譌 are identical. Additionally, A 13:8–18 has the line 侯王能守之而萬物將自㥶; in Mawangdui Copy B the corresponding passage is 侯王若能守之萬物將自化 (received *Laozi*, chapter 37). In the Guodian slips the 㥶 is a phonetic loan for 化, as demonstrated in the following. In the Mawangdui Copy A the character corresponding to 化 is also written 㥶, illustrating that the latter not only could be used as a loan for 偽, but also could be read as 化 and 譌. If we take it as a phonetic loan, then 㥶 can also be read as 義. This is because both 譌 and 義 have initials in the 疑 group and both are in the 歌 rhyme group: they share the same initial and rhyme group. Taking 㥶 as a phonetic loan for 義 is not only logical, but the meaning of the text is then also close to that of the Mawangdui *Laozi*.

In the Mawangdui copies, the previous sentence is 絕聖棄智, while the bamboo slips have 絕智棄攱. The 智 follows 絕 in the one, and 棄 in the other, but the meaning of these phrases is the same. Similarly, where the Mawangdui copies have 絕仁棄義, the bamboo-slip version is 絕義棄𡟰; again, one has 絕義, the other 棄義, but the meaning is the same. It is thus clear that although the traditional and bamboo-slip texts are not the same, they have a definite genealogical relationship.

As for the character 𡟰, in the *Guodian Chu Mu Zhujian* it is transcribed as 慮 and read as a phonetic loan for 詐. They explain that 慮 has the phonetic signifier 且, and is phonetically close to 詐. The Guodian bamboo-slip *Zi Yi* 緇衣 (slip 33) employs the same character, written as 𡟰. By comparing the latter with the corresponding character in the received *Zi Yi* (that found in the *Liji* 禮記), the affected sentence should read 慮其所終. Clearly, in Guodian *Laozi* A this character should also be transcribed as 慮. Ikeda Tomohisa's suggested transcription of 慮 is correct. If the character is indeed 慮, then it cannot be read as 詐; although its rhyme group is close, its initial consonant is too different. On the basis of the Mawangdui *Laozi*, I earlier suspected that the character should be read 仁, but although the initial consonants of 仁 and 慮 are close, their rhyme groups are very far apart. Thus, to take this character as a phonetic loan for either 詐 or 仁 seems inappropriate. How it should be read is difficult to determine at present. It will have to await further study, but it is also hard to avoid considering the possibility that there is a mistake in the text; like the 孝 in the line 民復孝慈 which was mistakenly written as 季.

A range of opinions is always preferable, so I will now raise a few other questions as a demonstration that other readings are also possible elsewhere in the text.

*#2. A 1:25 to 2:10*

| Guodian Laozi A 1:25 to 2:10 | Mawangdui Copies A and B |
|---|---|
| 三言以為貞不足, | 三言以為文未足, |
| 或命之或虖豆. | 故令之有所屬. |

The transcription in *Guodian Chu Mu Zhujian* takes 貞 as 弁, a phonetic loan for 辨; analyzes 虖 as 乎; and takes 豆 as a phonetic loan for 屬. Thus, the whole sentence reads: 三言以為辨不足, 或令之或乎屬. Qiu Xigui has added an additional note: "It seems 乎 ought to be read as 呼 here. I suspect that 或命之 and 或乎屬 should be read as two separate clauses." I think it is inappropriate to read 弁 as a loan for 辨 here; we should follow the Mawangdui silk-manuscript *Laozi*, and take it as a phonetic loan for 文. Thus, this line should be read as 三言以為文不足, equivalent in meaning to Mawangdui Copies A and B (see table above) ("These three sayings — their text is not yet regarded as sufficient"). In archaic Chinese, the initial of the character 弁 is in the 並 group and its rhyme group is 元; the initial for 文 is in the 明 group, and the rhyme group is 文. These two initial-groups are labials; and the rhyme groups are lateral conversions 旁轉, thus, 弁 and 文 had similar archaic pronunciations and were interchangeable.

Our reading of 或命之或乎屬 should also follow the Mawangdui silk manuscripts
— the second 或 should be taken as a loan for 有, thus the sentence should be read as:
或令之有乎（所）屬. The meaning of the bamboo slip-text is thus the same as the
corresponding passage in the silk manuscripts. The reading of 或 as a phonetic loan
for 有 is not only supported by the closeness of their ancient pronunciation, enabling
the potential for mutual phonetic interchange, but also by textual evidence. Examples
include:

 1. The "Wuyi 無逸" section of the *Shangshu* 尚書 (*Zhou Shu* 周書): 乃或亮
陰，三年不言. This line is quoted in the *Shiji* 史記 ("Lu Shijia 魯世家"), as 乃有
亮闇，三年不言.

 2. The "Wuyi" also has the line 亦罔或克壽, quoted in the *Hanshu* 漢書
("Zheng Chong Zhuan 鄭崇傳") as 亦罔有克壽.

 3. The line 小子無有宿問 in the *Da Dai Liji* 大戴禮記 ("Wudi De 五帝德")
occurs in the *Kongzi Jiayu* 孔子家語 as 小子無或宿問.

 4. In the *Liji* ("Yueling 月令") the line 無有斬伐, which in the *Lüshi
Chunqiu* 呂氏春秋 ("Ji Xia 季夏") is written 無或斬伐.

 5. The phrase 故有得神以興，亦有以亡 in the *Zuo Zhuan* 左傳 (Zhuang
Gong 莊公 32) is given as 故或得神以興，亦或以亡 in the *Guoyu* 國語 ("Zhou
Yu 周語").

 6. The *Zuo Zhuan* (Ai Gong 哀公 7) has 曹人或夢眾君子立於社宮而謀亡曹，
whereas the *Shiji* ("Cao Shijia 曹世家") quotes it as 曹人有夢眾君子立於社宮而
謀亡曹.

 7. The *Guoyu* ("Zhou Yu") has 而或專之，其害多矣, which is quoted in the
*Shiji* ("Zhou Shijia 周世家") as 而有專之，其害多矣.

From the above examples, it is clear that in ancient texts interchange between the two
characters 有 and 或 is extremely common, and this is also the case in the Guodian
*Laozi* phrase in question.

#3. A 7:31 to 8:3

| Guodian Laozi | Received Text | Mawangdui |
|---|---|---|
| A: 7:31 to 8:3 | Chapter 30 | Copies A  [and B] |
| 其事好長 | 其事好還 | □□□□  [其□□□] |

The Guodian slip has a short-stroke punctuation mark after the character 好, indicating the end of a sentence. Thus the *Guodian Chu Mu Zhujian* divided this section
after the 其事好 and made 長 the first character of the following sentence. But this
punctuation seems inappropriate. In the light of the context here, the entire section
ought to read: 以道佐人主者，不欲以兵強於天下．善者果而已，不以取強．果而弗伐，
果而弗驕，果而弗矜，是謂果而不強，其事好長. Mawangdui Copies A and B put 其事

好長 after the phrase 不以兵強於天下, thus giving a slightly different order from that of the Guodian *Laozi* bamboo slips. However, in both of the Mawangdui copies, the silk manuscript is damaged at this point: only the character 其 is still extant in Copy B and the following three characters are missing in both copies. In all received editions, there is the four-character phrase 其事好還 for this line. This corresponds to the 其事好長 of the Guodian slips and is sufficient evidence that the character 長 belongs to the preceding sentence.

Let us now consider the sentence that follows: 古之善為士者，必微妙玄達，深不可識 (A 8:4–18). This is equivalent to a part of chapter 15 of the received text. Neither the Mawangdui nor received text has 長 at the beginning of the above line, thus neither should it be here in the Guodian *Laozi*. From this it is clear that the punctuation mark *before* the 長 should have come *after* it. The scribe put his mark in the wrong place; we should correct this mistake rather than follow it.

### #4. B 5:1–11

| Guodian Laozi<br>B 5:1–11 | Received Text<br>Chapter 30 | Mawangdui<br>Copy B |
|---|---|---|
| 人之所褫（畏）， | 人之所畏， | 人之所畏， |
| 亦不可以不褫（畏）人． | 亦不可以不畏． | 亦不可以不畏人． |

The transcription in *Guodian Chu Mu Zhujian* punctuates just before the very last character, so that the last half of the passage reads 亦不可以不畏．This is a case of mistakenly adopting the reading of the received text. The Wang Bi and Heshang Gong editions both have 亦不可以不畏．However, Mawangdui Copy B supports exactly the reading of the Guodian *Laozi* given here. Obviously, the received text has omitted a character and should be emended on the basis of the other two. D. C. Lau made a penetrating analysis of this section of the *Laozi*:

> The meaning of the received text is "he whom others fear ought also to fear others," but the silk-manuscript meaning is that although others fear him (the ruler), he, too, must fear them in return. The import of the saying is very different in the two versions: the first offers a principle for anyone; however, the second is a principle for ruling offered to the man in power.[1]

If we then consider the text that follows in the Guodian, 人 is followed by 寵辱若驚, which is the same as the beginning of chapter 13 of the received text. Neither the Mawangdui Copies A and B nor the received text has a 人 before the characters 寵辱. In summary, to read it as part of the following sentence is incorrect.

---

[1] Liu Dianjue 劉殿爵, "Mawangdui Han Mu Boshu *Laozi* Chutan 馬王堆漢墓帛書老子初探," *Mingbao Monthly*, Sept., 1982; see also D. C. Lau, *Chinese Classics Tao Te Ching* (Hong Kong: Chinese University Press, 1989), p. 174.

# Some Methodological Issues in the Study of the Guodian *Laozi* Parallels

## HAROLD D. ROTH

The questioning of traditional assumptions about early Chinese thought has a very long history in China that goes back at least as far as the Han Learning Movement at the end of the seventeenth century.[1] In the twentieth century it assumed new significance under the leadership of such intellectual giants as Gu Jiegang 顧頡剛 , Guo Moruo 郭沫若 , and Qian Mu 錢穆 .[2] However, as important as these earlier movements were, the textual discoveries at Mawangdui 馬王堆 , now a quarter century old, ushered in a new and exciting era in the attempt to better understand the origins of early Chinese thought, one that continues to incorporate the new textual finds that seem to be announced almost annually. The brand new discovery of the cache of texts at Guodian 郭店, Hubei province, holds the potential of being every bit as significant as that of Mawangdui, especially for understanding the historical and philosophical origins and early development of the two traditions that have been called Daoism and Confucianism. If we are to maximize the opportunity for the reevaluation of early Chinese thought with which the Guodian discoveries present us, we must continue to be willing to criticize traditional beliefs in light of these discoveries in such a manner that all prior conclusions must be put up for discussion. In order to effectively accomplish such a thorough reevaluation we must proceed in a careful and systematic fashion.

Several related methodologies have been developed in a variety of academic disciplines in the West — most significantly in classical studies, biblical studies, and religious studies. They can be invaluable aids in examining the textual finds of the past quarter century in China. This article outlines four of the methodologies that I think are most relevant to the study of the meaning and significance of the Guodian *Laozi*

---

[1] For further information, see Benjamin Elman, *From Philosophy to Philology*, Harvard East Asian Monographs 110 (Cambridge, Mass.: Council on East Asian Studies, Harvard University, 1984).

[2] Their writings were published in numerous periodicals and collections. Representative works are: Gu Jiegang, ed., *Gushi Bian* 古史辨, 5 vols. (Shanghai: Shangwu Press, 1929–35); Guo Moruo, *Shi Pipan Shu* 十批判書 (Beijing: Kexue Press, 1956); Qian Mu, *Xian Qin Zhuzi Xinian* 先秦諸子繫年, 2 vols. (1st edn. 1935; 3d edn. Beijing: Zhonghua Shuju, 1984).

老子 parallels. I have organized them under the following general headings: textual methodologies, literary methodologies, philosophical methodologies, and religious methodologies. Each section presents the technical terms and examples most relevant to the study of the *Laozi*.

## TEXTUAL METHODOLOGIES

One of the most significant questions that confronts us in the study of the Guodian *Laozi* parallels is whether or not they are a version of the same text of the extant or "received" 81-chapter *Laozi* or whether they constitute a unique text or — rather — three unique texts in their own right. Western textual methodologies can shed considerable light on this problem.

There are two closely related methodologies for the critical study and analysis of texts: textual history and textual criticism. Textual history includes the study of textual transmission, textual stratification and authenticity, filiation analysis,[3] and the various aspects of bibliography and book production that have traditionally been subsumed in China under the headings *tushu banben xue* 圖書板本學, *mulu xue* 目錄學, and *shulin* 書林. Textual criticism takes the data obtained from textual history and uses it in the establishment of a critical edition of a given work that is as close as possible to the author's original text. It involves two processes: 1. *Recensio*: sifting through the variant readings that exist in all the important witnesses to a text that have been gathered through text-historical procedures and analyzing their patterns and constructing a genealogical tree (technically called a *stemma codicum*) that can then be used to decide logically which of these variants was most likely in the author's original text; and 2. *Emendatio*: emending those readings that cannot be established logically through this genealogical tree.[4] As an illustration of the first of these two stages I present the preliminary *stemma codicum* of the *Laozi* constructed by William Boltz.[5] In it the Mawangdui manuscripts A and B (ca. 205 and 190 BC, respectively) represent one side of the diagram and the two most fundamental recensions of the *Laozi* from the received tradition, the Heshang Gong 河上公 (of uncertain date, prob-

---

[3] Filiation analysis is a logical and systematic method for surveying the field of the available editions of a text and limiting the number of them that one must consult for obtaining the widest range of possibly authentic textual variants to an absolute minimum. See H. D. Roth, "Filiation Analysis and the Textual History of the Huai-nan Tzu," *Proceedings of the Conference of Orientalists in Japan* 60.2 (1982), pp. 60–81.

[4] For a discussion of the basic features of this methodology, see Harold D. Roth, "Text and Edition in Early Chinese Philosophical Literature," *Journal of the American Oriental Society* 113.2 (1993), pp. 215–16, 224–25. This is in turn based upon the single most influential statement of text-critical methodology, Paul Maas, *Textual Criticism*, translated by Barbara Flower (Oxford: Clarendon Press, 1958).

[5] William G. Boltz, "Manuscripts with Transmitted Counterparts," in Edward Shaughnessy, ed., *New Sources of Early Chinese History: An Introduction to the Reading of Inscriptions and Manuscripts* (Berkeley: Society for the Study of Early China, and Institute for East Asian Studies, 1997), pp. 253–83.

ably Han) and the Fu Yi 傅奕 (558?–639?) constitute the other side. Boltz here relies on his own prior research and on that of Rudolf Wagner, which indicates that the extant Wang Bi 王弼 recension contains, for the most part, the text of the Heshang Gong recension and therefore has little independent value for establishing a critical text, and, further, that the Fu Yi recension of the so-called "ancient edition" (*guben*) is extremely close in its readings to the otherwise lost Wang Bi redaction of the text.[6] Since all other complete recensions seem to be based upon these two, they are the two most fundamental for constructing a new critical edition.[7]

*Diagram: Preliminary Stemma Codicum of the* Laozi

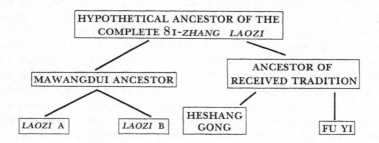

In order to establish the readings in the hypothetical ancestor of the complete *Laozi*, we need agreement between at least one edition in each of the two distinct branches (i.e., the Mawangdui ancestor and the ancestor of the received tradition). Thus, for example, if *Laozi* A from Mawangdui shares a reading with the Heshang Gong recension, then this reading can only have gotten into each of these sources if it came ultimately from their common ancestor.[8] This stemma is rather simplified, leaving out incomplete recensions, such as the Zhuang Zun 莊遵 (ca. 80 BC),[9] the Xiang Er 想爾 (ca. 250 AD), the Suo Dan 索紞 (ca. 270), and the many fragments from

[6] Boltz, "Manuscripts with Transmitted Counterparts," pp. 264–69; William G. Boltz, "The *Laozi* Text that Wang Bi and Heshang Gong Never Saw," *Bulletin of the School of Oriental and African Studies* 48 (1985), pp. 493–501; and Rudolf Wagner, "The Wang Bi Recension of the *Laozi*," *Early China* 14 (1990), pp. 27–54.

[7] According to Boltz, the so-called "Imperial Commentary version," established by Tang Emperor Xuanzong in 735, conflated textual readings from a number of independent recensions of the *Laozi* and so has no independent value for establishing such a critical edition of the text. See Boltz, "Lao tzu Tao te ching," in Michael Loewe, ed., *Early Chinese Texts: A Bibliographical Guide* (Berkeley: Society for the Study of Early China, and Institute for East Asian Studies, 1994), pp. 279–80.

[8] This rule discounts the always present possibility of conflation. Here it is not possible, since the Mawangdui manuscripts were buried for over 2,000 years.

[9] Zhuang Zun is commonly known by the name Yan Zun 嚴遵 because his biographer, Ban Gu, was

Dunhuang.[10] Nonetheless, it can still demonstrate how this type of logical analysis is an invaluable tool in making objective decisions among textual variants. Of course not every textual variation can be decided by the stemma. In those cases we must resort to all the various tools of the *emendatio* stage of textual criticism, including historical phonology and historical linguistics.

Textual criticism further provides us with a number of valuable definitions of terms that can facilitate our analysis of the Guodian *Laozi* material:

A *text* is a unique complex and expression of ideas created by an author or authors. Throughout the course of its transmission from creation down to the present moment, a text will be transformed into the various unique states created by subsequent copyists and editors, each containing their own unique textual variations. The actual physical objects in which the states of a text are embodied are technically called its "records," and it is these records that constitute the "editions" of a text. So we can speak of the *Sibu Congkan* or the *Sibu Beiyao* editions of the text called *Laozi*. Of course, we also use the term "text" to distinguish the main body of an original work from its commentaries.

A *recension* is a unique foundational state of a text, one that has undergone editorial modifications that have resulted in some aspect of the format or organization of the text being altered. Recensions are often associated with a particular commentary, such as the Heshang Gong and Wang Bi. As a foundational state of a text, a recension persists through many generations of records or editions. The most important of these editions are called "redactions," each of which constitutes a new record of the text with a unique format and arrangement of text and commentary and a distinctive pattern of textual variations. There may be many redactions of a particular recension, but the oldest identifiable one is what I have called the "ancestral redaction."[11] It contains the recension in its original and uncontaminated form. For example, the Wang Bi recension of the *Laozi* today exists in a conflated redaction in which the commentary is Wang's but the text contains for the most part the readings from the Heshang Gong recension and is thus far removed from the ancestral redaction of the Wang recension.

With these definitions we can speak of a number of distinct recensions of the *Laozi*: the Mawangdui, represented by the two editions A and B; the Wang Bi, which Boltz and Wagner have clearly shown does not survive in its original form; the Heshang Gong; the Fu Yi, which Wagner has shown is close to the ancestral redaction of the

avoiding one of the taboo names of the previous emperor. For a biography of Zhuang, see Aat Vervoorn, "Zhuang Zun: A Daoist Philosopher of the Late First Century B.C.," *Monumenta Serica* 38 (1988–89), pp. 69–94.

[10] For an overview of all extant redactions of the *Laozi*, see Boltz, "Lao tzu Tao te ching," pp. 269–92.

[11] An ancestral redaction may also be the oldest extant edition in a unique lineage of editions as identified by filiation analysis. See, Harold D. Roth, "Text and Edition," p. 225.

text of the Wang Bi recension; and the various incomplete recensions. The He and Wang recensions contain numerous editions and the Fu Yi has a number of important descendants.

Scholars also frequently speak of the "received text" (*textus receptus*) but often do not adhere to the above distinctions between the terms "text" and "edition." What this term really refers to is the total number of recensions of a text that are still extant. For example, until the Mawangdui discoveries, there were probably only three extant recensions: the conflated He/Wang that goes under Wang's name; the Heshang Gong; and the Fu Yi. Now with the addition of the Mawangdui recension we can speak of the "received tradition" (a term that I prefer to "received text") as containing four recensions. One of the most interesting questions to be pursued in studying the Guodian materials is whether or not the *Laozi* parallels can truly be said to constitute a new and distinct recension of the text.

The thirty-three parallel passages to the received *Laozi* found at Guodian, which come from thirty-one different chapters, occur in three distinct bundles of bamboo slips. In each bundle the parallel passages occur in an order that bears little relationship to that of the received *Laozi*. The final bundle also contains a text heretofore unknown, that the scholars who worked on the discovery have named after its initial sentence: "Vast Unity Gives Birth to Water" (*Tai Yi Sheng Shui* 太一生水 ).

The *Laozi* parallels are indicated in the table on the following page.[12] A striking aspect of the table is that less than half of the parallels are complete. Even if we remove those that are missing four or fewer lines, we are still left with eleven partial parallels. Upon examining them, it is clear that each can stand on its own, both semantically and syntactically. If this is true, then we must acknowledge the possibility that the versions of these passages in the received *Laozi* were built up from small distinct units, as Michael LaFargue has postulated.[13]

[12] The table is based upon the text of the Guodian *Laozi* parallels found in Jingmen Bowuguan 荆門 博物館 , *Guodian Chu Mu Zhujian* 郭店楚墓竹簡 (Beijing: Wenwu Press, 1998), pp. 111–21. The line numbers of the received *Laozi* are taken from materials presented by Robert Henricks at the Dartmouth Conference on the Guodian *Laozi*.

[13] Michael LaFargue, *The Tao of the Tao Te Ching* (Albany: State University of New York Press, 1992), and *Tao and Method: A Reasoned Approach to the Tao Te Ching* (Albany: State University of New York Press, 1994).

## Table 1. Guodian Laozi Parallels with Corresponding Laozi Passages

| Guodian *Laozi* Slips (Slip no.: char. no.) | Received *Laozi* Passages (Traditional Chap. no.) | Guodian Passage (Ryden Chap. no.) |
|---|---|---|
| | | JIA 甲 BUNDLE A |
| A 1:1 to 2:18 | 19 | A:I |
| 2:19 to 5:13 | 66 | A:II |
| 5:14 to 6:16 | 46 (missing lines 1-2) | A:III |
| 6:17 to 8:3 | 30:1-2; 6-13 (of 16 lines) | A:IV |
| 8:4 to 10:21 | 15 (missing lines 4, 12, 16-17) | A:V |
| 10:22 to 13:2 | 64:10-18 | A:VI |
| 13:3 to 14:13 | 37 (missing lines 2, 10) | A:VII |
| 14:14 to 15:7 | 63:1-4; 14-15 | A:VIII |
| 15:8 to 18:8 | 2 (missing lines 9, 13) | A:IX |
| 18:9 to 20:28 | 32 | A:X |
| 21:1 to 23:12 | 25 (missing line 5) | A:XI |
| 23:13 to 23:19 | 5:5-7 (of 9 lines) | A:XII |
| 24:1 to 24:25 | 16:1-6 (of 17 lines) | A:XIII |
| 25:1 to 27:2 | 64:1-9 | A:XIV |
| 27:3 to 29:16 | 56 | A:XV |
| 29:17 to 32:22 | 57 (missing line 5) | A:XVI |
| 33:1 to 35:17 | 55 | A:XVII |
| 35:18 to 37:3 | 44 | A:XVIII |
| 37:4 to 37:27 | 40 | A:XIX |
| 37:28 to 39:9 | 9 | A:XX |
| | | YI 乙 BUNDLE B |
| B 1:1 to 3:7 | 59 | B:I |
| 3:8 to 4:7 | 48:1-4 (of 7 lines) | B:II |
| 4:8 to 5:11 | 20:1-7 (of 24 lines) | B:III |
| 5:12 to 8:23 | 13 | B:IV |
| 9:1 to 12:17 (slip 12 damaged) | 41 | B:V |
| 13:1 to 13:20 | 52:5-10 (of 15 lines) | B:VI |
| 13:21 to 15:14 | 45 | B:VII |
| 15:15 to 18:25 (slip 18 damaged) | 54 (missing line 9) | B:VIII |
| | | BING 丙 BUNDLE C |
| C 1:1 to 2:21 | 17 | C:I |
| 2:22 to 3:22 | 18 (missing line 2) | C:II |
| 4:1 to 5:21 | 35 | C:III |
| 6:1 to 10:14 | 31:4-18 | C:IV |
| 11:1 to 14:7 | 64:10-18 | C:V |

Given the above contrasts between the Guodian parallels and the received *Laozi*, there are three possible relationships between them.[14] I have expressed these in terms of models: Anthology, Source, and Parallel Text.

*Model One: Anthology*
(Here, Guodian *Laozi* material constitutes extracts from the ancestral *Laozi*.)

ANCESTRAL 81-CHAPTER *LAOZI*

GUODIAN *LAOZI*   MAWANGDUI RECENSION   RECEIVED RECENSIONS

*Model Two: Source*
(Here, Guodian *Laozi* material would be one of the sources of the ancestral *Laozi*.)

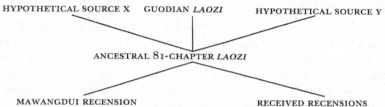

HYPOTHETICAL SOURCE X   GUODIAN *LAOZI*   HYPOTHETICAL SOURCE Y

ANCESTRAL 81-CHAPTER *LAOZI*

MAWANGDUI RECENSION   RECEIVED RECENSIONS

*Model Three: Parallel Text*
(In this model, Guodian *Laozi* material represents a unique text, which descends from a common ancestor or set of ancestral sources, as do the ancestral *Laozi* and other similar texts, most importantly the *Inward Training (Nei Ye)* text from the *Guanzi,* as I have found from my own research.)

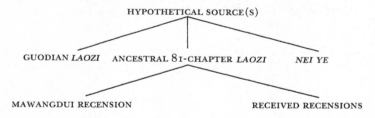

HYPOTHETICAL SOURCE(S)

GUODIAN *LAOZI*   ANCESTRAL 81-CHAPTER *LAOZI*   *NEI YE*

MAWANGDUI RECENSION   RECEIVED RECENSIONS

These diagrams raise the critical issue of precisely what constitutes a text. In Model I, the Guodian material does not constitute a text in its own right but is rather its own distinct abridged recension of the ancestral *Laozi*. In Models II and III the Guodian material does represent a text separate from that of the *Laozi*, not a recension, redaction, or edition of it. It is a distinct text because it meets the minimum definition of a

---

[14] These are not stemma but, rather, general diagrams.

text offered above: "a unique complex of ideas by an author or authors" that exhibits its own format and organization, even though it contains parallel material to the extant *Laozi*. Therefore the existence of such textual parallels does not — in and of itself — indicate that the Guodian *Laozi* material is actually taken from the complete 81-chapter *Laozi*, or even that there was a text called *Laozi* at the time the Guodian material was copied. The Guodian material could very well constitute its own text — or, rather, three distinct texts — composed of material that later found its way into the text we now know as *Laozi*.

Furthermore, there are a number of reasons to think that the three bundles of bamboo slips that contain the Guodian *Laozi* material did not even come from the same source. First there is the physical evidence that the slips in each bundle are of a different length, there are a different number of characters per slip in each bundle, and that there are variations in the style of the writing among the three bundles.[15]

Second, there is a strong textual evidence of this in the texts themselves. For example, compare the two parallel versions of the received *Laozi*, chapter 64, lines 10–18, as found in both Guodian bundle A 10:22 to 13:2 (A VI) and bundle C 11:1 to 14:7 (C V). Even a cursory attempt at textual criticism clearly indicates that they could not be taken from each other, nor could they have had a common source. In their nine lines, there are total of at least 33 textual variations.[16] Among the most significant is the apparent transposition of lines 15 and 14 of the received text in bundles A and C. Line 15 in A appears as line 14 in C and, furthermore, line 14 in A has nothing in common with line 15 in C, the line it appears to correlate with. Just given these two transpositions, A and C could not have been based on each other or on an immediate common ancestor. Their common ancestor must be several generations earlier, a textual "great-great-grandmother" rather than a "mother." This may become clearer if we look at these lines more closely:

[15] Cui Renyi 崔仁義, "Jingmen Chumu Chutu de Zhujian *Laozi* Chutan 荊門楚墓出土的竹簡老子初探," *Jingmen Shehui Kexue* 1997.5, p. 32.

[16] This is a conservative number, depending on how we deal with graphic variations. If we challenge the emendations of the authors of the book there may indeed be more.

Table 2. *Key Textual Variants between the Guodian and the*
*Received Versions of* Laozi *Chapter 64, Lines 14 and 15* [17]

| | | |
|---|---|---|
| *A VI (A 11:16-19)*<br>(line 14)<br><br>臨事之紀<br>The most important point<br>in regulating affairs | | |
| *A VI (A 11:20-28)*<br>(line 15)<br><br>慎終若始則無敗事矣<br>Is that if you are as careful at<br>the end as you are at the<br>beginning then you will have<br>no ruined affairs. | *C V (C 12:1-9)*<br>(line 14)<br><br>慎終若始則無敗事矣<br>Be as careful at the end as you<br>are at the beginning and you<br>will have no ruined affairs. | *Received*<br>(line 14)<br><br>民之從事<br>As for the conduct of<br>affairs by the people: |
| | | 恆於幾成而敗事<br>It is always when they are<br>about to succeed that they<br>ruin them. |
| | *C V (C 12:10-21)*<br>(line 15)<br><br>人之敗也<br>As for human beings'<br>ruining of their [affairs]: | *Received*<br>(line 15)<br><br>(故 {曰})*<br>(Therefore {it is said}) |
| | 恆於其幾成也敗之<br>It is always when they are about<br>to succeed that they ruin them. | 慎終若始則無敗事矣<br>Be as careful at the end as<br>you are at the beginning<br>and you will have<br>no ruined affairs. |

*Readings in Mawangdui silk-manuscript Copies A and B of the Laozi as follows: A 故; B 故曰.

If we look further at lines 14–15, there are a number of important things to note:

1. Line 14 in A VI: "The most important point in regulating affairs" is total-ly absent both from C V and from anywhere in the received tradition. Yet it makes perfect sense in the context of A VI.

2. A VI has no line corresponding to line 14 in the received *Laozi*, the general observation that, "As for the conduct of affairs by the people: It is always when they are about to succeed that they ruin them."

[17] I follow the conclusions of the editors of *Guodian Chu Mu Zhujian*, pp. 111–12, 121–22, about the graphic variations in these lines.

3. C V has its own unique version of this general observation that is missing in A VI but found in the received tradition: "As for human beings ruining [of their affairs]: It is always when they are about to succeed that they ruin them." Note that this follows the sentence that all sources share: "Be as careful at the end as you are at the beginning and you will have no ruined affairs." Yet if we compare these two lines with the received sources, their order is transposed in C V. Instead of placing the admonition drawn from the general observation about ruination on the verge of success after this observation, C V places the admonition *before* the observation, thereby using it to illustrate the reason for the admonition.

There are a number of observations to make about these extremely interesting textual variations:

The text of A VI, which does not contain the general observation about "ruination of affairs" found in C V, line 14, and received tradition, line 14, reads perfectly well without it. Its distinctive line, "The most important point of regulating affairs..." represents a unique attempt to introduce the admonition to be "as careful at the end as you are at the beginning."

Furthermore, the absence of this general observation from A VI does not appear to be a deliberate omission of this observation from a complete *Laozi* version because A VI does contain a unique line about the main point of regulating endeavors which, in effect, replaces this general observation. Therefore, A VI must either have had a source completely different from that of C V and the received tradition, or it represents a distinct attempt to compose a verse from a source or sources that it shared with the other two.

The transposition in the order of lines 14 and 15 between C V and the received tradition seems to be further indication of either different sources or different attempts to work with a common source or sources. In either case, it implies that the text of this verse was in flux — perhaps because it originated in an oral tradition in which there was no fixed version of the text. Given the close correspondences between the other lines of this passage (64, lines, 10–14 and 16–18) among the three sources, this explanation seems more likely than one arguing that A VI and C V took liberties with an already established text close to the ancestral redaction of the complete *Laozi*.

The fact that two such distinct versions of 64, lines 10–18, as we find in Guodian A VI and C V were both in circulation in the fourth century indicates a number of interesting things: a fluidity of the text of this verse could suggest that each was drawn from a source that represented a different stage in the accretion of the material that formed chapter 64, lines 10–18. This fact plus the occurrence of chapter 64, lines 1–9, on A 25:1 to 27:2 (Ryden A XIV), a completely different location in the text, suggests that the received *Laozi* chapter 64 was built up gradually in a process of accretion by several composers. It makes the scenario of a complete 81-chapter *Laozi* that the compilers of bundles A and C drew upon less likely than the other two possible scenarios, as represented by the "Source Model and the "Parallel Text Model."

A further significance of these three distinct versions of chapter 64, lines 14–15, is that it is unlikely that bundles A and C were part of one integral text. They appear to represent two unique texts and they were created by two different authors from two different sources. These indications that the text of the *Laozi* was in a state of flux at the time that the Guodian parallels were written down suggests that the work may not have been written at one point in time as an integral and complete text. The study of the possible literary genre of the *Laozi* that has been opened up by a number of literary methodologies can help to clarify this intriguing question.

## LITERARY METHODOLOGIES

Literary criticism has been used for the past half century by textual critics in biblical studies — particularly New Testament studies — in order to derive information about the possible historical conditions under which a text might have been created. Recently, in the analysis of early Chinese texts it has figured implicitly in the work of William Boltz, Victor Mair, and Bruce Brooks, and explicitly in that of Michael LaFargue.[18]

Biblical scholars have defined three closely related aspects of these methodologies which they refer to as "form criticism," "redaction criticism," and "composition criticism." Form criticism is the analysis of the standard genres or "forms" (stories, sayings, songs, poetic verse, and so on) in which the oral and early written tradition is cast in the effort to interpret each in the context of some concrete life setting in which it was originally used.[19] Redaction criticism attempts to identify the theological or ideological viewpoints of the people who assembled the various literary forms into the texts that we now have and to understand thereby their historical conditions.[20]

---

[18] William G. Boltz, "The Religious and Philosophical Significance of the 'Hsiang erh' *Laozi* in the Light of the Mawangdui Silk Manuscripts," *Bulletin of the School of Oriental and African Studies* 45.1 (1982), pp. 95–117; Victor Mair, *Tao Te Ching: The Classic Book of Integrity and the Way* (New York: Bantam, 1990), pp. 119–30; E. Bruce Brooks and A. Taeko Brooks, *The Original Analects: The Sayings of Confucius and His Successors* (New York: Columbia University Press, 1998); Michael LaFargue, *The Tao of the Tao Te Ching* and *Tao and Method*.

[19] Stephen D. Moore, *Literary Criticism and the Gospels: The Theoretical Challenge* (New Haven: Yale University Press, 1989), p. 180, and LaFargue, *The Tao of the Tao Te Ching*, p. 197. See also Edgar V. McKnight, *What is Form Criticism?* (Philadelphia: Fortress Press, 1969).

[20] Moore, *Literary Criticism*, p. 183, and LaFargue, *The Tao of the Tao Te Ching*, p. 197. See also Norman Perrin, *What is Redaction Criticism?* (Philadelphia: Fortress Press, 1969). For an application to early Chinese texts, see Harold D. Roth, "Redaction Criticism and the Early History of Taoism," *Early China* 19 (1994), pp. 1–46.

Composition criticism examines the literary techniques of the early redactors of a tradition and how they arranged and assembled their inherited material to create unified works.[21] A fourth criticism often included with the others is "narrative criticism," which analyzes the various literary devices used in narrative. Since there are no narratives in the *Laozi* material — indeed, this is one of its distinguishing features especially in contrast to texts like the *Zhuangzi* 莊子 and *Huainanzi* 淮南子 — it is not directly relevant to solving the problems raised by the Guodian *Laozi* parallels.[22]

When applied to the Guodian *Laozi* material, form criticism would lead us to focus on the individual units of text, many of which are marked off on the bamboo slips with a dark square mark. Like their parallels in the received *Laozi*, many appear to be in metered and sometimes rhymed verse. An excellent example of this is in B V (B 10:8 to 12:16), lines 5–17, the poetic lines that are said to be from the "Established Sayings" (*jianyan* 建言) that also appear in chapter 41 of the received *Laozi*. A form-critical analysis would focus on each unit of verse as the object of study and would suggest that such units are indicative of an earlier oral tradition whose memorization and transmission were facilitated by the presentation of ideas in poetic form. Indeed, if either the "Source Model" or the "Parallel Text Model" is correct, then in order to do systematic textual criticism on the Guodian *Laozi* material it is the individual units of verse that we should concentrate on.

Redaction and composition criticism would look for any evidence of ideological viewpoint in the very way in which the individual units of verse were assembled to create the three bundles of *Laozi* material at Guodian. What is the meaning of each of these passages, and is there a rationale behind their inclusion (and perhaps the omission of others now in the received *Laozi*)? Can we see a design in the order in which they are placed in each of the three bundles and is there an overriding philosophical viewpoint in each of them? If so, is it the same for all three or is it different? After working through the Guodian *Laozi* material initially I think that we *can* provide a definite answer to these questions and I present a few preliminary observations about this in the concluding section of this article.

One final, and relevant, element is related to form-criticism. It is the analysis of the poetic elements in the various units of verse in the *Laozi* material and their comparison to other roughly contemporaneous material. In a recently published article of singular importance, William Baxter presents an analysis of the rhyme-schemes and other rhetorical characteristics of the *Laozi*. He argues that four other extant texts share those characteristics, namely *Nei Ye* 內業 and the three other so-called "Xinshu"

---

[21] Moore, *Literary Criticism*, p. 179.

[22] For an example of this form of criticism applied to an early Chinese narrative, see Harold D. Roth, "The Yellow Emperor's Guru: A Narrative Analysis from Chuang Tzu 11," *Taoist Resources* 7 (1997), pp. 43–60.

心術 texts from the *Guanzi* 管子.[23] He suggests that all five are part of a distinct literary genre of "philosophical verse with strong oral elements and little concept of individual authorship" and need to be studied together:

> … Of course, these *Guanzi* chapters and the manuscripts from Mawangdui failed to reach the status of "classic," and, from a modern point of view, they may seem far less important than the *Laozi*. … But the compilers of these texts cannot have known in advance that the *Laozi* would win out in such spectacular fashion. If we wish to clarify the early history of the genre which the *Laozi* represents, these other texts could turn out to be as useful as the *Laozi* itself.[24]

My own research on *Nei Ye* has drawn me to the same conclusion, namely that both it and the *Laozi* are examples of a distinct literary genre of anonymous verse with Daoist philosophical content. Each text represents a unique collection of separate units of verse that may very well have been transmitted orally in these units for a considerable period of time before being assembled and written down.[25] If this is the case, rather than assuming the veracity of the "Anthology Model" for the relationship between the Guodian *Laozi* parallels and the received text, we must give very serious consideration to the hypothesis that each bundle of these parallels represents a different unique assemblage of these distinct units of verse, all of which were also later assembled into the *Laozi*. Should this prove true, then both the "Source Model" and the "Parallel Text Model" provide a more accurate way to understand the relationship between the Guodian *Laozi* materials and the received *Laozi*.

---

[23] William Baxter, "Situating the Language of the *Lao Tzu*: The Probable Date of the *Tao Te Ching*," In Michael LaFargue and Livia Kohn, eds., *Lao-Tzu and the Tao-Te-Ching* (Albany: State University of New York Press, 1998), pp. 231–54. Baxter identifies the following rhetorical characteristics of the *Laozi*:
1. rhyme: frequent rhymes with no dominant pattern (Karlgren, "The Poetical Parts in Lao Tsï," *Götesborgs Högskolas Årsskrift* 38.3 [1932], p. 4);
2. rhythm: the rhymed parts of the *Laozi* are often in four-character (tetrasyllabic) lines;
3. semantic parallelism and antithesis: rhymed and unrhymed lines are often related through these two devices, with distinct subjects and predicates in line x having parallel meanings or antithetical meanings with those in line y as in *Laozi* 81;
4. repetition:
   a. chain repetition: "if x then y, if y then z…" (*Laozi* 59)
   b. repetition of the same word over several lines (*Laozi* 19);
5. paradox (*Laozi* 45);
6. absence of narration: in contrast to the *Analects*, *Mencius*, *Zhuangzi*; and
7. framing of passage with introductory and concluding comments.

[24] Baxter, "Situating the Language of the *Lao Tzu*," pp. 231–54.

[25] We find further examples of this genre scattered throughout the *Zhuangzi*, such as the teachings of Guang Chengzi and "Vast Obscurity" in chapter 11, and the teachings of Guanyin in chapter 33. This is also the form in which Guang Chengzi's inner cultivation ideas are presented in *Huainanzi* 14, and it is also found in the "Dao Yuan" and "Jing Fa" and "Shiliu Jing" (Yandanzi teaches Yellow Emperor) texts within the *Huangdi Sijing* corpus.

## PHILOSOPHICAL METHODOLOGIES

Of course the hypothesis of the existence of a body of philosophical verse transmitted orally before being assembled into texts like the three bundles of Guodian *Laozi* parallels, the *Laozi*, and *Nei Ye* raises the most important historical question of who might have transmitted these units of verse. A minimal assumption — justified by their very existence — is that of some kind of master-disciple lineage centrally concerned with Daoist philosophy. But just what does the term "Daoist" even mean if we subscribe to the conclusion — as many scholars now do — that Laozi is not a historical figure and that the *Laozi* text and the legend of Lao Dan as its author did not appear until the third century BC?[26]

In surveying the range of texts in late-Warring States and early-Han China that could possibly be classified as Daoist, I have come up with three general categories under which the distinctive philosophical ideas we find in these "texts" can be organized.

1. cosmology: based upon the Dao as the dominant unifying power in the cosmos;

2. self-cultivation: the attainment of the Dao through a process of emptying out the usual contents of the mind until a profound state of tranquillity is achieved; and

3. political thought: the application of the cosmology and the self-cultivation methods to the problem of rulership.

Based upon these three general philosophical categories we can organize the surviving textual sources of early Daoism into the following three general philosophical types, all of which share a common cosmology and self-cultivation agenda but which differ in the area of political thought. The latter of these types have been suggested by A. C. Graham, Benjamin Schwartz, and Liu Xiaogan 劉笑敢.[27] Individualist (represented by *Nei Ye* and the *neipian* of *Zhuangzi*); Primitivist (represented by the *Laozi* and chapters 8–11 [first third] and 16 of *Zhuangzi*); and Syncretist (represented by a wide variety of texts including much of chapters 12–14 and 15 and 33 in *Zhuangzi*, the other "Xinshu" texts in *Guanzi*, *Jing Fa* 經法, *Huainanzi*, and others).

In my opinion, Sima Tan 司馬談 seems to have had in mind the Syncretist category when he defined "Daojia" 道家 in his famous discussion of the "Six Schools." While all three types existed in the century preceding the *Huainanzi*, the Syncretist

---

[26] For the influential analysis of how the legend of Lao Dan as the author of the *Daodejing* originated and developed, see A. C. Graham, "The Origins of the Legend of Lao Tan," in *Studies in Chinese Philosophy and Philosophical Literature* (rpt.; Albany: State University of New York Press, 1990), pp. 111–24.

[27] A. C. Graham, "How Much of *Chuang Tzu* Did Chuang Tzu Write?" in *Studies in Chinese Philosophy and Philosophical Literature*, pp. 283–321; Benjamin Schwartz, *The World of Thought in Ancient China* (Cambridge, Mass.: The Belknap Press of Harvard University Press, 1985); Liu Xiaogan, *Zhuangzi Zhexue ji qi Yanbian* 莊子哲學及其演變 (Beijing: Chinese Social Sciences Press, 1987).

strain is the only one that survived into the Han. It is what Sima Qian 司馬遷 labeled "Huang-Lao 黃老."

Organizing extant Daoist textual sources under these three general types avoids the difficulties that arise with the usual labels for early-Daoist texts. The two most important of these latter are "Lao-Zhuang" and "Huang-Lao." Both have come under criticism in recent Western scholarship as being retrospective labels with little basis in actual historical fact. Returning to the three general philosophical types, described above, which are simply heuristic devices for organizing textual sources, might they in fact refer to actual master-disciple lineages? It is possible that the Guodian *Laozi* material, which would clearly fall into the "Primitivist" type, will help us to answer this question.

## RELIGIOUS METHODOLOGIES

An important aspect of the critical study of religion in the West has focused on the psychology of the unusual states of consciousness attained through various methods of religious practice. Pioneered by the work of William James in *The Varieties of Religious Experience*, this aspect has been pursued under the general heading of the comparative study of mystical experience, and it has much to bear on our understanding of early-Daoist thought and its possible historical context.[28]

One of the three general categories, mentioned above, of philosophical concepts in early-Daoist works is that of self-cultivation. It entails a systematic cultivation of states of profound tranquility and emptiness, primarily through breath cultivation or breathing meditation. These profound states produce noetic insights into the nature of the cosmos that are embodied in the distinctive cosmology we can label as "Daoist." Knowledge of breathing meditation has a long history in China: the oldest extant source for it is the famous "Duodecagonal Jade Table Inscription" that dates to around the fourth century BC.[29] In my reading of *Nei Ye*, this type of "mystical practice" — which I have deemed "inner cultivation" — is absolutely central to its twenty-six verses, and I would argue that there is evidence of it throughout all of the texts of early Daoism, even those with well-developed political agendas.[30]

If we examine the Guodian *Laozi* parallels, there are nine verses in bundles A and B that deal in some fashion with inner-cultivation theory. For example, A XIII (re-

---

[28] William James, *The Varieties of Religious Experience* (1902; rpt. New York: Penguin Books, 1982).

[29] For information on this important inscription, see Guo Moruo, "Gudai Wenzi zhi Bianzheng de Fazhan 古代文字之辨證的發展," *Kaogu* 1972.5, pp. 2–13, and Li Ling 李零, *Zhongguo Fangshu Kao* 中國方術考 (Beijing: People's China Press, 1993), pp. 319–24.

[30] For a complete version of this hypothesis, see my *Original Tao: Inward Training and the Foundations of Taoist Mysticism* (New York: Columbia University Press, 1999), chapter 5.

ceived chapter 16) advocates attaining emptiness (*zhixu* 至虛 ) and guarding one's core (*shouzhong* 守中). A XV (received chapter 56) presents the self-cultivation practices of eliminating sense-perception, thought, and emotion that result in the "profound merging" (*xuantong* 玄同 ), and the uniting of the sage with the Way.

Such methods are found elsewhere in cultures associated with breath meditation. A XVII (received chapter 55) speaks of breath or *qi* 氣 cultivation and links inner power (*de* 德 ) to the high degree of vital essence (*jing* 精 ) possessed by the young child. *Nei Ye* too makes the same associations between *de* and *jing*. In addition, this passage implies that longevity is the outcome of such attainments, and this result is also spoken of in passages A XVIII (received chapter 44) and B I (received chapter 59), whose advice of "being sparing from an early age" echoes *Lüshi Chunqiu* 2.3, "The Essential Desires" ("Qing Yu 情欲").[31] These associations and others — such as the ocurrence of the bellows analogy in A XII that Donald Harper has convincingly demonstrated is associated with breath cultivation in "macrobiotic hygiene" texts from Mawangdui and Zhangjiashan 張家山 — indicate that the mystical practices of inner cultivation share important aspects with what Harper and Li Ling 李零 have so insightfully studied in recent years and which the former refers to as "*fang*-literature."[32] It further suggests that the composers of the A and B bundles of *Laozi* parallels from Guodian also regarded such practices as an integral part of their own philosophies.

So if we are to hypothesize the existence of one or more closely related master-disciple lineages that were involved in the production of the distinct units of verse that were combined into the *Laozi*, *Nei Ye*, and the Guodian *Laozi* parallels, I would argue that the religious practices of inner cultivation were a central element in both their teachings and in the manner in which they defined themselves as a group.

Some scholars may be concerned that I am somehow attempting to denigrate the widely hallowed philosophy of the *Laozi* by linking it with religious practice. I would answer that, on the contrary, it does not denigrate philosophy in the least to say that it includes within its purview the profound states of consciousness attained through religious practice. Indeed, why should it be limited to what can be apprehended through common perception alone? To say this implies that one adheres to a relatively recent Western philosophical bias — whether one defines it as beginning with Descartes or Kant or even Ayer. It is not any less scientific to include these mystical states in one's

---

[31] D. C. Lau, and Chen Fong Ching, eds., *A Concordance to the Lüshi Chunqiu*, Ancient Chinese Texts Concordance Series, Philosophical Works 12 (Hong Kong: Commercial Press, Institute of Chinese Studies 1994), vol. 2, part 3, p. 9, line 6.

[32] Donald Harper, "The Bellows Analogy in *Laozi* V and Warring States Macrobiotic Hygiene," *Early China* 20 (1995), pp. 381–92.

analysis of the great variety of aspects of human experiences and the knowledge about the world that they yield. If we are to classify significant aspects of the philosophy of the *Laozi* as "religious thought," it in no way detracts from its value or significance.

## CONCLUDING OBSERVATIONS

One is tempted to see in the Guodian *Laozi* parallels concrete evidence for the existence of a complete 81-chapter *Laozi* at the approximate time Guodian Tomb Number One was sealed, circa 300 BC. This would fit well with a traditional idea that the text was the work of the shadowy sixth-century BC figure Lao Dan and that he founded a school of Daoist philosophy that continued into the fourth century BC. Even those who would agree that we cannot accept this traditional authorship and that we should place the text two centuries later, as many modern critical scholars do, might be tempted to conclude that the Guodian parallels prove the existence of a complete *Laozi* from which these passages were taken, a situation I have characterized as the "Anthology Model."

However, this would preclude two other logical possibilities, what I have deemed the "Source" and "Parallel Text" Models. We cannot accept the first of the three models without ruling out the possibility of the other two. Yet when we consider the data in light of the four types of critical methodologies I have presented in this article, the "Anthology Model" — at least at first glance — seems the least likely of the three.

To begin with, the arrangement of passages in the Guodian parallels is totally different from those found in the received text; more than half of these passages are incomplete; and most contain important lexical — and not just graphic — variations. This indicates at the very least that if they represent an anthology, their source text was a very different recension of the complete *Laozi* from all others heretofore known.

Textual variations such as the ones briefly discussed (that between the two versions of chapter 64, lines 10–18, found in bundles A and C of the Guodian parallels) demonstrate that the compilers of each could not have drawn on the same edition of the *Laozi* text. Furthermore, the fact that there are so many partial parallels — eleven Guodian passages that contain only part of their corresponding chapters in the received text — and that all of them can stand on their own both semantically and syntactically argues strongly that the individual verse is the meaningful unit of textual transmission, not the complete text. A form-critical analysis would argue precisely this.

If the individual verse is the meaningful unit of transmission, what is the significance of how they were assembled together to form the three distinct bundles? My preliminary redaction-critical analysis, done in light of the observations on the religious and philosophical context made above, indicates that if there is an overall theme to the Guodian *Laozi* parallels, it is that of the benefits of Daoist inner-cultivation practice to rulership. As noted above, the topic of inner cultivation is central: it is found in A XII, XIII, XV-XVIII, and in B I, II, and VI. Moreover many other passages talk about two of the specific psychological benefits attained through inner-cultivation practice: becoming desireless (*wuyu* 無欲) and acting effortlessly (*wuwei* 無為). These are discussed in A I, III, VI, VII, XVI, and A VI-IX, B II, respectively. Further passages present elements of the activity of the Way or the "Way of Heaven" that provide a cosmological basis for these psychological experiences (e.g., A X-XIV, XX, and B VII). In other words, this Way is itself desireless and acts effortlessly, yet accomplishes everything.

Finally, a specific set of passages talks about the qualities of a sage-ruler and illustrates how the psychological states attained through inner cultivation are useful for governing. This set includes A I-VIII, XVI; B IV, VII, VIII; and C I, III-V. Noticeably absent here are many of the passages on governing and warfare that we find in the received *Laozi* in such chapters as 36, 50, 60, 61, 65, 67–69, 74, 76, 78, and 80. What this indicates is that whoever compiled the Guodian bundles was more concerned with the self-cultivation of the ruler than with specific principles of sagely government. This message is certainly also found in the received *Laozi*, but since it is mixed with many other ideas it is comparatively diluted.

When we consider the results of this preliminary form- and redaction-criticism of the Guodian parallels in light of the gradually increasing amount of evidence that indicates that rhymed and metered verse comprised a principal form for the communication of early Daoist thought, the likelihood that these parallels were taken from a more general body of philosophical verse rather than from a complete text of the *Laozi* only increases. They appear to represent an attempt to assemble these verses into a text or texts that was unique and different from the editorial assemblage of the received *Laozi*. Further research on the Guodian passages may be able to clarify whether the compilers of the received *Laozi* drew upon them or whether they both drew on a common fund of verses. Whatever the ultimate results of this research, the four types of critical methodologies outlined here can only benefit the overall project of unraveling the mysteries of early Daoism and its relationship to the other intellectual traditions of the time.

# On the Formal Treatment of Textual Testimony

## *P. M. THOMPSON*

his paper presents a sample collation of a short text from the *Laozi*. Its purpose is to illustrate some of the problems faced during the first stage of the process of textual criticism, namely, the management of textual testimony. It is hoped that this exercise may also illuminate, to some extent, the principles which underlie the production of a rigorous edition of an ancient text; especially, as in this case, one possessed of a rich history of transmission and of a number of newly discovered ancient manuscript witnesses. It is further hoped that the contemplation of the difficulties of such a task will inspire young sinologues to take up the challenge of the many important ancient texts in this category.

### THE TEXT: LAOZI (GD-A1.2, A 2:19 to 5:13; zh. 66)

The text I have chosen for this illustration appears among the Guodian manuscripts of the *Laozi* (GD). It is a passage in the first series (bamboo slips 1–20) of the *jia* 甲 manuscript (GD-A1). It begins at the 19th character of the second slip and ends with the 13th character of the fifth slip (2:19 to 5:13). This passage corresponds to *zhang* 66 in the received tradition of the *Laozi*. Though marked in the manuscript before 2:19 with a separator dot, its end point, 5:13, is not marked. It is the second of ten such passages that make up the first series of the A manuscript, each of which corresponds to the whole, or a part, of one of the traditional eighty-one *zhang*.

*Zhang* 66 is traditionally divided into four constituent subunits, known as *ju* 句. Each *ju* is treated as a discrete unit of collation. I have departed from the traditional interpretations of this *zhang* by taking the phrase, 天下樂推而弗厭也 (the reading of Mawangdui Copy A), as the beginning of the final *ju*, rather than as the ending of the third. This should be a salutary reminder that, in spite of the goal of achieving greater rigor in the processes of textual criticism by postponing subjective judgement until objective analysis has been exhausted, "interpretation of text" remains both the starting point and the conclusion of the critical task. The higher principle, I believe, should rather be "transparency"; that is to say that the procedures followed and the bases of decisions taken should be clear to the reader and where there is a possibility that they may not be, they should be stated explicitly.

## THE TESTIMONY

In this collation the direct testimony is divided into four categories:

A. *The Guodian bamboo manuscripts of the Laozi (late fourth century BC).*

Published in the *Guodian Chu Mu Zhujian* 郭店楚墓竹簡, 1998; Jingmen Municipal Museum, ed. Beijing: Wenwu.

B. *The Mawangdui silk manuscripts of the Laozi.*

B¹: Manuscript Copy A (late third century BC) and

B²: Manuscript Copy B (early second century BC)

Both published in the *Mawangdui Han Mu Boshu* 馬王堆漢墓帛書, vol. 1, 1980. Beijing: Wenwu.

C. *Redactions of Tang or earlier date which seem to have drawn from textual traditions that did not survive in the redactions of the Laozi which have been accepted as standard since Tang times (see below, category D).*

C¹: The *Daode Zhenjing Zhigui* 道德真經指歸, 13 *juan*

This work is attributed to Yan Zun 嚴遵 (fl. late first century BC) and is supplied with a commentary by a certain Gushenzi 谷神子, a *hao* known to have been used by Zheng Huangu 鄭還古 of the late Tang (*jinshi* before 821; rose to be a scholar of the Guozi Jian 國子監). It is a redaction of the *Laozi* with Yan Zun's *Zhigui Lun* 指歸論 distributed, *zhang* by *zhang*, over the text. This is the only witness to the *Zhigui Lun* which has been transmitted with a text of the *Laozi*. Its survival is due to its inclusion in the *Dao Zang* 道藏, but it appears that by the time of the recompilation of the latter in the Zhengtong 正統 (mid-fifteenth century) redaction, the first six *juan*, comprising the *Daojing* section, could not be found or replaced from other sources. Thus only the *Dejing* section (*juan* 7–13), in which *zhang* 66 occurs, now survives.

*Dao Zang* (1436–1449); woodblock print. See *Zhongguo Congshu Zonglu* 中國叢書綜錄 2, p. 687, col. 1. Photo-facsimile, Yan Lingfeng 嚴靈峰, *Laozi Jicheng* 老子集成, 1st ser., vols. 3–5. Taiwan: Yiwen, 1965.

C²: The *Daodejing Guben* 道德經古本, 2 *juan*

This is a redaction edited (*jiaoding* 校定) by Fu Yi 傅奕 (555–639). Apart from minimal phonetic-semantic glosses (see, e.g., *zh.* 19) there seems to be no commentary. Whether it derived simply from a single manuscript in Fu Yi's possession or whether it was the result of a more ambitious exercise involving conflation from a number of *Laozi* manuscripts (*guben* 古本 in the plural) of which he was a keen collector, is a question which does not yet have an answer.

*Dao Zang* (1436–1449); woodblock print. See *Zhongguo Congshu Zonglu* 2, p. 686, col. 2. Photo-facsimile, Yan Lingfeng, *Laozi Jicheng*, 1st ser., vol. 17. Taiwan: Yiwen, 1965.

### D. Representatives of the received standard.

D$^1$: The Jinglong 景龍 stele

A stone stele erected at the Longxing 龍興 monastery in Yixian 易縣, engraved in the
2d year of the Tang Jinglong 景龍 period (708). The text of this inscription is both
complete and pre-Kaiyuan and so free of imperial interventions.

> Facsimile published in the *Guben Daodejing Jiaokan* 古本道德經校刊, 3 vols., Archeologi-
> cal Monograph Series, vol. 1, part 2, edited and published by the Guoli Beiping Yanjiu Yuan
> Shixue Yanjiu Hui Kaogu Zu 國立北平研究院史學研究會考古組, 1936. I have not been
> able to consult this source, but have used here the text provided in Zhu Qianzhi's 朱謙之
> detailed study of this inscription, the *Laozi Jiaoshi* 老子校釋, 1975. Reprinted in *Xinbian
> Zhuzi Jicheng* 新編諸子集成. Beijing: Zhonghua, 1984.

D$^2$: The Wang Bi 王弼 "text"

It may be presumed that in its early history Wang Bi's famous commentary was transmitted independently. The text referred to here is the text which eventually came to
be its vehicle of transmission, no doubt because it had achieved a widespread accep-
tance as an authoritative text of the *Laozi*, and certainly not because it represented the
state of the text which was addressed by the commentary.

> *Guyi Congshu* 古逸叢書, listed as 老子道德經二卷; woodblock facs. of 集唐字 edn. See 中
> 國叢書綜錄 2, p. 687, col. 2. Photo-facsimile. Taiwan: Yiwen, 1958.

D$^3$: The Heshang Gong 河上公 "text"

The relationship between the Heshang Gong commentary and the text with which it
has been transmitted is, as in the case of the preceding item, not original. The collation of *zhang* 66 in these three witnesses shows them to be a very close group, differing by only one or two variations, involving unique omissions. It is probably wise to
wait until the influence of the 4,999–character redactions is better understood before
the significance of such omissions is assessed.

> *Sibu Congkan* 四部叢刊, listed as 老子道德經二卷; facs. edn. of the Song Jian'an Yu Shi
> Jiashu 宋建安虞氏家塾 woodblock edition. See 中國叢書綜錄 2, p. 686, col. 2, bottom.
> Photo-facsimile, Yan Lingfeng, *Laozi Jicheng*, 1st ser., vol. 8. Taiwan: Yiwen, 1965.

## FORMAL FEATURES OF THE COLLATION

The collation proper consists of two blocks, which display respectively the direct and
indirect testimony to the passage under study. The direct witnesses, A to D, are those
described above. For the indirect sources, E$^1$ to E$^3$, see the section entitled "The Pur-
suit of Reconciliation," below. The third block shows the result of an analysis of the
direct testimony, namely an "evidential base," intended as a starting point for the editorial phase of the text critic's task. The indirect testimony has not been analyzed. I
believe that, where a rich, direct textual tradition exists, the use of indirect testimony
should not anticipate the determination of the direct evidence. I have, however, noted
in the list of variations at the bottom of each page of collated text occasional agree-

ments of the indirect sources with the ancient manuscripts, which are not reflected in the received tradition.

## Alignment

The key feature of the formal presentation of the testimony is strict alignment (at right angles to the linear direction of the text) in order to provide an immediate view of variations at any *point of text* without abstraction from the *line of text*. The convenience of this can be appreciated by comparing the conventional notation for the variation at, say, point 11 of the first *ju* (1.11) from the note at the bottom of the first page of the collation (11 □AD$^1$: 者B$^1$CD$^2$: [■B$^2$]), with the vertical expression of that variation in the collation itself, where one can *see* an omission in A and D$^1$ opposed to a 者 in B, C and D$^2$).

Note that variations between witnesses are *products* of collated testimony, and, strictly speaking, do not need to be shown in notational form below the collation as in this specimen. This is not to say that lists of variations are not valuable for other purposes (at subsequent stages of the text-critical process), particularly for the filiation of witnesses and for the determination of rules of evidence. What is important for the design of the collation is that it should make it easy to generate the variations automatically and to sort them by type as needed.

A contrast between standard and italic styles is used in the vertical display to distinguish the terms of a variation, that is to say the *variant types*. Once again the purpose is to make it easier to read the variations directly from the collation. I have applied the rule that the most frequent positive variant is in standard style, and a second positive variant is in italic style. A third positive variant occurs only in two variations. See 3.5 and 3.19, where I have used a reduced font size.

## Polygraphic Variations

Typologically, ancient Chinese seems to have been "vocalically reductive," in the sense that its words characteristically retained a single vocalic focus while suppressing vocalization at the junctures with affixes. In the development of the script this agglutinated, monosyllabic, pseudo-monomorphic lexeme became the primary object of graphic representation. Thanks to this script/language relationship, the great majority of variations consist of contrasts between single-syllabic words occupying a point of text equal to a single character, that is to say, are monographic. This feature is a great convenience for the alignment of texts, but it is not sensible to make a general principle of it. There are a number of categories of polysyllabic words and phrases whose entry into variations should be recognized. The following types occur in our short passage:

a. Polysyllabic words. (E.g., 3.1 ☐ A: 故 BC$^1$: 是以 C$^2$D)

To treat this variation as two separate monographic variations is not helpful. Should it be ☐ A: 故 BC$^1$: 是 C$^2$D and ☐ A: ☐ BC$^1$: 以 C$^2$D, or should it be ☐ A: ☐ BC$^1$: 是 C$^2$D and ☐ A: 故 BC$^1$: 以 C$^2$D? Neither pair provides any explanation of the transmissional change nor of the relationship between the pairs.

b. Short clausal structures. (E.g., 1.16 為百谷下 A: 下之 BCD)

This type is clearly more important. What varies in this example are the syntactic relationships, "to become the-mountain-streams' inferior" in A and "to go-below them" in BCD. In A, 下 is a locative noun and the head of the noun phrase 百谷下; in BCD, 下 is a verb of motion governing the locative argument 之, a pronoun referring back to the 百谷 in the previous clause. At whatever point this divergence between A and the other witnesses took place, it can hardly be put down to a copyist's error. Does it reflect a transition from the oral to the written tradition? Does it point to a redactor's preference determined by time, or place, or style? Or is it the characteristic symptom of indirect transmission — paraphrase? What is important here is that our way of collating the testimony does not hide such questions from view.

At the same time I should point out that the collator should not have to interpret variations in advance of his collation, and that clear criteria to establish explicit categories of polygraphic variations do not exist and are a task for the future. But, even at the risk of a certain loss of "transparency," I feel that there is more to gain than to lose by marking variations of this kind.

A variation occupies a single point of text. Single character variations do not need to be marked. Polygraphic variations, whose length is determined by their longest variant, are referred to by the first of the series of numbers which label their position in the collated testimony (top row). All except the first number in such a sequence are printed in gray, marking the fact that the corresponding sequence of graphs, in each of the witnesses collated, participates in a single variation and is treated as a single point of the text to which they testify.

*Points of Text*

It should be noted that only *variations with respect to the direct testimony* are marked here in this way. *Agreements*, even where they may be polysyllabic words or syntactic structures, are left unmarked as they normally are by the script (i.e., no spaces between words). In summary, agreements are, for the purposes of collation, always treated as monographic; variations may under certain conditions be treated as polygraphic. The number of points of text in a collated text database is equal to the sum of the agreements and the variations. In the collation this number is given to the right of the row of position numbers.

## Text Reversal

A serious obstacle to strict vertical alignment is presented by disordered sequences. These are common to all transmissional systems. Most are cases of simple reversal, which are, in effect, two-term reversal variations. This is true of the two cases which appear in our sample (see *ju* 2 and *ju* 3). I have marked the "reversed testimony" there by underlining with a wavy line [∿] in the row below the direct testimony, and have indicated the point around which the reversal takes place by a "pivot" marker [△]. In order to maintain alignment, I have reversed the order actually found in the witnesses with the "less frequent order variant," and have substituted the "alert" sign [ ※ ] for the pivot.

## Lacunae and Omissions

Another important consideration for the maintenance of strict alignment is the distinction between omissions and lacunae. A *lacuna* (∎) results from the loss of, or damage to, the physical (graphical) representation of the text. It exists of itself, quite independently of other testimony and represents the *absence of testimony* at a given point of text. It neither agrees nor disagrees with other variants. From it, as in the juridical analogy of the silent witness, no implications ought to be drawn; on it no evidence may be based. The complete agreement of other witnesses standing against a lacuna does not constitute a variation. In lists of variations, I note lacunae only where a variation does exist among other witnesses, but then, in square brackets, as a reminder that the variation in question is not based on the full number of witnesses. It is important that for ancient Chinese manuscripts a standard method for approximating the number of lacunae is agreed. Such a standard would safeguard against the risk, in collation, of adjusting the number of lacunae to the positive testimony, rather than *vice versa*.

An *omission* ( ☐ ), on the other hand, leaves no trace in the physical representation of the text. It is not perceived as an incomplete state of the text. That is an editorial judgement. It exists only *relative to other testimony*. Its presence always signals a variation. If, at the editorial stage, it is deemed to be the better reading, then the positive variants become "errors by addition"; if a positive variant is judged superior, then the negative variant is declared an "error by omission." Thus, editorially, we may, for instance, think of the 皆 in the variation at point 4.5 as an unwarranted addition in $B^2$, or, somewhat less probably, we may conclude that each of the other witnesses has an omission at that point. If we keep the collational and editorial tasks strictly separated, this use of the term "omission" causes no difficulty.

To mark this fundamental difference in the "relationship to evidence" of the omission and the lacuna, it is important to maintain distinct markers for these two forms of negative testimony.

## HISTORICAL PROBLEMS

*Graphic Variations*

Throughout the foregoing discussion it has been assumed that a comparison at each point in a well-constructed collation will immediately reveal the variations from which an editor may form a view of the changes in the state of a text through time. This assumption has ignored the fact that the script itself has undergone major historical changes. This section is concerned with the implications, for the text critic as collator, of this fact.

In the first place, the problem is not exclusively related to the existence of newly discovered early manuscripts. The texts we have received by transmission from antiquity have all been subjected, at different periods of their history, to the processes of "modernization" and standardization. The effect of these processes has not been uniform. Consider, for instance, the relative neglect accorded the text of the *Mozi* 墨子 . The most striking evidence of this uneven historical process of standardization is the very high number of *graphic variants*. The list 異體字表 in vol. 8 of the *Hanyu Da Zidian* 漢語大字典 occupies 125 pages. Where such variants are strictly orthographic, that is to say, represent the same linguistic unit as that represented by the "standard form 正體" and nothing else, then their inclusion in the collation in opposition to the standard form will present false variations. Such purely orthographic variations hide the true textual agreement at the point in question. Under these circumstances it is better to standardize the graphic form in the collation while registering the original form against the witness in whose testimony it occurs. When, however, a graphic variant has a conditioned relationship to more than one standard form, or is disputed, or not well documented, is better to let it stand in the collation and to deal with the uncertain textual variation at the editorial stage.

In the second place, the recent ancient manuscript discoveries have presented us with a wide range of new graphic variants, associated with particular times and places, and are of immense value for epigraphy, on which the study of ancient texts so heavily depends. Epigraphic editions of such manuscripts routinely transcribe the script into modern forms, and where the result of direct transcription is thought to be a graphic variant the proposed standard form is normally supplied in brackets. In collating these manuscripts, it is wise to cite and follow a particular edition, and to register the superceded variants. As editor, the text critic cannot avoid engagement with epigraphic problems; but as collator, he should try to do so as far as possible.

On the question of the registration of graphic variants, a list should be kept of the variant forms, if any, in each witness, which are regularly replaced by a "standard" graph in the collation. Such a register should be archived in the same way as full collations and (unlike collations) published with critical editions of the text. One advantage is that only deviations from the register would require noting in the collation or in the *apparatus criticus*. Another is that if produced conscientiously by text critics, such registers might make a contribution to an epigraphic database. In this sample collation, I have simply noted epigraphic variants, if any, after the testimony from each witness.

### Taboo Avoidance Forms

The somewhat different case of substitute forms for tabooed imperial names would, if not corrected, have a similar effect of creating false variations. In this short passage, the only taboo respected is the graph 民 in deference to Li Shimin 李世民, the founder of the Tang dynasty; and then, among the direct witnesses, only by D1, the Jinglong stele, which replaces 民 in all of its four occurrences — twice in *ju* 2 and twice in *ju* 3 — with the graph 人. This seems perfectly normal in that it was an inscription exposed to public view engraved shortly after the restoration of the Tang line, upon the death of the Empress Wu in 705. It is, however, unusual, for two reasons. One is that elsewhere in the inscription, 民 is not avoided; the other is that an order published in 626, as Li Shimin assumed the imperial title, explicitly removed the taboo from the individual components of his personal name, 世 and 民, except when they occurred together in order.

I have marked taboo variants in this collation in the same fashion as graphic variants, but have preceded the substitute form with a capital T.

## USES OF THE COLLATION

### The Assessment of Witnesses

In the study of a particular text, even a small set of collations may be sufficient to offer a solution to the problem of deciding which further witnesses need to be collated for inclusion in the set. This problem is particularly acute in the case of the Chinese textual tradition, where printing became a standard for transmission much earlier than in the West. This has the consequence that the exclusive use of early manuscripts is too severe a rule and the inclusion of printed books too lenient. The problem can be stated thus: How to discover which witnesses need not be collated (because they bring no useful new information to the reconstruction of earlier states of the text) without actually collating them to find out.

The following example is based on the alleged Dunhuang manuscript of the *Laozi* copied in 270 (2d year of the Jianheng period of the Three Kingdoms state of Wu, 建衡二年) by Suo Dan 索紞, a member of an important Dunhuang family, some of whom achieved very high rank at the Jin 晉 court. This manuscript contains *zhang* 51–81 of the *Laozi*, in sequence and marked by starting each *zhang* with a new line. It has been in private hands since its discovery. It is reputed to have been acquired by Li

Shengduo 李盛鐸 (1860–1937) through his family connections with He Yansheng 何彥昇 , who had been responsible for the collection and shipment to Beijing of the remaining Dunhuang treasures under an order of the imperial government in 1910. On the death of Li Shengduo, his collections were broken up. The only person who claimed to have seen the manuscript while it was in Li s possession was Ye Xia'an 葉遐庵. It was through Ye that it was introduced to the world. It passed through a number of hands in Japan and in China and was made available to Rao Zongyi 饒宗頤 for study in the early 1950s. It is now held in the Gest Library at Princeton. In recent years, many scholars in China have expressed doubts about this manuscript. These doubts concern, first, the account of its discovery and the circumstances of its introduction to the public, and, in addition, the compatibility of its hand with its claimed date of copying.

I have collated *zhang* 66 from this manuscript against the collations made for the present exercise, using for the purpose the photographs published by Rao Zongyi in 1955 as an appendix to his article, "索紞寫本道德經殘卷," *Journal of Oriental Studies* 東方文化 , vol. 2.1. If it were, in fact, a physical witness from the end of the 3d century, we might reasonably hope for the preservation of a few ancient readings, earlier than B, whether or not in agreement with A. In other words, one might expect it to fall into category C (see above, "The Testimony"). Where it turns out actually to belong, however, is quite firmly into the "received standard" category (D). In fact, for this *zhang*, the Suo Dan testimony differs from all of our three D-witnesses only at one point. It adds a 民 after 4.12. Otherwise it is textually identical to $D^3$, the Song woodblock edition of the redaction with the Heshang Gong commentary.

Though this means that this manuscript is unlikely to provide exciting new evidence of early states of the *Laozi* text, not too much should be read into this conclusion from a single *zhang*. It would certainly require two or three more test collations of other *zhang* to determine, without further evidence, whether a full collation of the Suo Dan manuscript would be useful to an editor of the *Laozi*. One must, of course, take pains to include in the basic test set of collations all early manuscripts and other witnesses known to have played an important role in the history of the text. If that condition is satisfied, then this means of excluding supernumerary witnesses will not only save time, but can make the difference between the feasibility or otherwise of undertaking an edition.

## The Determination of Evidence

### Rules of evidence based on historical and textual data

The primary use of collation is to present in a systematic form the textual variations between the key witnesses to a text. The analysis of those variations, in combination with historical (i.e. bibliographical) information about the witnesses in question, may allow the reconstruction of the relationships between the witnesses, and thereby provide a basis for assessing the testimony within a given variation. It is by the generalization of this principle that the formulation of rules of evidence for earlier states of a text is achieved. However, because this sample collation is so short, it is not possible to hope for more than some preliminary and tentative rules.

Our knowledge of the witnesses collated, independent of their testimony, is minimally their relative dates. These allow us to say with confidence, for instance, that the agreement of the Guodian (A) and Mawangdui (B) testimony is "evidential" against any variant of a later date. For the remaining variations, where A and B disagree, the distribution of agreement from CD is not equal between A and B. B attracts the overwhelming support of later testimony, as the appended Table of Variations shows. It appears, in other words, that from the testimony of *zhang* 66, it may be the case that the A manuscripts form a branch on the transmissional tree of the *Laozi*, which though old, has not left us any direct descendants. It is also clear that the B manuscripts are in effect the "modern" redaction, so we may not use the agreement of their own descendant affines to give the testimony of B the greater weight when in opposition to A. On the other hand, the survival among some medieval witnesses of positive disagreements with B while agreeing with A, suggests an older tradition ancestral to both A and B. The Table of Variations sorts the 54 variations, identified by the collation of this passage, by "rules" based on historical considerations of this kind. These rules are necessarily tentative due to the size of the sample collated.

*Group D witnesses provide no evidence*

It will be observed below that the formulation of the rules of evidence for this *zhang* does not require any appeal to the testimony of group D. Of the 54 variations, only two are *determined by* the testimony of D witnesses. Those variations are 4.29 (omission in $D^1$) and 2.3 (omission in $D^2$). In both those variations, the reading in $D^3$, at the point of text in question, differs from $D^1$ and $D^2$ and agrees with all other witnesses. In one other variation, 1.11, which is otherwise characterized by the difference between A and BC, $D^3$ differs from $D^1$ once again, in such a way that the former agrees with BC while the latter agrees negatively with A. In all other variations the testimony among the group D witnesses is in agreement. These three variations are as follows:

2.3　聖人 $ABCD^1D^3$ : $\square\ D^2$
4.29　能 $ABCD^2D^3$ : $\square\ D^1$
1.11　$\square\ AD^1$ : 者 $BCD^2D^3$

In the first two, $D^2$ and $D^1$, with unique omissions in opposition to a positive variant common to *all* other earlier witnesses, are clearly in error. In 1.11, the agreement of $D^1$ with A sets up a real variation, but the case for the rule "AD:B implies AD = evidence," is far weaker than the same rule with respect to C (see item iii in the next paragraph). There are two reasons for this. Firstly, examples of this type of variation with D are rare in the extreme. Besides 1.11, just cited, there is only one clear example, at 4.18 (see table). Secondly, D follows C so closely that it seems unlikely that a second rule can be justified. D has, for instance, no positive variants, and only one negative variant in addition to those referred to above, that do not agree with one or both of the C witnesses. Most importantly, however, is the consideration that even for C, the proposed rule is not safe for negative agreements with A. I conclude, therefore, that D contributes nothing to the evidence of *zhang* 66 of the *Laozi*.

### The rules of evidence

The Table of Variations lists all the variations in *zhang* 66 in the order of the rules set out below. For the time being, these rules are divided into two groups, those that apply to *non-unique variations* and a smaller group that apply to unique variations. A unique variation is a variation, which consists of a positive variant in a single witness opposed to omissions in all other witnesses.

A. For non-unique variations

i. AB[+] (evidence)

Where A and B are in agreement, then a positive variant to which they testify is taken to be evidence to the text at the point in question, despite the testimony of other witnesses.

ii. AC[+] : B  (AC = evidence)

Where A differs from B but a positive variant in one of the C witnesses is in agreement with A, then the testimony of AC is taken to be evidential.

iii. A : BC[+] (evidence equivocal)

Where A differs from B, even though a positive variant in one of the C witnesses is in agreement with B, the testimony of A and B cannot be resolved by rule and the evidence is therefore equivocal.

B. For unique variations

iv. A[+] : BC[-] or AC[-] : B[+] (equivocal evidence)

The first of these two types of variation shows a unique positive variant in A, opposed to an omission in the other collated witnesses. It is in fact the inverse of Rule iii. The critical feature is that, whether the agreement of C with B is positive or negative, the post-Mawangdui tradition of this text provides no confirmation of the Guodian testimony so that the difference between A and B cannot be resolved by rule. The second type covers a unique positive variant in both the B witnesses. Here the balance of evidence between A and B cannot be affected by the negative agreement of C with A, because of the possibility of its arising from the tradition of reducing function words in the *Laozi*.

v. $AB_iC[-] : B_j[+]$ or $AB[-] : C[+]$  (AB = evidence)

In the first pattern, the negative agreement of AC and one B witness should probably be given more weight than a unique positive variant in the other B witness. In the second pattern, the agreement of A and B, albeit negative, must also be taken as evidential. It is interesting to note that where there are positive variants in C, it is rare that one or both fail to agree with either A or B. The only cases, other than those listed under this rule in the Table of Variations, are:

| | |
|---|---|
| 2.5 | 之 AB : 其 $C^1$ : □ $C^2$ |
| 3.27, 4.13 | 弗 AB : 不 C |
| 3.3 | 其 A : □ $BC^1$ : 聖人 C |

But even in these cases, C has clear links with A or B below the surface disagreements. Against this background of close dependence on the extant older witnesses, one cannot allow equal evidential value to the agreement of omissions in AB and to the unique variants of C. One must choose between the possibility of coincidental omissions in the separate traditions of A and B on the one hand, and, on the other, the well-established probability that *unique variants in naturally transmitted texts are errors*, a probability that increases with the distance in time from the oldest witness.

I should also point out that I have included in this section on unique variations those numbered 4.16 and 3.21, even though their positive variants are not unique to single witnesses, but merely to their group (B and C respectively). In neither case however is the argument about the quality of their testimony affected by this accommodation.

### The textual evidence

The "evidence" for a text is the text generated by the application of "rules of evidence" to the conflicting testimony of its witnesses. The minimum case is the text known only through, say, a single manuscript. The testimony of that manuscript *is* the evidence for that text. More complex rules can also be applied quite easily. In the case of our exercise on this short text, the collation indicates ninety-three "points of text." Fifty-two show variations over the eight witnesses collated (see Table of Variations: fifty-four items less two non-punctal reversal variations). Forty-one text points show agreement across all the witnesses. The rule for the agreements is, of course, the same as that applied to the single witness text. Below the Collation for each *ju*, the results of that rule, and of the rules proposed above, have been read into positions aligned with the testimony from which they were derived. It will be noticed that the evidence is presented separately for the Guodian manuscript and the rest of the textual tradition. This is in no sense because the evidence gives any indication that, at the hypotext level at which it has been examined, *zhang* 66 is anything but a single text with an identity derived from the common ancestor of all its witnesses. I have done so to show clearly where the two traditions are already in agreement (70%) and where equivocal testimony cannot be reconciled by rule (30%). The text points where the latter occur are marked with an asterisk and, in the case of polygraphic variants, with dotted lines (---) following an asterisk.

## THE PURSUIT OF RECONCILIATION

An editor working from this evidence might feel able to propose quite convincing conjectures for the reconciliation of some of these conflicts. But if we are to take full advantage of the phenomenal Guodian discovery, we must first exhaust the search for more objective means to reduce the degree of equivocation, which exists between the testimony of the Guodian manuscript and the other witnesses. There are a number of tasks that could be done. One is the collation of the other eighty *zhang* of the *Laozi*; in particular, of course, the thirty-odd *zhang*, which we also know from the Guodian manuscript. This would allow the determination of rules of evidence from a much broader basis. Another is the search for other witnesses to the *Laozi*, which may fall into category C. The Dunhuang *Laozi* manuscripts are, possibly, the most likely source of these.

A third task, which should be examined once again in the light of the Guodian discovery, is the indirect tradition of the *Laozi*. I have, for the present exercise, divided indirect sources into three types:

E[1] The approximately 10 philosophical works of the 3d and 2d centuries BC of which the *Hanfeizi*, including *pian* 20 "Jie Lao 解老" and *pian* 21 "Yu Lao 喻老," is particularly important.

E[2] The *Laozi* commentaries, especially those attributed to Yan Zun, Wang Bi, Heshang Gong, Xiang Er, and also other commentaries among the *Laozi* manuscripts from Dunhuang. The implications of many of these commentaries for the text of *Laozi* have been very carefully scrutinized. Most notably in recent years, the Wang Bi commentary has been the object of a number of studies by Rudolf Wagner.

E[3] The literary and political anthologies and their commentaries, and the encyclopedias.

I have included one or two indirect witnesses in each category. It should be noted that the date of indirect testimony is crucial, as it determines what direct testimony would have been available to the author of the indirect source. It appears, for instance, that, from this *zhang* Wei Zheng 魏徵 is citing a group D direct source in the *Qunshu Zhiyao* 群書治要 (cf. E[3] with D[3] in *ju* 1–3).

I have added to the variations, listed at the bottom of each page of the Collations, occasional references to indirect testimony cited. Though such testimony cannot simply be taken as having the authority of direct testimony, in the Heshang Gong commentary, two agreements with the Guodian manuscript are particularly interesting (see 2.7 在民上 and 2.22 在民前 ).

# A Collation of *Zhang* 2 of Series 1 of the "A" Bamboo Manuscript of the Laozi from a Chu Tomb at Guodian, Hubei

郭店楚墓竹簡老子甲篇第一系列第二章的校讎

|   | 1 | 2 | 3 | 4 | 5 | 6 | 7 | 8 | 9 | 10 | 11 | 13 | 14 | 15 | 16 | — | — | 20 | 22 | 23 | 24 | 25 | 26 | 27 | 28 | Points 23 |  |
|---|---|---|---|---|---|---|---|---|---|---|---|---|---|---|---|---|---|---|---|---|---|---|---|---|---|---|---|
| A | 江 | 海 | □ | 所 | 以 | □ | 爲 | 百 | 谷 | 王 | □ | 以 | 能 | 爲 | 百 | 谷 | 下 | □ | 是 | 以 | 能 | 爲 | 百 | 谷 | 王 | 。 | 鄠本 2 |
| B1 | ■ | 海 | □ | 所 | 以 | 能 | 爲 | 百 | 谷 | 王 | 者 | 善 | □ | 其 | 能 | 善 | 下 | □ | 是 | 以 | 能 | 爲 | 百 | 谷 | 王 | 。 | 馬甲 61 |
| B2 | 江 | 海 | □ | 所 | 以 | 能 | 爲 | 百 | 谷 | ■ | ■ | ■ | ■ | ■ | □ | 下 | 之 | □ | 是 | 以 | 能 | 爲 | 百 | 谷 | 王 | 。 | 馬 203A |
| C1 | 江 | 海 | □ | 所 | 以 | 能 | 爲 | 百 | 谷 | 王 | 者 | 以 | 其 | 善 | □ | 下 | 之 | □ | 故 | □ | 能 | 爲 | 百 | 谷 | 王 | 。 | 嚴遵 |
| C2 | 江 | 海 | □ | 所 | 以 | 能 | 爲 | 百 | 谷 | 王 | 者 | 以 | 其 | 善 | □ | 下 | 之 | 也 | 故 | □ | 能 | 爲 | 百 | 谷 | 王 | 。 | 傅奕 |
| D1 | 江 | 海 | □ | 所 | 以 | 能 | 爲 | 百 | 谷 | 王 | 者 | 以 | 其 | 善 | □ | 下 | 之 | □ | 故 | □ | 能 | 爲 | 百 | 谷 | 王 | ; | 龍碑 |
| D2 | 江 | 海 | □ | 所 | 以 | 能 | 爲 | 百 | 谷 | 王 | 者 | 以 | 其 | 善 | □ | 下 | 之 | □ | 故 | □ | 能 | 爲 | 百 | 谷 | 王 | ; | 王本 |
| D3 | 江 | 海 | □ | 所 | 以 | 能 | 爲 | 百 | 谷 | 王 | 者 | 以 | 其 | 善 | □ | 下 | 之 | □ | 故 | □ | 能 | 爲 | 百 | 谷 | 王 | ; | 河上 |
| E1 | 江 | 河 | □ | 所 | 以 | 能 | 爲 | 百 | 谷 | 王 | 者 | □ | 能 | 下 | 之 | □ | □ | 也 | 是 | 以 | 能 | 上 | 之 | □ | □ | ◦ | 淮南說 1l, p525 |
| E3 | 江 | 海 | □ | 所 | 以 | 能 | 爲 | 百 | 谷 | 王 | 者 | 以 | 其 | 善 | 下 | 之 | □ | □ | 是 | 以 | 能 | 爲 | 百 | 谷 | 王 | ; | 群書治要 |

Note: E1 agrees with A at 15

是宇衛有失權能下之五字

|   | 1 | 2 | 3 | 4 | 5 | 6 | 7 | 8 | 9 | 10 | 11 | 13 | 14 | 15 | 16 | — | — | 20 | 22 | 23 | 24 | 25 | 26 | 27 | 28 | |  |
|---|---|---|---|---|---|---|---|---|---|---|---|---|---|---|---|---|---|---|---|---|---|---|---|---|---|---|---|
| 郭本 | 江 | 海 | □ | 所 | 以 | 能 | 爲 | 百 | 谷 | 王 | □ | 以 | 其 | 能 | 爲 | 百 | 谷 | 下 | □ | 是 | 以 | 能 | 爲 | 百 | 谷 | 王 | Characters: 22 |
| 傅本 | 江 | 海 | □ | 所 | 以 | 能 | 爲 | 百 | 谷 | 王 | 者 | 以 | 其 | 善 | 下 | 之 | □ | □ | 是 | 以 | 能 | 爲 | 百 | 谷 | 王 | 。 | Characters: 23 |
|  |  |  | * |  |  | * |  |  |  |  | * |  |  | * | * | — | — | — |  |  |  |  |  |  |  |  | Equiv. points: 5 |

3 □AB²CD : 之 B¹  6 □A : 能 BCD  11 □AD¹ : 者 B¹C²D² : 善 B²C¹D : □C¹ : [■B²]  15 能 A(E¹) : □ B²  16 爲百谷下 A : 下之 BCD

20 □AB¹C¹D : 也 B³C²  22 是以 AB : 故 CD

| | 1 _ 3 _ 5 6 7 _ 10 | 12 13 14 15 16 17 | 20 21 22 _ 25 | 27 28 29 30 31 32 | Points: 22 | |
|---|---|---|---|---|---|---|
| A | 是以□□□聖人之□在民上也 | ，□以□言下之 | ；□其□在民前也 | ▲□其□身後之 | 郭甲3 | 7,22 才 |
| B1 | 是以聖人□欲□上民■ | ，必以其言下之 | ；△□其欲□先民■ | ，必以其身後之 | 馬甲62 | |
| B2 | 是以聖人□欲□上民也 | ，必以其言下之 | ；△□其欲□先民也 | ，必以其身後之 | 馬乙203B | |
| C1 | □□□聖人其欲□上民□ | ，□以□言下之 | ；△□其欲□先民□ | ，□以□身後之 | 嚴遵 | |
| C2 | 是以聖人其欲□上民□ | ，必以其言下之 | ；△□其欲□先民□ | ，必以其身後之 | 傅奕 | 9,24 丁人 |
| D1 | 是以聖人□□□上民□ | ，必以其言下之 | ；△□其欲□先民□ | ，必以其身後之 | 龍碑 | |
| D2 | 是以聖人□□□上民□ | ，必以其言下之 | ；△□其欲□先民□ | ，必以其身後之 | 王本 | |
| D3 | 是以聖人□□□上民□ | ，□以□言下之 | ；△□其欲□先民□ | ，□以□身後之 | 河上 | |
| | | | ▲ | | | |
| E1 | 古之聖王—————□以其下民 | ——夫欲□上民者 | —□以□先民者 | △□以其身後民之 | 文子符言 4.23, p74 | 17,32 丁人 |
| E2 | ———聖人□欲在民上□ | ——欲在民前□ | ——□□先民前 | △□以□身後之 | 文子道德 5.11, p89 | 9,24 丁人 |
| | | | | | 河上公注 | 民後有之字 |
| E3 | 是以聖人□欲□上民□ | ，必以其言下之 | ；△□其欲□先民□ | ，□以□身後之 | 群書治要 | 9 丁人 |

Note: E2 agrees with A at 7 & 22

| | 1 _ 3 _ 5 6 7 _ 10 | 12 13 14 15 16 17 | 20 21 22 _ 25 | 27 28 29 30 31 32 | Characters: | |
|---|---|---|---|---|---|---|
| 郭本 | □□是以□聖人之□在民上也 | ，□以□言下之 | ；□其□在民前也 | ，▲□其□身後之 | 20 | |
| 傅本 | 是以聖人之欲上民也 | ，必以其言下之 | ；其欲先民也 | ，必以其身後之 | 26 | |
| | * — — * | * | * — — * | * | | |

Equivocal points: 9

1 □A：是以 BCD
7 在民上 A(E²)：上民 BCD
19 ▲ A：△ BCD
25 也 AB²：□CD

3 聖人 AB²CD^{r3}：□D²：[□人 B^r]
10 也 AB：□CD
20 其 ABC^r：□C²D
27 □AC^rD：必 BC²

5 之 AB：其 C^r：□C²D
12 □AC^r：必 BCD
21 □A：欲 BCD
29 □AC^rD：其 BC²

6 □A：欲 BCD
14 □AC^rD：其 BC²
22 在民前 A(E²)：先民 B²CD：[先 B^r]

Guodian LaoziA1.2 (zhang 66), Ju 2: Sample Collation.   P. M. Thompson

| | 1 --- 3 --- 5 6 7 8 9 11 12 13 14 15 18 19 20 21 22 23 25 26 27 28 29 | Points: 23 | |
|---|---|---|---|
| A | □□□*其*在民□上也，□民*弗厚*也；△其在民□前 也，□民弗害也。 | 郭甲 4 | 5, 19 才 |
| B1 | *故*□□□*居*□□上□，而民*弗*重也；▲□*居*□□前 □，而民弗害也。 | 馬甲 63 | |
| B2 | *故*□□□*居*□□上□，而民*弗*重也；△□*居*□□前 □，而民弗害□。 | 馬乙 204A | |
| C1 | *故*□□□在□□上□，而民不重□；△□*居*民之前 □，而民不害□。 | 嚴遵 | |
| C2 | 是以聖人處□之上□，而民*弗*重□；△□處□之前 □，而民不害也。 | 傅奕 | |
| D1 | 是以聖人處□□上□，而民不重□；△□處□□前 □，而民不害□。 | 龍碑 | 12, 26 T 人 |
| D2 | 是以聖人處□□上□，而民不重□；△□處□□前 □，而民不害□。 | 王本 | |
| D3 | 是以聖人處□□上□，而民不重□；△□處□□前 □，而民不害□。 | 河上 | |
| | ▲ | | |
| E1 | —————居□□上□，而民不重□；△□居□□前 □，而衆不害□。 | 文子道德 5.11, p89 | |
| | 是以□□處□□上□，而民不重□；△□居□□前 □，而民不害□。 | 文子道原 1.6, p10 | 26 T 人 |
| | 是以□□處□□上□，而民弗重□；△□居□□前 □，而衆不害□。 | 淮南原道, p11 | |
| E3 | 是以聖人處□□上□，而民不重□；△□處□□前 □，而民不害□。 | 群書治要 | |

Note: E1 (HNT) agrees with ABC$^2$ at 13

| | | | |
|---|---|---|---|
| 郭本 | □□□其在民□上也，□民弗厚也；△其在民□前也，□民弗害也。 | Characters: 18 | |
| 傳本 | 故□□□在□□上□，而民弗重也；△□居民□前□，而民弗害也。 | 16 | |
| | * --- * --- * * * * * * * * | Equivocal Points: 10 | |

1 □A：故 BC$^1$：是以 C$^2$D　3 □其 A：□□BC$^1$：聖人 C$^2$D　5 在 AC$^1$：居 B：處 C$^2$D　6 民 A：□BCD　7 □ABC$^1$D：之 C$^2$
9 也 A：□BCD　11 □A：而 BCD　13 弗 ABC$^2$(E$^1$)：不 C$^1$D　14 厚 A：重 BCD　15 也 AB：□CD
17 ▲ B$^1$：△ AB$^2$CD　18 其 A：□BCD　19 在 A：居 BC$^1$：處 C$^2$D　20 民 AC$^1$：□BC$^2$D　21 □ABD：之 C
23 也 A：□BCD　25 □A：而 BCD　27 弗 AB：不 CD　29 也 AB$^1$C$^2$：□B$^2$C$^1$D

Guodian LaoziA1.2 (zhang 66), *Ju* 3: Sample Collation.　P. M. Thompson

| | 1 | — | 3 | 4 | 5 | 6 | 7 | 8 | — | — | 12 | 13 | 14 | 15 | 16 | 18 | 19 | 20 | 21 | 22 | 23 | 25 | 26 | 27 | 28 | 29 | 30 | 31 | 32 | Points: 26 | |
|---|---|---|---|---|---|---|---|---|---|---|---|---|---|---|---|---|---|---|---|---|---|---|---|---|---|---|---|---|---|---|---|
| A | □ | □ | 天 | 下 | □ | 樂 | 遝 | □ | □ | — | 而 | □ | 厭 | □ | | □ | 以 | 其 | 不 | 爭 | 也 | | 故 | 天 | 下 | 莫 | 能 | 與 | 之 | 爭 。 | 郭甲 4 | 15 點：22, 32 / 靜：25 古 |
| B1 | □ | □ | 天 | 下 | □ | 樂 | 推 | □ | | | 而 | 弗 | 厭 | 也 | | 非 | 以 | 其 | 無 | 爭 | 與 | | ■ | ■ | ■ | ■ | ■ | 與 | 之 | 爭 。 | 馬甲 63 | 7 隼：22, 32 靜 |
| B2 | □ | □ | 天 | 下 | 皆 | 樂 | 推 | □ | | | 而 | 弗 | 厭 | 也 | | 不 | 以 | 其 | 無 | 爭 | 與 | | 故 | ■ | 下 | 莫 | 能 | 與 | 之 | 爭 。 | 馬乙 204A | 7 讋 |
| C1 | □ | □ | 天 | 下 | □ | 樂 | 推 | 而 | 上 | 之 | 而 | 不 | 知 | 厭 | □ | 非 | 以 | 其 | □ | 爭 | 與 | | 故 | 天 | 下 | 莫 | 能 | 與 | 之 | 爭 。 | 謝遴 | |
| C2 | 是 | 以 | 天 | 下 | □ | 樂 | 推 | □ | | | 而 | 不 | □ | 厭 | □ | 不 | 以 | 其 | □ | 爭 | 與 | | 故 | 天 | 下 | 莫 | 能 | 與 | 之 | 爭 。 | 傅奕 | |
| D1 | 是 | 以 | 天 | 下 | □ | 樂 | 推 | □ | | | 而 | 不 | □ | 厭 | □ | □ | 以 | 其 | 不 | 爭 | | | 故 | 天 | 下 | 莫 | □ | 與 | 之 | 爭 。 | 龍碑 | |
| D2 | 是 | 以 | 天 | 下 | □ | 樂 | 推 | □ | | | 而 | 不 | □ | 厭 | □ | □ | 以 | 其 | 不 | 爭 | 與 | | 故 | 天 | 下 | 莫 | 能 | 與 | 之 | 爭 。 | 王本 | |
| D3 | 是 | 以 | 天 | 下 | □ | 樂 | 推 | □ | | | 而 | 不 | □ | 厭 | □ | □ | 以 | 其 | 不 | 爭 | 與 | | 故 | 天 | 下 | 莫 | 能 | 與 | 之 | 爭 。 | 河上 | |
| E1 | □ | □ | □ | □ | □ | □ | □ | □ | □ | | 而 | 不 | □ | 厭 | □ | — | — | — | — | — | — | | — | — | — | — | — | — | — | — | 文子符言 4.23, p74 | 厭後有而 p.74 重四字 |
| | | | | | | | | | | | | | | | | — | — | — | — | — | — | | — | — | — | — | — | — | — | — | 文子道德 5.11, p89 | |
| | | | | | | | | | | | | | | | | — | — | — | — | — | — | | — | — | — | — | — | — | — | — | 文子道原 1.6, p10 | 爭後有於萬物 三字 |
| | | | | | | | | | | | | | | | | □ | 以 | 其 | 無 | 爭 | 與 | | 故 | □ | 下 | 莫 | 敢 | 與 | 之 | 爭 。 | 淮南道應 p11 | |

Note: E1 (HNZ) agrees with B at 21

| | 1 | — | 3 | 4 | 5 | 6 | 7 | 8 | — | — | 12 | 13 | 14 | 15 | 16 | 18 | 19 | 20 | 21 | 22 | 23 | 25 | 26 | 27 | 28 | 29 | 30 | 31 | 32 | Characters: | |
|---|---|---|---|---|---|---|---|---|---|---|---|---|---|---|---|---|---|---|---|---|---|---|---|---|---|---|---|---|---|---|---|
| 郭本 | □ | □ | 天 | 下 | □ | 樂 | 遝 | □ | | | 而 | 弗 | 厭 | 也 | | □ | 以 | 其 | 不 | 爭 | 也 | | 故 | 天 | 下 | 莫 | 能 | 與 | 之 | 爭 。 | 20 | |
| 傅本 | □ | □ | 天 | 下 | □ | 樂 | 推 | □ | | | 而 | 弗 | 厭 | 也 | | 非 | 以 | 其 | 無 | 爭 | 與 | | 故 | 天 | 下 | 莫 | 能 | 與 | 之 | 爭 。 | 22 | |

Equiv. points: 4

1 □ABC¹：是以 C²D    5 □AB⁴CD：皆 B²    7 遝 A：推 BCD    8 □ABC²D：而上之 C¹    13 弗 AB：不 CD

14 □ABC⁵D：知 C¹    16 □ACD：也 B    18 □AD：非 B¹C¹：不 B²C²    20 其 ABC⁵D：□C¹    21 不 AC⁵D：無 B(E¹)：□C¹

23 也 A：與 B：□CD    29 能 AB²CD²³：□D¹：[■B⁷]    31 乙 ACD：□B

Guodian LaoziA1.2 (zhang 66), fu 4: Sample Collation.    P. M. Thompson

## i. AB [positive]   (evidence)   14

| | A | B¹ | B² | C¹ | C² | D¹ | D² | D³ |
|---|---|---|---|---|---|---|---|---|
| 2.10 | 也 | 也 | 也 | □ | □ | □ | □ | □ |
| 2.25 | 也 | ■ | 也 | □ | □ | □ | □ | □ |
| 3.15 | 也 | 也 | 也 | □ | □ | □ | □ | □ |
| 3.29 | 也 | 也 | □ | □ | □ | □ | □ | □ |
| 4.23 | 也 | 與 | 與 | □ | □ | □ | □ | □ |
| 2.5 | 之 | 之 | 之 | 其 | □ | □ | □ | □ |
| 2.20 | 其 | 其 | 其 | 其 | □ | □ | □ | □ |
| 4.20 | 其 | 其 | 其 | □ | 其 | 其 | 其 | 其 |
| 3.13 | 弗 | 弗 | 弗 | 不 | 弗 | 不 | 不 | 不 |
| 3.27 | 弗 | 弗 | 弗 | 不 | 不 | 不 | 不 | 不 |
| 4.13 | 弗 | 弗 | 弗 | 不 | 不 | 不 | 不 | 不 |
| 1.22 | 是以 | 是以 | 是以 | 故 | 故 | 故 | 故 | 故 |
| 2.3 | 聖人 | ■人 | 聖人 | 聖人 | 聖人 | 聖人 | □ | 聖人 |
| 4.29 | 能 | 能 | 能 | 能 | 能 | □ | 能 | 能 |

## ii. AC [+] : B   (AC = evidence)   5

| | A | B¹ | B² | C¹ | C² | D¹ | D² | D³ |
|---|---|---|---|---|---|---|---|---|
| 4.21 | 不 | 無 | 無 | □ | 不 | 不 | 不 | 不 |
| 3.5 | 在 | 居 | 居 | 在 | 處 | 處 | 處 | 處 |
| 3.20 | 民 | □ | □ | 民 | 民 | □ | □ | □ |
| 4.31 | 之 | □ | □ | 之 | 之 | 之 | 之 | 之 |
| 3.17 | △ | ※ | △ | △ | △ | △ | △ | △ |

## iii. A : BC   (evidence equivocal)   23

| | A | B¹ | B² | C¹ | C² | D¹ | D² | D³ |
|---|---|---|---|---|---|---|---|---|
| 1.6 | □ | 能 | 能 | 能 | 能 | 能 | 能 | 能 |
| 1.11 | □ | 者 | ■ | 者 | 者 | □ | 者 | 者 |
| 2.1 | □ | 是以 | 是以 | 是以 | 是以 | 是以 | 是以 | 是以 |
| 2.6 | □ | 欲 | 欲 | 欲 | 欲 | 欲 | 欲 | 欲 |
| 2.21 | □ | 欲 | 欲 | 欲 | 欲 | 欲 | 欲 | 欲 |
| 3.1 | □ | 故 | 故 | 故 | 是以 | 是以 | 是以 | 是以 |
| 3.11 | □ | 而 | 而 | 而 | 而 | 而 | 而 | 而 |
| 3.25 | □ | 而 | 而 | 而 | 而 | 而 | 而 | 而 |
| 2.12 | □ | 必 | 必 | □ | 必 | 必 | 必 | 必 |
| 2.27 | □ | 必 | 必 | □ | 必 | 必 | 必 | 必 |
| 4.18 | □ | 非 | 不 | 非 | 不 | □ | □ | □ |
| 2.14 | □ | 其 | 其 | 其 | 其 | □ | □ | □ |
| 2.29 | □ | 其 | 其 | □ | 其 | □ | □ | □ |
| 1.20 | □ | □ | 也 | □ | 也 | □ | □ | □ |
| 1.15 | 能 | 善 | ■ | □ | 善 | 善 | 善 | 善 |
| 3.14 | 厚 | 重 | 重 | 重 | 重 | 重 | 重 | 重 |
| 3.19 | 在 | 居 | 居 | 居 | 處 | 處 | 處 | 處 |
| 4.7 | 進 | 推 | 推 | 推 | 推 | 推 | 推 | 推 |
| 1.16 | 爲百谷下 | 下之 | 下之 | 下之 | 下之 | 下之 | 下之 | 下之 |
| 2.7 | 在民上 | 上民 | 上民 | 上民 | 上民 | 上民 | 上民 | 上民 |
| 2.22 | 在民前 | 先■ | 先民 | 先民 | 先民 | 先民 | 先民 | 先民 |
| 3.3 | 其 | □ | □ | □ | 聖人 | 聖人 | 聖人 | 聖人 |
| 2.19 | ※ | △ | △ | △ | △ | △ | △ | △ |

## Unique Variations

### iv. A[+] : BC[-] or AC[-] : B[+] (evidence equivocal);   v. ACBᵢ[-] : Bⱼ[+] or AB[-] : C[+] (AB = evidence)   12

| | A | B¹ | B² | C¹ | C² | D¹ | D² | D³ |
|---|---|---|---|---|---|---|---|---|
| 3.6 | 民 | □ | □ | □ | □ | □ | □ | □ |
| 3.9 | 也 | □ | □ | □ | □ | □ | □ | □ |
| 3.18 | 其 | □ | □ | □ | □ | □ | □ | □ |
| 3.23 | 也 | □ | □ | □ | □ | □ | □ | □ |
| 4.16 | □ | 也 | 也 | □ | □ | □ | □ | □ |
| 1.3 | □ | 之 | □ | □ | □ | □ | □ | □ |
| 4.5 | □ | □ | 皆 | □ | □ | □ | □ | □ |
| 4.14 | □ | □ | □ | 知 | □ | □ | □ | □ |
| 4.8 | □ | □ | □ | 而上之 | □ | □ | □ | □ |
| 3.7 | □ | □ | □ | □, | 之 | □ | □ | □ |
| 4.1 | □ | □ | □ | □ | 是以 | 是以 | 是以 | 是以 |
| 3.21 | □ | □ | □ | 之 | 之 | □ | □ | □ |

# The Confucian Texts from Guodian Tomb Number One: Their Date and Significance

## LI XUEQIN

The contents of the bamboo slips from Guodian Tomb Number One can be divided into three main categories. The first category consists of the Daoist *Laozi* 老子 — in bundles A, B, and C; the C bundle includes the *Tai Yi Sheng Shui* 太一生水. The second category is composed of Confucian works, which can be divided into two groups. The first consists of six texts: *Zi Yi* 緇衣, *Wu Xing* 五行, *Cheng Zhi Wen Zhi* 成之聞之, *Zun De Yi* 尊德義, *Xing Zi Ming Chu* 性自命出, and *Liu De* 六德. The second group contains two texts: *Lu Mu Gong Wen Zisi* 魯穆公問子思 and *Qiong Da yi Shi* 窮達以時. This leaves only the *Zhong Xin zhi Dao* 忠信之道 and *Tang Yu zhi Dao* 唐虞之道, which, although maintaining a Confucian tone, are specifically concerned with abdication, and I suspect they are related to the ideas of Su Dai 蘇代 and Cuo Maoshou 厝毛壽, who may be labeled as "vertical and horizontal strategists 縱橫家" (a type of political philosophy so called in early texts and bibliographic lists). The third category contains the four bundles known as the *Yu Cong* 語叢, which are a mixture of sayings from the Hundred Schools and were probably used for teaching purposes. Below, I discuss only the second of these groups — the Confucian texts.

In order to examine these Confucian texts in the context of Chinese intellectual history, we must first determine the date of the slips. The nature and period of the archeological culture to which Guodian Tomb Number One belongs are clear. The tomb is in a cemetery of the Ying 郢 capital of the Chu state. The archeological sequence for Chu tombs in this area is already relatively well known, allowing the tomb to be dated to the late mid-Warring States period. More specifically, the tomb closely resembles the nearby Baoshan Tombs Number One and Number Two, the second of which contained a divination slip that mentions an event which we know to have occurred in 323 BC. At the same time, Baoshan Tombs Number Four and Number Five are later than Tombs One and Two, but are still typical Chu tombs and, therefore, cannot date to after 278 BC, when Qin occupied this area. We can deduce from this that the date of Guodian Tomb Number One cannot be later than 300 BC. Of course, the bamboo slips would have been written down somewhat earlier, and the composition of the works themselves would have been earlier still.

Let us now compare the dates of the leading Confucian teachers from Confucius onwards. The following table is based on Qian Mu's 錢穆 *Xian Qin Zhuzi Xinian* 先秦 諸子繫年:[1]

| | |
|---|---|
| Confucius 孔子 | 551–479 BC |
| Zengzi 曾子 | 505–436 BC |
| Zisi 子思 | 483–402 BC |
| Zishang (子上, Zisi's son) | 429–383 BC |
| Mencius 孟子 | 390–305 BC |
| Xunzi 荀子 | 340–245 BC |

Confucius lived from the second half of the sixth century to the beginning of the fifth century BC. Some of his seventy disciples would probably have lived until the middle of the fifth century BC. After this, his teachings passed on to the so-called "disciples of the seventy disciples," who lived in the middle-to-late fifth century BC. Mencius, who flourished in the mid- to late-fourth century, is a further generation removed from the "disciples of the disciples." Thus, we may conclude that Guodian Tomb Number One dates to the period when Mencius was an old man, and the works that were found in the tomb are texts that he could have read. If we consider that Mencius composed the *Mencius* in his old age, the Guodian texts ought to be earlier than the *Mencius*.

There were many developments in Confucianism after the death of Confucius. According to the "Xian Xue 顯學" chapter of the *Hanfeizi* 韓非子, the Confucian school divided into eight groups: that of Zizhang 子張, Zisi 子思, Yan Shi 顏氏, Meng Shi 孟氏, Qidiao Shi 漆雕氏, Zhongliang Shi 仲良氏, Sun Shi 孫氏, and Yuezheng Shi 樂正氏.

The corpus of Confucian texts suffered huge losses during the Qin burning of the books, but the number of Confucian works recorded in the "Yiwen Zhi 藝文志" section of the *Hanshu* 漢書 is still quite large. Unfortunately, there have been further losses since that time, and the great majority of the texts listed there have not been transmitted. From the late-Qing dynasty on, the tendency to "doubt antiquity 疑古" resulted in suspicion being cast upon the few remaining texts, with the result that the sequence of transmission of early Confucianism was completely obscured. The period between Confucius and Mencius, in particular, appeared to be a blank, leading to a proliferation of conjecture and supposition. When one realizes that the discovery of the Guodian Confucian works fills this gap, it becomes easy to appreciate their great importance.

---

[1] Published by Hong Kong University Press, 1956.

I have already mentioned the eight-fold division of the Confucian school. I believe that the group of Guodian texts that includes the *Zi Yi* belongs to the Zisi school and quite possibly constitutes, or is at least related to, the work known as the *Zisizi* 子思子 , as recorded in the "Yiwen Zhi."[2] The *Zi Yi* is found in the received text of *Xiao Dai Liji* 小戴禮記 . Shen Yue 沈約 , quoted in the "Yinyue Zhi 音樂志 " section of the *Suishu* 隋書 , states that the *Zi Yi* was originally part of the *Zisizi*. The fact that two lines attributed to the *Zisizi* in the Tang-period *Yi Lin* 意林 both appear in the *Zi Yi* is clear evidence for this.

We can see from the "Fei Shier Zi 非十二子 " chapter of the *Xunzi* 荀子 that the doctrines found in the excavated *Wu Xing* are those of Zisi, and that these were later adopted and developed by Mencius. The Guodian *Wu Xing* only has the text of the *Wu Xing* itself, whereas the Mawangdui silk-manuscript *Wu Xing* includes the commentary of Shizi 世子 , one of the "disciples of the seventy disciples." (Shizi's name was Shuo 碩 , and he came from the state of Chen 陳 .) That he wrote a commentary for the *Wu Xing* suggests that the *Wu Xing* was composed by Zisi.[3]

In the early Han, Jia Yi 賈誼 quoted from the *Wu Xing* in the "Liu Shu 六術 " chapter of his *Xinshu* 新書 . Furthermore, both this chapter and the chapter linked to it, the "Dao De Shuo 道德說 ," quote material found in the Guodian *Liu De* text. The *Liu De* and the *Wu Xing* ought, therefore, to be from the same school. The *Cheng Zhi Wen Zhi* frequently quotes the *Shangshu*, and its stylistic form is the same as that of the *Zi Yi*. Furthermore, the discussion about "*liu wei* 六位 " at the end of this text is related to the *Liu De*. The line in the *Xing Zi Ming Chu* that reads: 性自命出，命由天 降 ("nature emerges from order, the order comes down from heaven") is the equivalent to the line: 天命之謂性，率性之謂道 ("heaven's order, we call nature; following nature, we call the way") in the "Zhongyong 中庸 " chapter of the *Liji*. The "Kongzi Shijia 孔子世家 " section of the *Shiji* also informs us that Zisi wrote the "Zhongyong." Some of the lines in the *Zun De Yi* are originally from the *Analects* 論語 ; and some are similar to lines in the "Quli 曲禮 " chapter of the *Liji*. There are also similarities with the "Zhongyong" and other such works.

If we further recall that the Guodian slips also include the *Lu Mu Gong Wen Zisi*, we realize that all these Confucian works are, to a greater or lesser extent, associated with Zisi. As other scholars have already explained, the *Mencius* and the Mawangdui silk-manuscript *Wu Xing* text and commentary are related.[4] We also find sections in

---

[2] See also Li Xueqin, "Jingmen Guodian Jian zhong de *Zisizi* 荊門郭店簡中的《子思子》," *Wenwu Tiandi* 1998.2; also published in *Zhongguo Zhexue* 20 (1999), pp. 75–80.

[3] See Li Xueqin, *Zhouyi Jing Zhuan Suyuan* 周易經傳溯源 (Changchun: Changchun Press, 1992), for further discussion of Shizi.

[4] See Pang Pu 龐朴 , *Boshu Wuxing Pian Yanjiu* 帛書五行篇研究 (Jinan: Qi Lu Shushe, 1980).

the Guodian slips quoted in the *Mencius*. From this evidence, the succession of the Zisi-Mengzi school is now clarified.[5]

The Guodian Confucian slip-texts not only enable us to understand the true nature of Confucianism in the period between Confucius and Mencius, they also reveal the manner in which the early Confucianists perceived Confucius. Currently, people rely mainly on the *Analects* to research Confucius, but the *Analects* was produced by Confucius' disciples. The "Yiwen Zhi" of the *Hanshu* states:

> The *Lún Yu* 論語 is the words (*yu* 語) with which Confucius answered his disciples and contemporaries, and those they learned after they discussed what they had heard from the master with each other. At that time, the disciples all had their own records. After the master died, they collected these together and sorted (*lún* 論) and edited them, and so it was called the *Lún Yu* 論語 ("Assorted Words": "Analects").

The *Jingdian Shiwen* 經典釋文 quotes Zheng Xuan 鄭玄 as saying, "The *Analects* was written by Zhonggong 仲弓, Zixia 子夏, and others." Zisi was Confucius' grandson and studied under Zengzi; the records of the words and actions of Confucius as recorded by Zisi and his students ought to be relatively reliable.

The discovery of these Confucian works in the middle-Warring States capital of Chu is, in itself, most surprising. The occupant of the Guodian Tomb Number One was "Dong Gong zhi shi 東宮之師," a teacher of one of the Chu princes.[6] Clearly then, at this time the status of Confucianism was already very high in Chu. In fact, there was a large number of Confucian texts circulating in Chu. Another group of bamboo slips, unearthed a few years ago and bought by the Shanghai Museum in Hong Kong, also includes many Confucian works.[7] This illustrates that the influence of Confucianism in this period should not be underestimated.

Some scholars believe that Confucius only began to be revered as a sage 聖人 during the Han dynasty. If we look at the *Zhuangzi*, however, although there are sections mocking Confucius, such as the "Dao Zhi 盜跖," Confucius is, nevertheless, still referred to as a sage, which tells us that in this period Confucius' status as a sage was

---

[5] For example, the "Gongsun Chou 公孫丑, 上" section of the *Mencius* has the line: 孔子曰:德之流行,速于置郵而傳命, which is a quote from the *Zun De Yi*: 德之流,速于置郵而傳命. See *Guodian Chu Mu Zhujian*, p. 175.

[6] [Translators' note: Soon after the conference, Li Xueqin identified the prince as Crown Prince Heng 太子橫, who later became King Qing Xiang 頃襄王; Li Xueqin, "Xian Qin Rujia Zhuzuo de Zhongda Faxian 先秦儒家著作的重大發現," *Renmin Zhengxie Bao*, July 8, 1998; also printed in *Zhongguo Zhexue* 20, pp. 13–17].

[7] These include the *Zi Yi*, *Kongzi Xian Ju* 孔子閑居, and the *Shi Lun* 詩論. See "Zhanguo Zhujian Lu Zhen Rong 戰國竹簡露真容," *Wenhui Bao* (Shanghai), January 5, 1999.

already established.[8] This, of course, is related to the widespread circulation of Confucian works at that time.

The discovery of the Guodian Confucian slip-texts (and the slip-texts of the Shanghai Museum) is comparable in importance to the obtaining by King Xian of Hejian 河間獻王 and King Gong of Lu 魯恭王 of the old-script *Liji* at the beginning of the Han dynasty.[9] Moreover, the nature of these finds is similar.

To conclude, the discovery of the Guodian Confucian texts has opened up an entirely new area of study in the field of early Confucianism. These works, along with the soon to be published Shanghai Museum slips, will undoubtedly exert an enormous influence on the intellectual history of China.

---

[8] For the dating of the "Dao Zhi" to the late-Warring States period, see Li Xueqin, "Zhuangzi *Za Pian* Zhujian ji Youguan Wenti《莊子.雜篇》竹簡及有關問題," *Shaanxi Lishi Bowuguan Guankan* 5 (1998).

[9] See Li Xueqin, "Guodian Jian yu *Liji* 郭店簡與《禮記》," *Zhongguo Zhexue Shi* 1998.4.

# SECTION TWO:
# AN ACCOUNT OF THE DISCUSSION

# An Account of the Discussion

## SARAH ALLAN & CRISPIN WILLIAMS

In preparation for the conference, Sarah Allan and Robert Henricks divided the *Laozi* 老子 and *Tai Yi Sheng Shui* 太一生水 material according to the breaks in the Guodian 郭店 text — that is, in sections that begin at the top of a bamboo slip and end where black, square punctuation marks occur at the bottom of the bamboo slips — and assigned each section of continuous text to a small group of scholars. As we proceeded through the text, section by section, these groups presented their findings to the conference as a whole for discussion. The presenters were also encouraged to raise any general issues they wished to discuss at the time of their presentation. Since the texts are in Chinese and Chinese was our most common language, the discussions were conducted in Chinese, with only a minimal amount of translation.

This format worked well, allowing the conversation to range back and forth from the very specific to the very general throughout the course of the conference, without ever losing a central focus. It also provided a common ground for discussion to scholars from different disciplines and with different methodologies and interests. In the interests of clear exposition, however, we have rearranged and edited the following account of our discussions. Rather than presenting a verbatim chronological record, we have identified those topics to which the participants frequently returned, and taken the central themes and points of argument as the basis for our organization. We have also added a certain amount of explanatory material of our own in order to make our account more understandable to the reader, and some of the participants have further elucidated their own comments.

Part one, "The Tomb," includes questions about physical aspects of the tomb, the nature of the robbery that took place before the excavation, the date of the tomb, the preparation of the slips for publication, the possible identity of the occupant, and the role of the texts in their context as burial objects. Much of this discussion took place in response to the background talks by Li Boqian, Peng Hao, and Liu Zuxin on the first day of the conference, but we also returned to some of these issues at the end of the conference.

Most of the material in part two, "The *Laozi*," is taken from the presentations given in the course of reading the Guodian *Laozi* material and the discussions that followed. Although all of the sections of the text were discussed by the conference at large, the reader of this volume will find that, because of this format, many scholars are recorded as commenting in great detail about certain passages, but not about others. Generally, these detailed discussions concerned the sections that they had been assigned for presentation.

The Guodian texts other than the *Laozi* material are discussed in part three, "Other Texts and the Question of Philosophical Schools." The slips designated *Tai Yi Sheng Shui* are closely related to the *Laozi* material, and we read and discussed them in the same detail (for the question of the relationship between the *Tai Yi Sheng Shui* and the *Laozi*, see pp. 162–63, 168–69). The *Wu Xing* 五行 was also discussed extensively, even though it was not read in the same manner and is not included in Edmund Ryden's edition. This part also includes discussion of the relationship between the various texts found in the tomb and the question of philosophical schools.

The discussion of particular characters and suggestions for alternative readings are not included in the account of the discussion below, but in the apparatus of Edmund Ryden's edition of the Guodian *Laozi* and *Tai Yi Sheng Shui* in Section III of this book, below. Additional ideas concerning particular characters and afterthoughts, not expressed at the conference, are found in Section IV.

In the following discussion, references to passages from the Guodian text are by slip number and character number. *Laozi* "A," "B," and "C" refer to the slip-text groups, *jia* 甲, *yi* 乙, and *bing* 丙, as divided by the editors of the *Guodian Chu Mu Zhujian* 郭店楚墓竹簡 ; the first arabic number is the slip number, the second (separated by a colon) is the character number, as given in Edmund Ryden's edition. These can be readily matched to the photographs in *Guodian Chu Mu Zhujian*, where the reader wishes to examine the original writing (blank spaces are included in numbering where they can be reasonably estimated). The chapter number of the received text is given in square brackets. If the Guodian passage is only a part of a chapter division in the received text then "part," "a" (the beginning part) or "b" (the second part), is written to indicate this, as in Ryden's edition.

In this account, we have often used the term "received" text when the person actually said "current" (*jin* 今) or "Wang Bi" 王弼. The "Wang Bi" version of the text normally refers to an edition of the *Laozi* associated with the Wang Bi commentary, as opposed to versions associated with other commentators, such as Heshang Gong 河上公 or Yan Zun 嚴遵 .[1] It may also refer to the lost text that Wang Bi actually used in

---

[1] For a concise account of the bibliographic issues and textual history of the *Laozi* in English, see William Boltz, "*Lao tzu Tao te ching*," in Michael Loewe, ed., *Early Chinese Texts: A Bibliographical Guide*, Early China Special Monograph Series No. 2 (Berkeley: The Society for the Study of Early China and The

making his commentary.[2] In our discussions, however, scholars often used the terms "received text" and "Wang Bi" text loosely, sometimes meaning the entire corpus of transmitted editions, as opposed to the Guodian bamboo-slip material, with its unique features, and without reference to any particular edition, except when it became relevant because of variations in the text.

This imprecision reflects the fact that this is an account of an oral discussion among diverse specialists with varying styles of reference and different preferred editions. Nevertheless, we require a reference text for the purposes of this written account. Thus, in the following, we have used the edition of the text associated with the Wang Bi commentary found in Gao Ming 高明, *Boshu Laozi Jiaozhu* 帛書老子校注 (Beijing: Zhonghua Shuju, 1996), as the source of our citations to the "received text," as well as for the Mawangdui silk-manuscript copies.[3]

## PART ONE: THE TOMB AND ITS CONTENTS

### The Robbery

The tomb, designated Guodian Tomb Number One by the archeologists who excavated it, had been broken into in August and again in October of 1993. Thus, the excavation was not part of a preexisting plan, but undertaken as a rescue operation in order to protect the exposed tomb and salvage its contents. The archeologists who had participated in the original excavation, Peng Hao and Liu Zuxin, were asked to describe the nature of the robbery and questioned about whether bamboo slips might have been among the robbed items.

Liu Zuxin described how the robbers had dug a hole down from ground level to the southeast corner of the head compartment. The *Wenwu* excavation report states that the head compartment had been sawn into and the side compartment prized open.[4] Peng Hao further explained that water had entered the tomb. Most of the ob-

---

Institute of East Asian Studies, University of California, Berkeley, 1993), pp. 269–92.

[2] See Rudolf Wagner, "Wang Bi's Recension of the *Laozi*," in *Early China* 14 (1989), pp. 27–54, for the argument that the text used by Wang Bi is related to the anonymously transmitted *Laozi Wei Zhi Li Lüe*. For Wagner's reconstruction of the original Wang Bi text, see his "Wang Bi's Commentary on the *Laozi*: Critical Text, Extrapolative Translation, Philological Commentary," submitted for publication.

[3] Complete photographic facsimile reproductions of the Mawangdui manuscripts can be found in vol. 1 of Guojia Wenwuju Guwenxian Yanjiushi 國家文物局古文獻研究室, *Mawangdui Han Mu Boshu* 馬王堆漢墓帛書 (Beijing: Wenwu Press, 1980). Other editions, by conference participants, include: Chen Guying 陳鼓應, *Laozi Jinzhu Jinyi* 老子今註今譯 (Taibei: Taiwan Shangwu, 1997, 2d rev. edn.), and Xu Kangsheng 許抗生, *Boshu Laozi Zhuyi yu Yanjiu* 帛書老子註譯與研究 (Hangzhou: Zhejiang Renmin Press, 1985).

[4] According to the report in *Wenwu* 1997.7, pp. 35–48, one of the wooden pieces making up the top of the outer coffin had been sawn in half. Donald Harper pointed out, in conversation during the meeting, that diagram 5 in this report (p. 38) suggests that this board, numbered one, is at the west end of the tomb,

jects, including the bamboo slips, were sunk at the bottom of the outer coffin. He conjectured that the water would have made the removal of objects difficult and the robber could only have taken objects in the vicinity of the hole, including, possibly, some bamboo slips. However, considering their position in the tomb when they were excavated, both archeologists thought that it was unlikely that a large number of slips could have been removed.

Rumors had been circulating concerning bamboo-slip texts from a robbed tomb that were sold in Hong Kong and later acquired by the Shanghai Museum.[5] Donald Harper asked whether these slips could have been robbed from the Guodian tomb. Peng Hao said that it was not possible: the Shanghai slips are far too numerous. Moreover, the Guodian slip-texts are quite complete, without many missing sections, suggesting that only a few slips, if any, could be lost. Peng Hao's point here was that sentences usually continue from one slip to another, so missing slips result in incomplete sentences or passages. In the case of the *Laozi* material, some slips are damaged, but the number of characters missing on the damaged slips corresponds generally to what we would expect on the basis of the corresponding lines in the received text. There is no evidence of the type of discontinuity we would expect if whole slips were missing and it is unlikely that missing slips would correspond precisely to discrete sections of text that begin at the top of a slip and end at the bottom of another. The previously unknown texts are obviously more difficult to judge, but no one felt that there was evidence of any substantial loss.

## Dating

The date of the composition of the *Laozi* has long been disputed. Current opinions range from a date of the sixth century BC, based on the traditional identification of the author as a contemporary of Confucius, to the middle of the third century BC. Before the excavation of the Guodian tomb, the earliest extant copies of the *Laozi* were the two manuscript copies on silk, excavated from a Han dynasty tomb, Number Three, at Changsha Mawangdui 長沙馬王堆, Hunan province, in 1973. The tomb at Mawangdui is dated to 168 BC on the basis of a date on the burial inventory slips. This gives us an absolute date for the latest possible production of the silk manuscript copies. The older of the two copies, Copy A, observes no Han taboos, so it was written before the death of the first Han emperor in 195 BC.[6]

---

while the robbers are said to have entered from the southeast corner. We raised this point with Peng Hao who confirmed (fax, December 8, 1998) that the *Wenwu* diagram is incorrect; the robbers did indeed break into the southeast corner and the line indicating the saw cut should be at the lower end of board number 7.

[5] Since the conference, a preliminary report concerning these slips has been published in the Shanghai *Wenhui Bao*, January 1, 1999. There are over 1,200 slips, also containing philosophical texts.

[6] See note 3.

The Guodian slips do not include any dates, and there is no other dated material in the tomb. Therefore, the dating of the tomb inevitably relies on comparison of the burial style and the artifacts in the Guodian tomb with the typological sequences that archeologists have already established on the basis of other Chu tombs. Fortunately, due to the huge number of Chu tombs already excavated, numbering in the thousands, these typological sequences are very detailed. The archeologists with experience of Chu tombs in this region noted that changes in style, assemblage, and so on, can often be narrowed to time periods as short as twenty years (Li Boqian, Liu Zuxin, Peng Hao, Xu Shaohua).

Li Boqian and Liu Zuxin outlined the main features of these typological sequences and summarized the points of comparison that establish the date of Guodian Tomb Number One in their background talks (see pp. 9–32). Using material evidence and archeological methods, without reference to the texts, they arrived at a date for the tomb set from the middle-fourth to early-third centuries BC. In the discussion that followed these talks, the participants attempted to narrow this time span even further.

The latest possible date for the tomb can be fixed at 278 BC. This is the year in which the Qin army occupied the Chu capital at Ying 郢, and local burials after this date show clear Qin influence: the Guodian tomb does not. Moreover, the Guodian tomb artifacts are very similar to those seen in some other Chu tombs that can be dated with considerable accuracy, for example Tombs Number One and Two at Baoshan 包山, less than ten kilometers away. The similarity of the bronze mirrors found in these tombs was especially noted. However, the Baoshan site has other tombs which correspond to a later typological set, but still date to some time before the Qin invasion. This typological set can be given a period of usage of about twenty years, which therefore allows the date of the Guodian tomb to be pushed back to before 300 BC. The similarity to the Baoshan Tomb Number Two also enables us to supply an earliest date for the Guodian tomb. Baoshan Tomb Number Two is dated some time from 323 to 316 BC.[7] Given the similarity of artifacts in the Guodian tomb to those in this tomb, we can assume it was approximately contemporaneous, or only a few years later. A dating of late-fourth century BC was thus arrived at for Guodian Tomb Number One.

Susan Weld suggested several techniques that might assist with the dating of the tomb. Accelerator mass-spectrometry which, although the margin of error is wide,

---

[7] Some of the Baoshan slips are dated by the recording of a certain event to indicate the year, rather than by reign dates. Each year is identified by a notable event that took place in that year (or, some scholars have argued, the previous year). One such slip can be confidently identified with the year 323 (or 322) BC. For a study of the Baoshan tombs, see Hubeisheng Jingsha Tielu Kaogudui 湖北省荆沙鐵路考古隊, ed., *Baoshan Chu Mu* 包山楚墓 (Beijing: Wenwu Press, 1991); see appendix 2, by Liu Binhui 劉彬徽, for discussion of the dating.

would confirm that the suggested dating has no fundamental flaw. The timber of the coffin could also be used for tree-ring dating although this would depend on the construction of a tree-ring sequence for the region.

Having ascertained that the occupant of Guodian Tomb Number One was probably interred before 300 BC, we then had a latest date for the bamboo-slip texts. Two problems remained: when were they written on the slips found at Guodian? And when were they authored? The paleographers agreed that the script in which most of the texts in the tomb, including the *Laozi*, are written is typical of Chu writing in the Warring States period.[8] Thus, we know that these texts were current in the state of Chu at the end of the fourth century BC and at least some of the material now found in the received *Laozi* existed in written form before the third century BC.

The slips were buried at the end of the fourth century BC, but when were the texts composed? We cannot assume that the date when the texts were written on the bamboo slips is the date of composition of the texts recorded on them. Nor can we assume that all of the texts found in the tomb were originally composed at the same time. Some might have been written close to the date of the burial, while others might have been transmitted for generations. Thus, for example, Li Xueqin thought that we can reasonably assume that the Confucian texts predate the deceased, and belong at least to the generation of his teacher, but he thought that the *Tang Yu zhi Dao* is a more contemporary text concerned with political events later in the fourth century and written close to the time of burial.

What, then, does the date of the tomb tell us about the date of the *Laozi*? This question was complicated by the running debate among the participants about the nature of the *Laozi* material in the Guodian slips, a debate that remained unresolved. If we assume that the material recorded on the bamboo slips represents excerpts taken from a longer text, most probably a text much like the received *Laozi*, the Guodian material does not conflict with an assumption of an original date in the sixth century BC. Some scholars who took this position thought that it might nevertheless be based on an early version of the *Laozi* and thus preserve forms of wording that were changed in later versions. Others worked on the assumption that a "five-thousand-character" *Laozi* already existed and differences in wording between the received and/or Mawangdui versions of the *Laozi* and the Guodian material are due to idiosyncrasies of the Guodian *Laozi*, rather than its early date. If we assume, on the contrary, that what is written on the Guodian bamboo slips is an early form of the *Laozi* which had not yet developed into the received "five-thousand-character" text, then the Guodian text might well have taken its final form in the third century BC. We return to this question in part two.

---

[8] The exceptions are the *Tang Yu zhi Dao* and *Zhong Xin zhi Dao*, which Li Xueqin felt are not Chu script.

*Ordering the Slips and Preparing the Publication*

A number of scholars expressed appreciation for the exemplary manner in which the Guodian bamboo-slip texts were published. Looking at the finished work, with its clear calligraphy, the slips beautifully photographed and placed in order with transcriptions and annotations, it may be difficult to appreciate the achievement of the conservators and scholars who, working to a strict publication deadline, made sense of a disordered heap of bamboo strips, many of them damaged or broken, each with only some twenty or thirty characters written in a local script, recreating texts that they had never seen before, some perhaps not seen by anyone for more than 2,000 years. This is not to say that there are no mistakes or places where the present ordering is problematic, but rather to acknowledge how much was accomplished to get the texts into the form in which we find them in *Guodian Chu Mu Zhujian*.

The process by which the disordered clump of more than 700 blackened and fragmented bamboo slips were turned into a form suitable for publication for a modern audience was outlined by Peng Hao (see pp. 33–38). He explained that the slips were first cleaned, treated so that the characters became clearly visible, and then photographed. Only after that could they begin the work of joining slip fragments and placing the slips in order. This post-excavation process, by which archeologically excavated material (not necessarily textual) is systematically recorded, conserved, classified, and organized in a logical manner is known in Chinese as *zhengli* 整理, a term for which we have found no precise English equivalent. For bamboo-slip texts, the *zhengli* process includes joining broken slips, placing the slips in sequence, dividing them into coherent groups, and transcribing them for publication.

As Peng Hao and Qiu Xigui have discussed in their papers above, the main criteria used to put the slips in order and divide them in groups were: first, the physical form of the slips and calligraphic style of their writing; and second, their semantic content. The task was greatly facilitated when the slips could be matched to an extant text that included corresponding material, i.e. the *Laozi*, *Wu Xing*, and *Zi Yi* 緇衣, even though there were many differences. For most of the texts, however, there were no extant texts that could aid the task of ordering.

Peng Hao and Liu Zuxin did the work of putting the slips in order and writing the transcription and annotations. Wang Chuanfu 王傳富 also assisted with the transcription. After Peng Hao, who was the member of the *zhengli* group with primary responsibility for publication, submitted his manuscript to Wenwu Press, the press invited Qiu Xigui to be the reader for the manuscript. Peng Hao said that he then made extensive revisions on the basis of Qiu's numerous comments and suggestions. Qiu Xigui explained that, wherever he felt an original transcription was plausible he did not suggest a revision, even if his own analysis would have been different. He only suggested revision when he was confident that his own opinion was correct, or if he noted something that had been overlooked; in other cases, he put his opinion in a separate annotation — these are the notes prefixed with "Qiu *an* 裘按 ."

Qiu also observed that most of his time had been spent, not on the analysis and transcription of individual characters, but on ordering the slips and dividing them into separate texts. Peng Hao explained the criteria on which the slips were divided into separate texts. They included: similarity of the physical form of the slips — that is to say, length, distance between binding marks, shape of ends (beveled or straight) — and style of script, as well as the semantic content of the slips. He noted that there are examples of bundles of slips of exactly the same physical form, including style of script, being divided into separate texts on the basis of difference in content. In such cases, Qiu Xigui explained, where there was doubt about whether a series of slips represented an independent text, the general principle adopted when dividing the texts for publication was to split the material into smaller units, rather than lump potentially independent texts together. Supporting this method, Paul Thompson argued that it is preferable from the point of view of later research to split in the first instance and lump later.

The division of the *Laozi* group-C material from the *Tai Yi Sheng Shui* material is a pertinent example of this decision to split on the basis of content. The slips are identical in form and appear to have been written by the same scribe and bound together as one bundle. Qiu acknowledged this, but he felt that, on the basis of their style and content, it is unlikely that the *Tai Yi Sheng Shui* and the *Laozi* group-C were originally a single text, although the person who copied and bound them might have considered them as related to one another. Similar examples of texts separated on the basis of content are those assigned the titles *Lu Mu Gong Wen Zisi* 魯穆公問子思 and *Qiong Da yi Shi* 窮達以時; and the group of texts given the names *Cheng Zhi Wen Zhi* 成之聞之, *Zun De Yi* 尊德義, *Xing Zi Ming Chu* 性自命出, and *Liu De* 六德. These six texts are all written on slips of the same size and shape with the same distance between bindings, but they have been split up on the basis of content and what seem to be some differences in the style of the calligraphy. We should note, then, that these divisions are not final and can still be questioned; it may turn out that there should be further splits, some recombination of groups, and rearrangement of slips within groups. For example, Wang Bo suggested a rearrangement of the *Laozi* group-A slips. In debating the question of the philosophical schools to which the various texts might belong, some people also suggested different groupings of these texts on the basis of the similarities in physical form.

The titles of the texts were given by the annotators. The slips had no titles, with the possible exception of the *Wu Xing*, which has the words 五行 at the top of the first slip. Ikeda Tomohisa pointed out that in most examples of excavated texts with titles, the title is at the end of the text, not at the beginning. However, in received texts there are cases where the title comes at the start of a text, as, for example, in some sections of the *Xunzi* 荀子 . He therefore conjectured that this style of title might also have been used during the Warring States period.

## The Identity of the Tomb Occupant

Who was buried in the tomb? A peculiarity of Guodian Tomb Number One, in relation to the other excavated tombs in which texts have been discovered, is that it *only* contains philosophical texts. There are no divination texts, burial inventories, etc., as found in other tombs, or historical or personal records that could help to identify the occupant. The only other material with writing on it in this tomb is a lacquer cup with an inscription on the bottom. This inscription was originally read as *dong gong zhi bei* 東宮之杯 (*Wenwu* 1997.7, p. 41), but Li Xueqin pointed out that the last character is correctly read *shi* 師 , not *bei*, and this opinion was accepted.[9] What, then, can we surmise about the rank and the profession of the Guodian tomb occupant from the style and contents of the burial?

It was generally assumed, on the basis of the provenance, date, and similarity to other tombs in the area, as well as the presence of swords, that this was the tomb of a male noble of the state of Chu.[10] Donald Harper observed that the discovery of bamboo slips in Chu tombs suggests that the Chu nobles were literate. In his background talk, Liu Zuxin had categorized the coffin arrangement (one outer, one inner coffin) as typical of a Chu noble of the *shi* 士 rank (i.e., the lowest level of the aristocracy), with the qualification that the quality of some of the artifacts suggested that the family of the occupant might have been higher ranking than this coffin arrangement suggests.

Xu Shaohua further explained that the inner and outer coffins are more important than the burial goods in determining the rank of the deceased. According to Chu burial custom, the rank of the occupant is reflected in the number of inner and outer coffins and, especially, in the number of internal compartments within the outer coffin. This theory was based upon extensive archeological evidence in the region with a range of burials from those with nine-compartment coffins down to burials with no coffin. Guodian Tomb Number One has three compartments within its outer coffin, which Xu agreed fits the rank of *shi*.

Li Xueqin argued that the phrase on the bottom of the lacquer cup means that the deceased was the teacher of a royal prince; the *dong gong*, literally, "eastern pal-

---

[9] Although this view was accepted at the conference, in a paper presented at the International Symposium on Chu Slips of Guodian, Wuhan University, October, 1999, Li Ling supports the original reading of *bei*.

[10] The issue of gender was not discussed. The swords are evidence that the person buried in the tomb was male. However, a tomb in this region, which many people think is the source of the slips acquired by the Shanghai Museum after they had been robbed, was found upon later excavation to have a female occupant.

ace," was the princely residence and *shi* means teacher or tutor.[11] Dove-headed staffs 鳩杖 were for old men.[12] The buried texts were teaching materials — the four bundles of text with one-line statements, designated *Yu Cong* 語叢, are similar in form to primary teaching-texts in later times, and so are particularly good evidence of this. Thus, he was an "old professor."

This suggestion naturally pleased the conference participants, but questions were raised nevertheless. The term *shi* 師 does not refer only to teachers; e.g., it can be used for master musicians or artisans. Rudolf Wagner asked why, if the tomb occupant was a royal tutor, do we not see any one of the classic texts — no *Shangshu* 尚書, no *Shijing* 詩經, no *Chunqiu* 春秋 — yet there are three separate bundles of *Laozi* materials. Why were these considered to be so important and appropriate?

Paul Thompson questioned whether there was sufficient evidence to conclude that the occupant was the teacher to a royal prince. Both Paul Thompson and Peng Hao expressed reservations about relying too much on the cup with the 東宮之師 inscription to identify the tomb occupant, noting that we cannot be certain about its origin. Other explanations could account equally well for the cup's presence in the tomb. Could it, for example, have been given to the tomb occupant by the person for whom it was made?

Assuming that the tomb occupant was a teacher, and noting the three bundles of *Laozi* materials and the absence of the traditional classics, Paul Thompson wondered what the Chu court might have been looking for in a teacher and recalled the famous story in the "Qiushui 秋水" section of the *Zhuangzi* 莊子, in which a contemporary king of Chu sent officials to ask Zhuangzi to become the prime minister. If the Chu court was looking for teachers in this mold, then perhaps such teachers did not teach the classics. In this regard, Li Xueqin mentioned that there is a passage in the *Guoyu* 國語 which states that a Chu minister did teach the classics at the Chu court.[13]

Several scholars questioned whether a tutor to the crown prince would only have been of the relatively low rank of *shi*, as suggested by the scale of the burial. Li Xueqin said he was not convinced that the number of compartments did indicate such a low rank. Xing Wen suggested that the tomb occupant might have been demoted in rank later in life, perhaps as the result of displeasing the ruler in some way.

[11] At the conference, Li Xueqin did not identify the tomb as that of the crown prince or any particular prince, but simply as that of a royal prince. In an article published since then, however, he has identified the prince as Crown Prince Heng 太子橫, who later became the Chu king known as Qing Xiang 頃襄. See Li Xueqin, "Xian Qin Rujia Zhuzuo de Zhongda Faxian 先秦儒家著作的重大發現," *Renmin Zhengxie Bao*, July 8, 1998; and *Zhongguo Zhexue* 20 (1999), pp. 13–17.

[12] Eighty to ninety years of age, according to the *Hou Hanshu* 後漢書, "Liyi Zhi 禮儀志." Jiu 鳩, a species which includes doves and pigeons, suck liquids rather than sip and swallow. Thus, they "do not choke" and are a good omen for the elderly.

[13] *Guoyu* 國語 (Shanghai: Shanghai Guji, 1978), p. 528 ("Chu Yu 楚語").

Paul Thompson asked whether the size and types of the swords give any clue to the rank and status of the occupant. In reply, Peng Hao noted that swords are a standard feature of this type of Chu tomb and that they might have been given to the occupant especially for burial. The sword is long, but this does not relate to status; it relates to its use. Xu Shaohua further explained that most of the Chu Warring States tombs of male nobles that have been excavated have weapons and that the most common weapon found is the sword. This was a time of war; Chu was under frequent attack from the state of Qin. There is, however, also a distinctive regional burial pattern: Chu tombs have many more swords than those in the north. Robin Yates added that, at that time, it was customary for all male adults of a certain status to carry a sword; this would have been equally true for a philosopher or teacher. It need not imply that the person engaged in battle.

Susan Weld suggested that apart from using the burial goods to ascertain the rank and profession of the tomb occupant, one might be able to discover information about his life style and place of origin from studying the chemical make-up of his skeleton. Analysis of the isotopic ratios of carbon-12 to carbon-13 can shed light on his consumption of the key staples of millet and rice. Analysis of nitrogen isotope ratios and the concentration of strontium to calcium may tell us about the proportion of meat to plants in his diet. Weld also speculated that any specialized diet due to self-cultivation practices might also show up in bone chemistry analysis, especially if (as Donald Harper pointed out) it included some of the alchemical prescriptions traditionally related to self-cultivation. In addition, comparison of the strontium isotope levels in the teeth and bone can reveal whether the place of birth and later residence were the same — possibly bearing on the issue of whether the owner of the texts was a Chu native or an immigrant.[14]

*The Slips in the Context of the Tomb*

Of the thousands of Chu tombs excavated, only a small number have yielded texts, even when the conditions were conducive to their preservation. As Li Ling pointed out, writings were not placed in tombs in the course of some prescribed ritual or custom in the manner of bronze vessels. Clearly, texts were not considered to be essential burial goods like certain other objects (such as swords in tombs of male nobles). So why were some people buried with texts while the majority were not? And why were these particular texts placed in this tomb?

Rudolf Wagner raised the possibility that the artifacts in a tomb, including texts, were not necessarily chosen by the occupant, and some may have been gifts presented

[14] See Cai Lianzhen 蔡蓮珍 and Qiu Shihua 仇士華, "Tan Shisan Ceding he Gudai Shipu Yanjiu 碳十三測定和古代食譜研究," *Kaogu* 1984.10, pp. 949–55; and R. E. Taylor and Martin J. Aitken, eds., *Chronometric Dating in Archaeology* (Plenum Press: New York and London, 1997). See also the website <c14.sci.waikato.ac.nz/webinfo/index.html>, reviewed in *Science* 285 (July 16, 1999), p. 295.

posthumously. He noted, however, that there was no textual support for such a conclusion. Both Wagner and Li Ling preferred the theory that writings in tombs were
actually related to the concerns and habits of the tomb occupant. Both gave the example of Baoshan Tomb Number Two. The occupant of this tomb was very ill before
he died, and we find a large number of divination slips in the tomb relating to his last
illness, as well as judicial administration and inventory slips.

Marc Kalinowski and Rudolf Wagner noted the contrasting messages one gets
from the Guodian and Baoshan bamboo slips. The Baoshan slips include divinations
and indicate that the Chu noble class was participating daily in such activities. In
contrast, the Guodian tomb contains only philosophical texts. Moreover, in the
Guodian texts there are calls for the putting aside of such religious activity; the *Zi Yi*
緇衣 even says "do not perform divination," and "do not perform ritual." Wagner suggested that we might see this as a "counter tomb," that is, a tomb the contents of which
seem to show a programmatic rejection of a practice obviously very common among
the Chu nobility at the time and visible in the Baoshan finds. This would establish
some type of ideological dialogue between tomb occupants after their demise.

Wagner then asked what the function of these texts was in the tomb, in the
netherworld. Were they apotropaic, shielding the occupant from spirits and evil? Could,
for example, *Tai Yi Sheng Shui* have been included to act as a shield (for *Tai Yi*'s role in
repelling demons, see Li Ling's discussion of this text, pp. 163–65)? Wagner himself
felt that the *Tai Yi Sheng Shui* is not a cosmological work but a philosophical work
concerned with proving that all we see and all that happens around us is permeated
and suffused by the *Taiyi* which is not just at the "origin" but also "contained" in
everything in this world. He concluded that the texts were in the tomb because the
occupant, an old man, wanted to study them in the next world.

Robin Yates stressed that our reading of the texts themselves should be informed
by the context in which the texts were discovered; the burial provides the social and
ritual context for the texts. The Guodian *Laozi* may say that ideally one should be like
a child and discourage the use of weapons, but the occupant of the tomb also had
swords. One needs to remember, however, that the literati would have carried swords
as a social symbol. Yates' feeling was that the Guodian texts were of a very similar
nature to those in the Mawangdui tombs; they ask similar types of questions about
government and human nature and gave similar types of answer.

## PART TWO: THE LAOZI

Chinese scholars have been searching for early versions of ancient texts and producing critical editions since at least Han-dynasty times (206 BC - AD 220), when scholars
attempted to reconstruct that part of the literary tradition that the Qin had destroyed.
Since the Qin had also standardized the script in conformity with that of their own

state, a division opened up between ancient texts, like those found in the Guodian tomb, written in local or "old script" (*guwen* 古文 ) characters, and texts that were reconstructed from oral memory or transmitted in a copied form, written in the "modern" or "new script" (*jinwen* 今文 ).

As Rudolf Wagner observed, the hunt for "old manuscripts" of the *Laozi* has a very long history. Fu Yi personally inspected no less than nine "old manuscripts," the oldest being from the tomb of Xiang Yu's 項羽 concubine discovered in Peng Cheng 彭城 in AD 574. Since Xiang Yu died in 202 BC, and the concubine would not have been buried in such style had he been dead already, this manuscript is older than both of the Mawangdui manuscripts. Fu Yi's own *guben* 古本 edition is a first attempt to get a "critical text" established on the basis of a comparison of the different old texts in his hands.[15] Lu Deming 陸德明 (556–627) at three different places quotes readings from a *Laozi* text on bamboo slips in his *Laozi Yinyi* 老子音義 .[16]

Even before the Song-era fashion for old bronzes began, namely in the tenth and early eleventh centuries, we find paleographically oriented authors, such as Guo Zhongshu 郭忠恕 (10th century) tracking down an "old *Laozi*" 古老子 or "*Laozi* in old script" for use in his *Han Jian* 汗簡. Xia Song's 夏竦 (985–1051), *Guwen Si Sheng Yun* 古文四聲韻 also used many such materials.[17] These included two old *Laozi* manuscripts, namely a "*Laozi* in old script 古老子 ," and a *Daodejing* 道德經 , which also must rank among the "old" texts. Fan Yingyuan 范應元 (Song era) continued these efforts by publishing an edition explicitly comparing the various "old" versions then available in an attempt to get at another critical "old-text" reconstruction. This means that hidden in these surviving materials we have quite a few other old *Laozi* texts, some of which are older than the Mawangdui, and some of which might go back to the Guodian time horizon.

Moreover, Wagner further pointed out, people have been producing critical editions of the *Laozi* since the end of the Former Han at the latest, e.g., Liu Xiang 劉向 and Yan Zun 嚴遵 (i.e., Zhuang Zun 莊遵), and we have detailed reports of such editions from Fu Yi 傅奕 and other Tang authors. What they may have lacked in methodological rigor, they made up with broader familiarity with a historical record that was infinitely richer than what we see now. Thus, the process in which we are now engaging with these texts from Guodian should be seen as a continuation of this historic process.[18]

[15] See Wagner, "Wang Bi's Recension," pp. 35–37, for a translation of Fu Yi's report.

[16] See Boltz, "*Lao tzu Tao te ching*," pp. 269–92, for a concise summary of the textual history of the *Laozi* and the major bibliographic references.

[17] These two works were published together as *Han Jian, Guwen Si Sheng Yun* 汗簡・古文四聲韻 (Beijing: Zhonghua Shuju, 1983). See also Qiu Xigui, p. 54, and Li Xueqin, pp. 130–31.

[18] For a comparative edition of a representative selection of texts, see Shima Kunio 島邦男 , *Rōshi Kōsei* 老子校正 (Tokyo: Kyūko Shoin, 1973). For a nearly complete corpus of the extant transmitted

Nevertheless, the Guodian material is not simply another version of the *Laozi* and it presents a peculiar problem. The bamboo slips are clearly related to the text that we now know as the *Laozi Daodejing* — the received text with its approximately 5,000 characters divided into eighty-one chapters, but they do not relate to it in any simple manner. The Guodian material is divided into three groups of slips that were probably bound independently, but, taken together, they only constitute about a third of the received text. The individual lines on the slips correspond to lines in the received *Laozi*. However, there are many different characters within the lines, and lines are sometimes omitted or in a different order within the sections that correspond to chapters in the received text. Punctuation marks often occur where chapters now end, but the pattern is irregular. Moreover, where one chapter follows another in a sequence, the order is often radically different than that of the received text.

There are no historical references to a text in this form or with this sequence of material. In recent years, many scholars have discussed the question of the original structure of the received *Laozi*. This question is often linked to a theory about the origin of the text. For example, among prominent writers in English in recent years, D. C. Lau regards the text as an anthology of earlier material, and in his translation of the "Wang Bi" version of the text, he divided the chapters into smaller units that he hypothesized were originally independent. A. C. Graham, on the other hand, regarded the work as a long poem.[19]

At first glance, the Guodian material with its different order and early date might appear to support the "anthology" theory. Alternatively, since there is no evidence in the transmitted literature of the text's having existed in this form, it might constitute excerpts from a longer text similar to the traditional *Laozi*. The more the problem is considered, the more complex it becomes — and the more it is necessary to employ nuances in the potential solutions. At the root of much of our discussion during the conference was the fundamental problem: What is the Guodian *Laozi*? How does it relate to the transmitted text? And how can we decide? A further question — which depends upon the resolution of the first one — is: what do the Guodian slips tell us about the history of the *Laozi*?

In the following summary of our discussions, we begin with the textual problems and then proceed to the philosophical issues.

---

editions of the *Laozi*, see Yan Lingfeng 嚴靈峰 , comp., *Wuqiubeizhai Laozi Jicheng* 無求備齋老子集成 , *chupian* 初編 (160 冊 ), and *xupian* 續編 (280 冊 ) (Panqiao, Taiwan: Yiwen, 1965).

[19] D. C. Lau, *Lao Tzu: Tao Te Ching* (Harmondsworth: Penguin, 1963); A. C. Graham, *Disputers of the Tao* (La Salle: Open Court, 1989), p. 234.

*Textual Analysis*

### a. Methodology in graphic analysis

Different approaches to the decipherment of early characters were presented in the preceding papers (Section I) by William Boltz, Qiu Xigui, and Gao Ming. As we read through the *Laozi* material, various suggestions were made for the reading of particular characters. These are included in the apparatus and notes to Edmund Ryden's text (below, Section III). Thus we have not included the discussion of particular characters in the following summary of our deliberations.

The Guodian bamboo slips are written in the Chu script of the Warring States period and contain a large number of characters that denote words written differently in later standardized Chinese script. In order to make sense of these, we must identify them with known characters, i.e., ones that appear as words with attested meanings in known texts. In considering what texts may legitimately be used to determine standard variations in the script and possible loan characters, our individual practices diverged widely. Robin Yates, for example, argued that we should rely on texts known to have been contemporaneous with and circulated in the same area as the excavated materials in making such determinations. So, for the Guodian slips, we should base our decisions upon texts circulating in the state of Chu during the Warring States period.

Methodological issues were at the root of many of our discussions concerning individual characters. Generally speaking, characters that cannot be recognized are taken as loans 假借字, i.e., standard characters being used for a word usually denoted by another character; or as orthographic variants 異體字 , i.e, non-standard characters normally written in a different manner. Some such characters are locally standard (e.g., Chu script). Other characters may be scribal "mistakes," based on either the sound of the character, or the graphic form if it was copied wrongly. Since most loans are phonetic borrowings, and orthographic variants were often interpreted by taking one part of the character as a phonetic signifier, the most heated arguments occurred in decisions about phonological closeness. How similar in phonetic reconstruction must two characters be in order to identify them with one another? How important are attested examples in determining whether a character might be a loan?

Another issue was the strength that should be given to the evidence of the corresponding passages in the received and Mawangdui editions when we read a character as a loan or variant form. Should we begin with the received textual tradition and use it to make sense of the excavated material? Or should we try to make sense of the excavated material as it stands and then turn to the received tradition? Qiu Xigui's paper explained some of the methods he used to analyze individual characters. These include analysis of graphic form, i.e. the historical evolution of characters, including the particular evolution of Chu script, and historical phonology.

Gao Ming thought that our analysis should take more account of the two Mawangdui texts and the received tradition. Thus, he argued that, since the Guodian *Laozi* passages are generally close to corresponding passages in the other editions of the *Laozi*, then, where there are characters we do not recognize, we should as a matter of course consider whether they could denote the corresponding words in the received texts. If the characters in the excavated text appear to denote words with very different meanings than those in other editions, we should regard this as odd and reexamine them in light of the received text before accepting such a conclusion.

Qiu Xigui countered that we should not have a preplanned aim to match the characters of an excavated text to the corresponding characters in a received text or use phonetic closeness indiscriminately. If we allow series of loosely defined phonetic conversions, then any archeological text could be converted to a received text! Sarah Allan suggested that to see how close the excavated text can be made to correspond to the received text is, nevertheless, a legitimate and important exercise. If the *Laozi* passages in the Guodian were copied from a five-thousand-character text that is basically the same as the received *Laozi*, as many people believed, then we should expect to be able to achieve a high degree of correspondence.

Xu Kangsheng, on the other hand, suggested that if a character appears in a form we recognize and it makes sense in the context of the Guodian text, then there is no reason to treat it as a loan or variant, even if there is a corresponding passage in a received text and the corresponding character is different.

An interesting feature of the Guodian material that was touched on (but not analyzed in detail) during the conference was difference in grammatical markers. This is particularly apparent in the use of negatives in the Guodian material. The use of negatives in the Mawangdui silk-manuscript copies also differs from that of the received texts, but the Guodian pattern is often different from both the Mawangdui copies and the received text. Here, Rudolf Wagner observed that all the careful attention modern-day grammatical studies give to the different forms of negation and their very particular meanings falls shy of what the writers and scribes had in mind. Such studies describe what, in effect, is the result of a hardening of meaning and grammatical function of specific characters that came with the transfer of the old texts into the later standard script. Our grammatical analysis thus analyzes the interpretation given to the old texts by the people who managed this transfer, not what the old texts themselves might have wanted to suggest.

Li Xueqin observed that the characters of the Guodian bamboo slips are, in large part, the same as the old-script 古文 forms given as examples by Guo Zhongshu in the *Han Jian* and by Xia Song in the *Guwen Si Sheng Yun*. These old-script forms were previously rejected by scholars suspicious of forgery. However, with recent developments in Warring States epigraphy, the two works have been rehabilitated. The distinctive epigraphic forms in the Guodian slips are often the same, or similar, to the forms found in these two works. For example, the character 衍 is always read *dao* 道 in the Guodian slips. This character was previously seen in the Qin Stone Drums and the Mawangdui silk manuscript, where it is read *hang* 行 . However, in the *Han Jian* and *Guwen Si Sheng Yun*, it is recorded as the old-script form of *dao*, with examples taken from an "old" *Shangshu* 古尚書 and an "old" *Laozi* 古老子 . This accords precisely with the character in the Guodian slips. This, and the many similar examples, are clear evidence that old-script versions of the *Laozi*, *Shangshu*, and other texts said to have been handed down from earlier times did in fact exist and that the compilers of the *Han Jian* and *Guwen Si Sheng Yun* had seen Warring States texts similar to those written on bamboo slips in the Guodian tomb.

The so-called "old" *Shangshu* refers to the old-script bamboo-slip *Shangshu* discovered in the wall of Confucius' house in the early Han, traditionally said to have been hidden by Confucius' descendants at the time the order was given to burn the books during the Qin dynasty (213 BC). Confucius's house was in Qufu 曲阜 , originally part of the state of Lu 魯 . Lu was occupied by Chu in 256 BC and late-Warring States Chu artifacts are frequently excavated at Qufu. It is quite probable that the bamboo-slip texts hidden in Confucius' wall were written in Chu script, so it is natural that the old-script forms originating from Confucius' wall would be similar to the script of the Guodian slips.

The so-called "old" *Laozi* probably refers to the *Laozi* acquired from the tomb of Xiang Yu's concubine (mentioned above, p. 127). The Tang-period *Daodejing Guben Pian* 道德經古本篇 by Fu Yi is a comparative edition based upon this text. Xiang Yu was from Chu, so the *Laozi* in his concubine's tomb would most probably have been in Chu script.[20]

### b. Collation and comparison of editions

Robert Henricks produced an edition of the Guodian *Laozi* material, laid out line-by-line next to the Mawangdui, Copies A and B, and the received (Wang Bi) edition, for use in the conference.[21] His edition followed the arrangement given in *Guodian Chu Mu Zhujian*, but was divided into chapters following those in the received text. This method has the advantage that it allows ready comparison of the Guodian material with existing versions of *Laozi*. However, as a result, participants tended to refer to passages and characters by citing the traditional chapter numbers or the artificial chapter numbers provided by Ryden in his edition of the Guodian text. For example, the material in *Laozi* A, slip 1, character 1, to slip 2, character 18 (denoted herein,

[20] See also Li Xueqin "Guodian Chu Jian yu Ruxue Jingji 郭店楚簡與儒學經籍," in *Zhongguo Zhexue* 20 (1999), pp. 18–21.

[21] A revised version of this edition is published in Robert Henricks, *Lao Tzu's Tao Te Ching* (New York: Columbia University Press), forthcoming.

following Edmund Ryden, as A 1:1 to 2:18), would be called "chapter nineteen," after the received text (or else "chapter one," using Ryden's artificial Guodian "chapter" number).

Several scholars voiced concern that this gave the impression that it was a foregone conclusion that these chapter divisions already existed at the time of the copying of the Guodian *Laozi* and that the *Laozi* already existed in its current form. If this were accepted, it would further imply that the Guodian slips are simply a selection from that text. Edmund Ryden, Robin Yates and Donald Harper all advocated the use of slip and character numbers to refer to characters and passages rather than the chapter and line numbers of the received *Laozi*, which they felt would force an editorial decision about the chapter- and line-division on the reader.

A more elaborate method of collation, which could provide the basis for a text criticism methodology, was presented by Paul Thompson — see pp. 89–106 for an example of a section corresponding to chapter 66. Thompson's collation aligns the "witnesses" vertically and uses color coding — grey-scale and different fonts in the sample published herein — to classify different types of variation. Harold Roth suggested that Paul Thompson's analysis of the Guodian *Laozi* materials presupposes that the Guodian slips were copied from a redaction of the *Laozi* in the received form and argued that one must first be aware of the relationship between the redactions *before* applying this kind of collation. In reply, Paul Thompson said that we can analyze textual identity at the smaller level before identifying the larger level. He argued that his method of collation can itself lead to answers about the relationship between redactions. By laying out the texts so that they can be read vertically (to compare witnesses) as well as horizontally (to read them semantically), we get a sense of the relationship between the different versions that can develop into conjecture, and then a hypothesis that can be methodically analyzed on the basis of the texts as laid out.

Another example of how Thompson's method brings to light otherwise less obvious features is the apparent "eye skip" in the Guodian *Laozi* A 14:13 to 15:7. This section corresponds to chapter 63 of the received *Laozi*, but it omits several lines from the middle of the chapter. Paul Thompson's alignment of the witnesses brings to our attention the fact that the character 多 is the last character before the "missing" lines and also the last character of the section of missing lines. One explanation for this is that the copyist of the Guodian slips (or the ancestral copy from which the Guodian copy was made) having written down the first 多, then looked back at the slips from which he or she was copying, and his or her eyes, looking for 多, alighted on the next one in the text, accidentally skipping a section, and continued to copy from there, thus leaving out a whole section. Paul Thompson also pointed out that there are fifty-two characters missing, which would have been the equivalent of about two slips of characters: i.e., the two 多 characters could have been in approximately the same position on their respective slips.

In the three groups of *Laozi* materials, there is only one passage that is repeated: A 10:22 to 13:2 and C 11:1 to 14:7. These correspond to lines 10 to 18 in chapter 64 of the received text. Here, collation may be used to compare the different Guodian versions. For Harold Roth's discussion of this phenomenon, see his preceding paper (Section I). In discussing this passage, Xu Shaohua listed some of the differences between the *Laozi* A and C versions:

1. *Laozi* C has the line 人之敗也，恆於其且成也敗之, but this is missing from the *Laozi* A version. On the other hand, A has the phrase 臨事之紀, which is not in the C passage.

2. Character forms vary for corresponding words, or else the words used are actually different:

i. A uses 谷 for 欲 ; C uses 欲 .

ii. A has 孝 for 教 ; C has 學 in this position.

iii. A has 之所 written as two separate characters while in C the two are written in a combined form (*hewen* 合文 ).

iv. The characters in the line 慎終如始 (A 11:20–23; C 12:1–4) have several variant forms: in A it is written 誓冬女忊 while in C it is written 斩終若訂.

Xu Shaohua concluded that there are too many variations for these two copies to have originated from the same source-text. He further suggested that the different versions of the section of received text, chapter 64, may reflect different factions within the Daoist school at that time.

*The Scribes*

The Guodian slip texts were written in ink, by the use of brush on bamboo slips; and they were bound in bundles. Which bundles appear to have been written by the same hand? What does the calligraphy tell us about the literary level of the scribe(s)?[22]

Variations in handwriting (calligraphic style and the forms of particular characters) are evidence in determining whether the bamboo-slip bundles were written by more than one person. This, in turn, can help to decide how many different texts the bundles represent. In the discussions, Sarah Allan asked how many hands can be identified in the three *Laozi* bundles and the *Tai Yi Sheng Shui* (which was probably originally bound together with Guodian *Laozi* group-C). Peng Hao responded to this with

---

[22] The identity of the scribes was not a specific topic of discussion. There seemed to be a general assumption that the calligraphy on the slips was that of specialist scribes rather than the final user-owner of the slips (at least no one voiced the opinion that the slips were copied by the owner of the tomb or other reader). The conference participants also seem to have assumed that none of the texts was the original creation of the person whose writing we see; that is to say, that they were all copied or excerpted from existing written or oral texts.

the idea that the group-A bundle was written by a single scribe and that group-B may have been written by the same scribe; there are variations but not enough to differentiate clearly. Guodian *Laozi* group-C and the *Tai Yi Sheng Shui* were written by a single scribe who was not the one(s) who wrote the *Laozi* A and B bundles.

Peng Hao also noted that the calligraphic style in the *Tang Yu zhi Dao* 唐虞之道 is very particular. This suggests a different origin for this text. However, he further observed that one sometimes comes across the same unusual features in character structure in texts that have different calligraphy; thus, he wondered whether some scribes might have used a variety of styles.

Rudolf Wagner raised the question of the literary level of the scribes (for possible mistakes in punctuation, see below, p. 135). According to Qiu Xigui, the writing style was crude, with many basic mistakes in the characters, suggesting that the scribes were not highly educated. Li Xueqin agreed. He further pointed out that some excavated texts, in contrast to the Guodian slips, have a high standard of calligraphy which indicates that the scribes were highly skilled professionals. He noted, however, that beautiful calligraphy does not necessarily mean an accurate text; texts such as the silk-manuscript *Zhou Yi* 周易 from Mawangdui included basic mistakes which Li attributed to carelessness or simply irresponsibility.[23] Qiu Xigui noted that the types of mistake found on the Guodian slips, in contrast to such texts, indicate incompetence rather than carelessness.

Rudolf Wagner also raised the issue of whether the free use of non-standard characters might be because people in this period were not concerned about correct orthography; they simply wished to ensure that the writer and reader both knew which word was denoted. It was more important to convey meaning accurately than to observe rules. Robin Yates, however, pointed to the contrary example of the Qin-era (late-third century BC) legal texts on slips from Shuihudi 睡虎地 in which characters were written with great attention to scribal accuracy, perhaps because of the different nature of the material.

*Punctuation and the Question of Chapter Division*

Peng Hao introduced the punctuation symbols used in the Guodian texts (see his paper above, Section I). The marks include black squares, short lines, and a "tadpole"-shaped symbol. They are used as clause or sentence markers and to divide sections of text, but there is no obvious convention in their usage.

The questions of sentence punctuation and chapter division are closely tied, since the black squares and short strokes appear in both positions. The questions addressed

---

[23] Li cited the example of the character 象 , incorrectly written in the *Zhou Yi*, "Xici." See Li Xueqin "Boshu *Xici* Shangpian Xilun 帛書《繫辭》上篇析論," *Jiang Han Kaogu* 1993.1, p. 81. However, this example has been disputed; see Xing Wen 邢文 , *Boshu Zhou Yi Yanjiu* 帛書周易研究 (Beijing: Renmin Press, 1997), p. 49, and note 3, for citations to Rao Zongyi 饒宗頤 and Zhang Yongquan 張涌泉 .

below include: To what extent are marks used for grammatical punctuation? What is the meaning of the tadpole symbol? Do some of these marks imply chapter divisions? If they do mark chapter divisions, do they reflect an existing text with chapter divisions similar to the received *Laozi*?

### a. Punctuation

The conference discussed the apparent inconsistencies in the employment of punctuation marks and the implications of this phenomenon. For example, the black square is often found in places that correspond to chapter endings in the received text; however, not all such places are marked and it also occurs in places other than chapter endings. Usually it divides sections of at least several sentences, but it also occurs at the end of each one of the first five sentences in the *Laozi* A 1:1 to 2:18, a section equivalent to only one chapter (chapter 19) in the received text.

The short strokes marking phrases, clauses, or sentences are also used inconsistently. Wang Bo raised the issue of whether these marks have any significance at all, since their usage appears to be arbitrary and frequently appears not to make sense. Rudolf Wagner raised the further problem of the concept of grammatical division, questioning whether there was a clear concept of a clause or sentence at this time. Qiu Xigui and Li Xueqin both said that in other excavated texts these marks do function to divide sentences, but, they noted, there are a large number of such marks that we can be absolutely certain were placed incorrectly in those texts.

Xu Shaohua conjectured that inconsistencies in punctuation could reflect different habits of copyists. However, Peng Hao pointed out that although there are many such inconsistencies in, for example, the *Laozi* A material, the calligraphic style of the characters suggests it is the work of a single copyist. Robin Yates then raised the possibility that the copies were punctuated, not at the time of copying, but at a later date. He suggested testing the ink of the characters and the punctuation symbols to see if there were any indications that they were written at different times; he noted, however, that the cleaning process that the slips underwent may have affected the ink in such a way that such tests would not be effective. Sarah Allan noted, however, that the punctuation is given its own space within the lines, which suggests that it was not added later.

Peng Hao observed that there are later additions to the slips that do suggest proofreading after the text was completed. A clear example is found on slip 40 of the *Zi Yi* — namely, a sentence written on the reverse side that had been omitted from the text on the front.[24]

### b. Chapter divisions

Is there evidence in the Guodian *Laozi* material of chapter divisions, such as those

---

[24] See *Guodian Chu Mu Zhujian*, p. 20, for the photo of the slips, and p. 136, note 103.

found in the received eighty-one-chapter *Daodejing*? Do the black squares and short strokes correspond to the chapter divisions of the received *Laozi*? Rudolf Wagner felt that the Guodian *Laozi* is clearly divided into chapters. Sarah Allan objected to the assertion that the divisions clearly marked chapters. She noted that the sections of text marked off in the *Laozi* bundles do not all correspond to complete chapters in the received text, while several chapters in the received text are not marked off on the slips.

Wagner's point was that *zhang* 章 ("chapters") are nevertheless the basic textual unit; punctuation marks are only one, and a rather unstable, marker of *zhang* divisions.[25] This is evident, he argued, from both the Guodian and the Mawangdui finds. In the Mawangdui copies, the evidence for *zhang* is incontrovertible since the sequence of the *Laozi* segments in both Mawangdui manuscripts differs from the one used in all the extant editions. We can thus check whether *they appeared in their entirety as textual units in their different places or not*. In the Mawangdui manuscripts, we have the following four sequences that differ from the received editions: 38, 39, 41, 40, 42; 66, 80, 81, 67; 78, 79, 1; and 21, 24, 22, 23, 25. In every case where the Mawangdui order is different from that of the received text the *zhang* appears in its entirety. A similar situation prevails in the Guodian manuscripts, the sequence of which again is different from that in the Mawangdui manuscripts. While we do have cases of split *zhang*, Wagner felt that they generally reappear in their new place as intact textual units.[26]

Wagner added that this pattern of division does not lend credence to the theory that the *Laozi* was originally a collection of very short, independent passages or short proverbs later joined together. Peng Hao, on the other hand, noted that the Guodian *Laozi* material often only corresponds to short sections of the received chapters. Peng thought that this suggests that the *Laozi* was in fact originally composed of a large number of shorter chapters, rather than the longer *zhang* of the received text.

### c. The "tadpole" symbol

A symbol shaped like a tadpole occurs twice in the *Laozi* group-A bundle and in some of the other Guodian materials. Peng Hao compared its shape to that of the Eastern Zhou character 以 and suggested that its meaning is similar to that of 止 ("stop"). He noted that it is used to mark the end of large sections of text made up of

---

[25] Cf. Christoph Harbsmeier, *Language and Logic, Science and Civilisation in China* (Cambridge: Cambridge University Press, 1998) 7.1, p. 177.

[26] Wagner notes that Xie Shouhao's 謝守灝 (1134–1212) history of the transmission of the *Laozi* at one point says, "The manuscripts which are put together today are based on textual links (*wenlian* 文連). [Some] copyists have also given separate headings to each of the 81 *zhang*. But, as with the stanzas of the Old Poems, where each stanza is separated from the next through its literary cohesion, one can determine the [*Laozi*'s] subsections without the need for a separate heading for each *zhang*"; Xie Shouhao, *Hunyuan Shengji* 混元聖紀 (*Daozang*: HY 769, Schipper 770) 3, p. 18b. See also Wagner, "Wang Bi's Recension," pp. 47–49.

several individual chapters. In *Laozi* A, as edited for publication in *Guodian Chu Mu Zhujian*, this symbol appears as the last character on slip 32, with the remainder of the slip left blank, as well as at the end of the last slip, slip 39, thus dividing this bundle into two sections: the first one of 32 slips, the second of 7 slips.

Wang Bo suggested a reordering of this group of slips into two sections: (1) slips 1–20 with slips 25 to 32 and (2) slips 21 to 24 with 33 to 39. This reordering would leave both these sections with a tadpole symbol marking their end. Moreover, each section would have a thematic coherence (the thematic basis of Wang Bo's reordering is discussed below, p. 154).

Donald Harper argued that the tadpole symbol is actually a small version of the character 乙. The symbol is used elsewhere in the Guodian slips: in the *Cheng Zhi Wen Zhi*, *Xing Zi Ming Chu*, and *Liu De*, it appears at the end of the last slip. In the *Xing Zi Ming Chu* there is also one at the end of the text on slip 35 and no further text on this slip, as if this bundle can be seen as composed of two sections in the same way the *Laozi* A bundle is. Moreover, this symbol occurs on other excavated Chu slips — from Jiudian 九店 and Baoshan — where it is used as punctuation. Comparison of the so-called "tadpole" symbol with the Baoshan character 乙 in its meaning as the second of the ten stems (*tian gan* 天干), suggests that the punctuation symbol on the Guodian slips is a small version of the character 乙. Harper further pointed out that the latter's use as a stop mark is supported by a line in the *Shiji* which suggests that it was used by some to mark the place in a text where they stopped reading, as we might fold down a corner of a page or use a bookmark.[27] There is, however, possibly a difference between such usage and that of the Guodian texts, where it seems clearly to mark off large sections of text.[28]

---

[27] "人主從上方讀之,止,輒乙其處,讀之二月乃盡," *Shiji* (Beijing: Zhonghua Shuju, 1959) 126 ("Guji Liezhuan 滑稽列傳"), p. 3205. Donald Harper referred to Chen Mengjia 陳夢家, "You Shiwu Suojian Handai Jiance Zhidu 由實物所見漢代簡冊制度," in *Han Jian Zhuishu* 漢簡綴述 (Beijing: Zhonghua Shuju, 1980), pp. 291–315, which discusses this use of 乙. Chen thought that in the *Shiji* passage it is an error for 乚 (glossed in the *Shuowen Jiezi*, 14 *xia*, 戉 *bu*, as a punctuation marker), but the excavated Chu manuscripts suggest that the "tadpole" symbol and 乙 were interchangeable.

[28] Wagner notes that the *Shuowen* gives two explanations for interpunctuations: one for a kind of right-pointing hook, the other for a dot. Concerning the dot, the *Shuowen* writes: 有所絕止而識之也 ("it is something that reminds you of the fact that there is something like a stop there"). Concerning the hook, it says: 鉤識也 ("It is a reminder in the form of a [written] hook"); Duan Yucai comments: 鉤識者 用鉤表識其處也 … 今人讀書有所鉤勒即此 ("'A reminder in the form of a written hook' means that one uses a [written] hook to mark that place. It has [the same function] as the circles drawn by people nowadays [around important places they want to remember and find quickly] when they read books"). Cui Renyi, *Jingmen Guodian Chu Jian Laozi Yanjiu*, p. 62, note 223, identifies the tadpole as this right-pointing hook. See also Harbsmeier, *Language and Logic*, pp. 177–81, for an account of early interpunctuation with bibliographic references on related scholarship.

### d. Divisions and sequences

The following discussion centers on problematic points of punctuation, chapter divisions in the received text, and the implications of the Guodian sequences. The divisions in the Guodian text made by Sarah Allan and Robert Henricks on the basis of its own breaks, as marked by the conjunction of slip ends and marked stops, were: slips A 1–20, 21–23, 24, 25–32, 33–39; B 1–8, 9–12, 13–18; and C 1–3, 4–5, 6–10, 11–14. These are discrete sections of text in which the Guodian sequence of material is clear. According to Peng Hao and Qiu Xigui, the sequence of these sections in *Guodian Chu Mu Zhujian* is provisional and not based upon physical evidence.

The following are places where the junctures and/or sequences in the Guodian text were noted as particularly significant.

### Guodian *Laozi* A 5:14 to 6:16 [Chapter 46b]

Robert Henricks noted that this section is found in chapter 46 of the received text, but the received text chapter has an extra two lines, not found in the Guodian slips, at the beginning of the chapter: 天下有道卻走馬以糞，天下無道戎馬生於郊．Furthermore, although these lines do occur in the Mawangdui copies, they are marked off by punctuation marks in Mawangdui Copy A, as though they were considered to be a separate section. This suggests that this section was originally a separate chapter.

### A 6:17 to 8:3 [Chapter 30]

A question was raised about the short stroke between 好 (8:2) and 長 (8:3) at the end of this section. The *Guodian Chu Mu Zhujian* takes it as a punctuation mark ending a chapter. Qiu Xigui suggested that the mark was added some time after the writing of the text to indicate the omission of a character, in this case 還 (which ends this clause in the received text). Gao Ming, along with a number of other scholars, thought that this mark was misplaced and that the following character, 長, should be read as the last character in this section, resulting in the clause 其事好長．Views varied as to how to interpret 長．

Robert Henricks, following the latter reading, noted that the sentence occurs in different positions in the Mawangdui and received texts. Xu Kangsheng considered how this difference affects the meaning. The received version reads: 不以兵強天下，其事好還．師之所處，荊棘生焉．Xu Kangsheng interpreted this to mean that events can easily turn and develop in an opposite direction; the place at which an army arrives will inevitably grow thick with thorns (i.e., a victory may not have positive results). The Guodian text, on the other hand, reads: 是謂果而不強其事好長，which he interpreted to mean that if one can avoid being proud in victory, then victory can be maintained. This alteration to the text illustrates a change in the attitude towards war. The Guodian text advises one how to maintain victory by not being proud of one's success. The received version, on the other hand, opposes war on the grounds that even if one wins, things will go badly. Xu suggested that the widespread warfare of the mid-Warring States period led the Daoists to adopt this anti-war stance.

### A 33:1 to 35:17 [Chapter 55 part]

Marc Kalinowski pointed out, that in the received text, the last two phrases of this section: 物壯則老,是謂不道, are also found at the end of chapter 30 as well as in chapter 55. Previously, scholars noted that the repetition may have been a copyist's error due to the presence of the character 強 which precedes the two phrases in both chapters. In the section of the Guodian text corresponding to the received text chapter 30 (Guodian A: 6:17 to 8:3), we do not find these lines. Moreover, in the Guodian text corresponding to chapter 30, the line 其事好長 (A 7:31 to 8:3) follows 強 (in the received text this line occurs earlier in the same chapter.)

### A 37:4–27 [Chapter 40]

Marc Kalinowski noted that the position of the received text, chapter 40, has been the subject of controversy. In the Mawangdui silk-manuscript copies, it occurs between sections corresponding to received chapters 41 and 42. However, in the Guodian, the same text is placed between sections corresponding to received chapters 44 and 9; no one had suggested putting chapter 40 after 44.

### B 3:8 to 8:23 [Chapter 48a, Chapter 20a, Chapter 13]

The first line of chapter 20 in the received text is 絕學無憂 ("Eliminate learning and have no undue concern"). As Robert Henricks, Marc Kalinowski, and Carine Defoort pointed out, many scholars had already suggested that this phrase seems isolated at the beginning of chapter 20 of the received text and would make better sense as the last line of chapter 19, following 見素抱樸, 少私寡欲 ("... Lessen self-interest and make few your desires"), rather than preceding 唯之與阿, 相去幾何 ("Agreement and angry rejection; How great is the difference between them") as the beginning of chapter 20.[29] The Guodian slips call this theory into question because text corresponding to the first half of chapter 48 (rather than chapter 19) precedes chapter 20 on the Guodian slips. Moreover, the lines (corresponding to chapters 48 and 20) are divided in the Guodian slips with a short black stroke, not with the more prominent black square, and there is no gap after the short stroke.

Carine Defoort noted that if this line originally belonged to chapter 19, as many scholars have thought, and mistakenly got into chapter 20 of the received version, then we can infer from its presence in the Guodian material corresponding to chapter 20 (without chapter 19 in front of it) that the Guodian *Laozi* is copied from something like the received version. (That the Guodian texts include material correspond-

---

[29] Robert Henricks, trans., *Lao-tzu Te-Tao Ching*, pp. 224 and 226.

ing to chapter 19 without this line tends to further confirm this). Thus, she argued, chapter 20 in the Guodian *Laozi* contains a mistake that could only be explained by the chapter order of the received version.

As Paul Thompson and Wang Tao observed, there is a very clear and natural link in the Guodian slip-text, between the lines corresponding to the beginning of chapter 48 and the beginning of chapter 20, which immediately succeeds it. The former (B 3:8 to 4:7 學者日益，為道者日損，損之或損，以至亡為，亡為而亡不為 "He who pursues learning increases daily; he who follows the Way decreases daily. By decreasing and decreasing, he reaches the state of 'doing nothing'; in doing nothing, he leaves nothing undone") mentions study in a negative manner, and the latter (B 4:8–11 絕學無憂 "When one forsakes learning, one is free of cares"; Paul Thompson's translations) is a logical continuation. Thus, they argued, the short stroke on the bamboo slip at the end of the former section (after 4:7) may not indicate a chapter division.[30] Here, Andrew Meyer noted that we should not allow the chapter divisions of the received text to determine divisions in the Guodian text; the Guodian text has its own structure. In this case he thought that 絕學亡憂 relates to both the previous passage and that which follows.

Discussion then turned to the last sentence in the section corresponding to the first part of received chapter 20, which is followed by lines corresponding to received chapter 13. The question was whether the character 人 (B 5:11) should be read as the last word in the line 人之所畏，亦不可以不畏 (B 5:1–10) or as the first word of the next section, which reads 寵辱若驚，貴大患若身 (B 5:12–20). There is a small dot before the 人 in the Guodian slips, suggesting a break before it. However, Qiu Xigui and others thought that this was a scribal error and that the character should be placed with the previous line. There is support for such a reading in the Mawangdui copies and received editions. Mawangdui Copy B does have 人 after 畏, giving: 人之所畏，亦不可以不畏人 (Mawangdui Copy A is damaged here). Furthermore, none of the received editions or the Mawangdui copies begins the next section with 人 .

Chen Guying noted that, if we read 人之所畏，亦不可以不畏 , we have a version closer to the received edition: 人之所畏不可不畏 ("What others fear, one must also fear"; D. C. Lau's translation), while if we read this with the final 人 , then it is closer to the excavated Mawangdui editions: 人之所畏，亦不可以不畏人 ("He whom others fear ought also to fear others").[31] Chen made the general point that the Guodian text seems to be closer to the Mawangdui copies in some places, but closer to the received text in others. Therefore the received text may in some cases contain passages that

---

[30] See also Wang Tao, "Afterthoughts," pp. 241–42.

[31] D. C. Lau, trans., *Chinese Classics: Tao Te Ching* (Hong Kong: The Chinese University Press, 1989), pp. 29, 295.

reflect an earlier version than the Mawangdui copies. In other words, different editions have different sources ( i.e., the earliest edition is not necessarily to be preferred). Chen Guying said his preference was to read the line with 人 as the final character.

Ikeda Tomohisa, on the other hand, argued that 人 should be read with the next section (corresponding to the beginning of received chapter 13), as the punctuation indicates. He suggested that the Guodian text is the source of the received *Laozi*; thus this character was later mistakenly linked with the last line of the previous section (received text chapter 20). The first two lines of chapter 13 then become: 人寵辱若驚, 貴大患若身 … .

Considering such a reading, Wang Tao observed that 人 ("people"), would then parallel the 貴 in the second line, and 貴 would function as a noun, meaning "people of high status." If we follow the original punctuation of the Guodian text, reading the character 人 as the first word of the line that continues 寵辱若驚, 貴大患若身, we could interpret the line as: "when a man is favored or insulted, it is the same as a bad shock; when a man is honored, it is a great trouble, the same as one's [physical] body" (Wang Tao's translation). Chen Guying's reading of this line did not allow such an interpretation; he thought that the second line should be read 貴身若大患 ("treat one's body with respect as one would a great trouble"; editors' translation), and that it was inverted in the text so that the 身 would be at the end of the line and rhyme with the 驚 in the previous line.

Qiu Xigui argued that grammatically it is preferable to read the 人 with the previous line: 人之所畏, 亦不可以不畏人, reasoning that without it, the object of the final 畏 is unclear. Rudolf Wagner further observed that, when interpreting these sentences, it is important to bear in mind that 人 simply means 他人, "other people"; it does not become an abstract philosophical concept until the introduction of Buddhism into China. Before this, people were not conceptualized as a single category, but in ranks.[32]

### C 1:1 to 3:22 [Chapters 17 and 18]

Rudolf Wagner noted that in the Guodian slips this section is not divided into two chapters. He felt that the division in the received text is a logical one: the thought expressed in the two chapters is not only different, but the two are also structurally dissimilar. The Guodian and Mawangdui texts connect the two sections with a 故

[32] Wang Tao disagrees with Wagner's assertion that *ren* as an abstract concept only appeared later, after the arrival of Buddhism. In several places in the Guodian text it as an abstract category (e.g., A 22:5 to 23:5: 人法地, 地法天 … ["Man models himself on earth; earth models itself on heaven…"]). In a number of other early texts that predate the introduction of Buddhism, such as the *Huainanzi* 淮南子 and *Xiaojing* 孝經, it is discussed as a single abstract category; even the definition in the *Shuowen Jiezi* (ca. AD 100) (人, 天地之性最貴者) is too early for Buddhist influence.

("therefore"), but the received text omits it. Wagner suggested that it may have been removed from the received text by a later editor because of the differences in structure and content. The later editor was preoccupied with the use of standardized structures in texts; structures, which at an earlier time may not have been so rigidly adhered to or even recognized.[33]

### Relationship to the Received *Laozi*

Robert Henricks noted in his summing up speech at the end of the conference that two main possibilities had been proposed concerning the relationship between the received *Laozi* text and the three Guodian bundles that contain closely corresponding passages. One possibility is that the received *Laozi* already existed in written form and the Guodian slips are a selection of passages copied from such a text. The other possibility is that the Guodian bundles are a selection from a group of sayings that circulated orally and were later incorporated, along with materials from other sources, to form the received *Laozi*.

This summation covers the alternatives about the textual relationship broadly, but there are several more nuanced positions. For example, the *Laozi* may have existed as a written text, but it may not have included all of the sections that are in the received "five-thousand-character" classic. It may have had a form like the present one (divided into eighty-one or some other number of chapters); or it may have been a corpus of material with a common identity but with no given order. The material may have been originally written or originally transmitted orally; or, it may have been oral, then written, and then transmitted orally again before it reached its final written form. The order of the Guodian text may have been original, or it may have been reordered from the received form for a particular purpose, for example, for use in teaching.

Let us first consider the arguments for the theory that the Guodian *Laozi* slips are a selection of passages copied from an existing *Laozi* text with essentially the same form as the current *Laozi*. Chen Guying was a vocal supporter of this theory. Based upon his previous research, he held that the account in the *Shiji* concerning the *Laozi* and its author is correct. That is to say, the *Laozi* was written by one man, Lao Dan 老聃, in the early-fifth century BC. Chen noted that several other texts suggest that Lao Dan was from the state of Qi 齊; after Lao Dan wrote and compiled the book, there came to be several different versions.[34]

Chen Guying argued that the new finds support this view. First, we can see that the *Laozi* is an early text, earlier than many scholars have been suggesting in recent

---

[33] See "Afterthoughts" for Wagner's revised opinion about this section, pp. 240–41.

[34] See Chen Guying 陳鼓應, *Lao Zhuang Xin Lun* 老莊新論 (Shanghai: Shanghai Guji Press, 1992), especially pp. 43–58, for a detailed exposition of the history of Laozi and his work.

decades. Furthermore, the variants in the repeated section of chapter 64 (see p. 133) tell us that these two sections were copied from different editions. This supports the view that the original text had already been transmitted for a long time. The date of the Guodian tomb is not much more than 100 years after the death of Lao Dan (ca. 480 BC). Thus, this find does not conflict in any way with the theory that Lao Dan, that is to say Laozi, wrote this book in its present form.

While many scholars at the discussion sympathized with this view, others were not convinced. Robin Yates was willing to consider the possibility that a version of the received *Laozi* existed at the time the Guodian materials were written, but suggested that, in this case, it might not have been a complete text, but circulated in sections. He compared the Guodian bundles with the Mawangdui *Shiliu Jing* 十六經 (also known as the *Shi Da Jing* 十大經 and *Jing* 經 ), which he believed also circulated in separate units.[35] If the complete *Laozi* text existed at the time, he asked, why was the occupant of the Guodian tomb not buried with the full text; why did he have only these sections? It suggests that either he did not attach much importance to the complete text or, more probably, that there was none. A comparison can be made with the later Mawangdui tomb occupant who had two full versions of the *Laozi* buried with him, both of them essentially similar to the received text.

Another possibility that we considered was that the current *Laozi* existed and had been written down, but that it was passed down orally. It might then have been written down again but from memory rather than by copying from a text. The suggestion is, then, that the Guodian version might have been a selection from this orally-transmitted but complete *Laozi*. Sarah Allan posed the question that if the text was complete and memorized as a complete unit with a definite order, why would someone write down abbreviated sections ordered differently from that which they had memorized; surely, if it was written down based on memory, even extracts would tend to follow the order in which it was memorized. Wang Bo replied that the order of the passages might not have been fixed and that this is a phenomenon we see in other excavated texts where sections of a single text have different sequences from the corresponding received text.

Many in our discussion felt that the Guodian *Laozi* material has a more logical order than the received text. Does this mean that it was earlier? Li Xueqin pointed out that we should also not assume that our idea of logical order is the same as that of the ancients. In excavated texts we often find a group of passages selected from a complete text and placed together, but that the basis on which these selections was made is often unclear; this is true of some of the excavated examples of Qin and Han legal texts. On the other hand, we also have excavated texts in which the order appears

---

[35] See Robin D. S. Yates, *Five Lost Classics: Tao, Huang-Lao, and Yin-Yang in Han China* (New York: Ballantine Books, 1997), pp. 25–32.

logical, but we know that this was not the earliest sequence; an example of this is the Mawangdui *Zhou Yi* 周易, in which the order of the hexagrams is logical but we know that it is not the earliest form.[36]

On the subject of written texts and oral transmission, Li Xueqin observed that there were no printed books in ancient times, so texts were hard to come by. Many works were probably learned by heart and, if written down, they were written down from memory rather than copied from an earlier text. There is strong evidence of this phenomenon; for example, the *Zi Yi* found in Guodian Tomb Number One and a bamboo-slip version of this text discussed by Rao Zongyi probably have a similar place of origin and date of burial. However, characters in the two versions are used differently, suggesting they were being written from memory. [37]

Wang Bo added that he thought the *Laozi* would be easier to memorize in individual sections rather than as a whole work. Crispin Williams agreed, pointing out that, since the *Laozi* is not a narrative, it does not have a beginning and end; in that sense, the sections do not have a correct order. Rudolf Wagner observed that the order of sections is not important in early philosophical texts since each text has a central theme and all sections discuss this one theme.

A further alternative is that the Guodian bundles were a selection of orally transmitted teachings that were later incorporated, along with materials from other sources, to form the received *Laozi*. This was one of the three models presented by Harold Roth in his paper on the first day (see above, Section I), what he calls the "parallel text" model. In it the individual units of text in the Guodian *Laozi* bundles are considered to be the written expression of an earlier oral tradition in which Daoist philosophical ideas were presented in a poetic form. After a long period of oral transmission, these units of verse were assembled into various different written texts, of which the Guodian materials are examples. The received *Laozi* is simply a later assemblage from this tradition.

As for the form these smaller units would have taken, Harold Roth gave the example of poetic lines quoted in the text, such as B 10:8 to 12:17. Here a poetic passage is introduced by the words 是以建言有之 ("Thus, as the *Established Sayings* would have it …"). What follows are twelve lines of tetrasyllabic verse (two final lines are damaged) extolling the way and inner power. Elsewhere, Roth has theorized that such philosophical verse was the first form used for the transmission of the teachings of

[36] See Li Xueqin, "Boshu *Zhou Yi* de Guaxu Guawei 帛書《周易》的卦序卦位," in *Jianbo Yiji yu Xueshushi* 簡帛佚籍與學術史 (Taibei: Wenhua Congshu, 1995), pp. 239–51.

[37] Rao Zongyi notes that the slips under discussion had gone abroad, but were from the Chu region and date to the Warring States period; "*Zi Yi Ling Jian* 緇衣零簡," *Xueshu Jilin* 9 (Dec., 1996), pp. 66–68.

the early Daoists.[38] Susan Blader (Dartmouth College) noted that oral texts also quote from other materials; it is not only written texts that do this. Peng Hao, observing that we do find sections of chapters of the current *Laozi* occurring independently in the Guodian texts, agreed that this suggests the original *Laozi* was originally in shorter chapters.

Susan Blader and Bruce Brooks (University of Massachussetts, Amherst) made several further points about orally transmitted texts. Susan Blader suggested that many of the characteristics of the Guodian *Laozi* bundles might be explained if we take them to be part of an oral tradition (i.e., a written selection of orally transmitted units). The scribe while listening to someone else's recitation would have written these texts. She noted a strong oral element to these texts and conjectured that a large amount of phonetic borrowing could be a sign of this. She also observed that there are different types of orally transmitted texts: there can be a text that is fixed in a particular form orally, and then transmitted in that form; it does not have to have been written at all. On the other hand, a text that has been written down can be retransmitted orally (this point was also made by Li Xueqin, see above) and then written down again. Bruce Brooks suggested that there is a form of oral text (which he called "folklore") which has no fixed sequence, and when it is written down, it crystallizes into separate parts with only a very few similar sections.

Participants raised a number of objections to the theory that the Guodian slips are evidence of an orally transmitted text. Rudolf Wagner asked how it is that the Guodian *Laozi* slips have no passages that are not found in the present *Laozi*. That is to say, there is nothing in these texts to suggest they were taken from a source of oral literature that encompasses more material than found in the present *Laozi*, as the theory of oral transmission set out by Roth implies.[39] Paul Thompson also felt that the lack of repetition (only one exception) among the bundles suggested they were all copied from an existing text.

Li Xueqin further observed that people in ancient times felt free to alter texts to reflect their own personal thought and the ideology of the time. He gave an example from the Xiang Er *Laozi* 老子想爾注, which changes the last clause in the line 道大, 天大, 地大, 王亦大 to 生大 (chapter 25). Donald Harper stressed that written texts were nevertheless considered very important during this period. Harper cited the Mawangdui medical text *Shi Wen* 十問, in which the doctor Wen Zhi 文摯 had an audience with King Wei of Qi (齊威王; r. 357–320 BC), but was only allowed to say three words. He protested, "but my Dao has three hundred fascicles," suggesting that

---

[38] Harold D. Roth, *Original Tao: Inward Training (Nei-yeh) and the Foundations of Taoist Mysticism* (New York: Columbia University Press, 1999) pp. 12–17, 190–93.

[39] This assumes that the *Tai Yi Sheng Shui* is not part of the *Laozi*.

the doctor had a given set of written teachings that he could recite.[40]

Apart from these theories concerning the relationship between the Guodian *Laozi* material and the received *Laozi* text, Harold Roth's "source model" (see pp. 77–81) was also discussed. In this model, the Guodian *Laozi* slips represent one of a number of written sources for the received *Laozi*, which was compiled at a later date. Alternatively, Xing Wen hypothesized, both the Guodian *Laozi* and the received text derive from the same unknown source. He further suggested that the *Tai Yi Sheng Shui* and the *Laozi* C, which were written with one hand and probably bound together, may originally have been one text. This question is discussed again in part three, below.

*Text Structure*

Another question discussed was the relationship between text structure and meaning in the Guodian *Laozi*. Such analysis is based on the theory that the structure of a section of text indicates the semantic relationship between clauses in that section. If this structure is not recognized, the meaning of the passage, particularly the way ideas in it relate to one another, may remain unclear. Identifying such structures in the received *Laozi* aids in the understanding of the text. Rudolf Wagner, who had already introduced the concept of interlocking parallel structure in the *Laozi*, illustrated this methodology with two structural examples.[41] The first structure is found in Guodian *Laozi* A 10:22 to 11:15, which corresponds to the beginning of *Laozi* 64.

1. 為者敗之
2. 執者遠之
3. 是以聖人
4. 亡為故亡敗
5. 亡執故亡失

Phrases 1 and 2 are rigidly parallel, as are phrases 4 and 5. A linkage of content transcends the parallelism, bringing together the rigid couplets. The words *wei* 為 and *bai* 敗 from phrase 1 are taken up in phrase 4; the word *zhi* 執 from phrase 2 appears in phrase 5. It is evident from the hypothesis of interlocking structure that something is wrong with the second halves of 2 and 5. We have the standardized character 遠 in phrase 2, and a standardized 失 in phrase 5. A look at the Guodian manuscript quickly shows that the characters transcribed apparently so differently are actually similar,

---

[40] Donald Harper, *Early Chinese Medical Literature: The Mawangdui Medical Manuscripts* (London: Kegan Paul International, 1998), p. 406.

[41] This subject is explained in Rudolf Wagner, "Interlocking Parallel Style: *Laozi* and Wang Bi," in *Études Asiatiques* 34.1 (1980), pp. 18–58; idem, *The Craft of a Chinese Commentator: Wang Bi on the Laozi* (Albany: SUNY Press, 2000), pp. 53–113; and idem, "The Impact of Conceptions of Rhetoric and Style upon the Formation of Early *Laozi* Editions: Evidence from Guodian, Mawangdui and the Wang Bi *Laozi*," to appear in *Tōhō gakkai kiyō* 40.

the former having been a simple misspelling for the standard writing of 失 .[42]

Parallelisms with explicit linkage are the rule in "open interlocking parallel style." We thus have two pairs, 1/4 and 2/5, openly linked by common language and content, yet not parallel with each other. The five phrases therefore consist of two pairs linked by parallelism, 1/2 and 4/5, and two pairs linked by content, 1/4 and 2/5. The divide between the two parallel pairs is formed by number 3: "that is why the sage." Phrase 3 does not connect the immediately preceding to the immediately succeeding phrases, which would give an absurd sequence: "He who holds fast, loses them. That is why the sage does not interfere and thus does not destroy." This would connect the disconnected phrases 2 and 4. It actually performs a double linkage: 1 with 4 and 2 with 5; it is two occurrences of "that is why the sage" compressed into one. It thus establishes the connection between the pairs of phrases linked by content. Trivial as this might sound, it establishes a vital reading strategy for a proper handling of interlocking parallel style, namely spatial instead of linear reading. In spatial writing, the above section could be written:

I.          1|A              2|B

                    3|C

II.         4|A              5|B

While in terms of form the text might be described as two sets of parallel pairs, I and II, linked by a non-parallel phrase, in content the text consists of two interlocked strains, a and b, with a nexus formed by a third element. Focusing on content alone as visible in the words, one might unlock the text into two long parallel statements:

a: He who interferes, destroys them. That is why the sage does not interfere and thus does not destroy.

b: He who holds fast, loses them. That is why the sage does not hold fast and thus does not lose.

There is also a closed form of interlocking parallel style, which is indicated by strong parallelism, but the linkages are not as explicit as in the above. Guodian *Laozi* A 37:28 to 39:9 (corresponding to *Laozi* 9) is a difficult example of the kind.

1. 殖而盈之，不若其已．
2. 揣而群之，不可長保也．
3. 金玉盈室，莫能守也．
4. 貴富而驕，自遺咎也．
5. 功遂身退，天之道也．

---

[42] Rudolf Wagner states: "This slipped the attention of the *Guodian Chu Mu Zhujian* editors, but Cui Renyi 崔仁義 , *Jingmen Guodian Chu Jian Laozi Yanjiu* 荊門郭店楚簡老子研究 (Beijing: Kexue Press,

Wagner explained that the text here consists of neatly parallel pairs — 1/2 and 3/4. The first half of phrase 5 has a different grammar, with two full sentences of two characters each instead of one longer cohesive statement of four characters; and the second half is completely different in both grammar and content from the second halves of the previous two phrases. We thus have the same binary code as in the first example, and this marks phrase 5 as a summary statement pertaining to both previous chains. The 也 at the end of phrase 2 is a bit of an oddity because it has no parallel at the end of phrase 1, and the pattern in which it is used does not recur in 4 and 5. The Mawangdui manuscripts have the same pattern.

The received *Laozi*, to which Wang Bi's commentary is appended, takes out all the 也. This gives a more rigid parallelism. Nevertheless, the function of 也 in the Guodian *Laozi* is to separate the two pairs — not to mark the end of phrase 2, but the end of the statement consisting of two parallel phrases, 1 and 2. It signals that we do not have a chain of four phrases, but two pairs of two each, and the Guodian is thus providing an additional marker of this division (which does not exist in any available translation) by having the second halves of phrases 3 and 4 each with three characters plus a 也 instead of the four characters in the corresponding parts of phrase 1 and 2. This pattern prompts us to find the connections between the two pairs.

The above sort of connection is further indicated in the Guodian and the Mawangdui Copy A versions by the recurrence of the character 盈 in phrases 1 and 3. This tells us that phrases 1 and 3 are linked in content, and that phrases 2 and 4 are, by default, linked in the same way. In closed interlocking parallel style, such clues are not frequent, however, and the Wang Bi *Laozi* is in fact relatively more opaque in its use of 滿 instead of the second 盈. Furthermore, the Wang Bi commentary makes things easier by simply inserting the text of the second half of phrase 1 as a commentary under phrase 3, and doing the same with the second half of phrase 2 under phrase 4, thus establishing the links without any possible ambiguity. We thus have a structure very much like the one we had above in open interlocking parallel style:

|       |       |
|-------|-------|
| 1\|A  | 2\|B  |
| 3\|A  | 4\|B  |
|   5\|C  |       |

Our reading of this *zhang* has to take the above structure into account. The terms in the *Laozi* receive their meaning both from the semantic potential of the constituent words and from their structural positions.

---

1998), p. 65, note 266, spotted it correctly. I should point out that early editors were working with a conscious knowledge of this stylistic pattern and would often base their decisions for preferred readings (for example in this case) on knowledge of interlocking parallel style rules. We in fact have a fully parallel structure here."

Wagner translates:[43]

9.1
In maintaining [it] and then even adding
to it, one is not as well off as if one [had]
nothing.

9.2
By polishing [it] and then [further-
more] grinding it, one will be unable
to protect [oneself] for long.

9.3
    [Accordingly,]
no one who fills [his already sumptuous]
hall [furthermore] with gold and jades will
be able to preserve [them].

9.4
someone who is [already] wealthy
and honored but [in addition turns]
arrogant brings calamity upon himself.

9.5
To withdraw with one's person once the task is
achieved — that is the Way of Heaven!

The second structural feature that Wagner noted in the Guodian sections is that
of parallel series.[44] Here, he took the controversial A 1:1 to 2:18 as his example,
arguing that there was a clear, if inconsistent, editorial choice made here to change
the text.

絕知棄辯, 民利百倍.
絕巧棄利, 盜賊亡有.
絕偽棄詐, 民復孝慈.
三言以為辨不足, 或命之、或呼屬:
視素保樸, 少私寡欲.

The first problem is that the number of the items in the two series do not correspond:
one has three, the other two pairs or four items. Mawangdui Copy B inserts an 而 in
the middle of the last phrase, to get 少私而寡欲. While this does not fit the numbers
of characters it reduces the number of statements in the second series to three. Wang
Bi also comments and paraphrases this series as a sequence of three. In regular binary
interlocking parallel style, there is a frequent inversion within the middle of a sequence: ababc becomes abbac. This is not possible in parallel series of the form (also
occurring in the *Laozi*, but not in the Guodian groups):

---

[43] Wagner notes that his translation assumes that someone already has a sharp sword and then grinds
it even sharper, thus becoming an analogy for someone already in an honored position who brags about
it in public and draws the envy and opposition of everyone; the only point of importance in his translation is to make the structural links visible.

[44] See also Wagner's comments on *Laozi* 17/18, pp. 240–41.

1|A
   2|B
      3|C
         4|D
5|A
   6|B
      7|C
         8|D

with possible general statements between the two series or at the end. Lining up the parallel statements in the Mawangdui and Wang Bi *Laozi*, we get the combinations:

絕聖棄智      with
                          見素

絕仁棄義      with
                          抱樸

絕巧棄利      with
                          少私寡欲

In these combinations, the right-hand terms signal some sort of public political performance of the ruler. A bright commentator, such as Wang Bi, would directly link these parallel items; Wang Bi wrote:

竭聖智以治巧偽未若見質素以靜民欲
興仁義以敦薄俗未若抱樸以全篤實
多巧利以興事用未若寡私欲以息華競 .[45]

This establishes a tightly structured and tightly argued statement of the following form:

1|A
   2|B
      3|C
         4|X
5|A
   6|B
      7|C

(Above, X means "phrase pertaining to entire series"; it is not part of the series.)

In the Mawangdui texts, the above interpretation is also plausible. However, while the Guodian A keeps the text of the last items, its text for the first three is radically

---

[45] *Laozi Weizhi Li Lüe*, in Lou Yulie 樓宇烈 , ed., *Wang Bi Ji Jiaoshi* 王弼集校釋 (Beijing: Zhonghua Press, 1980, 2 vols.), p. 198.

changed both in vocabulary and in sequence. The combinations we would have for the Guodian text are:

絕智棄卞 (辯)　　　with

　　　　　　　　　　見素

絕巧棄利　　　　　with

　　　　　　　　　　保樸

絕偽棄詐　　　　　with

　　　　　　　　　　少私寡欲

The first conclusion is that these two lists do not match, which is most clearly evident in the third item. Here, 絕巧棄利 is the only possible partner for 少私寡欲, but it occurs elsewhere instead. Looking at it more closely, none of the three provides anything like a proper fitting. The first four items, to be abandoned with great benefit in the Mawangdui and Wang Bi texts, namely Sageliness, Knowledge, Humaneness, and Justice were clearly dear to Confucianists, even if we find much criticism (for example in the *Wu Xing*) of the superficial and external manner of people's adherence to these principles. The Guodian resets the target in the first three items against sly and cunning sophists of the Mohist kind. Wagner concluded that this was a conscious act of textual interference, but, simultaneously, the status of the text was already high enough to limit such interference to the absolute minimum. Therefore the last three items were not changed in their sequence and content. The jarring non-fit between the two lists signals this inconsistent interference.

Wagner further noted, with regard to the question of the correct transcriptions of the characters of the first Guodian list here into modern standard characters, that he did not consider the alternatives suggested on the basis of graphic and phonetic considerations as conclusive since sequences of value-laden terms (in this case, the parallel-style sequences) are not innocent but hierarchical. Normally the best is in the beginning and the worst at the end, though sometimes it is the other way around. Disclaiming sufficient knowledge to support or challenge the analysis of the characters given as 卞 (辯), 偽, and 詐, Wagner nevertheless pointed out that they are all controversial. However, he thought that a rule can be made that any analysis must take into account the hierarchical relationships between the terms. Thus, it is implausible that 卞 should be identified as 聖 since this would go against what he understood as the standard sequence, i.e. 聖智. Nor does it seem possible to identify 偽 and 慮 (which Qiu Xigui had suggested reading as 詐) with 仁 and 義 because in a sequence starting with 智, these terms could not come after 巧 and 利.

Xing Wen also discussed the order of key philosophical concepts in the texts with reference to the *Wu Xing*. His findings are discussed in detail in a later section (pp. 172–74); they support the idea that the order in which such concepts were presented was considered to be significant and that a particular order would be prevalent at a particular period of time. However, Xing Wen also gave an example of how the order could change over time; his research suggested that, at the time of the writing of the Guodian slips, the concepts 聖 and 智 were always presented in this order, but that at an earlier stage the order was 智 before 聖 .

Carine Defoort also analyzed the relationship between structure and meaning in the Guodian *Laozi*. Her assigned section was *Laozi* B, slips 1 to 8, which is a discrete section in the Guodian slips, containing a black square mark at its end. In this section, the topics of politics and self-cultivation are combined. The first nine lines, B 1:1 to 3:7 [chapter 59], are concerned with self-cultivation and have the structure of a chain. Each line proposes a main idea, which is followed up in the next line:

治人事天 , 莫若嗇.
夫唯嗇 , 是以早服 , 是以早服是謂 …
不克.
不克 , 則莫知其極 ,
莫知其極 , 可以有國.
有國之母 , 可以長…
長生久視之道也 .

Defoort also noted that the language of this section is particularly close to that of the Mawangdui silk-manuscript Copy B.

In the next section, B 3:8 to 4:7 [chapter 48a], clauses 1 and 2 and clauses 3 and 4 form contrasting pairs, leading to a climax and paradox, "doing nothing and leaving nothing undone":

1. 學者日益 ,
2. 為道者日損 .

3. 損之或損 , 以至亡為也 .
4. 亡為而亡不為 .

Here, there is merely cultivation, which might possibly result in political action.

In B 4:8 to 5:11 [chapter 20a], the first line stands alone. The phrases 2/3 and 4/5 are parallel pairs. Clauses 6 and 7 also form a pair, but their relationship with the previous lines is not clear. The character 人 belongs to the previous chapter in spite of the punctuation, as previously discussed.

1. 絕學亡憂 .

2. 唯與呵 ,
3. 相去幾何 ?

4. 美與惡 ,
5. 相去何若 ?

6. 人之所畏 ,
7. 亦不可以不畏人 .

The next section, B 5:12 to 8:23 [chapter 13], has a quite particular structure. The meaning of the first clause is explained by clauses 3 to 7, while the second clause is explained by clauses 8 to 11. Then, lines 12 to 15 give an opinion.

1. 寵辱若驚,

2. 貴大患若身.

3. 何為寵辱?
4. 寵為下也.
5. 得之若驚,
6. 失之若驚,
7. 是為寵辱若驚.

8. □□□□□若身?
9. 吾所以有大患者,
10. 為吾有身.
11. 及吾亡身,或何□

12. □□□□□為天下,
13. 若可以託天下矣.
14. 愛以身為天下,
15. 若何以迻天下矣.

Marc Kalinowski commented on variation in structure, specifically line length, between the Guodian *Laozi* materials and editions of the received *Laozi*. The example he gave was from A 33:1 to 35:17 [chapter 55]. In the Guodian materials, clauses 3 and 4 of this section are:

3. 虺蠆蟲蛇弗蓳,
4. 攫鳥猛獸弗扣,

Both clauses are made up of six characters; Kalinowski represents this structure as 6:6. In the Mawangdui copies these lines are also in the 6:6 pattern. If one looks at the seventeen received editions listed in Shima Kunio's *Rōshi kōsei* (Tokyo: Kyūko, 1973), p. 170, it appears that only one maintains this 6:6 pattern (Fan Yingyuan edition). It is noteworthy that all the Wang Bi editions follow a somehow distorted 6:4:4 pattern:

蜂蠆虺蛇不螫,
猛獸不據,
攫鳥不搏.

Whereas most of the other received editions have a 4:4:4 structure (eleven out of seventeen):

毒虫不螫，
猛獸不擔，
攫鳥不搏．

*Themes*

During our discussion sessions, several scholars suggested that there are a few main themes that run through the Guodian *Laozi* materials. Furthermore, some people conjectured that each of the *Laozi* slip-text groups (A, B, and C) has one or two characteristic themes particular to it. This led to the question of the relationship between the slip texts and to various theories about the compilation of the Guodian texts.

The question of thematic consistency was first raised by Harold Roth in his paper on methodological issues (see pp. 71–88). Roth had suggested that we should take the Guodian texts A, B, and C as integral texts and examine the ideology of the material from that point of view. In his opinion, inner cultivation and its application to rulership — rulership in the sense of the tools the ruler needs to govern effectively, rather than "government" or "politics" in general — make up the central theme, as well as a key to understanding the history of these texts as part of a larger corpus of related material. For the authors of the Guodian *Laozi* parallels, virtually the only one of these tools for governing of importance was breathing meditation, which they developed and advocated so as to cause rulers to have a selfless and dispassionate state of mind.

Wang Bo identified two main themes in the Guodian *Laozi* materials and suggested that the grouping of the slips in bundles was based on these themes. These themes were self-cultivation 修身 and state governance 治國. As noted above (p. 137), Wang Bo took the "tadpole" symbol as a section divider and reordered the slips in *Laozi* A, according to their content, into two subgroups:

Subgroup 1: slips 1 to 20, and 25 to 32
Subgroup 2: slips 21 to 24, and 33 to 39.

This rearrangement divides *Laozi* A into two sections, each punctuated at its conclusion with the "tadpole" symbol. The theme of the first is state governance; the theme of the second is self-cultivation, as well as *dao* 道 and *tian dao* 天道 , i.e., the "way" and "way of heaven."

Wang Bo further argued that the *Laozi* B materials are concerned with self-cultivation and *Laozi* C with governing. Thus, the two subgroups of slips in *Laozi* A form a pair, as do *Laozi* B and C taken together. These two pairs may have been compiled at different times and for different purposes. His conclusion was that there had existed already a "five-thousand-word *Laozi*," i.e., a version of the received text, and that the Guodian groups are selections from that text made on the basis of similarity in theme. The Guodian selection may have been made for a specific purpose, such as teaching.

According to Harold Roth's analysis, inner cultivation and its application to rulership are the main theme of all the Guodian *Laozi* materials. Roth gave the two following examples of sections which he believed contradicted Wang Bo's hypothesis of two paired, but distinct, themes. Both were in Wang Bo's *Laozi* A, subgroup 1, which he had identified as concerned primarily with governing. The first is A 27:3 to 29:16 [chapter 56], which Roth analyzed, and translated, as concerned with reducing sense perception (Harold Roth's translation):

知之者弗言，言之者弗知．
閉其兌，塞其門，和其光，
同其塵，銼其銳，解其紛，是謂玄同．
故不可得而親，亦不可得而疏；
不可得而利，亦不可得而害；
不可得而貴，亦不可得而賤．
故為天下貴．■

Those who know of this do not speak of it;
Those who speak of this do not know of it.

Close the holes.
Block the doors.
Blend the light.
Merge with the dust.
Sever the bonds.
Untie the knots.
This is called "the Profound Merging."

Therefore you cannot get close to it
Nor can you be far from it.
You cannot benefit it
Nor can you harm it.
You cannot ennoble it
Nor can you debase it.

Therefore it is valued by all under the heavens.

According to Roth, this passage begins by identifying its teaching as esoteric: it is really to be known directly through practical instruction from a teacher and not spoken of by anyone not so instructed. It then proceeds to describe, in deliberately allusive terms, a teaching of meditation in which one gradually restricts sense perception (closes the holes; blocks the doors), and relaxes attempts to control the many details of conscious experience (blends the light, merges with the dust) until one is able to sever the attachment to one's self and its turbulent emotional life (sever the bonds, untie the knots). It is at this point that one attains the most valued state of "Profound Merging," in which one directly attains union with the Dao.

Roth argued further that this passage presents a primary way of mystical self-cultivation found throughout the early Daoist tradition in which the adept practices a regular circulation of the breathing in order to first calm the mind and then to systematically empty out its normal contents until a profound state of tranquillity is attained in which one directly experiences the Dao, the primary power that underlies and infuses everything in the cosmos. He has termed the practice "inner cultivation" based on the oldest surviving work in which it is first presented, the "Nei Ye 內業" ("Inward Training") text from the *Guanzi* 管子,[46] according to which it would confer on the adept a much-prized mental clarity and physical vitality. A similar method is also described in the *Laozi* B materials (B 13:1–20), which Wang Bo also understood as dealing with self-cultivation. It contains the following parallel lines (Roth's translation):

閉其門, 塞其兌, 終身不棘.
啟其兌, 瘱其事, 終身不逑.

Close the doors.
Block the holes.
And your allotted years will be free from toil.
Open the holes.
Fill yourself with worldly affairs.
And your allotted years will never be reached.

In reply, Wang Bo noted that this section from *Laozi* B refers specifically to self-cultivation, with the term 終身, whereas the *Laozi* A section does not have this phrase; i.e., the connection to self-cultivation is not clear. Paul Thompson wondered who the 其 in these lines refers to: the sage-ruler or the people? Could this in fact be a lesson in rulership, a description of how to treat the people?

The second section Roth looked at was A 33:1 to 35:17 [chapter 55], which he felt was concerned with self-cultivation, not governing (Roth's translation):

含德之厚者, 比於赤子.
虺蠆蟲蛇弗螫,
攫鳥猛獸弗敏, 骨弱筋柔而捉固.
未知牝牡之合, 脧怒, 精之至也.
終日呼而不憂, 和之至也,
和曰常, 知和曰明.

---

[46] For details of the practice and its role in the foundational stages of "Daoism," see Roth, *Original Tao*.

益生曰祥 , 心使氣曰強 ,
物壯則老 , 是謂不道 .

Those who are filled with an abundance of inner power can be
  compared to baby boys.
Vipers, scorpions, insects, and snakes will not sting them.
Predatory birds and wild beasts will not strike them.
Their bones are soft, their muscles are supple, yet their grip is strong.
They get an erection before even knowing of the union of male and female: this is
  the perfection of the vital essence.
They scream all day without getting hoarse: this is the perfection of the harmony
  (of the vital breath).
This harmony is called the Constant.
Knowing this harmony is called Illumination.
Increasing vitality (through this harmony) is called good fortune.
(But) for the mind to control the vital breath is called "forcing."
For a thing in its prime to grow old, this is what we designate as "not the Way."

Some of the participants suggested that the two themes could be understood as
one, since the ruler might cultivate himself, by the means indicated, in order to be
able to govern. While agreeing that this interpretation was the principal theme of the
Guodian *Laozi* parallels as a whole, Roth insisted that this passage was primarily concerned with inner cultivation and did not discuss rulership. It is recommending the
cultivation of a relaxed and harmonious circulation of the vital breath, one in which
the mind does not forcibly control the breathing, as in Mencius' story of the "man
from Song" (*Mencius* 2A.2), which mentions that the practice increases vital essence,
inner power, and one's overall vitality, and prevents one from too quickly becoming
old when in the prime of life.

Many of the discussants, in their analyses of particular sections, addressed the
question of whether there is thematic consistency in the Guodian material. For example, Carine Defoort noted that in B 1:1 to 8:23 [corresponding to chapters 59, 48a,
20a, and 13] self-cultivation and politics are combined. The first part of this section is
concerned with self-cultivation; and in B 5:12 to 8:23, as well as in the last few lines of
B 7:21 to 8:23, the topic is *tianxia* 天下 ("below heaven"), i.e., "the world," which
implies discussion of governing:

□□□□□為天下 ,
若可以託天下矣 .
愛以身為天下 ,
若何以达天下矣 . ■

Chen Guying suggested that the main topic of this whole section is that one must 貴

身 ("value one's person") before one can 治國 ("govern the state"), so that this is still related to self-cultivation. Defoort further observed that in the section B 3:8 to 4:7, the topic is self-cultivation, whereas in the received and Mawangdui texts there are several additional lines, not found here, which discuss government:

取天下常以無事
及其有事
不足以取天下

Chen Guying added that there are two possible explanations for this: one, that the source from which the Guodian slips were copied did not have these lines; or two, that the copyist removed the section purposely because he was collecting sections concerning self-cultivation, not governing.

*Particular Concepts*

Although the lines in the Guodian *Laozi* materials correspond to lines in the received text, there are significant differences in wording. Some of these bear on our understanding of specific philosophical concepts as they appear in the *Laozi* and on the history of Daoist philosophy. Others are important in understanding the philosophical stance of the Guodian *Laozi* more generally.

The philosophical concepts discussed below include: 道 and 物; 聖人; 有 and 無; 守中; and 亡為而亡不為.

*a.* 道 *and* 物

Wang Bo discussed how the Guodian *Laozi* affects our understanding of how *dao* 道 was conceptualized in early Chinese philosophy. *Dao* is generally described as 無形 無象 ("without shape and without image"), but Zhang Dainian has suggested that in the received *Laozi*, *dao* is considered to be 無形而有象 ("without shape and yet having an image").[47] The difference, then, between *dao* and normal things is that *dao* has *xiang* 象, an "image," but is without *xing* 形, "shape."

This concept becomes more significant in light of the Guodian *Laozi*'s description of *dao* as 有狀混成 ("there is a *form*, formed from murk") (A 21:1–4), where the received text has 有物混成 ("there is a *thing*, formed from murk") [chapter 25]. Unlike the received *Laozi*, the Guodian *Laozi* does not describe *dao* as a *wu* 物 "thing." And elsewhere in the Guodian texts we actually find a definition of *wu* 物: 凡見者之 謂物, i. e., "everything that can be seen is called '*wu*'" (*Xing Zi Ming Chu* 性自命出 slip 12); but *dao* cannot be seen. The *Zhuangzi*, too, never describes *dao* using the term *wu*.

[47] Zhang Dainian 張岱年, "Daojia Xuanzhi Lun 道家玄旨論," *Daojia Wenhua Yanjiu* 4 (1994), pp. 1– 8; also Zhang Dainian, *Zhongguo Gudian Zhexue Gainian Fanchou Yaolun* 中國古典哲學概念範疇要論 (Beijing: Zhongguo Shehui Kexue Press, 1989), pp.103–9; translation by Edmund Ryden, Yale University Press, forthcoming.

So, the Guodian *Laozi* tells us that *dao* is not a *wu*, but it has a *zhuang* 狀, a "form." This reminds us of the line from chapter 14 of the received *Laozi*, not found in the Guodian materials, and already pointed out by Qiu Xigui in his discussion of the character 狀 : 無狀之狀, 無物之象, i.e., "a form without form, an image without substance." Here, both the terms *zhuang* 狀, "form," and *xiang* 象, "image," are used to describe *dao*, while the term *wu* 物 is specifically mentioned as a property the *dao* does not have.

Thus, from reading the Guodian *Laozi*, the difference between *dao* and *wu* becomes more apparent and supports the suggestion that in the *Laozi*, the *dao* is conceived as 無形而有象 ("without shape and yet having an image").

b. 聖人

Rudolf Wagner noted that in comparison with the received text of the *Laozi* we find relatively few examples in the Guodian *Laozi* materials of the phrase 是以聖人 ("this is why the sage…"), which links a given principle with the often-cited hallmark of wise conduct. In the received *Laozi*, of 81 chapters, we find this phrase in 28 chapters, just under 35%. In the Guodian materials the figures are laid out in the following:

| TOTAL NO. OF CORRESPONDING CHAPTERS IN EACH SLIP-GROUP | NO. OF CHAPTERS WITH PHRASE " 是以聖人 " | PERCENTAGE CHAPS. WITH " 是以聖人 " |
|---|---|---|
| *Laozi* A has 20 chaps. | 4 | 20 |
| *Laozi* B has 8 chaps. | 0 | 0 |
| *Laozi* C has 4 chaps. | 1 | 25 |

Here we have 5 chapters out of 32, a little more than 15%. Wagner concluded that the concept of the 聖人 ("sage") appears to be less important in the Guodian *Laozi* materials than in the received text. Thus, the slip-texts are less of a political treatise on how the ruler should behave and less concerned than the received text with opposing the doctrine of other schools.

c. 有 *and* 無

Chen Guying pointed out an important difference between the Guodian *Laozi* materials and the received text in their treatment of these terms:

Guodian A 37:5–27: 天下之物生於又 (有), 生於亡. ■

Received, chapter 40: 天下萬物生於有, 有生於無.

The received version suggests that 無 ("nothing") is equivalent to *dao*, while 有 ("something") is closer to 萬物 ("myriad things"). This however does not correspond with the treatment of those terms in chapter 1 of the received text: 同出而異名 ("they come from the same origin, but are different in name"); here both 有 and 無 refer to 道. The Guodian version solves the problem: the things of the world are generated from both "something" and "nothing." In fact, this also fits with the phrase from chapter 1 of the received, given just above. With this new reading, Chen observed, it becomes possible to talk about the ontology of the *Laozi*.

### d. 守中 *and* 守靜

Chen Guying noted that where the received text, chapter 16, contains the phrase 守靜 ("hold to stillness"), the Guodian A 24:1–25 gives us 守中 ("hold to the center"). This phrase also occurs in chapter 5 of the received text, 多言數窮,不如守中, and the *Zhuangzi* also speaks of 養中 "nourishing the center." Thus, he argued, the concept of *zhong* 中, "centrality," was important to the school of Lao-Zhuang, although many scholars have associated it only with the Confucian school.[48]

### e. 亡為而亡不為 *("when there is no doing, there is nothing not done")*

This line is found in the Guodian *Laozi* B 3:8 to 4:7. In the received text, the corresponding line is found in chapter 48: 無為而無不為 (see pp. 139–40 for previous discussion of this passage). Robert Henricks noted that the Mawangdui silk-manuscript copies do not have this line and that Gao Ming had suggested that this phrase might be a later addition or alteration. Henricks asked Gao Ming his thoughts about the phrase's appearance in the Guodian materials. Gao Ming pointed out that the Mawangdui copies have lacunae for this section and that his point was that there are several variations of this line in different editions. For example, Yan Zun's 嚴遵 *Daode Zhenjing Zhigui* 道德真經指歸 states " 無為而無以為 " in the corresponding line.

### Philosophical Stance

Robert Henricks noted that the very first lines of the Guodian material (A 1:1–24) are significant in helping us to understand its philosophical stance.

> 絕知棄辯,民利百倍. 絕巧棄利,盜賊亡有. 絕偽棄詐,民復孝慈 .[49] "Eliminate knowledge, get rid of distinction, and the people will benefit a hundredfold. Eliminate artistry, get rid of profit, and there will no longer be robbers and thieves. Eliminate transformation, get rid of deliberation, and the people will return to piety and compassion."

In contrast, we read in the corresponding part of the received text (chapter 19):

> 絕聖棄智,民利百倍. 絕仁棄義,民復孝慈. 絕巧棄利,盜賊無有 . "Eliminate sageliness, throw away knowledge and the people will benefit a hundredfold. Eliminate humanity, throw away rightness, and the people will return to filial piety and compassion. Eliminate craftiness, throw away profit, then we will not have

[48] See Chen Guying, "Chu Du Jianben *Laozi* 初讀簡本《老子》," *Wenwu* 1998.10, pp. 55–56, for a published version of this view and his following points.

[49] This reading follows the *Guodian Chu Mu Zhujian* and Qiu Xigui's annotations. For other readings of the characters in this line, see Edmund Ryden's apparatus and notes.

robbers and thieves" (Robert Henricks' translations.)

The Guodian advocates eliminating such vices as disputation, artifice, and deceit, but not the Confucian virtues of 仁 ("humaneness"), 義 ("rightness") or 聖 ("sageliness"), i.e., the objection is to learned rhetoric. On the basis of this line and the omission of certain other chapters of the received text from the Guodian *Laozi* materials, many of the discussants thought that the Guodian slips do not have the anti-Confucian stance found in the received *Laozi* because of their earlier date. Some felt that this language might be peculiar to the Guodian text.

Chen Guying argued that the Guodian slips are neither anti-Confucian, nor anti-Legalist. The treatment of the concepts of *ren* 仁 ("humaneness"), 義 ("rightness"), and 法 ("law") in the *Laozi* materials was adduced to support his claim. He noted that certain passages of the received *Laozi*, such as chapter 19 (text given just above), advocate eliminating *ren* and *yi*, thus leading scholars to conclude that the *Laozi* is critical of these Confucian doctrines, and that it presents a counter-argument to the *ren* and *yi* doctrine of Confucians, Mohists, or Mencians. But the Guodian text does not support this conclusion, since there is no attack on these concepts.

Chen noted that the phrase in chapter 8 of the received *Laozi*: 與善仁 ("in social intercourse, we value humaneness"; editors' translation) is not only not opposed to *ren*, but actually praises it. The Daoist opposition to *ren* and *yi* came later, and where it does occur, for example in the Waipian 外篇 portion of *Zhuangzi*, it does so as an attack on the use of *ren* and *yi* as mere tools of governing. This omission from the Guodian *Laozi* is important moreover because opposition to *ren* and *yi* in the *Laozi* has been used as evidence to argue that the *Laozi* must be later than the *Lunyu*, *Mozi*, and even the *Mencius*, all of which advocate them.

Sarah Allan and Qiu Xigui further observed that the contrast between *Laozi* C 2:22 to 3:6: 故大道廢，焉有仁義，and received text, chapter 18: 大道廢，有仁義，does not necessarily imply that the Guodian version opposes *ren* and *yi*, and in fact a possible translation is: "Thus, when the great way was abandoned, how could there be *ren* and *yi*?" Moreover, the two terms are paralleled with others in the same section that have a positive connotation, e.g., 孝慈 ("filial love and parental kindness") and 正臣 ("upright ministers").[50]

Chen Guying also discussed the stances towards *fa* 法 ("law") that are found in the received *Laozi*. The following line from chapter 57 has often been taken to show that the *Laozi* is anti-Legalist: 法令滋彰，盜賊多有 ("The better known the laws and edicts, the more thieves and robbers there are"; D. C. Lau's translation).[51] However,

---

[50] Alternatively, 焉, which appears as 安 (Copy B) and 案 (Copy A) in the Mawangdui *Laozi*, could be resumptive, as in Robert Henricks' translation, "Therefore, when the Great Way is rejected, it is then that we have the virtues of humanity and righteousness" (Henricks, *Lao-tzu Te-tao ching*, p. 222).

[51] *Chinese Classics: Tao Te Ching*, p. 83.

the corresponding section in the Guodian A 31:7–14 is: 法物滋彰 , 盜賊多有 . The Heshang Gong 河上公 edition has the same wording and glosses 法物 as 珍好之物 : "the more precious things are displayed, the more thieves and robbers there are" (editors' translation). Here, then, an increase in thieves and robbers is not correlated with an excess of laws and edicts, thus refuting the idea that the *Laozi* is opposed to Legalist thought.

Further discussion of the philosophical import of the Guodian *Laozi* may be found in part three, following, under the section "The Question of Philosophical Schools." For more on variant characters, which may have philosophical implications, see the notes to Ryden's edition of the text in Section III.

## PART THREE: OTHER TEXTS AND THE QUESTION OF PHILOSOPHICAL SCHOOLS

The conference proceeded to discuss the *Tai Yi Sheng Shui* 太一生水 in the same detail as it had the *Laozi* material. As we have already mentioned and will discuss again below, some of the participating scholars questioned the separation of this text from the *Laozi* material. Nevertheless, we include the discussion here under the rubric of "Other Texts." After the *Tai Yi Sheng Shui*, we spent a session on the *Wu Xing* 五行 , and this is summarized below. Li Xueqin then gave an overview of the other texts found in Guodian Tomb Number One (see pp. 107–11) and the group discussed them in a general manner. A few specific issues were raised concerning the *Tang Yu zhi Dao* 唐虞之道, the *Zhong Xin zhi Dao* 忠信之道, and the *Yu Cong* 語叢, and these are also summarized below. The more general problem of the implication of the texts as a corpus found together in a single tomb and the discussion concerning philosophical schools is summarized at the end of this part.

### Tai Yi Sheng Shui 太一生水

The group of slips designated *Tai Yi Sheng Shui* in *Guodian Chu Mu Zhujian* was probably originally bound together with the *Laozi* C material. Peng Hao explained that there is no physical distinction between the *Laozi* C and *Tai Yi Sheng Shui* slips, i.e., the shape of the slips, distance between the bindings, and calligraphy are the same as that of *Laozi* C. The separation into two texts in *Guodian Chu Mu Zhujian* is based entirely upon content. The editorial principle in writing the transcriptions was that, when in doubt, divide the text into smaller rather than larger units, for ease of analysis (see p. 122). An important question follows from this: what was the relationship, if any, between this text and the *Laozi*. Were they originally a part of the *Laozi*, or one of its source texts, discarded when the *Daodejing* reached its current form? Or was this an addendum or commentary created in the state of Chu around the time of the burial (the last quarter of the fourth century BC)?

The *Tai Yi Sheng Shui* is composed of three sections of continuous text. As with the *Laozi* material, their published order is tentative. Indeed, we do not know whether they were originally put at the end, beginning, or interspersed with the *Laozi* C passages. The longest, slips 1 to 8, is a continuous, well constructed passage that many of the conference scholars understood as the earliest known Chinese cosmogony. It begins with the line: 太一生水 ("The Great One generated water") and ends inconclusively, with a damaged slip: 君子知此之謂 ... ("the gentleman, knowing this, calls it…"). Slip 9 is also missing its bottom portion.[52] Since there is no clear continuity with either of the other sections, it constitutes a section by itself. Slips 10 to 12 are another section of continuous text.

The *Tai Yi Sheng Shui* has no parallel in the received tradition, and in that fact alone elicited immediate excitement. Cui Renyi 崔仁義 had already written about it before the publication of *Guodian Chu Mu Zhujian*, and Li Xueqin had made a tentative identification (on the basis of the material presented in Cui's articles) with a lost text known as the *Guanyin Shu* 關尹書 .[53] Li Ling, Isabelle Robinet, and Sarah Allan were assigned to present their views and lead discussion on it, but many of the other participants also expressed opinions about this text.

Li Ling, who had previously published on the cult of *Tai Yi* 太一 in the state of Chu during the Warring States period and its development in the Han and later periods, placed the Guodian text within the context of his earlier research.[54] In the notes to the text in *Guodian Chu Mu Zhujian*, 太一 is identified as *dao* 道. However, Li Ling observed that, before the Han dynasty, it was not simply an equivalent to *dao*, but referred to a linked set of concepts: an ultimate, a supreme spirit, an astral body, and the *dao*.

Li Ling stressed the importance of the *Tai Yi Sheng Shui* for the study of Chinese cosmology. First, he noted that its cosmological scheme is similar to Song period diagrammatic representations known as "Taiji tu 太極圖 " (see below, p. 167), although he emphasized that he was not suggesting that these Song diagrams are directly related to the *Tai Yi Sheng Shui*. He then discussed the Mawangdui "Bibing tu" 避兵圖 (see below). Li Ling argued that this drawing is an abstract representation of

---

[52] It is placed as part of the *Tai Yi Sheng Shui* because of the shape of the slip and style of the calligraphy, and because it has no corresponding material in the received *Laozi*; conversation with Peng Hao (Sarah Allan).

[53] See Cui Renyi, "Jingmen Chu Mu Chutu de Zhujian *Laozi* Chutan 荊門楚墓出土的竹簡《老子》初探 ," *Jingmen Shehui Kexue* 1997.5; idem, "Shilun Jingmen Zhujian *Laozi* de Niandai 試論荊門竹簡《老子》的年代," *Jingmen Daxue Xuebao* 1997.2, pp. 38–42; Li Xueqin 李學勤 , "Jingmen Guodian Chu Jian Suojian Guanyin Yishuo 荊門郭店楚簡所見關尹遺説 ," *Zhongguo Wenwu Bao*, April 8, 1998, p. 3. Note that the transcriptions used by Cui differ from those published in *Guodian Chu Mu Zhujian*.

[54] See Li Ling, "An Archeological Study of Taiyi (Grand One) Worship," translated by Donald Harper, *Early Medieval China* 2 (1995–96), pp. 1–39; idem, "Mawangdui Han Mu *Shenqi Tu* Yingshu Bibing Tu 馬王堆漢墓《神祇圖》應屬避兵圖 ," *Kaogu* 1991.10, pp. 940–42.

the *Tai Yi Sheng Shui*
text. The most impor-
tant part of the drawing
is the *Tai Yi* and the
three dragons.

Rao Zongyi had
suggested that these
three dragons are the
"three ones" 三一 men-
tioned in early texts.[55]
The "three ones" are Tian
Yi 天一, Di Yi 地一, and
Tai Yi 太一, and relate to
the San Huang 三皇 of
the Han dynasty dis-
cussed many years ago
by Qian Baocong 錢寶琮
and others.[56] Tian Yi

Mawangdui Bibing tu

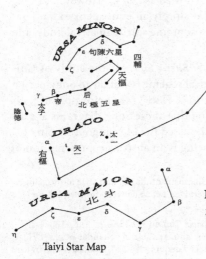

Taiyi Star Map

correlates with the three constellations
Tai Sui 太歲, the Big Dipper, and the
Green Dragon 青龍, and represents water. The Yellow Dragon is the earth
dragon and rests in water.

Li Ling then discussed the astronomical aspects of *Tai Yi* (see left; based on Qian
Baocong, p. 2465). He observed that *Tai Yi* has
been identified with different stars at different
periods due to the precession of the equinoxes.
Nevertheless, its philosophical and religious significance is clear, and it clearly served as an abstract astronomical marker. Analyzing the
Mawangdui "Bibing tu" in the light of the "Rui

[55] Rao Zongyi 饒宗頤, "Tu Shi yu Cifu — Mawangdui Xinchu *Da Yi Chuxingtu* Sijian 圖詩與辭賦馬
王堆新出《大一出行圖》私見," Hunansheng Bowuguan 湖南省博物館, ed., *Sishi Zhounian Lunwenji*
四十週年論文集 (n.p.: Hunan Jiaoyu Press, 1996), pp. 79–82.

[56] Qian Baocong, "Tai Yi Kao 太一考," *Yanjing Xuebao* 1932.12, pp. 2449–78.

*ying tu* 瑞應圖 ” from Dunhuang (Pelliot 2683), Li Ling constructed a diagram to help us read the *Tai Yi Sheng Shui*. Here, see below left, he posits a "sub-*Tai Yi*," as well as the primary *Tai Yi*, that functions on the same level as the 天一 ("celestial one") and 地一 ("earthly one").[57] Tian Yi is equivalent to the celestial (green) dragon 天龍 and represents 天 ("sky").

TAI YI
太一
|
sub-*TAI YI* 太一

Celestial One    Earthly One
天一              地一
|                |
Sky              Earth
天                地
|                |
Water            Fire
水                火
|                |
Wood             Metal
木                金

"Earthly one" is equivalent to the earthly (yellow) dragon 地龍 and represents 地 ("earth"). Furthermore, he noted, 天龍 is also a river dragon, and so also represents 水 , water.

Li Ling then constructed a diagram to represent the *Tai Yi Sheng Shui* text. Here we have a cosmogony, and creation occurs as we move down the page (see diagram, right).

Li Ling emphasized that the process of creation is actually circular; for example water and *Tai Yi* together produce sky, and sky and *Tai Yi* produce earth. He further noted that water plays a pivotal role in the process. Moreover, here *shen* and *ming* are treated separately, whereas, in many texts, they are a compound term, 神明 .

TAI YI
太一
|
Water
水

Sky          Earth
天            地

*shen*        *ming*
神            明
*yang*        *yin*
陽            陰
*spring,*     *autumn,*
*summer*      *winter*
春夏          秋冬
*heat*        *cold*
熱            滄
*dry*         *wet*
燥            濕

*year*
歲

Following Li Ling's presentation, Isabelle Robinet talked about the *Tai Yi Sheng Shui* in the context of Daoist religion. She argued that it is not only the earliest Chinese cosmogony, but a specifically Daoist one. She began with the cosmogonies we already know from Daoist literature and drew diagrams to illustrate these. The first cosmogony, found in the received *Laozi* (chapter 42), can be represented as a process of sexual union, as in the right-hand diagram.

*Dao* 道

One          Two

Three
|
The ten-thousand things

In the "Xici 繫辭 " section of the *Zhou Yi* 周易 and the *Lüshi Chunqiu* 呂氏春秋 ("Da Yue 大樂 "), the process is one of division:

太極 / 太一 (Grand Culmination/Tai Yi)

↓

兩儀 (Two principles)

↓

四象 (Four images)

[57] See Li Ling, "San Yi Kao 三一考 ," *Zhexue yu Wenhua Yuekan* 26.4 (April 15, 1999), pp. 359–67.

In the *Zhou Yi Weishu* 周易緯書 and the *Xiaojing Weishu* 孝經緯書, and in the *Liezi* 列子, the process is one of transformation 化生：

太易 (Grand Interchangeability)

↓

太初 (Grand Antecedence)

↓

太始 (Grand Initiation)

↓

太素 (Grand Simplicity)

↓

太極 (Grand Culmination)

These represent primal chaos which takes shape gradually. At each stage something appears: the *pneuma* (*qi* 氣), shape (*xing* 形), substance (*zhi* 質). It is a process of transformation.[58]

Robinet then illustrated the description of the cosmogonic process in the *Tai Yi Sheng Shui* with a series of diagrams, each one corresponding to a different section of the text:

*A. Slips 1:1–22*

太一 (1:1)        太一 +水 (1:8–9)        太一 +天 (1:17–8)

↓      反 (1:6)↗        ↓      反 (1:15)↗        ↓

水 (1:4,5)              天 (1:13,14)              地 (1:22)

With these three distinct operations, *Tai Yi* generates Water and Heaven and Earth (the three *guan* 官, "offices," of the Celestial Master Daoists). At first, *Tai Yi* operates alone, then is assisted by the entity it has created. This pattern can be compared with chapter 39 of the received *Laozi* where heaven, earth, and spirit 神明 obtain one 得一.

---

[58] Cf. Isabelle Robinet, "Lun *Tai Yi Sheng Shui* 論《太一生水》," *Daojia Wenhua Yanjiu* 17 (1999), pp. 332–39. See also, Isabelle Robinet, "Genesis and Pre-cosmic Eras in Taoism," forthcoming in the *Festschrift* in honor of Prof. Liu Ts'un-yan, University of Hong Kong Press.

*B. Slips 1:22 to 3:22*

天地 (1:23–24)

↓

神明 (2:5–6 and 2:7–8)

↓

陰陽 (2:16–17 and 2:18–19)

↓

°
°
°

濕燥 (3:19–20 and 3:21–22)

This section ends with the completion of one year 一歲 .

*C. Slips 4:3 to 6:7*

This reverses the above list: B 者, A 之所生也 ("B is that which was generated by A").

*D. Tai Yi: hides* 藏 *(6:12); moves* 行 *(6:15); circles and begins again* 周而又 始 *(6:18–21); mother* 母 *(7.3); principle* 經 *(7:13)*

*Tai Yi* is everywhere, hidden and circulating; it is that which the sky and earth, *yin* and *yang* cannot do, and it exceeds the sky and earth. Thus, it is everywhere, and not a god who has a location and a name.

*E. The Way* 道 *and the Celestial Way* 天道 *(9:1–2, 10:15, and 11.1) whose name is unknown*

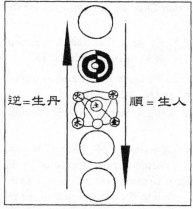

Robinet observed that there is a difference between Daoist and Confucian cosmogonies. Confucian cosmogony recognizes only the 順 (forward) direction, and ends with the creation of human beings. Daoism recognizes both the 順 and the 逆, i.e., the return process by which humans return to the source and 生丹 ("generate cinnabar"); the aim is to fuse with the Dao. The *Tai Yi Sheng Shui* description is typically Daoist: first descending and then ascending. Confucianism lacks this mysticism. And this is a distinction between the mysticism of Daoism and the religion of Confucianism.

After "Shang Yangzi Jin Dan Dayao Tu" 上陽子金丹大要圖 , *Daozang* (Ecole Française d'Extrême-Orient) 1067.3a.

In religion, the origin of the universe is a singular source, the *dao*, the ancestor 祖, *Tai Yi* 太一, or something else, but in mysticism this origin is everywhere and one fuses with it. In religion one uses *li* 禮 ("ceremony") to contact this origin. Confucius said he pays his respects to the gods, but keeps them at a distance; contact is made with them through ceremony. In Daoist mysticism there are no gods but there is *Tai Yi* which is everywhere; *Tai Yi* is not a god. The *Tai Yi Sheng Shui* is thus a specifically Daoist cosmogony.

The final presentation on the *Tai Yi Sheng Shui* was given by Sarah Allan. As in her recent book, *The Way of Water and Sprouts of Virtue*, Allan argued that water was the most important root metaphor for early Chinese philosophical concepts. The cosmology in the *Tai Yi Sheng Shui*, in which water is the origin of everything, is a theoretical formulation of an implicit idea that occurs more generally as a metaphor in a wide range of philosophical texts, though with especial emphasis in the *Laozi*. She then went on to discuss the *Tai Yi Sheng Shui* as it relates to the *Laozi*.[59]

Allan noted that the *Tai Yi Sheng Shui* slips were physically indistinguishable from the *Laozi* C materials and argued that it should be read as part of the same text: the last line, C 13:19 to 14:7 [chapter 64b], is 是以能輔萬物之自然, 而弗敢為 ("This is why he could assist the myriad things in what they do of themselves, yet does not presume to do so") is related in meaning and terminology to the *Tai Yi Sheng Shui*. The verb 輔 ("to assist" — but see Ryden's edition, p. 228, for Harper's suggestion that it should be read as 薄), the *wanwu* 萬物 ("myriad living things"), and the concept of *ziran* 自然 ("what is so of itself") in this line all point towards the language and ideas of what follows in the *Tai Yi Sheng Shui* text.

Allan observed other semantic connections. For example, the line in the *Lüshi Chunqiu* ("Da Yue"), which the annotators of *Guodian Chu Mu Zhujian* note for the identification of *Tai Yi* with the *dao*, reads:

道也者 ... 不可為形, 不可為名, 彊為之名, 謂之太一 ("As for the *dao* ... it cannot be given form; it cannot be named; forced to give it a name, I call it *Tai Yi*").

This is a paraphrase of a line that occurs in the Guodian *Laozi* A text and in the received text (chapter 25). The Guodian form of the line (A 21:21 to 22:6) reads:

未知其名, 字之曰道. 強為之名, 曰大 ("Not knowing its name, I give it the honorific *dao*. Forced to give it a name, I say 'great' ").

The character transcribed 太 in the name *Tai Yi* in *Guodian Chu Mu Zhujian* is written as 大 on the bamboo slips. (*Tai* 太 and *da* 大 were often not distinguished in the writing of this period.) Thus, the *Laozi*'s: "forced to give it a name, I say '*da*,'" may be an indirect reference to *Tai Yi*. This passage may also be linked to the first chapter of the re-

---

[59] See *The Way of Water and Sprouts of Virtue* (Albany: SUNY Press, 1997).

ceived *Laozi* in which the name of the *dao* is described as something that cannot be said: 道可道，非常道．名可名，非常名．無名天地之始，…（"The way that can be spoken of is not the constant way. The name that can be named is not the constant name. That which has no name is the beginning of the sky and earth…"）．

This same concern about the name of the *dao* also occurs in the *Tai Yi Sheng Shui* (slips 10–11):

道亦其字也．請問其名．以道從事者必託其名（"Dao is indeed its honorific, may I ask its name? He who would enact affairs by means of the dao must depend upon its name"）．

Li Xueqin had argued that the *Tai Yi Sheng Shui* acts as a commentary on the passage in the received *Laozi*: 道生一，一生二，二生三，三生萬物 (chapter 42, not in the Guodian material). Allan felt, however, that they might be linked in a general manner by the number one, but that the two passages cannot be reconciled as numerical sequences; they seem to be different systems (one to two to three, versus one to two to four).

In response to Li Ling's description of more than one star position for *Tai Yi*, Allan noted that regardless of astronomical realities, conceptually, *Tai Yi* was the center of the sky, i.e., the pole star seen as located at the center of the sky, in a position corresponding to the celestial north pole. This center may be understood as both an abstract concept and a spirit (the god of the pole star). As a spirit it was that which cannot be named; as an abstraction it was identified with the way (*dao*). The two are correlated with one another. This pattern of identification may explain the importance of not naming in the *Laozi* more generally.[60]

Following these three presentations, several other participants commented on the *Tai Yi Sheng Shui* and the points raised by the three speakers. Rudolf Wagner argued that the *Tai Yi Sheng Shui* text does not describe the cosmogenic or cosmological cycle, as argued by Isabelle Robinet. He agreed that the descending section of the description, from *Tai Yi* to "year," the section in the form "A generates B," is about cosmogony but that the next section, "B is that which was generated by A" (Robinet's process by which humans return to the source), is just a point of logic. The text has described how A produces B, B produces C and so on, and it then simply makes the logical, inductive observation that it must then be the case that C is that which is produced by B, B is that which is produced by A. Marc Kalinowski, however, wondered if the ancient Chinese divided physics and logic in the way Wagner implied.

---

[60] This argument was presented in more detail in S. Allan, "Tai Yi, Shui, Guodian *Laozi* 太一。水。郭店《老子》," presented at the International Symposium on Chu Slips of Guodian, Wuhan University, October, 1999, and in "The One, Water, and the Guodian *Laozi*," forthcoming.

Xing Wen noted that Li Ling's diagram did not properly describe the creation process given in the text and offered an alternative diagram (below). This chart, like Robinet's above, clarifies the role of water and sky, and also shows that 神明 are produced from 天 and 地 together; and, in the same way 陰 and 陽 are produced from 神 and 明 ; and so on.

Xu Kangsheng made the general point that this new text is important because, previously, the earliest example of a detailed cosmogony was that found in the *Huainanzi*; the cosmogonies in the *Laozi* and the *Guanzi* are very brief. Furthermore the description in the Guodian text differs from that in the *Huainanzi* in which the first thing generated by *dao* is *qi* 氣 , while in the *Tai Yi Sheng Shui* it is water. Previously, scholars concentrated on the role of *qi* since a cosmogonic role for water was not known; this still calls for further research.

Wang Bo thought that a detailed comparison should be made between the *Huainanzi* cosmogony and the *Tai Yi Sheng Shui*, since they appear to share some distinct features — for example the creation of 天 before 地 . The *Chuci* should also be compared, particularly to determine the relationship with the 東皇太一 of the "Jiu Ge 九歌 " section. Wang Bo also asked why this piece attaches so much importance to water. He wondered if it could have anything to do with the veneration of water in the Xia dynasty, or even with the man Laozi, who it is said was from the state of Chen 陳 , which also took water as its symbol.[61]

Wang Bo also discussed the nature of the *shen* and *ming*. In the *Tai Yi Sheng Shui* these terms occur in the text between "sky and the earth," which generated them, and *yin* and *yang*, which they, in turn, generated. He suggested that here they refer to the sun and the moon, a meaning also found in the *Zhuangzi*: 神何由降,明何由出. In the *Zhou Yi* ("Shuogua 説卦 " section) the line 幽贊于神明而生蓍 received the following commentary by the Han-era scholar Xun Shuang 荀爽：神者在天 , 明者在地 . 神以夜光 , 明以晝照 ("As for *shen*, it is celestial; *ming* is earthly. *Shen* shines by the night, *ming* shines by day"; editors' translation).

Marc Kalinowski remarked on the importance of water in Chinese cosmology, noting that in the "Shui Di 水地 " chapter of the *Guanzi*, water is taken as the source of all things on earth and that Joseph Needham had already remarked on the theoretical significance of this chapter for Chinese scientific thinking in his *Science and Civilisation in China*. He further noted that the *Tai Yi Sheng Shui* testifies to a specific link between philosophical cosmogonies and Daoism nearly two centuries before their

Diagram:

TAI YI 太一 → 水 天 地 → 神明 → 陰陽 → 四時 → 滄熱 → 濕燥 → 歲

---

[61] See *Zuo Zhuan* (Zhao Gong 昭公 , 5th year): 陳 , 水屬也 ("Chen is of the category water").

extensive use in the *Huainanzi*, especially in the astrological section "Tian Wen Xun 天文訓," and wondered if the Water-Heaven-Earth triad in the *Tai Yi* text might be somehow related to the Three Offices (*sanguan*) of Heaven, Earth, and Water in early Daoist religion.[62]

## *Wu Xing* 五行

The *Wu Xing* was allotted a morning for discussion after three days devoted to the *Laozi* and *Tai Yi Sheng Shui* slips. This text was unknown until a copy was discovered in the Mawangdui tomb in 1973.[63] Previously, the term *wu xing* was associated with cosmological theory of five elements, or five phases. However, the *Xunzi* ("Fei Shier Zi 非十二子") referred to Zisi 子思 and Mencius 孟軻 as advocates of *wu xing*. Since there are no textual references in the *Mencius* to the cosmological theory of five elements and most scholars do not think the theory had been formulated so early, this was difficult to explain. Since the discovery of the Mawangdui text, the *Xunzi* passage has been explained as a reference to the five principles of conduct found in the excavated text (*ren* 仁, *yi* 義, *li* 禮, *zhi* 智, *sheng* 聖). However, the Mawangdui tomb was closed in 168 BC, and most scholars considered the *Wu Xing* text found in it to be in fact later than the *Mencius*. The discovery of a version of this text in a tomb closed around 300 BC, i.e., close to the time of Mencius' death, is therefore of considerable significance to the history of early Chinese philosophical thought.

The conference participants asked to make presentations on the *Wu Xing* were Ikeda Tomohisa and Xing Wen. During and after the presentations other scholars raised further points. Below we have divided the discussion on the *Wu Xing* into three topics: comparison with the Mawangdui *Wu Xing*; philosophical content and the question of schools; and its relationship with the *Laozi*.

### a. Comparison with the Mawangdui Wu Xing

The major difference between the *Wu Xing* of the Guodian bamboo slips and that in the Mawangdui materials is the latter's commentary following the main text. The content of the main text of the two editions is basically the same, save for differences in the order of various sections of the text.

Ikeda Tomohisa, whose book *Maōtai Kanbo Hakusho Gogyōhen Kenkyū* 馬王堆 漢墓帛書五行篇研究 includes an annotated edition of the Mawangdui silk-manuscript *Wu Xing* and a Japanese translation, gave the first presentation.[64] He began by discussing the difference in the two editions of the *Wu Xing*: arguing that the

---

[62] See *Science and Civilisation in China* (Cambridge: Cambridge University Press, 1956) 2, pp. 55 ff.

[63] Guojia Wenwuju Gu Wenxian Yanjiushi 國家文物局古文獻研究室, ed., *Mawangdui Han Mu Boshu* 馬王堆漢墓帛書 (Beijing: Wenwu Press, 1980) 1, pp. 17–24.

[64] *Maōtai Kanbo Hakusho Gogyōhen Kenkyū* (Tokyo: Kyūko Shoin 汲古書院, 1993).

Mawangdui version is earlier because it is more clearly structured than the Guodian's version. Ikeda made three observations to support this. First, citations in the Guodian *Wu Xing* of the *Shijing* 詩經 have been abbreviated and are rather clumsy in comparison with those in the Mawangdui version: slip 12 (Mawangdui line 179; section 5a, as divided in Ikeda's text)[65] is missing two lines that are present in the Mawangdui version (which also precedes the citation with 詩曰 ["the ode says"]). Second, the Mawangdui has added material. Third, the order of key philosophical concepts is different: in Mawangdui, sections 10–12 (silk-manuscript lines 188–90) the order is 仁義禮智 聖 ,[66] whereas in the Guodian version the order is 智聖仁義禮 (slips 20:20 to 21:17). Ikeda also thought that the Mawangdui order is preferable from the point of view of literary style, because the order of these concepts corresponds to the order in which they are discussed in the text as a whole. For example, the last part (sections 23–26, lines 211– 212) talks about *zhi* 智 .[67]

Andrew Meyer asked whether the commentary was later or earlier than the Guodian text. Ikeda Tomohisa thought the commentary had been extant at the time of the Guodian copy. He said there were two possible explanations for the absence of the commentary in the Guodian *Wu Xing*. The first is that no commentary existed; the second, that it existed but was not always appended to every copy of the main text. Ikeda preferred the second explanation, arguing that the text would be very difficult to understand without the assistance of a commentary.

Xing Wen, on the other hand, thought that the Mawangdui commentary is later than the Guodian text. His evidence was the line on slip 28 in the Guodian *Wu Xing*: 聖智,禮樂之所由生也 ("Sagehood and wisdom are that from which the rites and music were generated"). In the Mawangdui text, this line (199–200) is damaged, but the commentary (line 285) has [ 仁 ] 義 , 禮樂所由生也 ("Humaneness and rightness are that from which the rites and music were generated). Xing's argument was that by the time the Mawangdui copy was produced, the principles of *sheng* and *zhi* had been replaced with *ren* and *yi* in the conventional sequence of conceptual importance, but that this evolution was not properly understood at the time of the alteration. Since the commentary follows the altered version, it must be later than the Guodian copy.

Xing Wen also took the Guodian *Wu Xing* to be earlier than the Mawangdui version. Here, again, his reasoning was based upon an historical evolution in the conceptual order in which *ren* and *yi* had replaced the earlier *sheng* and *zhi* in sequence of importance. Xing argued that the Mawangdui version is demonstrably a reordering of the Guodian version. The aim of this reordering was to make the sequence in which key concepts are discussed in the main body of the text parallel their sequence in the

---

[65] Ikeda, *Maōtai*, p. 187.

[66] Ibid., pp. 250, 259, 273.

[67] Ibid., pp. 501–46.

last section of the text. His argument follows.

The last section of the text in the Guodian *Wu Xing* reads: 聞道而悦者, 好仁者也. 聞道而畏者, 好義者也. 聞道而恭者, 好禮者也. 聞道而樂者, 好德者也. The Mawangdui version is essentially the same. The order of concepts is: 仁、義、禮、德. However in the main body of the Guodian *Wu Xing* the order in which these concepts are presented is 德、仁、義、禮. That this was the original order can be seen from the fact that the Mawangdui reordering has resulted in the separation of sections of related ideas. For example, the key concepts in the passage starting with the last character of slip 34 in the Guodian version are 簡 and 行: 不以小道害大道, 簡也. 有大罪而大誅之, 行也. This is followed by a further discussion of the two terms: 不簡, 不行. 不匿, 不辨於道 … . These two sections are clearly related, and their close proximity in the Guodian slips is intentional. In the Mawangdui version, however, they are separated by some seven lines of text (lines 195–202).

Xing Wen compared the Guodian and Mawangdui copies and described the alterations in the Guodian text that would be required to create the order of the Mawangdui texts. He then explained why he thought this reordering took place. He first proposed a reconstruction of how the Guodian copy was altered to produce the Mawangdui text:

1. Guodian, slips 20:20 to 21:17:

不聽不明, 不聖不智, 不智不仁, 不仁不安, 不安不樂, 不樂亡**德**. 不變不悦, 不悦不戚, 不戚不親, 不親不愛, 不愛不**仁**. 不直不迲, 不迲不果, 不果不簡, 不簡不行, 不行不**義**. 不遠不敬, 不敬不嚴, 不嚴不尊, 不尊不恭, 不恭亡**禮**.

The Mawangdui passage is identical, but the first line of the Guodian slip text is transposed to the end of the passage in the Mawangdui text (lines 188–190): 不變不悦, 不悦不戚, 不戚不親, 不親不愛, 不愛不**仁**. 不直不迲, 不迲不果, 不果不簡, 不簡不行, 不行不**義**. 不遠不敬, 不敬不嚴, 不嚴不尊, 不尊不恭, 不恭亡**禮**. 不聽不明, 不聖不智, 不智不仁, 不仁不安, 不安不樂, 不樂亡**德**. The effect of the alteration was to change the order of concepts from 德, 仁, 義, 禮 to 仁, 義, 禮, 德.

2. Guodian, slips 32:6 to 37:15:

顏色 … 禮也 is transposed in the Mawangdui text to just before slip 22:31.

Xing Wen explained the logic behind the reordering. The first alteration results in a change in the order in which key concepts are presented in this section of the text: from 德, 仁, 義, 禮 to 仁, 義, 禮, 德, which then conforms to the order in which these concepts are presented in the last section of the *Wu Xing* (slips 49:7 to 50:21). The second reordering moves the 顏色 … 禮也 section (slips 32:5 to 37:15) to follow directly after 不聽 … 亡德 (20:20 to 21:17). Since this second section first discusses the concepts 悦、戚、親、愛, and then goes on to 仁、義、禮, paralleling the discussion in the first section, these sections correspond to one another when they are placed together in this manner.

Although the reordering does not unduly disrupt the development of the discussion in the section that follows (beginning: 未嘗聞君子道,謂之不聰, then discussing the concepts 聰,明,聖, and 智, thus paralleling the last line of the first section: 不聰不明,不聖不智,不智不仁,不仁不安,不安不樂,不樂亡德), it causes disruption of the section dealing with 簡 and 行, which should follow the 顏色 … 禮也 section (32:6 to 37:15). Thus, it is the Guodian version that is earlier, i.e., the one that has been altered.

The original ordering found in the Guodian text gives a clear and well-ordered discussion, Xing Wen continued. He described this as follows:

a. slips 20:20 to 22:30 (quoted above) are a general discussion on 德, 仁, 義, 禮.

b. slips 22:31 to 32:5: 未嘗聞君子道, 謂之不聰 … 和則同, 同則善.

This section extends the discussion to include 聰, 明, 聖, and 智. It says that together the five principles 五行 (仁, 義, 禮, 智, 聖) are 德; and the four principles (仁, 義, 禮, 智) are 善. This reflects the first section in which 德 precedes 仁, 義, 禮.

c. slips 32:6 to 49:6: 顏色容貌溫變也 …. 其人施諸人, 僱也.

This section discusses 仁, 義, 禮 in detail.

d. slips 49:7 to 50:21: 聞道而悅者, 好仁者也. 聞道而畏者, 好義者也. 聞道而恭者, 好禮者也. 聞道而樂者, 好德者也.

This sums up the whole of this half of the text and echoes the beginning of the text where the five principles 仁, 義, 禮, 智, and 聖 are introduced.

*b. Philosophical content and school affiliation*

The meeting considered the question: to which philosophical school does the *Wu Xing* belong? The two main suggestions were, first, that the work reflects exclusively the thought of Zisi 子思, and, second, that the work was influenced by several philosophical schools. The most vocal supporters of the first theory were Li Xueqin and Xing Wen, while Ikeda Tomohisa advocated the second theory.

In his talk on the Guodian Confucian texts (see pp. 107–11), Li Xueqin proposed the theory that six of the Guodian texts, including the *Wu Xing*, contain the philosophy of Zisi. He pointed out that the content of the *Wu Xing* is related to other works that can be attributed to Zisi, for example the "Liu Shu 六術" section of Jia Yi's 賈誼 *Xinshu* 新書. Li Xueqin further observed that the tomb dates from the late fourth century BC, at which time the text of the *Mencius* was being written and not yet in wide circulation. According to Li Xueqin, then, the *Wu Xing* predates Mencius and is a book that Mencius might have read. It is not Mencian, but purely the philosophy of Zisi.

Xing Wen supported this theory and further argued that certain ideas in the *Mencius* were developments of ideas expressed in the *Wu Xing*.The example he used was that of the metaphorical use of the terms 金聲 ("peal of bronze") and 玉振 ("resonance of jade"). He cited passages from the two works, first from the *Wu Xing* (slips 18 to 20): 君子之為善也，有與始，有與終也；君子之為德也，有與始，無與終也．金聲而玉振之，有德者也．金聲，善也；玉音，聖也．善，人道也；德，天道也．唯有德者，然後能金聲而玉振之．("For a gentleman to be kind, there is a beginning and there is an end; for a gentleman to be virtuous, there is a beginning but there is no end. To peal with bronze and resonate with jade is like those who are virtuous. The peal of bronze is kindness; the sound of jade is sageliness. Kindness is the way of humans; virtue is the way of Heaven. It is only those who are virtuous who can peal with bronze and resonate with jade"; Xing Wen's translation.)

Second, a passage from the Mencius (5B.1, "Wanzhang 萬章，下"): 孔子之謂集大成．集大成也者，金聲而玉振之也．金聲也者，始條理也；玉振之也者，終條理也．始條理者，智之事也；終條理者，聖之事也．智，譬則巧也；聖，譬則力也．("Confucius was the one who gathered together all the great merits. To achieve this is like pealing with bronze and resonating with jade. To peal with bronze is to begin in an orderly fashion; to resonate with jade is to end in an orderly fashion. To begin in an orderly fashion pertains to wisdom; to end in an orderly fashion pertains to sageliness. Wisdom is like skill; sageliness is like strength"; Xing Wen's translation.)

He argued that in the *Wu Xing* the "peal of bronze" and "resonance of jade" are symbols of 善 ("kindness") and 德 ("virtue") rather than of 智 ("wisdom") and 聖 ("sageliness"), and these virtues are considered to be on a higher level than 智 and 聖. Xing saw the symbolic association in the *Mencius* of 金聲 and 玉振 with 智之事("wisdom") and 聖之事 ("sageliness") as a development of the way 智 and 聖 are treated in the *Wu Xing*. He concluded that the *Wu Xing* is earlier than the *Mencius* is and that the *Mencius* further develops the teachings in the *Wu Xing*.

Ikeda Tomohisa agreed that the *Wu Xing* is principally a Confucian text, but argued that the work also draws on the thought of other schools, such as the Daoists, Mohists, and Legalists. He also thought that it does show the influence of the *Mencius*, although it is not specifically attributable to the Zisi-Mengzi school. Examples of the influence of other schools include the mention of the Mohist concept of 慎獨 ("being cautious when alone") in slips 16 to 18. He also noted the lines: 目而知之，謂之進之．俞［喻］而知之，謂之進之．譬而知之，謂之進之 (slip 47). The term 目 is a term used by Mohist logicians and is defined in the "Xiao Qu 小取" chapter of the *Mozi* 墨子，45, where it is written with the homonym 牟：牟也者，比辭而俱行也 ("'Adducing' is saying: 'If it is so in your case, why may it not be so in mine too?'"). The 譬 which also occurs in this line is another term used by the Mohist logicians, and is defined in the same section of the *Mozi* as 辟也者，舉也（他）物而以明之也 ("'illustrating' is referring to other things in order to clarify one's case").[68]

---

[68] These translations are from A. C. Graham, *Later Mohist Logic, Ethics, and Science* (Hong Kong: The

Ikeda saw Legalist influence in the phrase: 有大罪而大誅之，行也 ("When there is great crime, greatly punish it; this is proper conduct"; editors' translation) of slip 35. He argued that this is not typical Si-Meng thought. From these observations he concluded that the *Wu Xing* draws on the thoughts of many schools.

Wang Bo asked Ikeda if he therefore believed that the *Wu Xing* is a later work than the *Mencius*, to which Ikeda replied that he did. Wang Bo went on to ask how Ikeda then explained the appearance of the *Wu Xing* in a tomb dated to the late fourth century BC when Mencius himself lived from 390 to 305 BC and the *Mencius* was only written towards the end of his life. Ikeda said that his conclusions were based on a philosophical analysis rather than an archeological or historical one. Edmund Ryden suggested that, even if the text of the *Mencius* was later, Mencius' thought may already have been well known in his lifetime, in which case it could have influenced the *Wu Xing*. Chen Guying asked whether it was possible to push Mencius' dates back to an earlier time, but Li Xueqin observed that Mencius' dates are based on datable historical incidents recorded in the *Mencius*, which makes his dates quite specific and difficult to alter.

Xing Wen, commenting on Ikeda's two conclusions (that the *Wu Xing* is not in the Si-Meng school; and that it is later than the *Mencius*), felt the evidence given in Li Xueqin's background talk is convincing, especially that concerning the concepts of 聖 and 智. He further observed that these concepts in the *Wu Xing* are used in the same manner as in the *Zhongyong* 中庸, which is associated with Zisi. Xing Wen also observed that the concepts also appear in the bamboo-slip *Wenzi* 文子 excavated at Dingxian Bajiaolang 定縣八角廊 in Hebei province, but the thought expressed about them in each case is different and indicates that the concept had developed.[69]

Xing Wen conjectured that comparison between the Guodian *Wu Xing* and the Mawangdui edition indicates there were at least two separate groups within the Zisi school in the state of Chu. The group represented by the Guodian edition basically followed Zisi's original thought while the group represented by the Mawangdui edition reflects the thought of the Shizi 世子 school: the alterations to the text, discussed above, show that the Shizi school's understanding of the same two concepts 聖 and 智 in the original *Wu Xing* was unclear.

With regard again to those terms, Paul Thompson suggested that whereas in the Guodian edition they are two of the five *xing* 五行, in the Mawangdui edition they have become a single concept, with 聖 an adjective modifying 智 ("sagely wisdom"). In response, Xing Wen suggested that, in fact, the discussion of these concepts is the same in both editions: in the first part of the Guodian *Wu Xing* they are discussed as

---

Chinese University Press, 1978), p. 483.

[69] See Xing Wen, "*Wenzi Sheng Zhi* Tanlun 《文子·聖知》探論," *Xueshu Jilin* 10 (1997), pp. 198–203.

separate concepts, and, then, in the second part they are discussed together as a combination. The Mawangdui edition is no different but, due to the alteration in the textual sequence, the discussion of 聖智 is no longer clear.

Ikeda Tomohisa gave a detailed account of his understanding of the philosophy of the Guodian *Wu Xing*, which we summarize here. Ikeda understands the *Wu Xing* to be saying that at birth everyone has five sprouts 端 that are got from *tian* 天 : they are 恷 (愛 )、直 , 嚴 , 聰 , and 明 . Through conscious effort one can transform these into, respectively, the five *xing*: 仁 , 義 , 禮 , 聖 , 智 .[70] The text uses the terms 志 , 為志 , 思 , and 進 in the description of this process.[71] Once one has realized the five *xing*, the aim is then to harmonize them.[72] The harmonizing of the four *xing* (the five minus 聖 ), results in "goodness 善 ," which is "the way of man 人道 ." The harmonizing of the *Wu Xing* adds the 聖 to the other four. The harmonization of the five *xing* brings about 德 , "virtue," which is the "celestial way 天道 ." Ordinary people are not able to harmonize all five *xing*; only sages 聖人 are able to do this. The text gives an example of one such man, King Wen of the Zhou 周文王 , in section 18 (Guodian slips 29 to 30).

### c. The relationship of the Wu Xing to the Laozi

Xing Wen observed that both the Guodian tomb and the Mawangdui tomb have copies of *Laozi* materials and the *Wu Xing*. In the case of the Mawangdui silk manuscripts, the *Laozi* and the *Wu Xing* are on a single piece of silk, which suggests that the person who copied these texts (or had them copied) considered them to be somehow complementary. In the Guodian tomb, the bamboo slips of the *Laozi* materials group-A are almost identical in form to those of the *Wu Xing*. What do these texts share that might explain their association with one another? Xing Wen suggested that both texts discuss the concepts of 天道 and 德 . Chen Guying agreed with this suggestion.

### Tang Yu zhi Dao 唐虞之道 and Zhong Xin zhi Dao 忠信之道

The content of the *Tang Yu zhi Dao* is a version of the myth of the abdication by Yao to Shun. Here, we find that the reason Yao decided to give up the throne to Shun was that he had become old and feeble. Sarah Allan, who had discussed the various transformations of this story in her book *The Heir and the Sage: Dynastic Legend in Early China*, argued that this version of the story does not occur in the extant corpus of philosophical texts and that it cannot be attributed to any particular school. It is

[70] For 仁 , see Ikeda, *Maōtai*, sections 10, p. 250 (silk manuscript lines 188–89), and 14, p. 301 (lines 191–92); for 義 , see sections 11, p. 259 (line 189), and 15, p. 318 (lines 193–94); for 禮 , sections 12, p. 273 (line 190), and 16, p. 336 (lines 194–95); for 聖智 , sections 6, p. 193 (lines 182–84), and 17, p. 349 (lines 196–97).

[71] Ibid., sections 3, p. 177 (line 176); 4, p. 187 (line 178); 5, 6, p. 187–93 (lines 178–84); and 21, p. 446 (line 206).

[72] Ibid., sections 1, p. 163 (lines 170–73); 5, p. 178 (lines 187–81); 6, p. 193 (lines 181–84); 18, p. 364 (lines 198–200); 19, p. 398 (lines 201–2), 28, p. 570 (lines 213–14).

noticeably different from the Confucian versions of the story.[73] As Allan explained, each philosophical school had its own transformation of the story of the abdication by Yao to Shun. The *Mencius* and *Xunzi* both deny that kings can "abdicate"; they explain the change in leadership in the predynastic period using the concept of *tian ming* 天命 as a decision of heaven, manifested in the movement of the people, rather than due to a decision made by the ruler. Thus, Allan felt these schools would not have used the version of the myth found here in the *Tang Yu zhi Dao*.

Wang Bo argued that this text can be seen as a summary of the "Yaodian 堯典" chapter of the *Shangshu* 尚書, and pointed to similar language in the *Mencius*. Allan noted, however, that the philosophical implications of the detailed description of abdication in the *Tang Yu zhi Dao* are distinctive.[74] On a similar note, Qiu Xigui said his impression was that the *Tang Yu zhi Dao* emphasizes the importance of handing power to someone virtuous, as opposed to hereditary succession from father to son, which is quite different from Confucian thought on the matter.

Marc Kalinowski noted that, in the *Tang Yu zhi Dao*, the abdicating emperor is supposed to practice self-cultivation 養生 after he steps down. Kalinowski wondered if this linked the text with the Huang-Lao school. Here Allan argued that we should not assume that these texts belong to known schools. Paul Thompson noted that in the version of the myth in which Yao tries to give up the throne to Xu You 許由, Xu You refused, probably for the same reason — that he wanted to 養生. Marc Kalinowski also noted that the *Tang Yu zhi Dao* might be included in the group of texts which Li Xueqin regards as works of the Zisi school since it shares many characteristics with them.

Li Xueqin observed that, as Peng Hao and Qiu Xigui had already pointed out, the characters of both the *Tang Yu zhi Dao* and the *Zhong Xin zhi Dao* texts are written in a very particular style. Li thought that, unlike the other texts in the tomb, they are not in Chu script. Furthermore, from the point of view of language and content, rather than philosophy, we can conclude that within the context of the tomb they are relatively late works related to the *Mencius*. The question of abdication was an important political issue at the end of the fourth century BC. Advocates of abdication traveled around spreading the word; e.g., Cuo Maoshou 厝毛壽 and King Kuai of Yan 燕王噲. Abdication was being promoted, and the fiercest opponent of abdication as a political philosophy was Mencius. Thus, this particular text may have been written in this period in response to this argument, and it may be later than some of the other texts in the tomb.[75]

---

[73] See Sarah Allan, *The Heir and the Sage: Dynastic Legend in Early China* (San Francisco: CMC, 1981).

[74] Relevant passages in the *Mengzi* 孟子 include: 5A.1–6, "萬章, 上."

[75] Li Xueqin has discussed this political situation in an article "Pingshan San Qi yu Zhongshan Guo Shi de Ruogan Wenti 平山三器與中山國史的若干問題," originally published in *Kaogu Xuebao* 1979.2, reprinted in *Xin Chu Qingtongqi Yanjiu* 新出青銅器研究 (Beijing: Wenwu Press, 1990), especially pp. 195–97.

Li thought that there was also a relationship between these two texts and Zisi. The similarities with the *Mencius* include the story about Shun 舜 and Gu Sou 瞽瞍 and the phrase 養天下之老也 ("nurturing the elders of the world"). Moreover, in the *Zhong Xin zhi Dao* (slip 5), the phrase 口凷 (惠) 而實弗從 is very close to a phrase in the *Biaoji* 表記 attributed to Zisi: 口惠而實不至 (*Liji* 禮記). On these grounds Li Xueqin concluded that these two texts are approximately contemporaneous with the *Mencius*.

## Yu Cong 語叢

The *Yu Cong* phrases are one-line sayings, each on its own slip. Li Xueqin suggested that they might have a teaching purpose. Robin Yates observed that the *Yu Cong* should not be dismissed as a jumbled group of relatively unimportant sayings. They are on the shortest of the slips uncovered from the Guodian tomb and Yates noted that in other finds the most important slip-texts are often written on the shortest slips. He pointed to the example of slip 1 of the second (*yi* 乙) group of *Yu Cong*: 情生於性, 禮生於情 ("natural endowment is generated by nature and the rites are generated by endowment") as particularly worthy of attention and research. He felt that these slips were not produced for school use; they are not similar to the "Tan Cong 談叢" chapter of Liu Xiang's 劉向 *Shuoyuan* 説苑. He suggested that the *Yu Cong* may be addressing very specific philosophical themes, perhaps in reply to the *Mozi*. Yates further compared the *Yu Cong* to the *Cheng* 稱 from Mawangdui, which have some similarities as a type of text and may be related to the *Guanzi*, "Shu Yan 樞言" section.

## The Question of Philosophical Schools

Guodian Tomb Number One, taken as a whole, has two striking features. One is that all of the texts found in it are philosophical, as opposed, for example, to the divination manuals, medical, legal, historical, and personal records found in other tombs. Some of the other excavated tombs in which texts have been preserved have included philosophical texts, but no other tomb has yielded only philosophical texts. Moreover, the texts are not only philosophical; they are, within the Chinese tradition, particularly abstract in nature. We mentioned Li Xueqin's conjecture that the tomb was that of an "old professor." If so, then we may suppose that the texts buried with him were his teaching materials, and thus had a practical purpose in his lifetime. This surmise, however, makes the other striking feature of the tomb even more remarkable: that is, the mix of texts from different philosophical schools within a single tomb.

The question of philosophical schools in the Warring States period and the relationship between the early philosophical texts has been hotly disputed in recent years; the characterization of these texts in terms of schools was itself contested. Previously, most scholars have seen a relatively clear division between Daoist and Confucian works. Li Xueqin identified the *Laozi* materials and the *Tai Yi Sheng Shui* as Daoist; the six texts: *Zi Yi, Wu Xing, Cheng Zhi Wen Zhi, Zun De Yi, Xing Zi Ming Chu, Liu De*, as

Confucian. The other texts in the tomb may be Confucian, Daoist, or belong to other schools. In Li's analysis, the common characteristic of the Guodian Confucian texts is that they expound theoretical and philosophical questions. The concepts of *tian* ("heaven"), *dao* ("way"), *xing* ("nature"), *ming* ("order"), and others that reflect the main trends in early Confucian philosophy are all discussed here.

Li Xueqin not only identified certain texts as Confucian, he placed them within a historical construct of the early development of the Confucian school, noting that they confirm many of the ideas that were current among scholars in the Song dynasty. He suggested that these six texts are not only related to one another, at least two of them (the *Zi Yi* and *Wu Xing*) may clearly be identified with the philosopher Zisi, the grandson of Confucius.

Li Xueqin further argued that the Guodian texts provide evidence for the view that Zisi wrote the *Zhongyong* and for a relationship between Zengzi 曾子 and the *Daxue* 大學 . He noted in this regard that many of the categories advanced in the *Daxue*, such as *xiu shen* 修身 , *shen du* 慎獨 , and *xin min* 新民 , are discussed repeatedly and developed in the bamboo slips. Moreover, the structure of the *Daxue*, a main text followed by a commentary, is very similar to that of the Mawangdui *Wu Xing*, with its text and commentary.[76]

In the Song dynasty, neo-Confucianists venerated the *Daxue* and *Zhongyong* as the embodiment of the theory and ideals of Confucius' disciples, and Zhu Xi 朱熹 ranked these two texts together with the *Lunyu* and the *Mencius* as two of his "four books" 四書. One of the most important aspects of the Confucian texts in this tomb, Li argued, is that they confirm the opinion of the Song-period scholars, often disputed in more recent years, of the historical relationship of these two texts to Zisi and their importance in the early historical development of Confucian thought.

If the Guodian tomb does, indeed, include a number of the core Confucian texts, later lost, why are they together with the *Laozi* and *Tai Yi Sheng Shui*? Did the teacher use both as part of his corpus of teaching materials? Were they not considered to be in contradiction to one another? Many scholars noted that the Guodian *Laozi* does not include the specifically anti-Confucian language of the received text. Perhaps the followers of Confucius and Laozi were not yet opposed to one another; or, perhaps, the Guodian *Laozi* material and *Tai Yi Sheng Shui* should not be considered purely Daoist. Some scholars also questioned Li Xueqin's characterization of some of the texts as Confucian and, more specifically, the possible identification of certain texts with Zisi or the Si-Meng school.

Here, Chen Guying argued that his general impression was of a harmonious mixture of (what later came to be regarded as) Daoist and Confucian thought in the

---

[76] Cf. Li, "Xian Qin Rujia Zhuzuo."

Guodian texts. Whereas many scholars thought the slip text designated *Zhong Xin zhi Dao* was Confucian, Chen Guying observed that his personal impression on first reading was that it was a *Laozi* type work. He pointed out that the *Laozi* emphasizes the concepts of 忠信, as does the *Zhong Xin zhi Dao*. He gave the following example: 至忠如土, 為物而不發 ("The greatest loyalty is like the earth; it makes the living things, yet does not make a show of it"; editors' translation) (*Zhong Xin zhi Dao*, slip 2). Similar lines exist in the received *Laozi*: 萬物恃之而生而不辭, 功成而不名有 ("The myriad creatures depend on it for life yet it claims no authority. It accomplishes its task yet it lays claim to no merit"; D. C. Lau's translation) (chapter 34), and 是以聖人為而不恃,功成而不處 ("Therefore the sage benefits them yet exacts no gratitude, accomplishes his task yet lays no claim to merit"; D. C. Lau's translation) (chapter 77).

Moreover, the concept *ji* 積 found in the *Zhong Xin zhi Dao* is an important idea in the *Zhuangzi* (e.g., "Xiaoyao You 逍遙遊": 水之積也不厚,則其負大舟也無力, "When the accumulation of water is not great, then it does not have the power to carry a large boat"; editors' translation). Chen Guying suggested that a tradition concerning moral conduct was passed down from the Western Zhou period and that, not only the Confucians, but the Confucian and Laozi schools were both carrying on this tradition.

Chen Guying further argued that neither *Xing Zi Ming Chu* nor *Liu De*, both of which, it had been suggested, could be attributed to the Si-Meng school, correspond to the thought of Mencius. The *Liu De* (slip 26) has the phrase 仁內義外 ("humaneness is inner and rightness outer"), which is the philosophy of Gaozi 告子 that Mencius opposed and criticized. The *Xing Zi Ming Chu* speaks of *you* 游 ( 游樂 and 游心 ; slip 33) in a manner which suggests the free-wandering joy of the heart/mind, found only in the *Zhuangzi*. So, Chen Guying's general impression was that the Guodian texts contain a mixture of thought from several different schools and cannot be categorized as works of individual schools.

Here, the question was raised about when the schools came to be seen as strictly opposed to one another and how much interchange of ideas there may have been in this period. A number of scholars objected to any neat division of the texts from this tomb into philosophical schools. Andrew Meyer cautioned, on methodological grounds, against using views of particular philosophical schools in order to categorize these texts, since different texts can disagree on many points, yet, in some cases, were still considered to be works of one school, for example, the Confucian school, which included Zisi, Gaozi, Mencius, and Xunzi. The criteria for these categorizations can change according to the historical and intellectual context.

Rudolf Wagner questioned the very idea of philosophical schools in this period, arguing that the division between schools did not become an issue until Sima Tan 司馬談 wrote his *Lun Liu Jia Yao Zhi* 論六家要指 in the Han dynasty. Xing Wen argued, in reply, that this concept was pre-Han, citing the examples of the "Fei Shier Zi" chapter of the *Xunzi* and the "Tianxia 天下" chapter of the *Zhuangzi*, which include references to philosophers in terms that suggest different schools.

Xu Kangsheng said that we cannot say there were not several philosophical schools (at this time), nor can we start redefining the philosophical schools on the basis of this tomb. In these Guodian texts, the *Laozi* materials and *Tai Yi Sheng Shui* belong to the Daoist school, and the *Wu Xing, Zi Yi*, and so on, are Confucian. The Daoist texts include some Confucian ideas, and the Confucian texts have some Daoist influence, but they are still fundamentally either Daoist or Confucian texts; they each have their own particular characteristics. It is also possible that there are texts that do not fit in any of the known schools, which we can attribute to some other previously unknown school.

At the root of the question of philosophical schools and their relationship with one another is the broader question of the nature of intellectual discourse at the end of the fourth century BC. Marc Kalinowski suggested that texts such as those found in this tomb were part of a larger discourse occurring in Chu about religion and philosophy, the physical world, and cosmology. Thus, he suggested, the *Laozi* and *Tai Yi Sheng Shui* might have been considered cosmological texts rather than philosophical ones. Donald Harper also said that we should bear in mind the situation during the second century BC in which there was a whole range of subjects that people studied, including philosophy, medical techniques, divination, and numerology, ceremony. The situation two centuries earlier may well have been similar, and we should be cautious in any attempt to characterize the nature of the texts in this tomb.

Rudolf Wagner noted that, from the Han period onwards, the picture of pre-Han philosophy is one of hardened schools of thought battling each other; it is a reconstruction of history attempting to give order to the universe. The Guodian texts show us a mix of schools and can be compared to the Jixia Academy, where scholars came together producing a fertile ground for debate. Although they are not easy to categorize we can say that the Guodian texts ask questions about life, ritual and so on. The "agenda" of Guodian Tomb Number One is one of intellectual fertility and openness.

## CONCLUDING REMARKS

In a talk on the last day of the conference, Marc Kalinowski summed up with the statement that while in the past, Chinese studies had been divided into *guoxue* 國學 ("national studies" — the research done by Chinese scholars), and *hanxue* 漢學 ("sinology" — that by non-Chinese scholars), he felt that the International Conference on the Guodian *Laozi* was an example of a new development: an "international Chinese studies." We hope that the easy exchange of ideas among all of the scholars throughout the conference will be apparent to the readers of this account.

Most of our time was spent concretely — reading and discussing the texts together, rather than presenting and listening to prepared papers; and this format undoubtedly contributed to the exchange. Although the use of Chinese as the language of the conference may have inhibited the Western scholars to a degree (and they have also been more avid in offering corrections and clarifications to this account), the desire to communicate, and the specificity of our focus on the Chinese text, usually overcame the difficulties. Each scholar brought his or her own specialist knowledge to the task, which resulted in a rich and varied exchange of ideas and opinions, the atmosphere was one of discovery, with everyone aware that this was a beginning, a chance to frame questions and try out answers, rather than finally to resolve these questions.

Some of the factual material presented above, such as the clarifications of the circumstances of the excavation of Guodian Tomb Number One and the initial process of ordering and transcribing the slips offered by the archeologists concerned, will be an important record for all future researchers. Some of the arguments and observations concerning the *Laozi* material and other texts from this Guodian tomb will also stand the test of time; others will fall by the wayside. More important than these specifics, however, is the range of questions that was raised and the variety of approaches and methodologies suggested for the possible resolution of these questions.

The importance of Guodian Tomb Number One, with its core texts from a critical period in the formation of the Chinese philosophical tradition, to Chinese intellectual history is such that the issues discussed in this first approach are likely to become more complex rather than reach a resolution. Nevertheless, we hope that this summary of our discussion will allow readers not only to understand the background to this major archeological discovery, but also to benefit from these first reactions and thoughts about the *Laozi* materials and other texts.

# SECTION THREE:

# EDITION OF THE BAMBOO-SLIP *LAOZI* A, B, AND C, AND *TAI YI SHENG SHUI* FROM GUODIAN TOMB NUMBER ONE

# Edition of the Bamboo-Slip *Laozi* A, B, and C, and *Tai Yi Sheng Shui* from Guodian Tomb Number One

## EDMUND RYDEN

In my earlier work and in a number of international conferences, I have argued for the importance of a critical apparatus in dealing with recently discovered texts. Having been assigned the task of one of the secretaries for the Dartmouth Guodian Conference, I made it a priority to familarize myself with the Guodian discoveries as much as possible. For this task I have adopted the same format for editing a text as I did with the Mawangdui *Huangdi Sijing* (Ryden, E., *The Yellow Emperor's Four Canons* [Taipei: Ricci Institute, 1997]). It is thus a great honor that the editors of the Conference proceedings have chosen to use my format of the original text. This format is based on the book edited by the Jingmen City Museum 荊門市博物館 and published by the Wenwu Publishing House, entitled *Guodian Chu Mu Zhujian* 郭店楚墓竹簡.

However, honor is not always a blessing. My original version was drawn up in one month and contained errors. This present version has been amended based on the comments of Professors Sarah Allan and Robert Henricks, Dr. Donald Harper, and Crispin Williams, as well as personal communications from Professor Li Ling and Fr. Jean Lefeuvre. Professor Henricks' comments can be studied in more detail in his *Lao Tzu's Tao Te Ching: A Translation of the Startling New Documents Found at Guodian* (New York: Columbia University Press, forthcoming). I have also taken into account the work of Professor Ding Yuanzhi of Fujen University, published after the Dartmouth Conference (Ding Yuanzhi 丁原植, *Guodian Zhujian Laozi Shixi yu Yanjiu* 郭店竹簡老子釋析與研究 [Taipei 臺北 : Wanjuanlou 萬卷樓圖書, 1998, 民87年 ]).

Having said this, a word of caution is required. It is not my intention here to present all the views of each member of the Conference on each graph for which the said member expressed an opinion. Nor do I pretend that the views presented represent a complete account of all possibilities for reading the text, either as presented at Dartmouth or later. Detailed information regarding the views of individual scholars is available in the Conference papers or in other articles already published or in the course of publication. Finally, it should be noted that the computer software used, good as it is, is not wholly stable. This makes every revision a perilous affair. I am assured by computer experts that the problem is totally unsolvable.

On a positive note I see this text as fulfilling three purposes. Firstly, it presents one possible edited version of the Guodian texts in a readable format, set out in neat lines of poetry without encumbrance or the need to read unfamiliar graphs. Secondly, it provides a standard way of referring to any graph in the original manuscript, based on the number assigned to the bamboo slips and the order of graphs on the slips. It also reproduces, as faithfully as possible, a standardized version of the original graph as written by the scribes. Thirdly, it presents a fairly complete, though not exhaustive, reading of each graph in those cases where scholars have differing opinions. If, fourthly, the notes help elucidate some of the reasoning behind these differences then that is all to the good but the notes do not summarize the Conference papers.

The question as to why an apparatus is necessary is not a trivial issue. Rather it highlights two different though complementary and at times overlapping tasks that face anyone dealing with ancient texts. Traditional Chinese methods of annotation using brackets and notes do not indicate these differences sufficiently. It is thus incumbent on me to spend some time outlining the differences.

## READING ANCIENT GRAPHS

The first and most obvious task is to identify the graphs used in a text, to determine how to read them, and to relate them to modern graphs. This task is of interest to the specialist in early Chinese writing and to the phonologist. Thus we discover that the graph 仁 ren was written 悥 in the Guodian slips and that 道 dao was sometimes written 行. In some cases the task of identification has yet to be undertaken, and this is a matter that was one of the main points of focus at Dartmouth.

More difficult are the loan characters. Moreover, in ancient times the Chinese often used more than one phonetically similar character to represent a single word. The problem for us is that we no longer live in the same context and we may have to make educated guesses as to which words are intended. Thus we find that the scribe of the *Tai Yi Sheng Shui* wrote 雀 (9:5), which the Wenwu Press editors read as a loan for 爵 jue; furthermore, Qiu Xigui suggests 削 xue. The choice will be dependent on knowledge of ancient phonology and practices but also on reading the character in a context. This latter task is an editorial one.

## EDITING

The editor makes decisions about how to read the text and seeks to establish a version that reflects what the scribe was actually writing. Editing goes behind the vagaries of personal style, mistakes, and phonetic loans to produce an accurate copy, which the hearers or readers could understand. It is this edition that we will compare with received versions of the text of the *Laozi*. Thus when we find that the Wang Bi *Laozi* writes 物 *wu*, whereas the Guodian *Laozi* writes 勿 *wu*, we cannot make a simple comparison between the two. The Wang Bi version is an edited version, written in a standardized script. The Guodian bamboo slips do not give us a version produced according to the same standardized script. It is necessary for the editor to standardize the script first before any meaningful comparison can be made.

Take an example from modern Chinese. If you buy a lunchbox from a Cantonese restaurant in Taipei, you may wonder what the character 立 *li*, "standing upright," could possibly mean. Once you realize that the cook is Cantonese the problem is resolved. The character 立 is read *laap* in Cantonese, and this is phonetically similar to 辣 *laat*, meaning "spicy." A busy cook can write 立 more quickly than 辣 . This does not mean that the cook cannot write Chinese, that he does not know which character is correct, but only that one is easier to write than the other. He will read it as 辣 , "spicy." That he actually wrote 立 is of interest to the phonetician but of no relevance to the cook or the buyer. Similarly, the meaning of an ancient text is not affected by 備 for 服 or 舊 for 久. This type of information is as irrelevant to understanding the text as the graph 立 is for the purchaser of spicy food. It is precisely this kind of information which should be kept in the apparatus.

Hence the apparatus provides a means of retaining all the information regarding the actual graphs on the manuscript itself, while at the same time distinguishing this task clearly from the work of editing. The advantage is that one can produce a readable edited version, set out in even lines, uncluttered by parentheses and fit for comparison with existing versions.

Naturally, there are problematic areas where the editor may make a decision that proves to be wrong. A character may be misread, another inserted or removed unnecessarily, but this work will all be recorded in the apparatus. A subsequent editor can challenge any given decision, revise the edition and note the revision in the same apparatus. This is standard procedure for all such editing and should not be considered abnormal.

### READING AN APPARATUS

A critical apparatus demands a simple means of communication with the edited text so that reference can be made from one to the other. In editing the *Huangdi Sijing*, I adopted the principle of using the line numbers assigned to the Mawangdui Silk Manuscript. The advantage of this choice is that these numbers are known to all who work on the same discovery. In the case of the Guodian finds, the same procedure has been adopted. Each slip is numbered in the left-hand margin. A superscript indicates where the slip begins and assigns a number to each graph in the line on that slip. This latter numbering is more problematic. It follows the actual graphs in the edited version, leaving out paragraph marks, ■, but including blanks where the number of such can be reasonably estimated. However, it should be pointed out that doubling of the characters marked with two short strokes (the ancient "ditto" symbol) may not be taken into account.

The apparatus itself is organized according to the slip numbers and the position numbers of each graph on that slip within each line. A typical lemma has two graphs. In first place comes the edited graph as it is found in the text above. Following this and in bold type, after the colon (:), is the graph as it is written on the bamboo:

*A 1:1* 絕 : 㞫

In most cases there are no more than two graphs but where an editor suggests an alternative reading this must be recorded, following a second colon (:). Thus we find a lemma such as this:

*A 1:2* 知 : **知** : 智 *DYZ*

The first graph is the graph adopted by the editor, the second, in bold type, is the original MS and the third is the reading adopted by a given scholar, here Ding Yuanzhi. In certain instances an editor may recommend one reading, while at the same time suggesting that an alternative is possible:

*A 9:16* 屯 : **屯** : 沌 *LL*: 敦 *LL alt*

Here Li Ling reads the MS 屯 as 沌 but thinks that 敦 is also plausible. At times the editor may be unclear as to which of two readings is the better, hence:

*A 24:20, 21* 芸 *Wang Bi*: **員** : 圓 *WBo*: 云 *LL*: 𩵋 *DYZ alt*: 運 *DYZ alt*

The present edition has followed Wang Bi 芸 ; Wang Bo reads 圓 ; Li Ling reads 云 , and Ding Yuanzhi proposes 𩵋 or 運 .

In cases where the editor has adopted a reading proposed by only one scholar in the face of the majority reading the initials of this scholar are duly mentioned, thus:

*Tai Yi Sheng Shui 7:9* 己 *QXG*: **忌** : 紀 *WW*

The edited graph 己 is the reading proposed by Qiu Xigui; the scribe wrote 忌 , and another possible edited form is 紀 .

Where the editor has added graphs believed to be missing in the original we find:

*Tai Yi Sheng Shui 4: 23–9* 者 , 四時之所生也 : **者**

This means that the scribe wrote 者 , but the editor has added 四時之所生也 .

Where an editor believes a graph should be excluded, this may be indicated either by simple omission in the edited slot as:

*A 38:2* 不 : **不不**

or by a ○ thus:

*B 1:11–12* 是以：是以：○ *LL*

Here the lemma means that the edited version reads 是以; the MS also reads 是以, but that Li Ling suggests eliding both characters.

Attention should be drawn to a number of graphs for which no acceptable edited form has yet been agreed upon. Since these graphs may puzzle the reader, they are recorded in the apparatus:

*B 8:20* 迖：迖

In some cases there are problems with transcription of the original graphs. This is due to several factors. The first is the problem of initial recognition. Thus the Wenwu editors identified A 2:17 as 須, but closer inspection of the photos, after the Conference, confirmed Li Ling's view that in fact the graph written was 寡, but that the bamboo had frayed leaving a few strokes off. In cases like this the apparatus must indicate that there are differences of opinion regarding the initial transcription, thus both graphs are presented in the slot for the original graph, separated by a vertical stroke, thus 寡 | 須, where the left-hand graph is the correct one and the right-hand graph is the initial transcription.

There is, however, a further problem with the transcription. In simple terms it is not a pure transcription but already an edited transcription. Thus the elements of each graph are reordered according to present usage. Thus, as Carine Defoort noted, the graph at B 2:13, 15 is clearly written 陕 and not 郏, as in the Wenwu transcription. Since this point was raised at the Conference, it is noted according to the same format as for misidentification, 陕 | 郏, but it would be impossible and unnecessary to indicate all such cases. For instance the 見 radical in the graph 覜 (A 1:13) is manifestly on the left of the phonetic 兆. The editors are not wrong to invert the order of radical and phonetic in their transcription, since in the modern script the radical 見 always occurs at the right of a character.

A third level of interpretation comes at the level of the gloss. In some cases this can be left to discussion in the notes, but when convenient or not immediately obvious the gloss is included in the lemma. Thus A17: 19 reads 始：訂：嗣 as 司 DYZ. This means that the MS has the graph 訂, which the majority of editors read as 始, but Ding Yuanzhi reads as 嗣, which he glosses as 司. In a case like this having both graphs helps the reader to see how a given editor has arrived at a particular reading.

No matter how complicated a lemma may become, the principle of placing the transcription of the original graph in second place and the preferred edited form in first place is always adhered to.

As with any tool, to learn to use an apparatus requires some effort but once learned, it provides a convenient manner of referring to graphs and dealing with editorial problems. Notes can be used to comment on the editorial process or point out difficulties in reading, but the evidence for the notes is all presented in the apparatus. It is the apparatus which is where the scholarly work is carried out. The rationale of this work is given in the notes and the fruit in the edited text. The tasks are clearly defined and confusion is avoided.

*SIGLA*

Black square      ■
Short stroke      ▬
"Tadpole"-shaped symbol   ↄ
Lacuna  □

The apparatus does not mark the following variant: *qi* 其 : 亓 or 丌

*Abbreviations*

| | |
|---|---|
| CD | Carine Defoort (Dartmouth Conference) |
| CGY | Chen Guying 陳鼓應 (Dartmouth Conference) |
| DH | Donald Harper (Dartmouth Conference) |
| DYZ | Ding Yuanzhi 丁原植 (published edition): |
| | 郭店竹簡老子釋析與研究。臺北：萬卷樓圖書，民 87 年 |
| IT | Ikeda Tomohisa 池田知久 (Conference edition of the text; comments) |
| LL | Li Ling 李零 (Conference: paper, comments and later observations) |
| LXF | Liu Xinfang 劉信芳 (unpublished MS quoted by Ding Yuanzhi) |
| MXL | Ma Xulun 馬敍倫 (as quoted by Ding Yuanzhi) |
| PT | Paul Thompson (Dartmouth Conference) |
| QXG[n] | Qiu Xigui 裘錫圭 (pre-Conference notes in Wenwu edition) |
| QXG | Qiu Xigui 裘錫圭 (Dartmouth Conference: paper and comments) |
| RH | Robert Henricks (Dartmouth Conference and published work): |
| | *Lao Tzu's Tao Te Ching*, New York: Columbia University P., forthcoming |
| RW | Rudolf Wagner (Dartmouth Conference) |
| WBo | Wang Bo 王博 (Dartmouth Conference) |
| WT | Wang Tao 汪濤 (Dartmouth Conference) |
| WW | Wenwu 文物出版社 (pre-Conference published book): |
| | 荊門市博物館。郭店楚墓竹簡。北京：文物出版社 1998 年 |
| XKS | Xu Kangsheng 許抗生 (Dartmouth Conference) |

*Divisions of the Text*

For convenience of comparison I have divided the Guodian text into paragraphs (numbered by Roman numerals) that correspond to the divisions of the received versions and of the Mawangdui version. It should be noted that these divisions are not original and could be suppressed. For this reason a comparative table of chapter divisions has been added which shows the actual divisions in the Guodian manuscript.

## SELECT BIBLIOGRAPHY

*Editions of the Guodian* Laozi

Jingmenshi Bowuguan 荊門市博物館 , ed. *Guodian Chu Mu Zhujian.* Beijing: Wenwu Publishing House, 1998.

Ding Yuanzhi 丁原植 . *Guodian Zhujian Laozi Shixi yu Yanjiu* 郭店竹簡老子釋析與研究 . Taipei: Wanjuanlou, 1998.

Henricks, Robert G. *Lao Tzu's Tao Te Ching: A Translation of the Startling New Documents Found at Guodian.* New York: Columbia University Press, forthcoming.

*Editions of Other Ancient Texts*

Gao Ming 高明 . *Boshu Laozi Jiaozhu* 帛書老子校注 . Beijing: Zhonghua Shuju, 1996.

Henricks, Robert G. *Lao-Tzu Te-Tao Ching: A New Translation Based on the Recently Discovered Ma-wang-tui Texts.* New York: Ballantine Books, 1989.

Ryden, Edmund 雷敦龢 . *The Yellow Emperor's Four Canons* (*Huangdi Sijing* 黃帝四經 ). Taipei: Ricci Institute, 1997.

Sha Shaohai 沙少海 and Xu Zihong 徐子宏 , tr. and ed. *Laozi Quan Yi* 老子全釋 . Guiyang: Guizhou People's Publishing House, 1989.

Yates, Robin D. S. *Five Lost Classics: Tao, Huang-Lao, and Yin-Yang in Han China.* New York: Ballantine Books, 1997.

*Reference Works*

Chen Fuhua 陳復華 and He Jiuying 何九盈 . *Gu Yun Tong Xiao* 古韻通曉 . Beijing: Chinese Academy of Social Sciences, 1987.

Hanyu Da Zidian Bianji Weiyuanhui 漢語大字典編輯委員會 , ed. *Hanyu Da Zidian.* 漢語大字典 . Wuhan: Hubei Dictionary Publishing House & Sichuan Dictionary Publishing House, 1993.

# COMPARATIVE TABLE OF
# TEXTUAL DIVISIONS
## 老子各版本分章欄

Bullet marks correspond to these paragraph marks: ⎰ ▬ ■ ⎰
子彈符號「•」等於郭店竹簡分段符號: ⎰ ▬ ■ ⎰

## Guodian Laozi A 郭店老子甲

| GD 郭店 | WB 王弼 | MWD 馬王堆 |
|---|---|---|
| • A Ia-d* | 19 | 63 |
| A II | 66 | 29 |
| A III | 46 | 9 |
| • A IV | 30 | 74 |
| • A Va | 15 | 59 |
| • A Vb | 15 | 59 |
| • A VI | 64 | 27 |
| A VII | 37 | 81 |
| • A VIII | 63 | 26 |
| • A IX | 2 | 46 |
| • A Xa | 32 | 76 |
| A Xb | 32 | 76 |
| A XI | 25 | 69 |
| • A XII | 5 | 49 |
| • A XIII | 16 | 60 |
| • A XIV | 64 | 27 |
| • A XV | 56 | 19 |
| A XVI | 57 | 20 |
| • A XVII | 55 | 18 |
| • A XVIII | 44 | 7 |
| • A XIX | 40 | 4 |
| A XX | 9 | 53 |

## Guodian Laozi B 郭店老子乙

| GD 郭店 | WB 王弼 | MWD 馬王堆 |
|---|---|---|
| • B Ia | 59 | 22 |
| • B Ib | 59 | 22 |
| • B II | 48 | 11 |
| • B III | 20 | 64 |
| • B IV | 13 | 57 |
| • B V | 41 | 3 |
| B VI | 52 | 15 |
| • B VIIa | 45 | 8 |
| • B VIIb | 45 | 8 |
| B VIII | 54 | 17 |

## Guodian Laozi C 郭店老子丙

| GD 郭店 | WB 王弼 | MWD 馬王堆 |
|---|---|---|
| • C I | 17 | 61 |
| C II | 18 | 62 |
| • C III | 35 | 79 |
| • C IV | 31 | 75 |
| • C V | 64 | 27 |

———— = Separates groups of strips 分冊.

════ = Separates groups of strips; indicates use of ⎰ 分冊亦表示「⎰」符號.

* = A I is divided into four paragraphs 分四段.

## A I    [Chapter 19 *complete* / MWD 63]

1:1     5

1    絕智棄辯，　民利百倍. ■

       10       15

    絕巧棄利，　盜賊亡有. ■

       20

    絕偽棄詐，　民復孝慈. ■

    25    2:1      5          10

2    三言以爲辨不足，或命之、或呼屬: ■

              15

    視素保樸，　少私寡欲. ■

---

**1** 1, 9, 17 絕: 凶; 2 智 QXG: 智: 知 WW; 3, 11, 19 棄: 弃;
4 辯: 㪟: 鞭 as 辯 QXG: 辨 RH; 8 倍: 伓; 10 巧: 攷; 13 盜: 規; 14 賊: 側;
16 有: 又; 18 偽: 惎 | 憍: 義 GM: 化 IT; 20 詐: 慮: 慮 IT; 22 復: 复; 23 孝: 季;
24 慈: 子

**2** 2 辨: 皀: 文 GM: 使 LL; 6 命 QXG^n: 命: 令 IT; 8 或: 或: 有GM, LL;
9 呼: 虖: 乎 LL; 10 屬 QXG^n: 豆; 11 示: 視; 12 素: 索; 14 樸: 僕; 16 私: 厶;
17 寡: 寡 | 須 WW error

---

NOTES :

The order of the 3 sayings (1:1–24) differs from that in all other versions. The six things to be rejected in other versions are *sageliness* 聖 , *knowledge/knowing* 智 , *benevolence* 仁 , *justice* 義 , *skill* 巧 and *profit* 利. Notice the items in italics, which are different here.

**1:1, 9, 17**    See Qiu Xigui, *On the Analysis*, pp. 53–63 [hereafter as Qiu Xigui], #3, and Gao Ming, *Some Observations*, pp. 65–69 [hereafter as Gao Ming], #1.

**1:2**    See Qiu Xigui, # 3; 1:4 See Qiu Xigui, #8; 1:10 See Qiu Xigui, #4.

**1:13–16**    See Qiu Xigui, #6.

**1:18, 20**    See Qiu Xigui, #9, & Gao Ming, #1; Gao Ming considers but rejects a reading of 1:20 as 仁 *ren*.

**2:5–10**    Punctuation of Qiu Xigui. For 2:5, 2:9–10 see Gao Ming, #2.

**2:11** On the reading of *shi* 視 as *shi* 示 , see Qiu Xigui, p. 59.

      For 1:17–24, see also Sect. IV, "Additional Textual Notes."

## A II  [Chapter 66 *complete*/MWD 29]

2/3  江海所以爲百谷王，以其能爲百谷下.

是以能爲百谷王.

聖人之在民前也，以身後之；

4  其在民上也，以言下之.

其在民上也，民弗厚也；

其在民前也，民弗害也.

5  天下樂進而弗厭，以其不爭也.

故天下莫能與之爭.

---

**2** 20 海: 洈; 25 谷: 浴;

**3** 4, 11 谷: 浴; 16, 25 在: 才;

**4** 5, 14 在: 才; 20 害: 害 | 害; 28 厭 WW: 詀: 詹 DYZ

**5** 4, 13 爭: 靜; 6 故: 古

---

NOTES:

There are two points of significance here. In the second line all other versions except the Yan Zun 嚴遵 version add the term *shan* 善, "good at": "is that they are good at being below them." The second difference is that other versions read *tui* 推, "promote," rather than *jin* 進, "advance": "All under heaven delight in drawing close to him."

**4:20**　Qiu Xigui (QXG[n]) discusses this way of writing 害 as 害.

**4:28**　Ding Yuanzhi reads as 詀 and notes that the *Yu Pian* 玉篇 defines this as "saying too much 多言" (see *Hanyu Da Zidian*, 詀 *zhan*), which is the same as the *Shuowen* definition for *zhan* 詹 (see *Shuowen Jiezi* 2 上, 八部 ).

## A III [Chapter 46b/ MWD 9]

/5
罪莫厚乎甚欲,

咎莫憯乎欲得,

禍莫大乎不知足.

知足之爲足, 此恒足矣. ▬

---

**5** 14 罪: 辠; 17, 23 乎: 虍; 18 甚: 甚: 貪 LL; 22 憯: 僉; 24 欲: 谷
**6** 1 禍: 化; 4 乎: 虍; 6, 8 知: 智; 14 恒: 亙

---

NOTES:

The order of the three phrases differs in other versions: the second and third being inverted. The only other significant difference is in the first line which reads: "As for crimes, there is none *greater* than the *potential for desire* 罪莫大於可欲 ." The nearest to the Guodian version is found in the *Hanshi Waizhuan* 韓詩外傳 : "As for crimes, there is none greater than much desire 罪莫大於多欲 ."

**6:14** See Qiu Xigui, #1.

## A IV [Chapter 30a/MWD 74]

6/7    以 道 佐 人 主 者， 不 欲 以 兵 强 於 天 下．

善 者 果 而 已， 不 以 取 强． ▬

果 而 弗 伐， 果 而 弗 驕，

果 而 弗 矜， ▬ 是 謂 果 而 不 强．

8    其 事 好 長． ▬

---

**6** 18 道: 衜; 19 佐: 差; 21 主: 宔; 24 欲: 谷
**7** 16 伐: 癹; 20 驕: 喬; 24 矜: 稴; 26 謂: 胃
**8** 2 好: 好: 好 還 QXG; 3 長 ▬: ▬長

---

NOTES:

The Guodian version is unique in reading "do not *desire* to use weapons" at 6:23–24. There is also variation in the order of the phrases 7:13–30, but no substantial differences from known versions.

Qiu Xigui suggested reading the last line as the displaced line: "Such deeds tend [*lit*. are good at] to rebound 其事好還." Qiu read the punctuation mark as a note added to indicate the omission of a character, viz. *huan* 還. Gao Ming, Xu Kangsheng and others maintained that the mark was a misplaced punctuation mark (see Gao Ming, #3).

**6:18** See Qiu Xigui, #2.

## A V [Chapter 15/MWD 59]

/8 古 之 善 爲 士 者, 必 微 妙 玄 達,

深 不 可 識, ▬ 是 以 爲 之 容:

9 豫 乎 如 冬 涉 川, 猶 乎 其 如 畏 四 鄰, ▬

嚴 乎 其 如 客, ▬ 渙 乎 其 如 凌 釋, ▬

屯 乎 其 如 樸, ▬ 沌 乎 其 如 濁 。

10 孰 能 濁 以 靜 者, 將 徐 清 。 ■

孰 能 安 以 動 者, 將 徐 生 。

保 此 道 者 不 欲 尚 盈 。

---

8　4 古: 古: 長 古 QXG; 11 微: 非; 12 妙: 溺: 汋 DYZ; 14 達: 達: 造 IT;
　　18 識: 志; 23 容: 頌: 頌 IT; 24 豫: 夜; 25, 31 乎: 虖;
　　26 如 QXGⁿ: 奴: 其 若 WW; 30 猶: 猷

9　1, 8, 13, 19, 24 如 QXGⁿ: 奴: 若 WW; 2 畏: 愄; 4 鄰: 哭; 5 嚴: 敢;
　　6, 11, 17, 22 乎: 虖; 10 渙: 觀; 14-15 凌 釋: 懌: 釋 LL: 液 DYZ;
　　16 屯: 屯: 混 LL: 敦 LL alt; 21 沌: 坉: 沌 LL: 淳 LL alt; 26 孰: 竺; 30 靜: 朿

10　2, 11 將: 酒; 3, 12 徐: 舍: 舍 DYZ; 5 孰: 竺; 7 安: 庀;
　　9 重 as 動 QXGⁿ: 迲: 延 as 行 XKS; 16 道: 衍; 19 欲: 谷; 20 尚: 端;
　　21 盈: 呈: 呈 XKS

---

NOTES:

The use of *shi* 士 rather than *dao* 道 in the first line is as in the received version. All versions repeat 8:12–13. In the following lines some but not all versions add a poetic *xi* 兮. The Guodian version is unique in not having the line "Broad like a valley 曠兮其若谷."

10:7 Xu Kangsheng notes that 庀 is glossed as 具 in the *Yu Pian* 玉篇。廣部, but since the meaning of 具 does not fit the present context, the graph must be a mistake for 安.

10:16 See Qiu Xigui, #2.

❧ For 9:16, see also Sect. IV, "Additional Textual Notes."

## A VI [Chapter 64b/MWD 27]

10/11 爲之者敗之， 執之者遠之.

是以聖人亡爲故亡敗;

亡執故亡失.

臨事之紀， 慎終如始， 此亡敗事矣.

12 聖人欲不欲， 不貴難得之貨,

教不教， 復衆之所過. ▬

13 是故聖人能輔萬物之自然， 而弗能爲.

---

**10** 30 遠: 遊 LL
**11** 8, 13 故: 古; 15 失: 遊; 20 慎: 訢; 21 終: 冬; 22 如: 女; 23 始: 訂; 31 欲: 谷
**12** 2 欲: 谷; 9, 11 教: 季; 15 所: 所 = ; 16 過: 華; 18 故: 古;
　　22 輔: 尃 薄 DH; 尃 DYZ; 24 物: 勿; 27 然: 肰

---

NOTES:

Other versions read *shi* 失 , "to lose," rather than *yuan* 遠 , "to distance," at 10:30. Line 11:16–19 is quite different from all other versions (Wang Bi/Heshang Gong: 民之從事，常於幾成而敗之 "People's dealing with affairs is always a case of ruining them just at the point of perfection"). As for line 12: 9–11, other versions read *xue* 學 , to study, rather than *jiao* 教 , to teach, as here.

**11:15** See Qiu Xigui, #7.

**11:20** QXG[n] notes that the graph here transcribed as 訢 should be considered in conjunction with C 12:1 transcribed 訢 and read as 慎 . He questions the validity of the transcription as 訢 .

**12:22** In commenting on C V 13:22, Harper read as *bo* 薄 . On this reading of *bo*, see *Hanyu Da Zidian*, p. 1378, *bo* as "to approach, draw close to."

　　🕭 For 12:15, see also Sect. IV, "*Additional Textual Notes.*"

## A VII     [Chapter 37 *complete*/MWD 81]

/13 道 恒 亡 爲 也， 侯 王 能 守 之， 而 萬 物 將 自 化.

化 而 欲 作， 將 鎭 之 以 亡 名 之 樸.

14 夫 亦 將 知 足， 知 足 以 靜， 萬 物 將 自 定. ■

---

**13** 3 道: 衍; 4 恒: 亘; 15 物: 勿; 16, 23 將: 酒; 18, 19 化: 惥 | 憍; 21 欲: 雒;
22 作: 乇; 24 鎭: 貞: 貞 DYZ; 30 樸: 叡
**14** 2, 11 將: 酒; 3 知: 智; 5-6 知 足: 智; 8 靜: 朿; 10 物: 勿

---

Notes:

All other versions are written in the first person, but in Guodian there is no "I," so we are at liberty to supply a third or first person pronoun before "calm (*zhen* 鎭)," or read as an imperative. Guodian does not repeat the phrase about the virgin wood 樸 *pu* and reads quite differently in 13:31 to 14:8.

In the final clause MWD reads "*zi zheng* 自正 : will be correct of their own accord," and both MWD MSS agree with Wang Bi/Heshang Gong in reading the subject of this clause as *Tian-di* 天地 , heaven and earth, rather than the myriad things.

**13:3–4** See Qiu Xigui, #2.

# A VIII   [Chapter 63 *part*/MWD 26]

/14 爲亡爲， 事亡事， 味亡味。

大小之， 多易必多難。

15 是以聖人猶難之， 故終亡難。 ∎

---

**14** 19, 21 味: 未; 23 小: 少; 26 易: 惕; 29 難: 戁
**15** 1 猶: 猷; 2, 7 難: 戁; 4 故: 古

---

NOTES:

The text of this section is not in itself very different from all other versions except that all others have several lines between 14:25 and 14:26. This may be an omission in the Guodian text (Paul Thompson) or the insertion of a commentary in other texts (Xu Kangsheng). [The comma at 14:24/25 is suggested by Xu.] The relevant deleted/inserted portion is highlighted below (Wang Bi edition):

大小多少，報怨以德。

圖難於其易，為大於其細。

天下難事必作於易，天下大事必作於細，

是以聖人終不為大，故能成其大。

夫輕諾必寡信，多易必多難，是以聖人猶難之，故終無難矣。

## A IX      [Chapter 2 *complete*/MWD 46]

/15  天下皆知美之爲美也，惡已；

皆知善，此其不善已。

16  有亡之相生也，難易之相成也，

長短之相形也，高下之相盈也，

音聲之相和也，先後之相隨也。

17  是以聖人居亡爲之事，行不言之教。

萬物作而弗始也，爲而弗恃也，功成而弗居。

18  夫唯弗居也，是以弗去也。 ■

---

15 11, 20 知: 智; 12 美: 散; 15 美: 散; 17 惡: 亞; 27 有: 又
16 1 難: 戁; 2 易: 惕; 8 短: 耑; 11 形: 型; 17 盈: 浧; 20 聲: 聖;
    23 和: 和: 舍 DYZ; 29 隨: 墮
17 13 教: 孝; 15 物: 勿; 16 作: 復; 19 始: 冂: 嗣 as 司 DYZ; 24 恃: 志;
    26-27 功 成: 成: 成 RH; 31 夫: 天

---

NOTES:

The text here is very close to the Mawangdui version. It has the *ye* 也 that characterizes Mawangdui. It also shares in common the absence of the clause *sheng er bu you* 生而不有 : "they are produced and he does not own them." A notable difference is that in common with the other versions and in contrast to Mawangdui there is not the final *heng ye* 恆也 : "these are all constants," after 16:30.

## A X [Chapter 32 *complete*/MWD 76]

/18 　道 恒 亡 名， 樸 雖 微， 天 地 弗 敢 臣，

19 　侯 王 如 能 守 之， 萬 物 將 自 賓． ■

　　天 地 相 合 也， 以 逾 甘 露．

　　民 莫 之 令， 而 自 均 焉．

　　始 制 有 名．

20 　名 亦 既 有， 夫 亦 將 知 止， 知 止 所 以 不 殆．

　　譬 道 之 在 天 下 也， 猶 小 谷 之 與 江 海． ■

---

**18** 10 恒: 亙; 13 樸: 僕; 14 雖: 唯; 15 微: 妻: 細 LL; 17 地: 陸; 23 如: 女
**19** 1 守: 獸; 4 物: 勿; 5 將: 酒; 7 賓: 宜; 9 地: 陸; 11 合: 合: 會 QXGⁿ;
　　14 逾: 逾: 逾 as 雨 XKS; 16 露: 零: 賈 LXF; 20 令: 命; 21 而: 天; 24 焉: 安;
　　25 始: 訂; 26 制: 折: 折 DYZ; 27 有: 又
**20** 3 有: 又; 6 將: 酒; 7, 9 知: 智; 14 殆 DYZ: 訂: 始; 15 譬: 卑; 18 在: 才;
　　22 猶: 獸; 23 小: 少; 24 谷: 浴: 谿 LXF; 28 海: 洰

---

NOTES:

Variations from known versions are found in a number of individual characters but with no great effect on the meaning. Hence *wei* 微 is used for "small" rather than *xiao* 小. *Yu* 逾 is used for the verb "to fall," as in the Mawangdui version (*yu* 俞). Finally rather than *chuan* 川, "river," in the last line there is the term *xiao*, 小, "small." Confusion of the two graphs 川 and 小 has probably led to the reading 川 in the received versions. The biggest difference of this kind is that the first line reads "heaven and earth, 天地" rather than "under heaven, 天下." More striking is the dot at 19:7–8 marking a division of the text, which does not correspond to known paragraph divisions.

**18:10** See Qiu Xigui, #1.

**19:14** Xu Kangsheng's reading as *yu* 雨 is based on a suggestion made by Gao Ming in his edition of the Mawangdui *Laozi*. Gao notes that here *yu* 雨 means *jiang* 降, "to rain down." See Gao Ming, *Boshu Laozi Jiaozhu*, pp. 398–99.

# A XI     [Chapter 25 *complete*/MWD 69]

21:1          5
21   有狀混成， 先天地生，
         10          15              20
     敓穆， 獨立不改， 可以爲天下母。
                     25              22:1              5
22   未知其名， 字之曰道， 吾强爲之名曰大。
                 10              15
     大曰澨， 澨曰遠， 遠曰返。
                     20
     天大， 地大， 道大， 王亦大。
     25          30
     國中有四大焉， 王居一焉。
     23:1          5                    10
23   人法地， 地法天， 天法道， 道法自然。 ∎

---

21 1 有: 又; 2 狀: 牀: 道 WW; 3 混: 蟲; 7 地: 陞; 9 敓: 㪅: 敦 DH: 寂 IT;
    10 穆: 㣎: 繆 LL; 11 獨: 蜀; 14 改: 亥: 咳 DH; 22 知: 智; 25 字: 绤; 29 吾: 虐
22 1 强: 弱; 9, 10 澨: 澨; 12, 13 遠: 連; 15 返: 反; 18 地: 陞; 27 有: 又;
    30, 34 焉: 安; 32 居: 尻: 處 LL
23 2, 3 地: 陞; 12 然: 狀

---

NOTES:

Like the Mawangdui version, Guodian does not have the phrase about the Way moving round in a circle:
" 周行而不殆 , *zhouxing er bu-dai*" at 21:14–15.

**21:2** The most notable feature is the term read as *zhuang* 狀 , "shape," by both Harper and Qiu Xigui,
while all other versions read *wu* 物 , "thing." See Qiu Xigui, #11.

**21:14** Harper's reading as 咳 is to be read according to the *Shuowen* as equivalent to *jian* 兼 , "paired
with," thus giving the reading "unique, without pair."

The character used at 22:9/10 is as yet unknown but may be the same as the more familiar, *shi* 逝 , written
in the Mawangdui version with the loan graph, *shi* 筮 .

Wang Bo held that sections A XI to XIII should be placed with XVII-XX.

&  *For A 21:14, see also Sect. IV, "Afterthoughts," pp. 238–39.*

## A XII　　　[Chapter 5b/MWD 49]

/23　天 地 之 間, 其 猶 橐 籥 與?

　　　虛 而 不 屈, 動 而 愈 出.　■

---

**23** 14 地: 陸; 16 間: 冽; 18 猶: 猷; 19 橐: 囝; 20 籥: 筶: 管 DH; 26 動: 迬

---

NOTES:

This version is exactly the same as known versions, bar a few graphic variants that do not affect the meaning. Of note is that the section concludes with a paragraph mark and is only 17 characters long. In all other versions this 17-character phrase forms the middle part of a complete chapter.

## A XIII     [Chapter 16b/MWD 60]

24:1                5
24    至 虛 極 也;  守 中 篤 也.
        10              15
      萬 物 旁 作,  居 以 須 復 也.
          20              25
      天 道 芸 芸,  各 復 其 根. ■

---

**24** 1 至: 至: 致 DYZ; 3 極 LL, LXQ: 亙: 恆 WW; 5 守: 獸; 6 中: 中: 盅 IT;
7 篤: 篙: 裻 DYZ; 10 物: 勿; 11 旁: 方: 並 LL: 方 DYZ; 12 作: 复;
18 天: 天: 夫 RW; 19 道: 道: 狀 RH;
20, 21 芸 Wang Bi: 員: 圓 WBo: 云 LL: 𢇍 DYZ alt: 運 DYZ alt; 25 根: 堇

---

NOTES:

The differences in this version are not trivial. Much depends on whether they are seen as graphic
differences or differences in meaning. For instance, if 24:18 does indeed read *tian* 天, "heaven," as in the
Mawangdui versions and not *fu* 夫, "this," as in the received texts, then this makes a difference.

**14:20–21**  has the graph *yuan* 員, which could be a phonetic variant for the *yun* 芸 of Wang Bi:
"Things are *plenteous* and each returns to its root."

At Dartmouth, Li Ling and Wang Bo held that 24:13 *ju* 居, "to dwell," is correct, whereas other versions
incorrectly read as *wu* 吾, "I." Wang Bo pointed out that this *ju* is in contrast to *zuo* 作 in the Mawangdui
*Four Canons of the Yellow Emperor* 111b 18–25 居則無法, 動作爽名. (Yates, *Five Lost Classics*, p. 127
[modified]: "at *rest* he lacks laws, and in *movement*, he is not in harmony with the correct names.")

**24:3**  should be read as *ji* 極 and not as *heng* 恆. Li Xueqin noted that the phrase *taiji* 太極 in the
Mawangdui texts is often written in a similar form. See also Qiu Xigui, #1.

> ❧ *For 24:3, see also Sect. IV, "Additional Textual Notes."*

## A XIV　　[Chapter 64b/MWD 27]

25 其 安 也, 易 持 也. 其 未 兆 也, 易 謀 也.

其 毳 也, 易 判 也. 其 幾 也, 易 散 也.

26 爲 之 於 其 亡 有 也.

治 之 於 其 未 亂.

合 □ □ □ □ □ □ 末,

27 九 層 之 臺 甲 □ □ □ □ □ □ □ □ □ 足 下. ▬

---

**25** 5 持: 枲; 9 兆: 芀; 12 謀: 悔; 15 毳 RH: 壨: 脆 WW; 18 判: 畔;
　21 幾: 幾: 微 LL; 24 散: 後

**26** 2 有: 又; 4 治: 絧: 鬜 as 治 DYZ; 17 末: 口 ; 19 層 LL: 成: 成 WW;
　22 甲: 甲: 作 WW: 蓋 LL: 己 as 起 IT

---

NOTES:

The first line reads as in the Mawangdui version, with *ye* 也 at the end of each phrase.

The graph at 25:15 is similar to the Heshang Gong version: 脆 *cui*.

The appearance of *jia* 甲 at 26:22 is worthy of note. Mawangdui reads *zuo* 作, "to set in motion," while other versions read *qi* 起, "to stir up." The Wenwu editors think that *jia* 甲 is a mistake for *zuo* 作. Ikeda held that the Guodian *jia* 甲 is a phonetic loan for *ji* 己, which he glossed as *qi* 起.

Wang Bo suggested sections A XIV-XVI should be placed with sections I-X. This would form a group of passages relating to how to govern.

## A XV    [Chapter 56 *complete*/MWD 19]

/27

知之者弗言, 言之者弗知.

閉其兌, 塞其門, 和其光,

28

同其塵, 副其籥, 解其紛, 是謂玄同.

故不可得而親, 亦不可得而疏;

不可得而利, 亦不可得而害;

29

不可得而貴, 亦不可得而賤.

故爲天下貴. ■

---

**27** 3, 12 知: 智; 13 閉: 閞:閟 LL; 15 兌: 逸; 16 塞: 賽; 22 同: 迵; 24 塵: 訢訢;
   25 副: 副: 副 IT: 削 DH: 刨 RH; 27 籥: 籥: 攖 IT: 彌 DH: 纓 RH
**28** 2 謂: 胃; 5 故: 古; 9 而: 天; 10 親: 新; 16 疏: 疋
**29** 6 亦: 亦 可; 11 賤: 戔; 12 故: 古

---

NOTES:

This text follows the Mawangdui version. Exceptions are the inversion of *bi* 閉, "to close," and *sai* 塞, "to shut up," at 27:13 and 27:16, and the addition of the pronoun *zhi* 之 after the verbs in the first line.

The graphs at 27:25 and 27:27 await identification. Ikeda read 27:25 as *fu* 副, meaning *pan* 判 "to cut, split" (*Shuowen* 4 下, 刀部). He read 27:27 as *ying* 攖, glossed in the *Guangya* as *luan* 亂. (*Hanyu Da Zidian* p. 833.) Thus the phrase would mean "sort out its confusion," that is, the primordial division of the cosmic soup. Harper read as *xiao qi mi* 削其彌, meaning that exaggerated speech should be cut down to size.

## A XVI [Chapter 57 *complete*/MWD 20]

29/30 以正治邦，以奇用兵，以亡事取天下。

吾何以知其然也。

夫天下多忌諱，而民彌叛。

民多利器，而邦滋昏。

31 人多知而奇物滋起。

法物滋彰，盜賊多有。

是以聖人之言曰：

我無事而民自富。

32 我亡爲而民自化。

我好靜而民自正。

我欲不欲而民自樸。乙

---

**29** 19 治: 之: 之 as 至 DYZ; 22 奇: **𢦏**; 23 用: **甬**
**30** 4 吾: **虗**; 5 何: **可**; 7 知: **智**; 9 然: **肰**; 12-13 天 下: **天**; 15 忌: **期**; 16 諱: **韋**; 19 彌: **爾**; 20 叛: **畔**; 27 滋: **慈**
**31** 1 知: **智**; 2 而: **天**; 3 奇: **𢦏**; 4, 8 物: **勿**; 5, 9 滋: **慈**; 6 起: **𨑹**; 10 彰: **章**; 11 盜: **覜**; 12 賊: **惻**; 14 有: **又**; 28 富: **𥙿**: 福 IT
**32** 7 化: **蠡**; 10 靜: **青**; 16, 18 欲: **谷**

---

NOTES:

This passage follows the preceding but is separated from it by a paragraph mark. In the received version the two are respectively chapters 56 and 57. At 30:20 all versions read as *pin* 貧, "poor," but here we find *pan* 畔, which the editors read as a loan for *pan* 叛, "to rebel." Otherwise the text follows Mawangdui though without *jia* 家 after *bang/guo* 邦 / 國 and with a distinctive order of the final four phrases 31:22 to 32:22. On 31:11–12, see Qiu Xigui # 6. The section ends with a punctuation mark in the form of 乙. Donald Harper noted this as found at A:39 and in *Cheng Zhi Wen Zhi* 成之聞之, slip 40, *Liu De* 六德, slip 49, and elsewhere. The *Shiji* records the use of *yi* 乙 as meaning "a stop in reading": 史記 126, "Guji Liezhuan 滑稽列傳," p. 3205: "The lord read from the top, and whenever he stopped would mark the place with an *yi*": 人主從上方讀之，止，輒《乙》其處.

❧ *For the* "乙" *see also Sect. II,* pp. 136–37.

## A XVII     [Chapter 55 *complete*/MWD 18]

**33:1**     5

33   含 德 之 厚 者, 比 於 赤 子,
10     15
　　　虺 蠆 蟲 蛇 弗 螫,
20          25       34:1
34   攫 鳥 猛 獸 弗 敂,　骨 弱 筋 柔 而 捉 固.
5            10
　　　未 知 牝 牡 之 合, 朘 怒, 精 之 至 也.
15          20
　　　終 日 呼 而 不 憂,　和 之 至 也,
25          30
　　　和 曰 常,　知 和 曰 明.
35:1          5
35   益 生 曰 祥,　心 使 氣 曰 强,
10          15
　　　物 壯 則 老,　是 謂 不 道. ■

---

33 1 含: 舍: 歙 DYZ; 2 德: 悳; 10 虺 LL: 蟲: 蚮 WW: 蝞 QXGⁿ; 13 蛇: 它;
　　15 螫: 蠚; 18 猛: 猒; 21 敂: 扣; 23 弱: 溺; 24 筋: 堇; 25 柔: 𣎳
34 3, 27 知: 智; 4 牝: 扎 | 牝 WW error; 5 牡: 戊; 8 朘: 肓: 然 LL: 家; 9 怒: 惹;
　　16 呼: 虐: 號 LL; 19 憂: 惥: 嚘 DYZ; 26 常: 尚; 27 知: 智 DYZ
35 1 益: 膥; 4 祥: 羕: 兼 DYZ; 6 使: 貞; 7 氣: 既; 9 强: 弜;
　　10 物: 勿; 11 壯: 臸; 15 謂: 胃

---

NOTES:

Again this text follows Mawangdui. It lacks, however, the last line known from all other versions: *bu-Dao zao yi* 不道早已, "what is not the Way terminates early."

**34:4** Li Ling notes that although the transcription 牝 is an error, the graph should be read this way. The original character is an alternative form of the character 必 *bi*.

The most difficult part of the Guodian text is 34: 8–9. QXGⁿ questions the transcription 然. The Mawang-dui versions read the equivalent of 34:8 as *zui [juan]* 朘, "male organ," whereas Wang Bi reads as *quan* 全, "completeness." Heshang Gong reads *zui* 峻, "male organ," and adds a note which provides the clue for the Guodian text: "The child does not yet know the union and mixing of male and female yet *yin* is excited to passion (*nu* 怒): 赤子未知男女之合而陰作怒者." In comments written after the Confer-ence, Henricks suggests that the graph is a form of *yang* 陽, i.e. "the penis."

Kalinowski noted that 35:10–17 is found in the received version in chapters 30 and 55. Ma Xulun 馬敍倫 (1884–1970) decided that its correct position was in ch. 30 and not in ch. 55. The Guodian version of ch. 30 (A IV, 6:17 to 8:3) does not contain the phrase. Hence Guodian disproves Ma's emendation.

Wang Bo read A XVII-XX as part of the same bundle of strips as XI-XIII. The topic discussed is personal cultivation relying on the Way.

## A XVIII    [Chapter 44 *complete*/MWD 7]

**35/36**   名 與 身 孰 親？ 身 與 貨 孰 多？ 得 與 亡 孰 病？

甚 愛 必 大 費， 厚 藏 必 多 亡.

**37**   故 知 足 不 辱， 知 止 不 殆， 可 以 長 久。 ∎

---

**35** 21 孰: 箸; 22 親: 新
**36** 1, 6 孰: 箸; 3 得: 𢍰; 5, 17 亡: 𠅃; 7 病: 疠; 9 愛: 忎; 12 費: 𧴥; 13 厚: 𠩺;
    14 藏: 𧤫; 18 故: 古; 19, 23 知: 智; 26 殆: 怠
**37** 3 久: 舊

---

NOTES:

The only point of difference with known versions — and this may simply be because the Mawangdui
versions are defective here — is the inversion of *duo* 多, "much," and *hou* 厚, "stress," at 36:13 and 16.
This difference does not affect the meaning.

## A XIX     [Chapter 40 *complete*/MWD 4]

/37 返也者, 道動也. 弱也者, 道之用也.
天下之物生於有, 有生於亡. ∎

---

**37** 8 動: 僮; 10 弱: 溺; 15 用: 甬; 20 物: 勿; 23-24 有 有: 又: 有 CGY

---

NOTES:

The editors note that *you* 有 , "being," should be repeated. They suggest that the repetition symbol has been omitted. However, Chen Guying argued against this, holding that "being" 有 and "beinglessness" 無 are names for the Way, hence the passage would read: 生於有, 生於亡 . He believed the sequence of "beinglessness" — "being" — "the myriad things" to be a later metaphysical construct. The implications of this reading are taken up by Ding Yuanzhi, pp. 213–20, and in his paper: "Problems of Ontology and Chinese Philosophy 存有論問題與中國哲學," given on January 8, 1999, at Fujen University, 8th Conference on Scholastic and Contemporary Philosophy.

*N.B.:* One might expect the particle *zhi* 之 between *Dao* 道 and *dong* 動 at 37: 7–8: "the movement of the Way."

## A XX    [Chapter 9 *complete*/MWD 53]

**37/38**    殖 而 盈 之，   不 若 其 已。

揣 而 群 之，   不 可 長 保 也。

金 玉 盈 室，   莫 能 守 也。

**39**    貴 富 而 驕，   自 遺 咎 也。

功 遂 身 退，   天 之 道 也。 ↲

---

**37** 28 殖: 柴: 持 IT; 30 盈: 涅
**38** 2 不: 不 不; 4-5 其 已: 已; 6 揣 PT: 湍: 湍 WW; 8 群: 群; 17 盈: 涅;
   21 守: 獸; 24 富: 福; 25-26 而 驕: 喬; 29 咎: 咎
**39** 2 功: 攻; 3 遂: 述

---

NOTES:

Guodian follows Mawangdui, most noticeably in reading *ying shi* 盈室 rather than *man tang* 滿堂, "fills the room," at 38:17–18.

The only peculiarity of Guodian is the absence of *er* 而, "yet," at 38:25. Might this be a scribal error?

The interpretation of the characters in the first and second lines, 37:28 to 38:5, is not clear. The editors suppose the first verb to be *zhi* 殖, "to fill up," though the received versions read *chi* 持, "to stand upright," and the Mawangdui version has a graph, *sic* 揸, that could correspond to either *zhi* or *chi*.

Paul Thompson's reading of 38:6 follows the received versions. The graph 揣 is read as *zhui* in this case, meaning "to hammer."

38:29  QXG[n] notes that the transcription of this graph as 咎 is problematic.

On the final punctuation mark in the form of ↲, see notes to A XVI above.

## B I  [Chapter 59 *complete*/MWD 22]

1:1          5
1    治人事天，莫若嗇.
          10           15          20
     夫唯嗇，是以早服，是以早服是謂……
     2:1
2    不克 ■
          5
     不克，則莫知其極，
     10           15
     莫知其極，可以有國.
               20
     有國之母，可以長……，
     3:1          5
3    長生久視之道也. ■

---

1 1 治: 紿; 11-12 是 以: 是 以:○ LL; 13-14 早 服: 枭:○ LL; 17 早: 枭;
   18 服: 備: 備 CD: 復 RW; 20 謂: 胃
2 7, 11 知: 智; 9, 13 極: 亙; 16, 18 有: 又; 17, 19 國: 哦 | 郯 WW
3 3 久: 舊

---

NOTES:

Aside from missing parts of the text this chapter displays no major differences with known versions. The only departure is the repetition of the phrase 1:11–12 "therefore."

On 1:18, Rudolf Wagner suggested the reading *fu* 復 and Qiu Xigui noted that the presence of the *chi* 彳 radical lent plausibility to this suggestion. Gao Ming's notes on the Mawangdui *Laozi* list six versions that read *fu* 復 ; see Gao Ming, *Boshu Laozi Jiaozhu*, p. 114.

On 3:4, see Qiu Xigui, #5.

**B II**      [Chapter 48a/MWD 11]

/3    學者日益, 爲道者日損.

4    損之或損, 以至亡爲也, ▬

亡爲而亡不爲. ▬

---

**3 8 學: 學: 聞 as 問 CGY: 爲學 DYZ; 16, 17, 20 損: 員**

---

NOTES:

The Mawangdui versions of this chapter are defective but even so, the Guodian text comes nearer to the received version. The first clause is unique in opening with *xue* 學, "to study," rather than with *wei* 爲, "in order to," as in all other versions. *Wei* is, however, found before *Dao* 道, "the Way" 3:13, as in the received versions. Qiu Xigui noted that grammar demands *wei* 爲 before *Dao* 道 but not before *xue* 學.

The presence of the particle *zhe* 者 at 3:9 and 3:14 follows Mawangdui.

In the second line, at 3:19, the MS reads *huo* 或, rather than *you* 又, as in the received versions. This is a graphic variant as the meaning is the same.

After *zhi* 至, "to come to," all versions agree on adding the preposition *yu* 於, "to." Its absence in Guodian is perhaps of grammatical interest but hardly effects the sense.

Carine Defoort notes that if the graph at 3:16 *et al.*, 員, is read as at A 24:20–21, then it would have the opposite meaning of that given here: A 24:20, 21 芸 : 員, but here the apparatus has B 3:16 損: 員.

The presence of 4:2–7 亡為而亡不為 "And with non-purposive doing there is nothing that is not done" is important. Gao Ming and D. C. Lau, noting the absence of this phrase in the Mawangdui versions, held that it was a later interpolation (Gao Ming, *Boshu Laozi Jiaozhu*, Beijing: Zhonghua Shuju, 1996, pp. 54–57). Guodian disavows that view.

As noted in the following section, Paul Thompson suggested that line 4:8–11 fits this section better than the following one, in which the Wenwu editors have put it.

## B III     [Chapter 20a/MWD 64]

/4     絕學亡憂。
<sup>(10 above 學)</sup>

    唯與呵, 相去幾何?
<sup>(15 above 呵)</sup>

    美與惡, 相去何若?
<sup>(20 above 美, 25 above 相)</sup>

5     人之所畏, 亦不可以不畏人。 ■
<sup>(5:1 above 人, 5 above 所, 10 above 不)</sup>

---

4 8 絕: 㠯; 11 憂: 惥: 憂 as 擾 CGY; 14 呵: 可 : 可 CD: 訶 IT; 18, 24 何: 可;
19 美: 뭐; 21 惡: 亞
5 4, 10 畏: 禔; 11 人 ■: ■ 人 [WW places this graph at the head of B IV]

---

NOTES:

This version is exactly the same as Mawangdui B except that, in common with the received versions, there is no *qi* 其 at 4:15 or 4:22.

Some scholars, such as Chen Guying, have previously argued that the line set out as 4:8–11 belongs to ch. 19. The Guodian version lacks the equivalent of ch. 19. Paul Thompson and others suggest that, in the Guodian context, this line fits better at the end of B II.

On the terms at 4:12 and 4:14, Carine Defoort proposed reading *wei* 唯, "to agree politely," and *ke* 可, "to merely acquiesce."

The punctuation mark on the MS is placed before 5:11 *ren* 人, hence Wenwu edited the text with this character at the beginning of the next paragraph (B IV). However, as Qiu Xigui and others made clear, this would produce a grammatically awkward sentence at the end of B III. A further consequence is to produce a peculiar reading for the first line of B IV. There was some discussion as to whether a reading of *ren*, people, in B IV could make sense. One proposal being that *ren* was opposed to *gui* 貴 (5:16), in the sense of the common people as opposed to the nobles. Rudolf Wagner noted that the theme of *ren*, the common people, had never been raised in the Warring States period. Hence it is more probable that the punctuation mark has been placed wrongly. See also Gao Ming, #4.

**B IV** [Chapter 13 *complete*/MWD 57]

15 20
/5 寵辱若驚， 貴大患若身。

6:1
6 何謂寵辱？

5
寵爲下也。

10 15
得之若驚， 失之若驚， 是謂寵辱若驚。

20 25 7:1
7 □ □ □ □ □ 若身？

5 10
吾所以有大患者， 爲吾有身。

15 20 25 8:1
8 及吾亡身， 或何 □ □ □ □ □ □ 爲天下，

5 10
若可以託天下矣。 ▬

15 20
愛以身爲天下， 若何以达天下矣。 ■

---

**5** 12, 23 寵: 慐; 15 驚: 纓: 纓 QXGⁿ; 21 何: 可; 22 謂: 胃
**6** 2, 16 寵: 慐; 9, 13 驚: 纓: 纓 QXGⁿ; 10 失: 遊; 15 謂: 胃; 18-19 若驚: ▬ 纓
**7** 3, 11, 15 吾: 虗; 6, 12 有: 又; 14 及: 返; 19 何: □
**8** 7 託: 厄: 厇 WW: 宅 DYZ; 11 愛: 炁; 18 何: 可: 可 DYZ; 20 达: 达

---

NOTES:

The opening lines of this chapter differ in other versions. Guodian brings a unique reading, which seems to make better sense of the passage. The question 何謂寵辱？ is found in this form in Heshang Gong but not in Wang Bi or Mawangdui. The reading 寵爲下 is that of Wang Bi and Mawangdui, but in Heshang Gong this has been changed to read 辱爲下 , and in one Japanese MS seen by Li Daochun 李道純 and Chen Jingyuan 陳景元 (d. after 1100): 寵爲上， 辱爲下 . (Wang Ka 王卡, ed., *Laozi Daodejing Heshang Gong Zhangju*, Beijing: Zhonghua Shuju 1993.) The Heshang Gong punctuation is, however, confirmed by the presence of *ye* 也 , and this in contrast to the Wang Bi punctuation confirmed by Wang Bi's own note.

On 5:12 see preceding section, B III, note on the punctuation mark at 5:11.

On 6:10 see Qiu Xigui, #7. At 6:18 the Wenwu editors assume the proofreader inserted a mark "▬" to indicate a missing graph.

The graph at 8:7 厄 is unattested. Yet, it surely must be read as similar to the graph in the next line of the received versions: *tuo* 託 . More problematic is the graph at 8: 20 达, which reads *tuo* 託 in the received versions. This graph is recorded in the *Hanyu Da Zidian*, p. 1591, as found by the Ming scholar Yang Shen 楊慎 (1488–1559) on a Han dynasty engraving. Yang adds that the meaning and sound of the graph are unknown.

## B V     [Chapter 41 *complete*/MWD 3]

9:1     5     10

**9**   上士聞道，勤能行於其中。

15

中士聞道，若聞若亡。

20     25

下士聞道，大笑之。

10:1     5

**10**   弗大笑，不足以爲道矣。

10

是以建言有之：

15     20     11:1

**11**   明道如費，夷道□□□道若退。

5     10

上德如谷，▬大白如辱，

15     20

廣德如不足，建德如□，□真如愉。

12:1     5     10     15

**12**   大方亡隅，大器晚成，大音祇聲，天象亡形，

道……

---

**9** 3, 13, 16, 21 聞: 昏; 5 勤: 董: 僅 QXGⁿ; 24 笑: 芺: 疑 DYZ

**10** 1 笑: 芺; 12 有: 又; 16 如: 女; 17 悖 as 費 XKS: 字: 悖 DYZ; 18 夷: 遲

**11** 5, 13, 18 德: 惪; 6, 10, 14, 19, 23 如: 女; 7 谷: 浴; 11 辱: 辱: 黣 DYZ;
12 廣: 坐; 17 建: 建: 健 DYZ; 20 □: □: 偷 DYZ: 如 RH;
21 □: □: 質 DYZ: 繽 RH; 22 真: 卣; 24 愉: 愉: 渝 DYZ

**12** 4 隅: 禺; 7 晚: 曼: 慢 QXGⁿ; 11 祇: 祇: 希 WW; 12 聲: 聖; 16 形: 坓; 17 道:□

---

NOTES:

9:6 reads *neng* 能, "be able," as in Mawangdui. Other texts read *er* 而, "yet." However, *neng* is a common loan for *er*. If the reading *neng* is adopted then Qiu's reading of 9:5 must be followed. 9:8–10: This phrase is found in no other version. 9:16: The recurrence of *wen* 聞, "to hear," at this point is unique and appears out of place. Other versions read *cun* 存, "to exist," which contrasts with the following *wu* 亡, "to not exist." This looks like a scribal error. At 9:27 the *da* 大, "great," of the preceding phrase is repeated, unlike other versions. 10:7 concludes with a final particle *yi* 矣. 10:17 reads *fei* 費, "wasteful," in Mawangdui B but Xu Kangsheng interpets this as a loan for the rare graph *fei* 費, "to be of poor eyesight." The order of the three clauses 10:14 to 11:3 is unique. 11:24 is read *yu* 渝 in the received text and *shu* 输 in the Fu Yi 傅奕 version. Mawangdui is deficient at this point. 12:7 *man* 曼 may simply be a phonetic borrowing for the more normal *wan* 晚, "late."

**12:11** QXGⁿ says *zhi* 祇 is read "only just," as the *xi* 希, "scarce," of the received versions. (Cf. *Shijing* No. 188 我行其野：不思舊姻；求爾新特；成不以富；祇亦以異.)

**12:13** As in Mawangdui, this phrase has *tian* 天, "heaven," rather than *da* 大, "great."

    ✍ For 10:7, 10:17, 12:5–8, see also Sect. IV, "Additional Textual Notes."

## B VI          [Chapter 52 *part*/MWD 15]

13:1                    5                    10

**13**     閉其門, 塞其兌, 終身不㻫.

15                   20

啟其兌, 塞其事, 終身不遝. ■

---

**13** 1 閉: 閟; 4 塞: 賽; 6, 13 兌: 逸; 10 㻫: 㻫: 勤 LL: 務 IT: 瞀 DYZ: 瘂 MXL;
14 塞: 賽: 塞 LL; 20 遝: 遝: 來 TI: 救 WT

---

NOTES:

Guodian is unique in the ordering of the first two commands. As in Mawangdui the word for "open" (13:11) is *qi* 啟 rather than *kai* 開. The use of *kai* for *qi* follows a taboo on the name of Emperor Jing of the Han dynasty, Liu Qi 劉啟; r. 157–141 BC.

Otherwise the only point of interest are the three characters at 13:10, 14, 20.

㻫: Ikeda read 13:10 as *wu* 務 glossed as *lao* 勞, "toil." Robin Yates noted that in the Guodian *Laozi* C 1:18 㦔 is read as 悔 and in the Guodian *Zun De Yi* 尊德義 1:23 㦔 is read as 務 (*Guodian Chu Jian*, p. 173). This would speak in favor of Ikeda's reading.

賽: Wang Tao read 13:14 as a mistake for a graph that must mean "to open."

遝: Wang Tao read 13:20 as meaning *jiu* 救, "to save," as in the received versions. In Mawangdui Copy B we find *ji* 棘 which was presumably a phonetic loan for *jiu* (Henricks, R. G., *Lao-tzu Te-Tao Ching*, New York: Ballantine 1989, p. 269, note 59). Ikeda reads 遝 as *lai* 來 which Han Kangbo 韓康伯 (d. *c.* 385) notes can be read as "returning" (Lou Yulie 樓宇烈, *Laozi, Zhouyi: Wang Bi Ji Jiaoshi* 老子, 周易: 王弼集校釋 [Taibei: Huazheng Shuju, 1983], p. 587). The sense is the same as *fan* 反, "to go back" as found in similar expressions in the *Zhuangzi*, thus *Zhuangzi* 24, "Xu Wu Gui 徐无鬼": 終身不反 ("without ever turning back their whole life long"), describing the ceaseless quest of ordinary, unenlightened people. In the *Laozi* the meaning is, however, positive.

## B VII                [Chapter 45 *complete*/MWD 8]

            21         **14**:1              5
**13/14**  大 成 若 缺， 其 用 不 敝． ▬

                                 10
           大 盈 若 盅， 其 用 不 窮． ▬

                15              20              **15**:1
**15**     大 巧 若 拙， ▬ 大 成 若 詘， 大 直 若 屈． ■

                5                   10
           燥 勝 滄， ▬ 清 勝 然， 清 靜 爲 天 下 正．

---

**13** 22 成: 成: 贏 LXF alt: 盛 LXF alt
**14** 1 缺: 夬; 3, 11 用: 甬; 5 敝: 幣; 7 盈: 浧; 9 盅: 中: 冲 WT; 13 窮: 穷;
    15 巧: 攷; 17 拙: 仳; 20 詘: 詘: 紬 RH; 23 直: 植
**15** 3 燥: 喿: 躁 RH, DYZ; 4, 7 勝: 剩; 5 滄: 蒼; 6 清: 青: 靜 QXG;
    8 然 as 燃 DYZ: 然: 熱 WW; 10 靜 QXG[n]: 清: 清 LXF; 14 正: 定

---

NOTES:

The problems raised by this chapter are mostly a matter of graphic variants. Thus 14:5 may be read as *bi* 敝 or *bi* 弊; 14:9 as *zhong* 盅 or *chong* 沖. These readings are all attested. There are also variations in the ordering of the elements in the third line, with the phrase at 14:18–21 being unique. It is also worth noting that the passage is divided by a paragraph mark at 15:2/3.

**14:21**    詘 *qu*. This term has the same meaning as *qu* 屈 , "bent." Here it must mean the opposite of "succesful, full of achievement." The *Hanyu Da Zidian* lists it as meaning "all used up" (p. 1647).

**15:3–8**    At the Dartmouth Conference Qiu Xigui noted that the standard interpretation of the received text could easily be read here, namely 躁勝滄, 靜勝熱 "move so as to overcome the cold, keep still so as to cope with the heat."

B VIII 　　　　[Chapter 54 *complete*/MWD 17]

> 15　　　　　20　　　　16:1
/15/16　善建者不拔，善保者不脱，
> 　　　5　　　　　　10
子孫以其祭祀不輟．
> 　　　　　　15
修之身，其德乃真．
> 　　　20
修之家，其德有餘．
> 　25　17:1　　　　　5
17　修之鄉，其德乃長．
> 　　　　　10
修之邦，其德乃豐．
> 　　　15　　　　　20　　　　　18:1
18　修之天下□□□□□□□□家，
> 　　　5　　　　　　　　10　　　　　　15
以鄉觀鄉，以邦觀邦，以天下觀天下．
> 　　　20　　　　　25
吾何以知天□□□□□．

---

**15** 19 拔: 朵 | 拔 WW error; 21 保: 仲
**16** 2 脱: 兌; 10 輟: 乇 | 屯 WW error; 11, 18, 25 修: 攸; 15, 22 德: 悳;
　　17 真: 貞; 20 家: 豙; 23 有: 又; 24 餘: 舍
**17** 2 鄉: 向; 4, 11 德: 悳; 7, 14 修: 攸; 13 豐: 奉; 16 下: □
**18** 1 家: 豙; 2, 5 鄉: 向; 16 吾: 虘; 17 何: 可; 19 知: 智

---

NOTES:

Unfortunately both Mawangdui texts are deficient in places, but where we have their reading it is clear that they are virtually the same as the Guodian text. There are then only three points to be raised.

As noted by the Wenwu editors the character at 15:21 仲 is manifestly a variant for *bao* 保 . This part of both Mawangdui MSS is deficient. Other versions read *bao* 抱 .

At 16:6 Guodian reads *qi* 其 , "its," unlike any other version.

Finally, at 16:10 乇 *zhe/tuo* is to be read as a phonetic loan for another graph. Other versions read *jue* 絕 or *chuo* 輟 , meaning, "stop, end." (Note: Chen Fuhua, He Jiuying, *Gu Yun Tongxiao*, p. 220, *tuo* is in *duo bu* [ 鐸部端母 ]; p. 232, *chuo* is in *yue bu* [ 月部端母 ].) QXG[n] considers the transcription 屯 erroneous.

## C I          [Chapter 17 *complete*/MWD 61]

1:1              5                    10
1    太 上， 下 知 有 之， 其 次， 親 譽 之，

              15
    其 次， 畏 之， 其 次， 侮 之.

    20        2:1
2    信 不 足， 焉 有 不 信.

      5
    猶 乎 其 貴 言 也.

    10            15                20
    成 事 遂 功， 而 百 姓 曰: 我 自 然 也.

---

**1** 1 太: **大**; 4 知: **智**; 5 有: **又**; 8, 16 次: **即**; 9 親: **新**; 13 次: **既**; 14 畏: **慢**; 17 侮: **癸**; 22 焉: **安**

**2** 1 有: **又**; 4 猶: **猷**; 5 乎: **虖**; 12 遂: **述**; 13 功: **杠**; 16 姓: **眚**; 20 然: **肰**

---

NOTES:

The Guodian version is very close to the Mawangdui version. The most notable feature is in the last line, where *gong* 功 is placed at the end of the phrase rather than at the beginning, as in all other versions.

**1:22** Xu Shaohua noted that, as on the Baoshan slips, the scribes had a special way of writing *an* 安 in those cases which we now transcribe as *yan* 焉. Thus it was always clear when the particle, now written *yan* 焉, is intended and when the word *an* 安 is meant. Li Ling confirmed the point too.

## C II [Chapter 18 *complete*/MWD 62]

3:1 5
2/3 故 大 道 廢， 焉 有 仁 義。

10
六 親 不 和， 焉 有 孝 慈。

15 20
邦 家 昏 亂， 焉 有 正 臣。 ■

---

**2** 22 故: 古;

**3** 2 廢: 癹; 3, 11, 19 焉: 安; 5 仁: 息; 8 親: 新; 14 慈: 孳; 16 家: 豕;
17 昏: 緍; 18 亂 QXG^n: 囗; 19 焉: 囗; 20 有: 又

---

NOTES:

This version is as Mawangdui B but differs from it, and all other versions, in not having the line about the loss of wisdom: 智慧出，有大偽 "When wisdom has gone there is great deceit."

**3:3, 11, 19** See note on C 1:22.

**3:5** QXG^n discusses this version of the graph 仁.

## C III          [Chapter 35 *complete*/MWD 79]

4:1                    5                          10
4     設大象，天下往．往而不害，安平大．
              15        20
      樂與餌，過客止．
                      25    5:1                5
5     故道口口口，淡呵其無味也．
                  10                15                20
      視之不足見，聽之不足聞，而不可既也．■

---

**4** 1 設 QXG[n]: 埶 | 執 WW error; 12 平: 坪; 17 過: 悆; 21 故: 古;
      25 口: 口: 口 口 DYZ
**5** 2 呵: 可; 11 聽: 聖; 15 聞: 䎽

---

NOTES:

The most notable feature here is the very last phrase. Other versions read 用之不可既 "Using it, it will not be used up."

**4:1**   See Qiu Xigui #10, where it is noted that *shi* is often borrowed for *she.* See *Xunzi* 22, "Zheng Ming":
無埶列之位．

**4:11**   See note on C 1:22.

**5:2**   According to Li Ling 呵 is equivalent to 兮．

**5:7**   Qiu Xigui believes that the Chu script maintained a distinction between *shi* 視 and *jian* 見 that was already manifest in the oracle bone script and in bronze script. At the Centenary Conference of the Discovery of the Oracle Bone Script 甲骨文發現一百周年學術研討會 , Taipei, May 8–10, 1998, Jean Lefeuvre 雷煥章 argued, against Qiu, that this distinction does not hold even in the bronze script, except when the terms refer to sacrificial rites. See Qiu Xigui, #5.

## C IV          [Chapter 31/MWD 75]

**6**    君子居則貴左, 用兵則貴右.

**7**    故曰: 兵者口口口口口不得已而用之.

恬礱爲上, 弗美也. 美之, 是樂殺人.

**8**    夫樂口口口以得志於天下.

故吉事上左, 喪事上右.

**9**    是以偏將軍居左, 上將軍居右,

言以喪禮居之也.

**10**   故殺口口, 則以哀悲莅之;

戰勝則以喪禮居之. ■

---

6  7 用: 甬; 12 故: 古; 21 不: 口
7  4 用: 甬; 6 恬 WW: 銛; 7 礱: 纑; 11 美: 媺; 13 美: 敳
8  7 故: 古; 18 偏: 麦; 19 將: 酒
9  5 將: 酒; 12 禮: 豊; 16 故: 古; 17 殺: 口
10 3 哀: 依; 5 莅: 位: 泣 LL alt; 8 勝: 勑; 12 禮: 豊

---

NOTES:

In terms of grammar, this passage varies here and there from known versions, in particular in the way 6:12–13 *gu yue* 故曰, "thus it is said," is used to introduce a saying. Guodian also lacks the famous opening phrase of the chapter, which is presumably repeated later in the chapter 6:14–20 (the text is defective): "Weapons are instruments of bad luck."

**7:6**  銛 Wenwu reads this graph as *tian* 恬, though Qiu Xigui was not so sure. From the photos it is clear that the radical is *jin* 金 rather than *xin* 心, as for *tian*. Both Mawangdui texts read 銛. Xu Shaohua said that the *jin* radical indicates that this is some kind of weapon, but most agreed that such a meaning would ill fit the context.

**7:7**  纑 This graph is unattested. The received versions read *dan* 淡, but Qiu Xigui noted that the graph at 7:7 could not possibly be a phonetic loan for *dan*. Mawangdui A has 龍 with the radical *yi* 衣; Mawangdui B has 龍 with the radical *xin* 心. It should be noted that a number of characters with the radical *gong* 廾 are variant forms in which this radical has been dropped in the modern versions. The graph *chong* composed of 龍 with the radical *mi* 糸 does exist but it is most probable that all three graphs are variants of a common version. Gao Ming suggested *zhe* 聾 ( 龍 with the radical *yan* 言 ), "to be cautious" (Gao Ming, *Boshu Laozi*, p. 390).

## C V     [Chapter 64b/MWD 27]

**11:1**          5               10

**11**   爲之者敗之, 執之者失之. ▬

          15

聖人無爲, 故無敗也;

          20

無執, 故 □ □ □.

**12:1**          5

**12**   愼終若始, 則無敗事矣. ▬

          10        15        20

人之敗也, 恒於其且成也敗之. ▬

              **13:1**      5          10

**13**   是以 □ 人欲不欲, 不貴難得之貨,

                  15

學不學, 復衆之所過. ▬

          20      **14:1**        5

**14**   是以能輔萬物之自然, 而弗敢爲. ■

---

**11** 9 失: 遊; 15, 21 故: 古
**12** 1 愼: 訢; 4 始: 訂; 9 矣: 喜; 14 恒: 亙; 17 且: 虘
**13** 7 難: 戁; 18 過: 迡; 22 輔: 柿: 薄DH; 23 萬: 㙟; 24 物: 勿
**14** 3 然: 肰

---

NOTES:

This version differs from the Guodian A version (A VI). It does not read *yuan* 遠, "to distance," in the first line, but a graph equivalent to *shi* 失, "to lose," as in the received versions.

As for line 13:11–13, it is also the same as other versions which read *xue* 學, "to study," rather than *jiao* 教, "to teach," as in A VI.

**11:9** See Qiu Xigui, #7.

**12:1, 9** See QXG[n].

**13:22** Harper read as *bo* 薄. On this reading of *bo*, see *Hanyu Da Zidian*, p. 1378, *bo* as "to approach, draw close to."

1  太 一 生 水， 水 反 輔 太 一， 是 以 成 天.

   天 反 輔 太 一， 是 以 成 地.

2  天 地 復 相 輔 也， 是 以 成 神 明.

   神 明 復 相 輔 也， 是 以 成 陰 陽.

   陰 陽 復 相 輔 也， 是 以 成 四 時.

3  四 時 復 相 輔 也， 是 以 成 滄 熱.

   滄 熱 復 相 輔 也， 是 以 成 濕 燥.

4  濕 燥 復 相 輔 也， 成 歲 而 止.

---

1  1, 8, 17 太: 大; 7, 16 輔: 補: 薄DH; 22 地: 陸; 24 地: 口;
   25-27 復 相 薄: 口 口 口

2  11, 22 輔: 補: 薄 DH; 16, 18 陰: 会; 17, 19 陽: 易: 易WW error

3  1-2 復 相: 復; 3, 14, 25 輔: 補: 薄 DH; 8,10 滄: 倉; 9,11 熱: 然;
   20, 22 燥: 澡; 28 歲: 戠

---

NOTES:

**1:7 *et al.*** Harper read as *bo* 薄, noting the frequent use of the phrase 相薄 *xiang bo* in cosmological texts. On this reading of *bo,* see *Hanyu Da Zidian,* p. 1378, *bo* as "to approach, draw close to."

/4 故 歲 者， 濕 燥 之 所 生 也． ▬

濕 燥 者， 滄 熱 之 所 生 也． ▬

滄 熱 者， 四 時 之 所 生 也．

5 四 時 者， 陰 陽 之 所 生 也．

陰 陽 者， 神 明 之 所 生 也． ▬

神 明 者， 天 地 之 所 生 也． ▬

6 天 地 者， 太 一 之 所 生 也． ▬

---

**4** 3 故: 古; 4 歲: 歲; 7, 13 燥: 澡; 15, 21 滄: 倉; 16, 22 熱: 然;
23-29 者, 四 時 之 所 生 也: 者
**5** 2, 8 陰: 侌; 3, 9 陽: 昜; 7 也: ▬; 21, 27 地: 陞
**6** 2 太: 大

---

NOTES:

A key question is how this text is related to Daoism:

• Isabelle Robinet noted the Daoist nature of this cosmogony. Having developed out of the Supreme One, it here returns to the One. This is a characteristic feature of Daoist as opposed to Confucian cosmogonies. It is related to Daoist mystical practice which requires the adept to become one with the origin.

• Yet, the *Daodejing* presents quite a different cosmogony, from the *Dao* via the One to the Two and the Three and thence to the myriad things.

• However, ch. 25 of the *Daodejing* gives the name of the *Dao* as *da* 大 "great," the same character as *tai* 太 "supreme." Could this provide a link between the *Laozi* and the *Tai Yi Sheng Shui*? In the Guodian MS a possible link is given in the last line of the C section (C 13:19 to 14:7) in which the sage "nestles against the naturalness of the myriad things and does not interfere with them" 薄萬物之自然而弗敢為 .

• Thus it would seem that it is not mere coincidence that the *Tai Yi Sheng Shui* and the *Laozi* C are copied by the same scribe on the same bundle of bamboo strips.

/6  是 故， 太 一 藏 於 水， 行 於 時， ▬

周 而 又 始， 以 己 爲 萬 物 母． ▬

一 缺 一 盈， 以 己 爲 萬 物 經． ▬

8  此 天 之 所 不 能 殺， ▬ 地 之 所 不 能 埋，

陰 陽 之 所 不 能 成．

君 子 知 此 之 謂……

---

**6** 9 故: 古; 10 太: 大; 12 藏: 臧; 18 周 QXG[n]: 迵; 20 又: 或; 21 始 QXG[n]: 囗;
22 以 己 爲 QXG[n]: 囗 囗 囗

**7** 1, 11 萬: 墒; 2, 12 物: 勿; 4, 6 一: 罷; 5 缺: 块; 7 盈: 涅;
9 己 QXG[n]: 忌: 紀 WW; 21 地: 陞

**8** 3 埋 LL: 奞 | 鼇 WW error; 4 陰: 会; 5 陽: 易; 13 知: 智; 16 謂: 胃

---

NOTES:

**8:3** Li Ling noted this phrase in the *Xunzi* 8, "Ru Xiao" (*Harvard-Yenching Index*, line 89) 天不能死，
地不能埋 "Heaven cannot slay them nor earth bury them."

9:1　　　　　5　　　　　　10　　　　　　　15

9　天道貴弱，削成者以益生者，伐於强，責於…

10:1　　　　5

10　下，土也，而謂之地。

10

上，氣也，而謂之天。▬

15　　　　　20

道以其字也。清昏其名。▬

11:1　　　　　5　　　　　　10

11　以道從事者必託其名，故事成而身長。

15　　　　　20　　　　　12:1　　　　　5

12　聖人之從事也，亦託其名，故功成而身不傷。▬

10　　　　　15　　　　　20

天地名字并立，故過其方，不思相當。

13:1　　　　　5

13　天不足於西北，其下高以强。

10　　　　　15

地不足於東南，其上□□□。

20　　　　14:1　　　　5

14　不足於上者，有餘於下；

10

不足於下者，有餘於上。■

---

**9**　4 弱: 溺; 5 削 QXGⁿ: 雀: 爵 WW; 14 强: 弜

**10**　5, 12 謂: 胃; 7 地: 陞; 9 氣: 毃; 18 字 QXGⁿ: 志●; 20 清 DH: 青: 請 WW; 21 昏DH: 昏: 問 WW

**11**　6, 22 託: 怳; 9 故: 古;

**12**　2, 15 故: 古; 3 功: 社; 8 傷: 剔; 10 地: 陞; 12 字: 志; 16 過: 悆; 22 當 QXGⁿ: □; 23-25 天不足 QXGⁿ: □ □ □

**13**　8 强: 弜; 9 地: 陞;

**14**　2, 11 有: 又; 3, 12 餘: 余

---

NOTES:

**9**　This slip is an isolated slip. Hence its exact location in the text is a matter for discussion. The image of paring away the mature/successful so as to give rise to life suggests the idea of fruit which when ripe rots and thus allows the new seeds to grow.

**10:18**　The dot ● placed after the graph does not seem to have any obvious meaning.

**10:20–21**　Donald Harper noted that the Wenwu reading 請問, which would introduce a question here "What is its name?", is linguistically odd. It is better to read 清昏 "bright-confused" (i.e. "obscure") as the name of the Way, a name which surpasses definition.

**12:23 to 14:14**　This passage refers to the tilting of the heavens to the NW, hence the need for the earth to be stronger at that point; and the incline of the earth to the SE where the sea is.

# SECTION FOUR:
## SUPPLEMENTARY MATERIALS

# Additional Textual Notes
*and*
# Afterthoughts

## ADDITIONAL TEXTUAL NOTES

### Gao Ming

The Guodian *Laozi* B 12:5–8 has the line: 大器曼成. The received texts all have 大器晚成 here. The Mawangdui Copy B text has 大器免成. Ryden has followed the received text. Scholars have previously debated whether this should be 晚 ("late") or 免. I suggest that the bamboo text 曼 is a loan for 免.

*Cf.* Gao Ming's *Boshu Laozi Jiaozhu*, pp. 24–25, where he argued that the Mawangdui Copy B form 免 is correct and cited Chen Zhu 陳柱, *Laozi Hanshi Shuo* 老子韓氏説 (Changsha: Shangwu Yinshuguan, 1939), who had already suggested that 晚 should be read as 免 which has a meaning similar to 無. Thus, 免成 would be read similarly to 無成, i.e., "incomplete."

### Xing Wen

#### A 12:15

The "=" symbol after the 所 is an erroneously placed *hewen* 合文 symbol. A *hewen* symbol indicates to the reader that the previous graph is a combined form made up of two characters to be read individually. The editors of the *Guodian Chu Mu Zhujian* read it as the identically written symbol that indicates a repetition of the previous character (a *chongwen* 重文), thus 所所 in this case. In fact, here the symbol was put in by a scribe who had meant to write a *hewen* combined form, for 之所, but had actually written the two characters separately and still included the *hewen* symbol. This is proved by the *hewen* of 之所 in the phrase 復眾之所過 in *Laozi* C 13:14–18.

#### A 24:3

The graph 亙 is read as 恆 in the *Guodian Chu Mu Zhujian*. In form the character is 恆; see C 12:14, but Li Xueqin and others believe that at A 24:3 it should be read as 極. The same usage is also found at B 2:9. This is relevant to the debate about the phrase 易有大恆 in the Mawangdui silk-manuscript *Zhou Yi*, "Xici" 周易繫辭. The Guodian *Laozi* demonstrates that, in Chu script, the character 恆 could be read as 極. The Mawangdui *Xici* phrase should, without doubt, be read 易有太極.

## Xu Kangsheng

A 1:18 為: 為; A 1:20 慮: 慮. A 1:17–20 should be read as 絕為棄慮. Proof of this may be found in the *Shangshu* 尚書, "Taijia 太甲" (*xia* 下), which has the line: 弗慮胡獲, 弗為胡成 ("if one does not think about it, how can one gain; if one does not act, how can one succeed"), in which 慮 and 為 are juxtaposed. In Qiu Xigui's annotation to the *Guodian Chu Mu Zhujian*, he says that: 慮 has 且 as a phonetic and is a loan for "詐." I believe this is an error. The graph in the Chu slip-text derives from 目 and 心 and I think it is the character 慮.

A 9:16 屯 should be read as 純.

A 10:7 厄. This should be read as: 安, not 具 (Xu Kangsheng has discarded his former opinion).

B 10:17 㫚 is the character 㫚. In Zuo Si's 左思 "Wu Du Fu 吳都賦" (found in the *Wenxuan* 文選), there is the line: 旭日暗㫚. Li Shan 李善 comments: 㫚亦暗也 (i.e. 㫚 has the same meaning as 暗 ["dark, dim"]). (See Ryden, p. 219; Xu Kangsheng has changed his opinion.)

B 12:7 曼. The "Shi Yan 釋言" section of the *Guangya* 廣雅 gives 無 as a gloss for 曼, so 曼成 is 無成 ("incomplete"). This matches 亡隅 ("without corners"), 祗聲 ("quiet"), and 亡形 ("shapeless") perfectly.

## Qiu Xigui

### A 1:17–24

In my paper "On the Analysis and Transcription of Ancient Chinese Characters: Examples from the Guodian *Laozi*" (pp. 53–63), I interpreted the phrase 絕𢤧(為)棄 𡪤(慮)[1] (A 1:17–20) as 絕偽棄詐. Several scholars have criticized this reading. They point out that, while people are generally opposed to 詐 ("deceit") and 偽 ("artifice," "falsehood"), this is not necessarily true for the other terms that this section proposes to abandon, i.e., 智 ("sageliness," "wisdom"), 辯 ("disputation," "rhetoric"; some scholars read this as 便 "advantage"), 巧 ("cleverness," "craft"), and 利 ("profit," "benefit"). They further observe that the semantic relationship between 偽 and 詐, terms similar in meaning, is different from that between both 智 and 辯, and 巧 and 利. Thus, the *Laozi* should not have a sentence like 絕偽棄詐 ("cut off artifice and discard deceit") here. These views are correct. I now agree that Xu Kangsheng is right when he reads this sentence as 絕為(偽)棄慮, and observes that 偽 refers to 人為 ("human action").[2]

---

[1] Note that the character here is transcribed with 目 and 一 components rather than the 且 used in the *Guodian Chu Mu Zhujian* transcription. This is done in order to avoid the implication that the graph must be interpreted as having the phonetic 虘.

[2] [Editors' note: see Xu Kangsheng's afterthought above and also his essay "Chudu Guodian Chu Jian *Laozi* 初讀郭店楚簡老子," in *Zhongguo Zhexue* 20.]

From the point of view of graphic form, the graph 慮 is probably better described as having the semantic signifier 心 and phonetic signifier 膚, than as being the character 慮. However, none of the readings suggested by taking 虍 as the phonetic signifier of this graph, that is 詐, 作, and 怚, are suitable in the context of this sentence. Since there are examples in the Guodian slips of the components 膚 and 庐 being muddled, it is possible to read the graph 慮 as 慮 Even if we could prove that the phonetic of the graph is 虍, it could still be a mistake for the graphically similar 慮 .

What the *Xunzi* refers to as 偽 is that which is not born of *tian* 天：可學而能，可事而成之在人者 ("That which people, of their own accord, through study become able to do and through pursuing, achieve"). The 為 which the Daoists oppose as 用己而背自然 ("acting according to one's own ideas and thus violating nature") is more or less the same as the 偽 of the *Xunzi* and the former is occasionally used in place of the latter (for example, in the "Geng Sang Chu 庚桑楚 " chapter of the *Zhuangzi* 莊子 ). For this reason the 為 of 絕為 may be read as 偽 or 為. Whichever character one chooses, it should be understood as "human action 人為 " that "violates nature 背自然 ," and not as the usual 為 meaning "to act, do, make" or 偽 in the sense of "false."

Daoism advocates 無為 ("not doing," "doing nothing") and 無慮 ("not considering," "having no anxieties") and the two terms sometimes occur together. *Xunzi* also discusses both concepts together. We can see, then, that it is appropriate to read this line as 絕偽棄慮 .

In the Guodian slips, 絕偽棄慮 is followed by: 民复季子 . Most scholars have interpreted this line in accordance with the received *Laozi*, reading 子 as 慈 and taking 季 as a scribal mistake for 孝. However others feel that 季子 are the characters which originally appeared in the *Laozi* and should not be changed on the authority of the received text. Considering our revised reading of the previous sentence as 絕偽棄慮 the latter view is probably correct. 民复季子 here means that the people will return to the pure state of a child.

For a more detailed account of the above, see my paper, "Jiuzheng Wo zai Guodian *Laozi* Jian Shidu Zhong de Yige Cuowu: Guanyu 'Jue Wei Qi Zha' 糾正我在郭店老子簡釋讀中的一個錯誤：關於絕偽棄詐," presented at the International Symposium on Chu State Slips of Guodian held at Wuhan University, October, 1999, to be published in a forthcoming collection of papers from that conference.

## AFTERTHOUGHTS

*Roger Ames[3]: Reinterpreting Chapter 25 (A 21:1 to 23:12)*

The recent recovery of new versions of existing texts, and the discovery of hitherto unknown ones, has occasioned the retranslation of many of the Chinese classics and provided an opportunity for us to rethink our standard readings. It has become a commonplace to assert that western humanists' attempts to make sense of the classical Chinese philosophical literature have inadvertently insinuated into it Western assumptions, and that such attempts have colored the very vocabulary through which an understanding must be articulated.

The Guodian *Laozi* is certainly an opportunity to learn more about the dating and the composition of the *Laozi* textual tradition. It is also an opportunity to reflect upon our present understanding of it.

One important example comes from the received text, chapter 25:

獨立不改，周行而不殆，可以為天下母.

In describing *dao* 道, the first phrase has been almost uniformly translated into English as some variation on "it stands solitary and does not change."[4] Yet we must ask what could it mean to assert that *dao* "does not change" in the "eventful" world of classical Daoism in which, to the contrary, *Laozi* chapter 60 claims 反道之動? We must allow that "change" is so real in fact that it is expressed in many different ways, *gai* 改 being only one of them. Hence, a translation of this passage might need to distinguish among several different senses of "change," some of which are:

1. *bian* 變 (change gradually across time);
2. *yi* 易 (change one thing for an other);
3. *hua* 化 (transform utterly, where A becomes B);
4. *qian* 遷 (change from one place to another);
5. *gai* 改 (correct, reform, improve upon X on the basis of some external and independent standard or model, Y).

A failure to make the "reforming" sense of *gai* clear has led to some classic misunderstandings in translating important texts, one of the most obvious perhaps being this particular passage.[5] While "does not change" might fall within the semantic toler-

---

[3] Roger Ames' necessity to leave the conference early resulted in the inclusion of his comments here.

[4] Yang Yu-wei and I were guilty of just such a reading in our translation of Chen Guying's popular translation, *Laozi Jinzhu Jinyi* 老子今注今譯, but we are in good company with James Legge, Bernhard Karlgren, Arthur Waley, D. C. Lau, W. T. Chan, Michael LaFargue, Robert Henricks, and a score of others. Interestingly, Fukunaga Mitsuji's *kanbun* reading with the benefit of the original character is *aratamezu*: "is not reformed, revised," and his interpretive translation is the passive-causative *kaerarezu*: "not made to change."

[5] See also the example in *Analects* 1.11 and our discussion of this passage in *The Analects of Confucius: A Philosophical Translation* (New York: Ballantine, 1998), Appendix 2, pp. 279–82.

ance of *gai*, the above translation is hard to square with the line immediately following in the received text:[6] 周行而不殆 ("Pervading everything and everywhere it does not pause"), and not insignificantly, everything else that is said about *dao* in the literature. The meaning here is not that *dao* "does not change," but being the *sui generis* and autopoeitic totality of all that is becoming (*wanwu* 萬物 ), *dao* is not open to reform by appeal to something other than itself. The Wang Bi commentary observes that *dao* has no counterpart – there is nothing beyond it. As we read further on in this same chapter, one thing might emulate another thing — that is, "humans emulate the earth, and the earth emulates the heavens." But because *dao* is everything, and everything is *dao*, what can it emulate? "*Dao* emulates itself 道法自然 ."

The variant in the Guodian *Laozi* is of some value in suggesting the intended meaning of this passage. It has 獨立不亥 (A 21:11–14), reinforcing Mawangdui Copy B, which has 亥 with the 玉 classifier. Don Harper has suggested that 亥 is a loan for the same character with the 日 classifier that the *Shuowen* takes as equivalent to 兼 ; Harper would understand the latter as "paired with," giving perhaps a meaning for the whole phrase: "solitary it has no counterpart." This is a reading close to that of Wang Bi.

Alternatively, making quite a different point, 亥 with the 日 classifier can mean "complete, all-in-all, entire," again consistent with 兼 or 備 as "the total." When we claim that 道 is everything and everything is 道 , we have to qualify this statement with the observation that 道 is processional and hence underdetermined. Hence it is described as the fecund mother of the world. Perhaps the point here is that 道 as 自然 entails the emergence of spontaneous novelty, and while always "great 大 " it is never complete. There is no finality or closure.

Or perhaps the text is making both points at the same time.

### Carine Defoort: Bruce Brooks' Theory of Accretion

Bruce Brooks has suggested an alternative view of the Guodian *Laozi*, somewhere between: (1) the view of a complete sixth century BC text and (2) the view that the text was still unformed at the time of the Guodian tomb and was only complete in the third century BC. According to his accretional theory, the three groups of *Laozi* sayings are indeed selections from a not yet complete *Laozi* but are not random collections of oral sayings, because they contain only future *Laozi* material. They are selected from a still incomplete phase of the later received *Laozi*, which at that time (288 BC) consisted of chapters 2 to 66, and continued to be added to after the Guodian date, eventually reaching its final eighty-one-chapter form, as many have concluded, at the middle of that century.[7]

---

[6] This phrase does not occur in the Guodian or in either of the two Mawangdui versions of the text.

[7] E. Bruce Brooks, *Warring States Working Group Newsletters* 9 (Sept. 1, 1998); 13 (March 10, 1999).

*Li Xueqin: Arrangement of Bamboo Slips in* Cheng Zhi Wen Zhi *and* Xing Zi Ming Chu

We should be extremely grateful for the work done in ordering of the slips and dividing them into texts in the *Guodian Chu Mu Zhujian* 郭店楚墓竹簡 . This provides a firm foundation for further research. Nevertheless, the Guodian slip texts are profound and complex works that cannot be fully understood in a short period of time. I give a couple of examples below.

Guo Yi 郭沂 has argued convincingly that slip 1 of the *Cheng Zhi Wen Zhi* should go after slip 30, so that by reading these together one gets: 是以君子貴成之.[8] According to the *Zhongyong* 中庸 :

誠者，天之道也；誠之者，人之道也．誠者，不勉而中，不思而得，從容中道，聖人也．誠之者，擇善而固執者也．

The 成之 of the *Cheng Zhi Wen Zhi* is the 誠之 of the *Zhongyong*. Since the *Zhongyong* is a work of the Zisi 子思 school, this passage is evidence that the *Cheng Zhi Wen Zhi* is also a work of that school.[9]

I also feel that the order of slips in the *Xing Zi Ming Chu* needs to be rearranged. These sixty-seven slips were not originally one text but two. Slips 1–36 are one text, the central discussion concerning music; slips 37–67 are the other text, discussing nature and natural endowment. The language and thought of the first piece is similar to the *Yueji* 樂記 of the *Liji* 禮記 . The *Yueji* was written by Gongsun Nizi 公孫尼子 , one of the "disciples of the seventy disciples" and a man who shared many of the views held by Zisi.[10]

*Rudolf Wagner: On C 1:1 to 3:22 (Received text chapters 17, 18)*

Chapters 17 and 18 of the *Laozi* are one of the very few examples of a sequence of chapters found together in all known editions: Guodian (C 1:1 to 3:22), both Mawangdui Copies A and B, and all received editions. The *gu* 故 linking the two makes sense structurally. Chapter 17 has a declining sequence of rulers: the best of them, the people only know exists somewhere up there; the next best the people get close to because he is good to them; the next, is one whom they fear because he uses the power of the state against them; and finally, there is the ruler whom the people fool. Even Wang Bi thought that this last type used an intelligence machinery to spy on people, who then thwart him with their collective wits. This sequence follows a historical decline.

The next segment of chapter 17 goes back to the great man of the first phrase and his relationship to the Hundred Clans. This is where the trouble is for the connection.

---

[8] Guo Yi 郭沂, "Guodian Chu Jian *Cheng Zhi Wen Zhi* Pian Shu Zheng 郭店楚簡成之之聞之篇疏證," *Zhongguo Zhexue* 20 (1999).

[9] See also p. 109.

[10] Li Xueqin, "Guodian Jian yu *Yueji* 郭店簡與樂記," to be published in a Festschrift for Zhang Dainian 張岱年 .

The *gu* does not link up with the immediately preceding thought about the ideal polity, but with the idea of the sequential decline of the beginning of chapter 17. Its steps *dao/ren/yi/zhihui* follow very much in the sequence of the beginning of chapter 17, a sequence that is echoed again in the beginning of chapter 38. Looking at it from the perspective of a Han-dynasty editor, the case for the link rests on this parallel sequence. The case against it rests on the fact that this sequence is topical and not the main argument, and that the *gu* has to link up with a statement already twenty-five characters away (in the Guodian *Laozi* group-C slips).

Fu Yi, who, for one, had hold of a manuscript that was even older than the Mawangdui manuscripts, decided against the *gu*. So did Lu Deming and Fan Yingyuan. It is possible, and even probable, that they had old manuscripts without it. I therefore think that the Han-dynasty editor had different copies giving him different options. He decided in favor of leaving the sequence, but not cutting the direct link through the *gu*.

## Wang Tao: The Case of 絕學亡憂 and the Problem of Chapter Division

Paul Thompson and I raised the question of whether the sentence 絕學亡憂 on the Guodian slips (B 4:8–11) might be better read together with the previous section: 學者日益，為道者日損，損之或損，以至亡為也，亡為而亡不為 , which is found in chapter 48 of the received text, rather than with the following text found in chapter 20: 唯與阿，相去幾何… . Scholars have long questioned the odd position of the sentence as the first line of chapter 20 and suggested that the sentence should be placed at the end of the chapter 19. The line appears between chapters 19 and 20 in the undivided text of Mawangdui Copy B (Mawangdui Copy A is damaged, giving a series of lacunae of an appropriate length). In the twelfth century, Chao Gongwu 晁公武 knew a Tang edition which exceptionally treated this phrase as the conclusion of chapter 19. In view of the palpable difficulty of reading it in its traditional position, modern scholars have frequently approved this division between the two *zhang*.[11] Though neither the sense nor the rhyme makes a perfect fit, the emendation is certainly the less difficult.

However, the Guodian manuscript places this phrase between chapters 48 and 20. In addition, it omits the final sentence in the received text of chapter 48. Thus Guodian points to an order where these four words were attached to the previous line of that chapter. This is a position where, contextually, they are also quite comfortable. In fact, Jiang Xichang and Zhu Qianzhi 朱謙之 had already noticed the relationship between this sentence and chapter 48.[12] Among the three possible readings, the re-

---

[11] See Gao Ming, *Boshu Laozi Jiaozhu*, pp. 315–16, where he cites the views of Yi Shunding 易順鼎, Jiang Xichang 蔣錫昌 , Li Dafang 李大防 , Ma Xulun 馬敍倫 , and Gao Heng 高亨 .

[12] Jiang Xichang's view is cited by Gao Ming, *ibid.*, pp. 315–16; Zhu Qianzhi's opinion is in his *Laozi Jiaoshi* 老子校釋 (Beijing: Zhonghua Shuju, 1984), p. 192.

ceived version (as chapter 20) is the weakest one; to tie 絕學亡憂 with either chapter 19 or 48 is a better choice. Nevertheless, we still cannot accept this as a final and definite solution. In the *Wenzi* 文字 citation of this line, it is placed before 絕聖棄智, 民利百倍. This suggests that there was probably still another different version of the text which the *Wenzi* followed. Thus, a sensible methodology is to treat the *Laozi* as an "open text" ("an anthology" in Lau's terminology)[13] which permits the different wordings and divisions of the text to be edited during the process of its transmitting.

[13] See D. C. Lau, *Lao Tzu Tao Te Ching* (Harmondsworth: Penguin Books, 1963), pp. 163–74.

# Scholarship on the Guodian Texts in China:
## A Review Article

## XING WEN

**T**he publication of the bamboo-slip texts from a Chu tomb at Guodian and the International Conference on the Guodian *Laozi* convened at Dartmouth College, May 21–26, 1998, have together attracted great interest in Chinese scholarly circles. Academic journals, such as *Guoji Ruxue Lianhehui Jianbao* 國際儒學聯合會簡報 (*Bulletin of the International Confucian Association*), *Wenwu* 文物 (*Cultural Relics*), and *Zhongguo Zhexue* 中國哲學 (*Chinese Philosophy*), etc., have all published reports on the Dartmouth conference,[1] and several of China's leading scholarly journals have published issues which took papers from this conference as their core.[2] Moreover, in response to the Dartmouth Conference, the International Confucian Association and the Institute of History of the Chinese Academy of Social Sciences jointly convened a conference on the "Bamboo Slips from the Chu Tomb at Guodian" on June 10, 1998, in Beijing, at which the Dartmouth Conference was specially introduced.[3] A year later, the Dartmouth Conference continues to receive attention in the Chinese academic world.[4]

The following is a review of Chinese scholarship on the Guodian texts, written at the request of the editors of the proceedings of the Dartmouth Conference, based on both presentations in conferences and published journals. I have not included works in English since such works are readily available to English-speaking readers and, in

---

[1] See "Meiguo Guodian *Laozi* Guoji Yantaohui Zongshu 美國郭店《老子》國際研討會綜述," in [2], reprinted in [4]; Xing Wen 邢文, Li Jinyun 李縉雲, "Guodian *Laozi* Guoji Yantaohui Zongshu 郭店老子國際研討會綜述," *Wenwu* 1998.9; Xing Wen 邢文, "Guodian Chujian Yanjiu Shuping 郭店楚簡研究述評," *Minzu Yishu* 3 (1998); Xing Wen 邢文, "Guodian Chujian yu Guoji Hanxue 郭店楚簡與國際漢學," *Shu Pin* 4 (1998); Wang Bo 王博, "Meiguo Damusi Daxue Guodian *Laozi* Guoji Xueshu Taolunhui Jiyao 美國達慕思大學郭店老子國際學術討論會紀要" [6].

[2] See Journals and Newletters [1] to [9] in the bibliography; see also *Wenwu* 1998.10.

[3] "*Guodian Chu Mu Zhujian* Xueshu Yantaohui Shuyao《郭店楚墓竹簡》學術研討會述要" [2], reprinted in [4]. Some of the ideas expressed at this conference can also be found in Pang Pu (3).

[4] Li Jinyun 李縉雲, "Guodian Chujian Yanjiu Jinkuang 郭店楚簡研究近況," *Guji Zhengli Chuban Qingkuang Jianbao*, April 1999.

any case, at the time of writing (September, 1999), no major articles are yet in print.[5] Nor have I included works in Japanese, though some important articles in that language have already been published.[6] I should also note that the second special issue of *Zhongguo Zhexue* (volume 21), will include a number of articles on the Guodian texts that are not reviewed herein.

I will first briefly introduce three workshops and conferences on the Guodian bamboo slip-texts held in China and then review various opinions on specific issues that have been offered over the past year.

The three workshops and conferences are: (1) the Workshop on the Guodian Chu slips, sponsored by the International Confucian Association; (2) the Conference on bamboo slips from the Guodian Chu tomb, sponsored by the International Confucian Association and the Institute of History, Chinese Academy of Social Sciences; and (3) the day-long Workshop on the Guodian Chu slips of the International Conference on "Perceptions of Being Human in Confucian Thought: Human Dignity, Human Rights and Human Responsibility." Moreover, another international conference on the Guodian bamboo texts, jointly sponsored by the Institute of Chinese Culture of Wuhan University, the Harvard-Yenching Institute of Harvard University, the International Confucian Association, the Chinese Society for History of Chinese Philosophy, and the Hubei Provincial Society for the History of Chinese Philosophy, will be held from October 15–18, 1999, at Wuhan University.

Sponsored by the International Confucian Association, the Workshop on the Guodian Chu slips was held in Beijing on May 2, 1998. This workshop was not public. Fifteen scholars from the Chinese Academy of Social Sciences, Peking University, and other institutions, discussed the Guodian texts one by one according to pre-assignments. The workshop proposed the following suggestions: (1) The Confucian texts in the Guodian Chu slips are generally relevant to the Zisi-Mengzi School and the date of those texts are earlier than that of the Mencius. (2) Since the discussions on the theory of mind and human nature, as well as the ethical theories proposed in the Chu slip texts, appeared during a period between Confucius and Mencius; they are particularly helpful in understanding the transition from the thought of Confucius to that of Mencius. (3) The content of some of the material in the Chu slips substantially affects traditional understandings of the *Liji* 禮記 and both the new and old text ver-

---

[5] There has, however, been some important discussion by Bruce Brooks in his *Warring States Working Group Newsletter* (see 9 [Sept. 1, 1998] and 13 [March 10, 1999]).

[6] Most importantly, the Japanese journals *Tōhōgakuhō* 96 (July, 1998) and *Chūgoku Shutsudo Shiryō Kenkyū* (July, 1998) include reports by Ikeda Tomohisa on the Dartmouth Conference, and the March 1999 issue of the latter journal has a number of articles on the Guodian slips, including Japanese translations of articles by Chinese scholars. I would also like to thank Ikeda Tomohisa for his assistance in compiling this bibliography.

sions of the *Shangshu* 尚書 . This has important consequences for research on the history of Confucianism and on Chinese thought more generally.

Cosponsored by the International Confucian Association and the Institute of History of the Chinese Academy of Social Sciences, the Conference on Bamboo Slips from the Guodian Chu tomb was held on June 10, 1998. This was the first conference on the Guodian texts openly held in China. More than thirty participants attended from such institutions as the Chinese Academy of Social Sciences, Peking University, Tsinghua University, the Palace Museum, the Chinese Institute of Cultural Relics, Beijing Normal University, Zhonghua Shuju 中華書局, etc. Keynote presentations were made by Li Xueqin (Chinese Academy of Social Sciences), Pang Pu (Chinese Academy of Social Sciences), and Xing Wen (Peking University). Li Xueqin discussed the date of the Chu slips, their connection with the *Mencius*, the principles used for transcribing and ordering the Chu slips, and their significance. Pang Pu further discussed the significance of the slips from the perspective of both Daoist and Confucian studies. Xing Wen reviewed the main arguments made at the Dartmouth Conference. The participants' discussion following these talks covered the content, the schools, and the transcription and paleography of the Guodian Chu slips. This discussion is included in the review below.[7]

The International Conference on "Perceptions of Being Human in Confucian Thought: Human Dignity, Human Rights and Human Responsibility," held in Beijing from June 15 to 17, included twenty-five participants from the United States, mainland China, Taiwan, Hong Kong and Europe. It concentrated on the issues of Confucian thought and human rights, but the last day of the conference was specially arranged as a discussion on the Guodian texts. Du Weiming (Wei-ming Tu) (Harvard University) gave the keynote speech and Pang Pu introduced the slip-texts. These talks were followed by discussion of the content and titles of the Guodian slip-texts, as well as various related problems.

In the following, I will introduce and discuss the major arguments and suggestions made in these conferences and Chinese publications since the Dartmouth Conference, according to the sequence of the Account of Discussion section in this book.

## THE TOMB AND ITS CONTENTS

### The Identity of the Occupant

Cui Renyi (1) was the first to identify the occupant of Guodian Tomb Number One as a literary figure closely associated with the Chu royal house, most likely the teacher of the crown prince (who resided in the Eastern Palace), on the basis of the

---

[7] The discussion and major papers for this conference are included in the bibliography [4].

inscription on the bottom of the lacquer ear-cup, which he read as: 東宮之不 (杯). Li Xueqin (2) was the first to point out that: 東宮之不 should be read as: 東宮之帀(師).[8] Li Xueqin (3) further observes, on the basis of the date of the burial in Guodian Tomb Number One at the end of the fourth century BC, that the "teacher of the Eastern Palace" would have been tutor under Qingxiang Wang 頃襄王 of Chu, and the Crown Prince was Heng 橫 who later ruled as Huai Wang 懷王 of Chu. Li Cunshan (1) supports this view with more detail. Jiang Guanghui (3) is also of the opinion that the "teacher of the Eastern Palace" was tutor for Qingxiang Wang and further hypothesizes that the "teacher of the Eastern Palace" was most likely the Chen Liang 陳良 mentioned in the *Mencius* 3A, "Teng Wen Gong 滕文公 , 上 ."

Liao Mingchun (4) argues that the tomb occupant was a disciple of Zisi 子思 . Gao Zheng (1) is of the opinion that the occupant was no less than the famous Chu poet Qu Yuan 屈原 .

Worth noting here is that the various hypotheses concerning the identity of the tomb occupant are based upon the determination of the date of the tomb made by the archeologists. However, there is not universal agreement among scholars concerning the date of the tomb. Wang Baoxuan (1) contends that the two factors upon which the date of the tomb was determined are both inaccurate. He argues that: (1) the burial date of the occupant of Baoshan Tomb Number Two, which serves as a reference point for Guodian Tomb Number One, is not 292 BC, but 284 BC; and (2) after Bai Qi captured the Chu capital of Ying, the Chu cultural tradition was still preserved in the Jiangling region. Thus Wang offers the alternative opinion that the date of Guodian Tomb Number One is between 278 and 227 BC.

In my own opinion, the identification of the occupant of the tomb as the "teacher of the Eastern Palace" tallies with the books found in the tomb and the bird-headed staffs, but the evidence is insufficient to ascertain with certainty the precise identity of the occupant. I also think that the date of the tomb can not be determined solely by reference to textual evidence. For a reliable date, the literary evidence must be considered in combination with an analysis of the typology of the objects excavated from the tomb. The suggestion of a mid-third century date for the Guodian tomb does not take sufficient account of the archeological evidence and does not include any typological analysis.

## The Contents and Date of the Bamboo Slips and the Names of the Texts

At the Dartmouth Conference, Rudolf Wagner remarked that it is surprising, if the occupant of the tomb was a royal tutor, that the texts included in his tomb include

---

[8] [Editors' note: This reading, which was accepted at the Dartmouth Conference, was recently challenged by Li Ling at the International Symposium on the Chu Slips from Guodian (*Guodian Chu Jian Guoji Xueshu Yantaohui* 郭店楚簡國際學術研討會 ), Wuhan University, October 15 to 18, 1999. See Bibliography [8]. Li Ling suggests that the reading should be *bei* 杯 , as in the original *Wenwu* excavation report.]

only the *Laozi* and Confucian, or other, philosophical texts, but no classics such as the *Shangshu*, *Shijing* or *Chunqiu*. Why were philosophical texts so favored by the tomb occupant? In this regard, Liu Zonghan (1) theorizes that moral education would be the major principle in the teaching of the crown prince, and, for this purpose, the Confucian texts would have been used. However, Chu was a state in which the noble houses held extraordinarily great power. In the time of Dao Wang 悼王 of Chu, Wu Qi 吳起 revised the laws in a manner that diminished some of the advantages enjoyed by the nobility. Wu Qi was subsequently executed and it became necessary for the royal tutor to instruct the crown prince in techniques of ruling such as "meeting action with stillness" and "doing nothing and nothing is not done." In this context, the Daoist teachings of the *Laozi* were particularly favored.

With regard to the date of the composition of the texts found in Guodian Tomb Number One, Wang Baoxuan (1) is of the opinion that: the *Liu De* was written during the period between 278 and 227 BC; the four texts *Xing Zi Ming Chu*, *Zun De Yi*, *Tang Yu zhi Dao*, and *Zhong Xin zhi Dao* are earlier than the *Xunzi*; and the *Zun De Yi* and *Zi Yi* are even earlier than those four texts.

Li Xueqin (2) expresses the opinion that the name *Liji* 禮記 was not used in the pre-Qin period; there were only scattered works — some of which later came to be part of the *Liji* — by the seventy disciples of Confucius and their followers. Such texts as the *Zi Yi*, *Zun De Yi*, and *Lu Mu Gong Wen Zisi* were works in the teaching lineage of Zisi and it is appropriate to call them the *Zisizi* 子思子. Chen Lai (1) proposes that, when compared to corpuses of texts found in the received tradition, the content of fourteen of the Guodian texts are closest to the *Liji*, and so they should be called the Guodian *Liji*.

Other suggestions concerning the division into texts and the titles of the bamboo-slip texts include Zhang Liwen (1) who suggests that *Qiong Da yi Shi* should be called *Tian Ren* 天人 and *Zhong Xin zhi Dao* simply *Zhong Xin*; and Liao Mingchun (4) who proposes *Qiu Ji* 求己 as a title for *Cheng Zhi Wen Zhi*.

## THE LAOZI

### The Arrangement of the Slips

That material corresponding to the *Laozi* in the Guodian slips should be divided into three groups is apparent from the physical shape and form of the bamboo slips. In the Jingmenshi Bowuguan's *Guodian Chu Mu Zhujian* (pp. 111–26), the slips are divided into *jia* 甲 (A), *yi* 乙 (B), and *bing* 丙 (C), in which *Laozi* A includes five sections of text on 39 bamboo slips; *Laozi* B, three sections of text on 18 bamboo slips; and *Laozi* C, three sections on 14 bamboo slips. The *Tai Yi Sheng Shui*, which is on slips with the same shape and form and calligraphy as the *Laozi* C, is treated as a separate text in that publication.

Cui Renyi 崔仁義 , of the Jingmenshi Bowuguan, also provides an edition of the *Laozi* in his *Jingmen Guodian Chu Jian Laozi Yanjiu* 荊門郭店楚簡老子研究 together with a set of photographs different to those found in *Guodian Chu Mu Zhujian*. Cui's edition divides the slips into texts according to the length and form of the bamboo slips and he divides the *Laozi* material into a *Laozi* A, *Laozi* B, and *Laozi* C that are different from those found in *Guodian Chu Mu Zhujian*. Cui's "*Laozi* B" and "*Laozi* C" are, respectively, the *Laozi* B ( 乙 ) and A ( 甲 ) of that work. Moreover, whereas the *Guodian Chu Mu Zhujian* establishes two different texts, *Laozi* C ( 丙 ) and *Tai Yi Sheng Shui*, they are a single text (*Laozi* A) in Cui's edition. The division in the *Guodian Chu Mu Zhujian* takes account of the content of the slips, as well as their physical shape, and the separation of *Tai Yi Sheng Shui* and *Laozi* C ( 丙 ) into two texts reflects the cautious approach of the compilers. Cui Renyi's method of dividing the texts, which is based entirely upon the physical shape and form of the bamboo slips, avoids being overly influenced by the received tradition during the process of putting the slips in order, but the slip sequences in his "*Laozi* C" are unconvincing in some places.

Discussions about joining slips include both the joining of broken slips and textual sequences. Li Jiahao (1, 2) points out that the Guodian *Laozi* B, slip 10, can be joined to slip fragment 20; this results in a section that corresponds to chapter 41 in the received text. Xing Wen (4) suggests that the slips in *Laozi* C should be reordered into a sequence of: 1, 2, 3, 6, 7, 8, 9, 10, 4, 5, 11, 12, 13, 14 (using the *Guodian Chu Mu Zhujian* slip numbers). I also argue therein that *Tai Yi Sheng Shui* should be a part of *Laozi* C and placed at the beginning of the C sequence on the basis of its content.

*The Relationship of the Guodian Bamboo-Slip Material to the Received* Laozi

Xu Kangsheng (1) holds that the *Laozi* of the Guodian bamboo slips is earlier than the current text. In Xu's opinion, the Guodian *Laozi* was not divided into chapters and this is the earliest form of the text, followed by the Mawangdui *Laozi* which is divided into two parts, a *De* and a *Dao*. The latest form is that of the current text (with eighty-one chapters, divided into *Dao* and *De*). Wang Zhongjiang (1), on the basis of a comparison between the Guodian, Mawangdui, and received versions of the *Laozi*, also argues that the Guodian *Laozi* is earlier than the received text. Guo Yi (4) not only takes the Guodian *Laozi* to be earlier than the received version, but goes a step further, proposing that it is by Lao Dan 老聃 and the received version by Taishi Dan 太史儋 . The Guodian *Laozi* is, at present, the earliest, complete, and most primitive form of the *Laozi* and the variant characters in this text should generally be given precedence over those in the current text.[9] Yin Zhenhuan (1) challenges some of the opinions expressed by Guo Yi.

[9] This was expanded upon by Guo Yi at the Workshop on the Guodian Slip-texts held in Beijing on June 10, 1998.

Although much of the research concerning the relationship of the Guodian bamboo slips to the received *Laozi* is of high quality, some of the articles that discuss the relationship between the Guodian *Laozi* and the received text are impressionistic, suggesting that the authors first formed imaginative opinions and then looked for examples to illustrate their viewpoints. In their anxiety for new knowledge concerning Laozi as a person and his book, some people have raced to establish fanciful theories that are not based upon any hard evidence. Although these theories have had some influence, they need not be rebutted herein.

### A1:17–20 絕偽棄詐

At the Dartmouth Conference, Gao Ming suggested that this line should be read as: 絕仁棄義. This proposal excited an intense argument. Since the Dartmouth Conference, other scholars have offered further proposals. Pang Pu (2) argues that 偽 ("artifice") and 詐 ("deceit") are inherently undesirable so that there is no philosophical significance in suggesting that they should be rejected and discarded. The line should instead read: 絕為棄作 ("reject action and discard innovation"). Xu Kangsheng (1) argues on the basis of the *Shangshu* 尚書, "Taijia 太甲," that the character read as "詐" should be: 慮 .[10]

The argument that ensued at the Dartmouth Conference with regard to Gao Ming's proposals was as much about the methodology of analysing and transcribing characters as about different transcriptions. Since the Dartmouth Conference, a methodological trend towards considering the meaning of the text within a philosophical context without reference to paleographical considerations has appeared. Thus, the theory that this line should be read as 絕為棄作 is based on the analysis that the philosophical statement 絕偽棄詐, 民復孝慈 is philosophically insignificant. It omits comparison between the manner in which the characters read here as 偽 and 詐 are written on the Guodian bamboo slips and the forms of writing 為 and 作 found on these or other Chu slip-texts. Although the history of thought provides an intellectual context that is useful in making a correct paleographical analysis, any suggestion of possible alternatives for a character must also be based on a sound analysis of the paleographical potential of the character.

### B 4:2–7 亡為而亡不為

The phrase 無為而無不為 ("do nothing and there is nothing not done"), which appears in chapters 37 and 48 of the received *Laozi*, is absent from Copies A and B of the Mawangdui *Laozi* manuscripts.[11] Robert Henricks noticed that it appears in the Guodian *Laozi* (with the variant 亡 for 無 ), and discussed this with Gao Ming at the

---

[10] [Editors' note: See also pp. 236–37, for Xu Kangsheng's "Afterthought" and Qiu Xigui's revised opinion in light of Xu's suggestions.]

[11] See Gao Ming 高明, *Boshu Laozi Jiaozhu* 帛書老子校注 (Beijing: Zhonghua Shuju, 1996), pp. 421–25.

Dartmouth Conference. Liao Mingchun (5) looks at this question in detail, arguing that the original *Laozi* must have had the phrase 無為而無不為.

### B 12:13–16 天象無形

The expression 大象無形 ("The great image is shapeless") in chapter 41 of the received *Laozi* was written as 天象無形 ("Heaven's image is shapeless") in Copy B of the Mawangdui *Laozi*.[12] Xu Kangsheng (1) notes that the Guodian *Laozi* B also has the expresson 天象無形 and argues that "heaven's image" refers to the sun, the moon, and the constellations. Wang Zhongjiang (1) further points out that the expression 天象無形 was the original form, and 大象無形 was the result of a later revision.

### 一 ("one")

That "one" is a particularly important concept in the *Laozi* is generally acknowledged. For example, the received text of the *Laozi* has the phrase 載營魄抱一 "the soul embracing the one" in chapter 10; 聖人抱一為天下式 ("the sage embraces the one and acts as a model for the world") in chapter 22; 天得一以清, 地得一以寧, 神得一以靈, 谷得一以盈, 萬物得一以生, 侯王得一以為天下正 ("Heaven, obtaining one, becomes clear. Earth, obtaining one, becomes tranquil. Spirit, obtaining one, becomes divine. The valley, obtaining one, becomes full. The myriad things, obtaining one, are alive. The lords and kings, obtaining one, become the right people of the world") in chapter 39; and 道生一, 一生二, 二生三, 三生萬物 ("The *dao* generates one; one generates two; two generates three; three generates the myriad things") in chapter 42. Xing Wen (4) observes that all these occurences of "one" in the received *Laozi* are absent from the Guodian *Laozi*, and takes them as a mark of distinction between two different *Laozi* traditions. In the Guodian *Laozi*, "Tai Yi generates water" 太一生水, and water assists Tai Yi to form heaven, earth, *shen* and *ming*, *yin* and *yang*, the four seasons, …, with the year as the end. This is similar to "the *dao* generates one; one generates two; two generates three; three generates the ten thousands things." If the concept, "Tai Yi generates water," in the Guodian *Laozi* corresponds to the "*dao* generates one" of the received *Laozi* and the "one" theory of the received *Laozi* is absent from the Guodian *Laozi*, then we can reasonably deduce that the Guodian *Laozi* and the received *Laozi* belong to two different traditions.

At the time of writing, a number of important articles on the Guodian *Laozi* and *Tai Yi Sheng Shui* are soon to be published as a special issue of *Daojia Wenhua Yanjiu* (volume 17). This volume includes essays by a number of the participants at the Dartmouth conference (Wang Bo, Peng Hao, Qiu Xigui, Chen Guying, Edmund Ryden [Lei Dunhe], Isabelle Robinet [He Bilai], Carine Defoort [Dai Kalin], Ikeda Tomohisa

---

[12] See Xu Kangsheng 許抗生, *Boshu Laozi Zhuyi yu Yanjiu* 帛書老子註譯與研究 (Hangzhou: Zhejiang Renmin Press, 1985), p. 40.

[Chitian Zhijiu], Robert Henricks [Han Lubo], Harold Roth [Luo Hao], Li Xueqin, and Li Ling, as well as Ding Yuanzhi, Zhang Liwen, Wei Qipeng, Zhao Jianwei, Pang Pu, Qiang Yu, Li Zehou, Li Cunshan, and Bai Xi. Volume 21 of *Zhongguo Zhexue* 中國 哲學 is also in press with articles on the Guodian *Laozi* by Qiu Xigui, Shen Qingsong, and Zeng Xiantong, as well as articles on other Guodian texts.

Besides Cui Renyi, *Jingmen Guodian Chu Jian Laozi Yanjiu*, mentioned above, two further editions of the Guodian *Laozi* have been published already: Ding Yuanzhi, *Guodian Zhujian Laozi Shixi yu Yanjiu* 郭店竹簡老子釋析與研究 ("Analysis and Research on the Guodian Bamboo-slip *Laozi*") and Liu Xinfang, *Jingmen Guodian Zhujian Laozi Jiegu* 荊門郭店竹簡老子解詁 ("Expositions of the Jingmen Guodian Bamboo-slip *Laozi*"). Peng Hao's *Guodian Chu Jian Laozi Jiaodu* 郭店楚簡老子校讀 is also forthcoming. This book includes a commentary on the Guodian *Laozi*, Peng Hao's own transcription of the Guodian *Laozi*, and comparisons among the Guodian *Laozi* and the main received versions, etc. It focuses on the arrangement of the slips and explanation of the differences between the Guodian *Laozi* bamboo-slip version and the Mawangdui silk copies, and provides more interpretation. The original authors of *Guodian Chu Mu Zhujian* (Peng Hao, Liu Zuxin, and Wang Chuanfu) are also preparing a *Pujiben* 普及本 ("ordinary edition") together with Qiu Xigui (reader for *Guodian Chu Mu Zhujian*), to be published by Wenwu Press. This edition will also include some corrections and revised opinions.

## OTHER TEXTS AND THE QUESTION OF PHILOSOPHICAL SCHOOLS

The Guodian material includes some fourteen texts other than the *Laozi* and *Tai Yi Sheng Shui*. Li Xueqin was specially requested to summarize their contents at the Dartmouth Conference and a written version of this paper is included in this volume. Du Weiming (Wei-ming Tu) was also invited to address the Confucian texts at the International Conference of "Perceptions of Being Human in Confucian Thought: Human Dignity, Human Rights and Human Responsibility." Du Weiming (1) points out that the Guodian bamboo-slip texts reflect various developments in pre-Qin Confucianism, and have two major points of significance: (1) they provide a source for the study of the early Confucian teaching tradition as it developed after the time of Confucius, filling the interim between Confucius and Mencius; (2) they provide materials for research on philosophical schools other than Confucianism. Du further discussed the significance of the Guodian texts from the perspective of four aspects of Confucian values (respect for the individual, social group, nature, and the way of Heaven), noted the spirit of social criticism found in pre-Qin Confucianism, the trend towards moral idealism, and discussed the issue of elitism. He observed that it will be necessary to rewrite Chinese intellectual history in the light of this material, and to reconsider Chinese traditional culture as a whole.

Jiang Guanghui (4) reinterprets the Confucian tradition on the basis of the Guodian texts. Jiang points out that the Guodian texts reflect the thought of the first and second generation students of Confucius and thus represent the core of Confucian theory, i.e., the social ideal of a "great commonality" 大同, the political theory of "abdication" 禪讓 based upon merit, and the life philosophy of "valuing emotion" 貴情. The recipients of these core theories were Ziyou 子游, Zisi, and Mencius; and the real successors of this Confucian system were not the Confucian scholars of the Han, Tang, Song and Ming dynasties, such as Zhu Xi 朱熹, Wang Yangming 王陽明, and Liu Zongzhou 劉宗周, but those Qing scholars, represented by Huang Zongxi 黃宗羲, Dai Zhen 戴震, and Kang Youwei 康有為, who developed and practised the democratic ideas of early Confucianism, which have similarities to democratic systems and ideas found in the West.

## Tai Yi Sheng Shui 太一生水

Li Xueqin and Sarah Allan discussed connections between *Tai Yi Sheng Shui* and Guan Yin 關尹 at the Dartmouth Conference. Further research by Guo Yi (2) supports the attribution of *Tai Yi Sheng Shui* to Guan Yin, and dates this text as later than the received *Laozi*. Li Xueqin (11) relates the *Tai Yi Sheng Shui* to divination rather than cosmogenesis. Li Zehou (1) argues that the idea of Tai Yi generating water came from the primitive shamanism of early people, and that the *Tai Yi Sheng Shui* is most likely a rationalized transformation of early people's observation of shamanistic dancing in prayer for rain.

## Wu Xing 五行, Liu De 六德

At the Dartmouth conference, Ikeda Tomohisa suggested that although the archeologically determined date of Guodian Tomb Number One is earlier than the *Mencius*, the *Mencius* is nevertheless earlier than the Guodian *Wu Xing* from the perspective of the history of the philosophical ideas discussed in the text. Xing Wen (5) returns to this argument and contends that the Guodian *Wu Xing* is earlier than the *Mencius* in this respect.

At the Dartmouth Conference, I also proposed that the Mawangdui silk-manuscript *Wu Xing* was later than the Guodian Chu-slip *Wu Xing*, and that the differences in the sequence of sections between these two versions were intentional revisions by the compiler of the Mawangdui silk version. This is discussed in Xing Wen (2). Pang Pu (5), on the other hand, argues that the logic of the Mawangdui *Wu Xing* is more reasonable than the Guodian *Wu Xing* and concludes that the Mawangdui is probably earlier. In this article, the first two characters of the Chu-slip version (*wu xing* 五行) are taken as the title of the text given by the scribe. However, the transcribers of archeological texts conventionally use key words of the first sentence as a title of the text, and the title of the Guodian *Wu Xing* simply follows this convention. Moreover, titles of bamboo or silk texts were usually written at the end of the document rather than the beginning.

At the Conference on Bamboo Slips from the Chu Tomb at Guodian (Beijing, June 10, 1998), Yu Dunkang 余敦康 pointed out that the six positions — of the emperor and minister, father and son, and husband and wife — discussed in the *Liu De* reflect a societal question and an important aspect of the Confucian theory of mind and nature in which one should serve the world/society and apply theory to practice. Qian Xun (1) contends that the *Liu De* discusses *ren* 仁 ("humaneness"), *yi* 義 ("rightness"), *zhong* 忠 ("doing one's best") and 信 *xin* ("trustworthiness") without the basic spirit implicit in the Confucian idea of humaneness (*ren*), so that it presents a technique of ruling that is not consistent with Confucianism as known from the Confucius-Mencius tradition.

## *Tang Yu zhi Dao* 唐虞之道 *and Zhong Xin zhi Dao* 忠信之道

Li Xueqin (3) argues that both *Tang Yu zhi Dao* and *Zhong Xin zhi Dao* stress abdication to an unusual degree and suggests that these texts belong to the Zong Heng 縱橫 ("Vertical and Horizontal" or "Strategist") school. Li further surmises that they are connected with a specific event in the late-fourth century BC, King Kuai 噲 of Yan's abdication to Zizhi 子之 under the influence of Su Dai 蘇代 and Cuo Maoshou 厝毛壽. Yu Dunkang (Conference on Bamboo Slips from the Chu Tomb at Guodian, June 10, 1998) and Jiang Guanghui (1), on the other hand, argue that the Zong Heng school has no political ideal, that it is the Confucian school that attributed their political ideal to Tang and Yu, and that abdication is the essence of early Confucian thoughts. Li Cunshan (1) argues that the attribution of *Tang Yu zhi Dao* to the Zong Heng school lacks evidence because abdication is an idea that is common to the Confucian, Mohist, Daoist, and other schools. Liao Mingchun (4) contends that Gu Jiegang 顧頡剛 and Tong Shuye 童書業's theory that the story of Yao and Shun's abdication originated with the Mohists is actually a misunderstanding, and that the Guodian texts suggest that the abdication theory must have originated with Confucianism.

Li Cunshan (1) suggests that the *zhong xin* 忠信 of *Zhong Xin zhi Dao* was intended as a topic of study for the ruler, rather than ordinary people, and may be the work of one of the eight schools of Confucianism, known as the "Zhongliang 仲良" school. Liao Mingchun (4) suggests that *Zhong Xin zhi Dao* is a treatise by Confucius' student, Zizhang 子張, based on Confucius' teachings. He notes that since Zizhang's son, Shenxiang 申祥, and Zisi both served Duke Mu of Lu, both Zizhang and Zisi's works might be found in the Chu region.

*Zi Yi* 緇衣 , *Qiong Da yi Shi* 窮達以時 , *Cheng Zhi Wen Zhi* 成之聞之 , *and Xing Zi Ming Chu* 性自命出

Rao Zongyi (1) offers the first reading of a broken bamboo slip in a Hong Kong collection, which he identifies as coming from a Chu slip-text of the *Zi Yi*. Li Xueqin (5) further discusses the connections between the Guodian *Zi Yi* and *Liji*. In Li Xueqin (7), he deciphers the character 祭 in the Guodian slips, and further points out that the so-called Hui Gong 慧公 in Western Zhou bronze inscriptions is the famous Cai Gong Moufu 祭公謀父. Peng Hao (2) discusses the textual division of the *Zi Yi* and related questions in the Guodian Chu slips. On the basis of a comparison between parts of the bamboo version *Zi Yi* with the received *Zi Yi*, Zhou Guidian (1) suggests that the received *Zi Yi* has some misordered sections (due to misarranged slips) and added passages. A number of further studies on the *Zi Yi* are forthcoming.

Zhang Liwen (2) suggests that whereas 窮達 occurs as a compound term in *Qiong Da yi Shi*, 窮 and 達 are parallel words in the *Mencius*, so the text of *Qiong Da yi Shi* probably dates to the end of Mencius' life or somewhat later.

Pang Pu (8) suggests that *Xing Zi Ming Chu* and *Yu Cong* reflect the general features of an early Confucian theory of nature, which includes nature and fate, nature and emotion, and nature and mind. Chen Lai (2) considers *Xing Zi Ming Chu* as adhering to the theory of natural human nature, which was in the mainstream of pre-Qin thought, including pre-Qin Confucianism. From the perspective of philosophical schools, Chen believes that it was connected with Ziyou 子遊, Gongsun Nizi 公孫尼子 and Zisi, with Gongsun Nizi, the more likely. Peng Lin (1) was the first to compare a shared passage found in *Xing Zi Ming Chu* (slips 34 and 35) and the "Tangong" chapter of the *Liji*.

Guo Yi (3) discusses and revises the slip sequence of *Cheng Zhi Wen Zhi*, changing the title to *Tian Jiang Da Chang* 天降大常, and provides a general explanation of the text as a whole. Guo also takes the text as written in the generation between Zisi and Mencius, its author a student of Zisi and the teacher of Mencius. Chen Lai (2) discusses the *Xing Zi Ming Chu* and stresses the importance of Confucius' teachings and theories in the Guodian slip-texts.

*The Question of Philosophical Schools*

Li Xueqin's suggestion at the Dartmouth Conference that many Guodian documents belong to the Zisi school led to an animated discussion among the conference participants. Jiang Guanghui (2) further suggests four criteria to be used in examining the relationship between the Guodian slips and Zisi. Jiang also points out that the Guodian slip-texts make it possible to reevaluate early Confucianism. For example, the reference to "Confucianists dividing into eight" in the *Hanfeizi* 韓非子 may not necessarily mean eight Confucian schools, but refer to the eight most influential Confucianists and their followers, including Ziyou, Zisi, Mencius' Hong Dao 弘道 ("Enlarging the Way") School, Zixia's Chuan Jing 傳經 ("Transmitting Classics") School, Zengzi 曾子 's Jian Lu 踐履 School which stressed the practice of filial piety, and Zizhang's Biao Xian 表現 ("Expression") School. Chen Lai (1) and Liao Mingchun (4) support Li Xueqin's argument.

Li Xueqin also pointed out that the second half of *Xing Zi Ming Chu* is similar to Gongsun Nizi's *Yueji* 樂記 , and that Gongsun Nizi's viewpoint was similar to that of Zisi. At the "Conference on Bamboo Slips from the Chu Tomb at Guodian" (June 10, 1998, Beijing), Kong Fan 孔繁 pointed out that the identification of the *Wu Xing* texts from Mawangdui and Guodian with the *wu xing* 五行 of Zisi and Mencius criticized in the "Fei Shier Zi 非十二子" chapter of the *Xunzi*, is difficult to verify. Kong further observed that although the Chu slips have ideas consistent with the *Zhongyong* 中庸 , we cannot say with certainty that the *Zhongyong* was the work of Zisi, and noted that the academic tradition of the Philosophy Department of Peking University is to not accept that there was a school of Zisi and Mencius in the pre-Qin period.

Li Cunshan (2) argues that the Guodian Chu slips are works of the Chen Liang 陳良 school of Confucianism, a branch of Confucianism in the Chu state that had Daoist characteristics.

In my opinion, we need to recognize the difference between pre-Qin schools of thought and the modern idea of a philosophical school before we can address this question properly. Furthermore, we cannot ignore the influence of local cultural characteristics on pre-Qin schools. We cannot simply refuse to recognize a known school or invent a non-existing one. A judgement about the existence of a school in this period should be based on a study of members of the school (including leading figures and followers), their theories (including their background, works and ideas), influences (transmission and regional characteristics), and the state of literary and scientific knowledge of the historical period as evidenced in contemporaneous literature.

*Paleographic Problems*

Li Xueqin (6) includes new analyses of *dao* 道 and other characters in the Guodian texts, not presented at the Dartmouth conference. Du Weiming (1) observes, from the perspective of the graphic construction of the characters used to denote key concepts on the Guodian slip-texts, that they take the body and mind/heart (*shen xin* 身心) as "humane" (*ren* 仁), the upright mind/heart (*zhi xin* 直心) as "virtuous" (*de* 德), one's own mind/heart (*wo xin* 我心) as "right" (*yi* 義), the blocked mind/heart (*ji xin* 旡心) as "covetous" (*ai* 愛), and the personal mind/heart (*ge xin* 各心) as "desiring" (*yu* 欲). These concepts now require a philosophical reconsideration from the perspective of body, mind, nature and fate as found in the Guodian slip-texts.

Li Jiahao (2) points out some problems in both the transcriptions and annotations of the *Guodian Chu Mu Zhujian*, and raises various issues in the transcription of the Chu slips, such as omissions, inaccurate characters, mistranscriptions, and problems in the annotations, including errors and omissions. Liu Lexian (1) discusses the relationship between the Guodian Chu slips and the Chu slips discovered at Jiudian, Jiangling, Hubei province and their transcriptions. Liu Yu also discussed the significance of the Guodian Chu slips for paleographic research at the Conference on Bamboo Slips from the Chu Tomb at Guodian, June 10, 1998, Beijing.

Zhang Guangyu and Yuan Guohua's *Guodian Chu Jian Yanjiu* includes the text and further paleographical research. There are also a number of other publications on this subject by scholars from Hong Kong and Taiwan.[13]

In the above, I have summarized a few of the most important issues that have been raised by Chinese scholars in the year following the Dartmouth Conference. The Guodian texts have received an extraordinary level of interest and a great many articles have been published in a very short period of time. Much of the scholarship is of high quality. However, there are also important problems with some of the research thus far published which could have serious consequences if attention is not drawn to them. The first is the most obvious; that is, the rush to publication, the deliberate formulation of new theories without sufficient consideration, and a lack of thoroughness in research. Another is lack of attention to related disciplines that require specialized training, such as paleography and archeology. The most serious of all is the usurpation of other scholars' ideas. Admittedly, this problem is limited, but it is nevertheless objectionable whenever it occurs.

The received texts are the key to the interpretation of the excavated texts. For example Peng Lin (1) compares a passage from *Xing Zi Ming Chu* to a passage to the "Tangong" chapter of the *Liji* and Li Jiahao (2) compares a passage from *Cheng Zhi Wen Zhi* to the "Yueji" chapter. Both are successful examples of such an approach. However, if we read the archeological texts only from the perspective of the received texts, we will inevitably misread individual characters and distort the meaning of the text as a whole.

The relationship between excavated texts from different sites is an aspect of research that is too readily neglected. Furthermore, with regard to the Guodian Chu slip-texts, the relationships between the different texts from this one tomb have not yet been systematically studied. The transcribers and annotators of the *Guodian Chu Mu Zhujian* have provided a firm foundation for future research from the point of view of paleography and archeology. They have also provided a provisional division into texts, and a sequence for reading the slips. However, their research awaits verification and further development. For example, the relationship between the *Laozi* and the *Tai Yi Sheng Shui* and that between the *Zi Yi*, *Zun De Yi*, and *Xing Zi Ming Chu*,

---

[13] See Ji Xusheng (1), Zhou Fengwu (1) and (2), Cheng Yuanmin (1), Chen Gaozhi (1), Yan Shixuan (1), Huang Ren'er (1).

etc., still require comparative and comprehensive research and analysis. They can provide us with a foundation for a new understanding of the history and development of pre-Qin thought. Du Weiming has described the Guodian texts as the tip of an iceberg and suggested that they should be researched together with the still unpublished Chu bamboo slips in the Shanghai Museum. It is this type of comparative and comprehensive research which is likely to achieve the most significant results in the future.

International Sinology represents "the rock of another mountain used to break open jade." In this article, I have only reviewed the research of Chinese scholars. I have not discussed the publications by foreign scholars in Chinese. This does not mean that foreign scholarly research can be neglected. On the contrary, research such as Sarah Allan's use of root metaphors, or Donald Harper's philological analysis, are stimulating, but since they are likely to be available to English readers in other forms, I have not included them herein.

At present, there are two basic approaches to the study of the Guodian Chu slips, those of the specialists in Daoism and Confucianism. The Dartmouth Conference focused on the *Laozi* and *Tai Yi Sheng Shui*. The workshop and conferences sponsored by the International Confucian Association have focused on the Confucian texts. Obviously every scholar's individual research is based upon his or her own background and interests. However, for the general understanding of the Guodian documents as a whole, any bias towards Confucianism or Daoism will inevitably affect our understanding of the intellectual significance of the Guodian tomb. The special significance of the Guodian texts is that Confucian and Daoist texts have been unearthed from the same tomb. Not only does this fail to reflect the attitude of opposition between Daoism and Confucianism with which we are familiar from later times, but furthermore, in some important passages, we find a sharing of ideas by the Daoist and Confucian schools. Thus, if we are to understand the Guodian Chu texts from the perspective of intellectual history in the pre-Qin period more generally, we must rethink the connection between pre-Qin Daoism and Confucianism. If we neglect this, the academic significance of the Guodian Chu slips will be greatly reduced, and we will miss the great opportunity which these newly discovered texts present to us for research in the coming century.

*BIBLIOGRAPHY OF CHINESE LITERATURE ON THE GUODIAN TEXTS*

*Books*

Cui Renyi 崔仁義 . *Jingmen Guodian Chu Jian Laozi Yanjiu* 荊門郭店楚簡老子研究 . Beijing: Kexue Press, 1998.

Ding Sixin 丁四新 . *Guodian Chu Mu Zhujian Sixiang Yanjiu* 郭店楚墓竹簡思想研究 . Wuhan University: Doctoral Dissertation, April 18, 1999.

Ding Yuanzhi 丁原植 . *Guodian Zhujian Laozi Shi Xi yu Yanjiu* 郭店竹簡老子釋析與研究 . Taibei: Wanjuanlou Tushu, 1998.

Jingmenshi Bowuguan 荊門市博物館 . *Guodian Chu Mu Zhujian* 郭店楚墓竹簡 . Beijing: Wenwu Press, 1998.

_____. *Guodian Chu Mu Zhujian Pujiben* 郭店楚墓竹簡普及本 . Beijing: Wenwu Press. Forthcoming.

Liu Zuxin 劉祖信 . *Guodian Chu Jian Shufa* 郭店楚簡書法 . Forthcoming.

Liu Xinfang 劉信芳 . *Jingmen Guodian Zhujian Laozi Jiegu* 荊門郭店竹簡老子解詁 . Taibei: Yiwen Yinshuguan, 1999.

Peng Hao 彭浩 . *Guodian Chu Jian Laozi Jiaodu* 郭店楚簡老子校讀 . Wuhan: Hubei Renmin Press. Forthcoming.

Pian Yuqian 駢宇騫 and Duan Shu'an 段書安 . *Ben Shiji Yilai Chutu Jianbo Gaishu* 本世紀以來出土簡帛概述 . Taibei: Wanjuanlou Tushu, 1999.

Zhang Guangyu 張光裕 and Yuan Guohua 袁國華 , eds. *Guodian Chu Jian Yanjiu* 郭店楚簡研究 (*Wenzi Bian* 文字編 ). Taibei: Yiwen Yinshuguan, 1999. Vol. 1.

*Journals and Newsletters with Special Issues*

[1] *Guoji Yixue Yanjiu* 國際易學研究 . Vol. 4. 1998.

[2] *Guoji Ruxue Lianhehui Jianbao* 國際儒學聯合會簡報 . No. 2. June, 1998.

[3] *Jianbo Yanjiu* 簡帛研究 . Vol. 3. 1998.

[4] *Zhongguo Zhexue* 中國哲學 . Vol. 20. 1999. Special Issue: *Guodian Chu Jian Yanjiu* 郭店楚簡研究 .

[5] *Zhang Yiren Xiansheng Qizhi Shouqing Lunwenji* 張以仁先生七秩壽慶論文集 . Part One. Taibei: Xuesheng Shuju, 1999.

[6] *Daojia Wenhua Yanjiu* 道家文化研究 . Vol. 17. 1999. Special Issue: *Guodian Chu Jian Zhuanhao* 郭店楚簡專號 .

[7] *Zhongguo Zhexue.* Vol. 21. Special Issue: *Guodian Jian yu Jingxue Yanjiu* 郭店簡與經學研究 . Forthcoming.

[8] *Guodian Chu Jian Guoji Xueshu Yantaohui* 郭店楚簡國際學術研討會 (*The International Symposium on Chu State Slips of Guodian*). Wuhan University. October 15–18, 1999. Publication of symposium papers forthcoming.

*Articles*

N.B. If an entry is followed by a number, e.g. "in [2]," the article was published in the collection cited above with the corresponding number.

Bai Xi 白奚 . (1) "Guodian Ru Jian yu Zhan'guo Huang-Lao Sixiang 郭店儒簡與戰國黃老思想 ." In [6].

Bai Yulan 白于藍 . (1) "Guodian Chu Mu Zhujian Shiwen Zhengwu Yili 郭店楚墓竹簡釋文正誤一例 ." *Jilin Daxue Shehui Kexue Xuebao* 吉林大學社會科學學報 . No. 152. 1998.2.

Chen Gaozhi 陳高志 . (1) "Guodian Chu Mu Zhujian *Zi Yi* Pian Bufen Wenzi Liding Jiantao 郭店楚墓竹簡緇衣篇部分文字隸定檢討 ." In [5].

Chen Guying 陳鼓應 . (1) "Chudu Jianben *Laozi* 初讀簡本老子 ." *Wenwu* 文物 . 1998.10 (October).

———. (2) "Cong Guodian Jianben Kan *Laozi* Shang Ren ji Shou Zhong Sixiang 從郭店簡本看老子尚仁及守中思想 ." In [6].

———. (3) "*Tai Yi Sheng Shui* yu *Xing Zi Ming Chu* Fawei 太一生水與性自命出發微 ." In [6].

Chen Lai 陳來 . (1) "Guodian Jian Ke Cheng *Jingmen Liji* 郭店簡可稱《荊門禮記》." *Renmin Zhengxie Bao* 人民政協報 . August 3, 1998.

———. (2) "Guodian Chu Jian zhi *Xing Zi Ming Chu* Pian Chutan 郭店楚簡之性自命出篇初探 ." *Kongzi Yanjiu* 孔子研究 . 1998.3 (September).

Chen Ming 陳明 . (1) "*Tang Yu zhi Dao* yu Zaoqi Rujia de Shehui Li'nian 唐虞之道與早期儒家的社會理念 ." In [4].

Chen Ning 陳寧 . (1) "*Guodian Chu Mu Zhujian* zhong de Rujia Renxing Yanlun Chutan 郭店楚墓竹簡中的儒家人性言論初探 ." *Zhongguo Zhexue Shi* (Ji Kan) 中國哲學史 ( 季刊 ). No. 24. 1998 (November).

Chen Wei 陳偉 . (1) "Guodian Chu Jian Bieshi 郭店楚簡別釋 ." *Jiang Han Kaogu* 江漢考古 . 1998.4.

———. (2) "Wenben Fuyuan Shi Yixiang Changqi Jianju de Gongzuo 文本復原是一項長期艱巨的工作 ." *Hubei Daxue Xuebao* (*Zhexue Shehui Kexue Ban*) 湖北大學學報 ( 哲學社會科學版 ). 1999.2 (March).

Cheng Fuwang 成復旺 . (1) "*Xing Zi Ming Chu* Jianlun 性自命出簡論 ." In [6].

Cheng Yuanmin 程元敏 . (1) "*Liji: Zhongyong, Fangji, Ziyi* Fei Chu yu *Zisizi* Kao 禮記・中庸、坊記、緇衣非出于子思子考 ." In [5].

Chitian Zhijiu 池田知久 (Ikeda Tomohisa). (1) "Shangchu Xingcheng Jieduan de *Laozi* Zui Gu Wenben — Guodian Chu Jian *Laozi* 尚處形成階段的老子最古文本-- 郭店楚簡老子 ." In [6].

Cui Renyi 崔仁義 . (1) "Jingmen Chu Mu Chutu de Zhujian *Laozi* Chutan 荊門楚墓出土的竹簡老子初探 ." *Jingmen Shehui Kexue* 荊門社會科學 . 1997.5.

———. (2) "Shi Lun Jingmen Zhujian *Laozi* de Niandai 試論荊門竹簡老子的年代 ." *Jingmen Daxue Xuebao* 荊門大學學報 . 1997.2.

Dai Kalin 戴卡琳 (Carine Defoort). (1) "*Tai Yi Sheng Shui* Chutan 太一生水初探 ." In [6].

Ding Sixin 丁四新 . (1) "Lue Lun Guodian Jianben *Laozi* Jia Yi Bing Sanzu de Lishixing Chayi 略論郭店簡本老子甲乙丙三組的歷時性差異 ." *Hubei Daxue Xuebao (Zhexue Shehui Kexue Ban)* 湖北大學學報 ( 哲學社會科學版 ). 1999.2 (March).

Ding Yuanzhi 丁原植 . (1) "Jiu Zhujian Ziliao Kan *Wenzi* yu *Jie Lao* Chuancheng 就竹簡資料看文子與解老傳承 ." In [6].

Du Weiming 杜維明 (Wei-ming Tu). (1) "Guodian Chu Jian yu Xianqin Ru Dao Sixiang de Chongxin Dingwei 郭店楚簡與先秦儒道思想的重新定位 ." In [4].

Gao Ming 高明 . (1) "Du Guodian *Laozi* 讀郭店《老子》 ." *Zhongguo Wenwu Bao* 中國文物報 . October 28, 1998.

Gao Zheng 高正 . (1) "Lun Qu Yuan yu Guodian Chu Mu Zhu Shu de Guanxi 論屈原與郭店楚墓竹書的關係 ." *Guangming Ribao* 光明日報 . July 2, 1999.

Guo Qiyong 郭齊勇 . (1) "Guodian Rujiajian de Yiyi yu Jiazhi 郭店儒家簡的意義 與價值 ." *Hubei Daxue Xuebao (Zhexue Shehui Kexue Ban)* 湖北大學學報 ( 哲 學社會科學版 ). No. 26. 1999.2.

Guo Yi 郭沂 . (1) "Cong Guodian Chu Jian *Laozi* Kan Laozi Qi Ren Qi Shu 從郭 店楚簡老子看老子其人其書 ." *Zhexue Yanjiu* 哲學研究 . 1998.7.

_____ . (2) "Shitan Chu Jian *Tai Yi Sheng Shui* ji qi yu Jianben *Laozi* de Guanxi 試探楚簡太一生水及其與簡本老子的關係 ." *Zhongguo Zhexue Shi* 中國哲學 史 . 1998.4.

_____ . (3) "Guodian Chu Jian *Tian Jiang Da Chang (Cheng Zhi Wen Zhi)* Pian Shuzheng 郭店楚簡天降大常 ( 成之聞之 ) 篇疏證 ." *Kongzi Yanjiu* 孔子研究 . 1998.3.

_____ . (4) "Chu Jian *Laozi* yu Laozi Gong'an — Jian ji Xianqin Zhexue Ruogan Wenti 楚簡老子與老子公案 - - 兼及先秦哲學若干問題 ." In [4].

_____ . (5) "Guodian Chu Jian *Cheng Zhi Wen Zhi* Pian Shuzheng 郭店楚簡成之 聞之篇疏證 ." In [4].

Han Dongyu 韓東育 . (1) "Guodian Chu Mu Zhujian *Tai Yi Sheng Shui* yu *Laozi* de Jige Wenti 郭店楚墓竹簡太一生水 與老子的幾個問題 ." *Shehui Kexue* 社會 科學 . 1999.2.

Han Lubo 韓祿伯 (Robert G. Henricks). (1) "Zhiguo Dagang — Shidu Guodian *Laozi* Jiazu de Diyi Bufen 治國大綱 - - 試讀郭店老子甲組的第一部分 ." In [6].

Han Renzhi 韓忍之 . (1) "Han Fei Zhu *Jie Lao Yu Lao* Shi *Wu Qian Yan* Shifou Yi Ming Wei *Laozi* — Jian Lun Sima Qian Panduan de Shizai Xing 韓非著解 老喻老時〝五千言〞是否已名為老子 - - 兼論司馬遷判斷的實在性 ." *Dongbei Shida Xuebao (Zhexue Shehui Kexue Ban)* 東北師大學報 ( 哲學社會 科學版 ). 1999.2 (March).

He Bilai 賀碧來 (Isabelle Robinet). (1) "Lun *Tai Yi Sheng Shui* 論太一生水 ." In [6].

He Feng 何鋒 and Xu Yide 徐義德 . (1) "Jingmen Chutu *Laozi* deng Wu Bu Dianji Zhujian wei Wo Guo Muqian Faxian Zui Zao, Zui Wanzheng, Shuliang Zui Duo zhi Chu Jian 荊門出土《老子》等五部典籍竹簡為我國目

前發現最早、最完整數量最多之楚簡." *Renmin Ribao* (*Haiwaiban*) 人民日報 - 海外版 . Feb. 7, 1995.

_____. (2) "Jingmen Chutu *Laozi* deng Wu bu Zhujian Dianji 荊門出土《老子》等五部竹簡典籍." *Zhongguo Wenwu Bao* 中國文物報 . March 19, 1995.

Huang Ren'er 黃人二 . (1) "Guodian Chu Jian *Lu Mu Gong Wen Zi Si* Kaoshi 郭店楚簡魯穆公問子思考釋." In [5].

Ji Xusheng 季旭昇 . (1) "Du *Guodian Chu Mu Zhujian* Zhaji: Bian, Jue wei Qi Zuo, Min Fu Ji Zi 讀郭店楚墓竹簡札記：卞、絕為棄作、民復季子." *Zhongguo Wenzi* 中國文字 . *Yiwen Yinshuguan*. New series. No. 24. December, 1998.

Jiang Guanghui 姜廣輝 . (1) "Guodian Chu Jian yu Yuandian Ruxue — Guonei Xueshujie Guanyu Guodian Chu Jian de Yanjiu (1) 郭店楚簡與原典儒學 - - 國內學術界關於郭店楚簡的研究（一）." *Shu Pin* 書品 . 1999.1.

_____. (2) "Guodian Chu Jian yu *Zisizi* — Jian Tan Guodian Chu Jian de Sixiangshi Yiyi 郭店楚簡與子思子 - - 兼談郭店楚簡的思想史意義." *Zhexue Yanjiu* 哲學研究 . 1998.7. Reprinted in [4].

_____. (3) "Guodian Yihao Mu Muzhu Shi Shui 郭店一號墓墓主是誰?" In [4].

_____.(4) "Guodian Chu Jian yu Zaoqi Daojia — Guonei Xueshujie Guanyu Guodian Chu Jian de Yanjiu (2) 郭店楚簡與早期道家 - - 國內學術界關於郭店楚簡的研究（二）." *Shu Pin* 書品 . 1999.2.

Jingmenshi Bowuguan 荊門市博物館 . "Jingmen Guodian Yihao Chu Mu 荊門郭店一號楚墓." *Wenwu* 文物 . 1997.7 (July).

Lei Dunhe 雷敦和 (Edmund Ryden). (1) "Guodian *Laozi*: Yixie Qianti de Taolun 郭店老子：一些前提的討論." In [6].

Li Cunshan 李存山 . (1) "Du Chu Jian *Zhong Xin zhi Dao* ji Qita 讀楚簡忠信之道及其他." In [4].

_____. (2) "Cong Guodian Chu Jian Kan Zaoqi Dao Ru Guanxi 從郭店竹簡看早期道儒關系." In [4], [6].

Li Jiahao 李家浩 . (1) "Guanyu Guodian *Laozi* Yi Zu Yi zhi Can Jian de Pinjie 關於郭店《老子》乙組一支殘簡的拼接." *Zhongguo Wenwu Bao* 中國文物報 . October 28, 1998.

_____. (2) "Du *Guodian Chu Mu Zhujian* Suoyi 讀郭店楚墓竹簡瑣議." In [4].

Li Jinyun 李縉雲 . (1) "Guodian Chu Jian Yanjiu Jinkuang 郭店楚簡研究近況." *Guji Zhengli Chuban Qingkuang Jianbao* 古籍整理出版情況簡報 . April 1999.

Li Ling 李零 . (1) "Du Guodian Chu Jian *Tai Yi Sheng Shui* 讀郭店楚簡太一生水." In [6].

_____. (2) "Guodian Chu Jian Jiaodu Ji 郭店楚簡校讀記." In [6].

Li Xueqin 李學勤 . (1) "Jingmen Guodian Chu Jian Suojian Guan Yin Yishuo 荊門郭店楚簡所見關尹遺說." *Zhongguo Wenwu Bao* 中國文物報 . April 8, 1998. Reprinted in [4].

_____. (2) "Jingmen Guodian Chu Jian zhong de *Zisizi* 荊門郭店楚簡中的子思子." In *Wenwu Tiandi* 文物天地 . 1998.2. Reprinted in [4].

_____. (3) "Xian Qin Rujia Zhuzuo de Zhongda Faxian 先秦儒家著作的重大發現." *Renmin Zheng Xie Bao* 人民政協報. June 8, 1998. Reprinted in [4].

_____. (4) "Cong Jianbo Yiji *Wu Xing* Tandao *Daxue* 從簡帛佚籍五行談到大學." *Kongzi Yanjiu* 孔子研究. 1998.3 (September).

_____. (5) "Guodian Jian yu *Liji* 郭店簡與禮記." *Zhongguo Zhexue Shi* 中國哲學史. 1998.4.

_____. (6) "Shuo Guodian Jian *Dao* Zi 說郭店簡 ˋ道 ´字." In [3].

_____. (7) "Shi Guodian Jian Cai Gong zhi Guming 釋郭店簡祭公之顧命." *Wenwu* 文物. 1998.7 (July). Reprinted in [4].

_____. (8) "Guodian Chu Jian yu Rujia Jingji 郭店楚簡與儒家經籍." In [4].

_____. (9) "Tian Ren zhi Fen 天人之分." In *Zhongguo Chuantong Zhexue Xinlun* 中國傳統哲學新論. Jiuzhou Tushu Press, 1999.

_____. (10) "Lun Shanghai Bowuguan suo Cang de Yizhi *Zi Yi* Jian 論上海博物館所藏的一支緇衣簡." *Qi Lu Xuekan* 齊魯學刊. 1999.2.

_____. (11) "*Tai Yi Sheng Shui* de Shushu Jieshi 太一生水的數術解釋." In [6].

_____. (12) "Guodian Jian yu *Yueji* 郭店簡與樂記." *Zhang Dainian Xiansheng Zhushou Lunwenji* 張岱年先生祝壽論文集. Forthcoming.

Li Zehou 李澤厚. (1) "Chudu Guodian ZhujianYinxiang Jiyao 初讀郭店竹簡印象紀要." *Shiji Xinmeng* 世紀新夢. Hefei: Anhui Wenyi Press. October 1998. Reprinted in [6].

Liao Mingchun 廖名春. (1) "Chu Jian *Laozi* Jiaoshi zhi Yi 楚簡老子校釋之一." *Huaxue* 華學. Vol. 3. 1998.

_____. (2) "Guodian Chu Jian Rujia Zhuzuo Kao 郭店楚簡儒家著作考." *Kongzi Yanjiu* 孔子研究. 1998.3 (September).

_____. (3) "Chu Jian *Laozi* Kaoshi (2) 楚簡老子考釋 ( 二 )." In [3].

_____. (4) "Jingmen Guodian Chu Jian yu Xianqin Ruxue 荊門郭店楚簡與先秦儒家." In [4].

_____. (5) "*Laozi* Wuwei er Wu Buwei Shuo Xinzheng 老子無為而無不為說新證." In [4].

Liu Lexian 劉樂賢. (1) "Du Guodian Chu Jian Zhaji San Ze 讀郭店楚簡札記三則." In [4].

Liu Zonghan 劉宗漢. (1) "Youguan Jingmen Guodian Yihao Chu Mu de Liangge Wenti — Mu Zhuren Shenfen yu Ru Dao Jianxi" 有關荊門郭店一號楚墓的兩個問題 - - 墓主人身份與儒道兼習." In [4].

Liu Zuxin 劉祖信. (1) "Jingmen Chu Mu de Jing Ren Faxian 荊門楚墓的驚人發現." *Wenwu Tiandi* 文物天地. 1995.6 (November).

Liu Zuxin 劉祖信 and Mei Xun'an 梅訓安. (1) "Jingmen Chutu Wo Guo Zui Zao Zhujian *Laozi* 荊門出土我國最早竹簡老子." *Renmin Ribao (Haiwaiban)* 人民日報 - 海外版. Feb. 8, 1995.

Liu Zuxin 劉祖信 and Cui Renyi 崔仁義. (1) "Jingmen Zhujian *Laozi* bing fei Duihua Ti 荊門竹簡《老 子》并非對話體." *Zhongguo Wenwu Bao* 中國文物報. August 20, 1995.

Luo Hao 羅浩 (Harold Roth). (1) "Guodian *Laozi* Duiwen zhong Yixie Fangfalun Wenti 郭店老子對文中一些方法論問題." In [6].

Pang Pu 龐朴. (1) "Ru Lian Zhaokai — *Guodian Chu Jian* Yantaohui 儒聯召開《郭店楚簡》研討會." In [2].

_____. (2) "Gumu Xinzhi — Man du Guodian Chu Jian 古墓新知 - 漫讀郭店楚簡." In [2]. Reprinted in [4].

_____. (3) "Chu Du Guodian Chu Jian 初讀郭店楚簡." *Lishi Yanjiu* 歷史研究. 1998.4.

_____. (4) "Kong Meng zhi Jian — Guodian Chu Jian de Sixiangshi Diwei 孔孟之間 - 郭店楚簡的思想史地位." *Zhongguo Shehui Kexue* 中國社會科學. 1998.5.

_____. (5) "Zhu Bo *Wuxing* Pian Bijiao 竹帛五行篇比較." In [4].

_____. (6) "Fu XinYue Pi 撫心曰闕." In [4].

_____. (7) "*Yucong* Yishuo 語叢臆説." In [4].

_____. (8) "Kong Meng zhijian — Guodian Chu Jian zhong de Rujia Xin Xing Shuo 孔孟之間 - - 郭店楚簡中的儒家心性説." In [4].

_____. (9) "Yizhong Youji de Yuzhou Shengcheng Tushi — Jieshao Chu Jian *Tai Yi Sheng Shui* 一種有機的宇宙生成圖式 - - 介紹楚簡太一生水." In [6].

Peng Hao 彭浩. (1) "Tan Guodian *Laozi* — Fen Zhang he Zhang Ci 談郭店老子 - - 分章和章次." *Zhongguo Wenwu Bao* 中國文物報. October 28, 1998.

_____. (2) "Guodian Chu Jian *Zi Yi* de Fenzhang ji Xiangguan Wenti 郭店楚簡緇衣的分章及相關問題." In [3].

_____. (3) "Guodian Yihao Mu de Niandai yu Jianben *Laozi* de Jiegou 郭店一號墓的年代與簡本老子的結構." In [6].

Peng Lin 彭林. (1) "Guodian Chu Jian *Xing Zi Ming Chu* Bushi 郭店楚簡性自命出補釋." In [4].

Qian Xun 錢遜. (1) "*Liu De* Zhupian Suojian de Ruxue Sixiang 六德諸篇所見的儒學思想." In [4].

Qiang Yu 強昱. (1) "*Tai Yi Sheng Shui* yu Gudai de Tai Yi Guan 太一生水與古代的太一觀." In [6].

Qiu Xigui 裘錫圭. (1) "Jiaguwen zhong de Jian yu Shi 甲骨文中的見與視." Zhongyang Yanjiuyuan Shiyu Yanjiusuo and Taiwan Shifan Daxue, eds. *Jiaguwen Faxian Yibai Zhounian Xueshu Yantaohui Lunwenji* 甲骨文發現一百週年學術研討會論文集. May, 1998.

_____. (2) "Guodian *Laozi* Jian Chutan 郭店老子簡初探." In [6].

Rao Zongyi 饒宗頤. (1) "*Zi Yi* Ling Jian 緇衣零簡." *Xueshu Jilin* 學術集林. Vol. 9. 1996. Reprinted in *Qin Han Shi Lun Cong* 秦漢史論叢. Vol. 7. 1998.

Wang Baoxuan 王葆玹. (1) "Shilun Guodian Chu Jian Gepian de Zhuanzuo Shidai ji qi Beijing — Jianlun Guodian ji Baoshan Chu Mu de Shidai Wenti 試論郭店楚簡各篇的撰作時代及其背景 - - 兼論郭店及包山楚墓的時代問題." *Zhexue Yanjiu* 哲學研究. April, 1999. Reprinted in [4].

Wang Bo 王博. (1) "Guodian Zhujian zhong Suojian Ru Dao zhi Guanxi 郭店竹簡中所見儒道之關系." In [6].

_____. (2) "Guanyu Guodian Chu Mu Zhujian *Laozi* de Jiegou yu Xingzhi — Jianlun qi yu Tongxing Ben *Laozi* de Guanxi 關于郭店楚墓竹簡老子的結構與性質－－兼論其與通行本老子的關係." In [6].

_____. (3) "Zhang Dainian Xiansheng Tan Jingmen Guodian Zhujian *Laozi* 張岱年先生談荊門郭店竹簡老子." In [6].

Wang Zhongjiang 王中江. (1) "Guodian Zhujian *Laozi* Lueshuo 郭店竹簡老子略説." In [4].

Wei Qipeng 魏啟鵬. (1) "Chu Jian *Laozi* Jianshi 楚簡老子柬釋." In [6].

Xing Wen 邢文. (1) "Guodian Chu Jian Yanjiu Shuping 郭店楚簡研究述評." *Minzu Yishu* 民族藝術. 1998.3.

_____. (2) "Chu Jian *Wu Xing* Shilun 楚簡五行試論." *Wenwu* 文物. 1998.10 (October).

_____. (3) "Guodian Chu Jian yu Guoji Hanxue 郭店楚簡與國際漢學." *Shupin* 書品. 1998.4.

_____. (4) "Lun Guodian *Laozi* yu Jinben *Laozi* Bu Shu Yixi — Chu Jian *Tai Yi Sheng Shui* jiqi Yiyi 論郭店老子與今本老子不屬一系－－楚簡太一生水及其意義." In [4].

_____. (5) "*Mengzi Wanzhang* yu Chu Jian *Wuxing* 孟子·萬章與楚簡五行." In [4].

Xu Hongxing 徐洪興. (1) "Yigu yu Xingu — cong Guodian Zhujian Ben *Laozi* Chutu Huigu Benshiji Guanyu Laozi Qiren Qishu de Zhenglun 疑古與信古－－從郭店楚簡本老子出土回顧本世紀關于老子其人其書的爭論." *Fudan Xuebao (Shehui Kexue Ban)* 復旦學報(社會科學版). Nov. 1, 1998.

Xu Kangsheng 許抗生. (1) "Chudu Guodian Chu Jian *Laozi* 初讀郭店楚簡老子." In [4].

_____. (2) "Chudu *Tai Yi Sheng Shui* 初讀太一生水." In [6].

Yan Shixuan 顏世鉉. (1) "Guodian Chu Jian Qianshi 郭店楚簡淺釋." In [5].

Yin Zhenhuan 尹振環. (1) "Ye Tan Chu Jian *Laozi* qi Shu — yu Guo Yi Tongzhi Shangque 也談楚簡老子其書－－與郭沂同志商榷." *Zhexue Yanjiu* 哲學研究. April 1999.

Yuan Guohua 袁國華. (1) "Guodian Chu Jian Wenzi Kaoshi Shiyi Ze 郭店楚簡文字考釋十一則." *Zhongguo Wenzi* 中國文字. New series. No. 24. December, 1998.

Yue Jin 躍進. (1) "Zhenfen Ren Xin de Kaogu Faxian — Lueshuo Guodian Chu Mu Zhujian de Xueshu Shi Yiyi 振奮人心的考古發現－－略説郭店楚墓竹簡的學術史意義." *Wen Shi Zhishi* 文史知識. 1998.8.

Zhang Jiliang 張吉良. (1) "Cong Lao Dan *Laozi* dao Taishi Dan *Daodejing* 從老聃老子到太史儋道德經." *Jiangxi Shehui Kexue* 江西社會科學. 1999.2.

Zhang Liwen 張立文. (1) "Guodian *Chu Mu Zhujian* de Pianti 郭店楚墓竹簡的篇題." In [4].

_____. (2) "*Qiongda Yi Shi* de Shi yu Yu 窮達以時的時與遇." In [4].

_____. (3) "Lun Jianben *Laozi* yu Rujia Sixiang de Hubu Huji 論簡本老子與儒家思想的互補互濟." In [6].

Zhao Jianwei 趙建偉. (1) "Guodian Zhujian *Laozi* Jiaoshi 郭店竹簡老子校釋." In [6].

_____. (2) "Guodian Zhujian *Zhong Xin Zhi Dao, Xing Zi Ming Chu* Jiaoshi 郭店竹簡忠信之道、性自命出校釋." In [6].

_____. (3) "Guodian Chu Mu Zhujian *Tai Yi Sheng Shui* Shuzheng 郭店楚墓竹簡太一生水疏證." In [6].

Zhou Fengwu 周鳳五. (1) "Guodian Chu Jian *Zhong Xin zhi Dao* Kaoshi 郭店楚簡忠信之道考釋." *Zhongguo Wenzi* 中國文字. New series. Vol. 24. 1998 (December).

_____. (2) "Guodian Chu Jian Shizi Zhaji 郭店楚簡識字札記." In [5].

Zhou Guidian 周桂鈿. (1) "Jingmen Zhujian *Zi Yi* Jiaodu Zhaji 荊門竹簡緇衣校讀札記." In [4].

Zuo Peng 左鵬. "Jingmen Zhujian *Laozi* Chutu Yiyi 荊門竹簡《老子》出土意義." *Zhongguo Wenwu Bao* 中國文物報. June 25, 1995.

*Conference Reports*

"Meiguo Guodian *Laozi* Guoji Yantaohui Zongshu 美國郭店《老子》國際研討會綜述." In [2]. Reprinted in [4].

"*Guodian Chu Mu Zhujian* Xueshu Yantaohui Shuyao 《郭店楚墓竹簡》學術研討會述要." In [2]. Reprinted in [4].

"Guoji Rulian Shouci Chu Jian Yantaohui 國際儒聯首次楚簡研討會." In [4].

Wang Bo 王博. "Meiguo Damusi Daxue Guodian Laozi Guoji Xueshu Taolunhui Jiyao 美國達慕思大學郭店老子國際學術討論會紀要." In [6].

Xing Wen 邢文. "Ruxue de Renlun: Guoji Xueshu Yantaohui Shuyao 儒學的人論國際學術研討會述要." *Guoji Ruxue Yanjiu* 國際儒學研究. No. 5. November, 1998.

Xing Wen 邢文 and Li Jinyun 李縉雲. "Guodian *Laozi* Guoji Yantaohui Zongshu 郭店老子國際研討會綜述." *Wenwu*. 1998.9.

Zhang Yukun 張玉昆. "Beijing Guodian Chu Mu Zhujian Xueshu Taolunhui Zongshu 北京郭店楚墓竹簡學術討論會綜述" *Guoji Ruxue Yanjiu* 國際儒學研究. No. 5. November, 1998.

*News Items*

"Wo Guo Kaogu Shi shang You Yi zhong Da Faxian — Zui Zao Zhujian *Laozi* deng Dianji zai Jingmen Chutu 我國考古史上又一重大發現 – – 最早竹簡老子等典籍在荊門出土." *Hubei Ribao* 湖北日報. December 15, 1994.

"Jingmen Chutu Zhanguo Shiqi Wu Bu Dianji " 荊門出土戰國時期五部典籍." *Zhongguo Wenwu Bao* 中國文物報. January 25, 1995.

"Bamboo Slips of Classics Unearthed." *Beijing Review*. April 13–16, 1995.

"Zhanguo Zhujian Lu Zhen Rong 戰國竹簡露真容." *Wen Hui Bao* 文匯報.

January 5, 1999.

"Shanghai Bowuguan Cong Xianggang Gouhui Hanjian Zhanguo Zhujian Chu Lu Zhen Rong 上海博物館從香港購回罕見戰國竹簡初露真容." *Aozhou Xin Bao* 澳洲新報 . January 8, 1999.

"Guodian Chu Jian Yanjiu Zouxiang Shijie — Shi *Laozi* Chengwei Zhongguo Dianji zhong Zui Wanzheng de Banben Xulie 郭店楚簡研究走向世界 – – 使《老子》成為中國典籍中最完整的版本序列." *Changjiang Ribao* 長江日報 . July 11, 1997 (afternoon edition).

# INDEX

abdication and succession 107, 177–178, 252, 253
    origin of theory 253, SEE ALSO *Tang Yu zhi Dao* 唐虞之道, *Zhong Xin zhi Dao* 忠信之道

accelerator mass-spectrometry 119–120; SEE ALSO archeological methods

accretion of textual material 80–81
    accretion of *Laozi* 老子 239; SEE ALSO models

additions 94; SEE ALSO lacunae, textual errors

administrative texts 126

affiliation of texts 39; SEE ALSO filiation

*ai* 愛 255

allographs; SEE orthography

*an* 安 199, 223, 236

*Analects*; SEE *Lunyu* 論語 ; SEE ALSO Confucianism

ancient Chinese 53, 58, 60, 62, 67, 92, 129
    paleographic material 53, 57; script 66, 129; SEE ALSO linguistics

anthologies (literary and political) 101

anthology model; SEE model

arrangement of passages 36, 60, 65, 74, 87, 144; SEE ALSO *zhang* 章, *ju* 句, bamboo slips (arrangement, punctuation and chapter divisions, reconstruction), Guodian (arrangement of chapters)

archeological methods 119, 256
    material evidence 119, SEE ALSO carbon dating, chemical analysis, tree ring dating; *zhengli* 整理 (post-excavation work) 121

astronomy 164, 231, 250
    equinoxes 164; pole star, SEE *Tai Yi* 太一

artisans 124; SEE ALSO *shi* 師

authenticity; SEE textual history

authorship 74, 78, 81, 82–83, 87

bamboo objects 26, 27–28
    tablets 11–12

bamboo slips 11–12, 19, 30, 35–36, 55–58, 62, 107, 110, 121, 123, 125–126, 179, 189–190, 231
    dating of 107, 120, 135, 245; physical appearance 30, 33–34, 78, 121, 122, 133, 162, 247; script 78, 120, 121, 127, 129; state of 33, 118, 121; damaged slips 30, 33, 36, 118, 121, 191, 248, 254; intact slips 30; cleaning, conservation and treatment 4, 33, 121, 135; separation 33–34, 65, 121, 122; punctuation and chapter divisions 4, 33, 34–36, 65, 68, 82, 89, 115, 134–135, 135–142, 152, 190, 195, 210, 217, 248, black squares 34–35, 134, 135, 136, 152, short strokes 34–35, 134, 135, 136, 140, tadpole mark 35–36, 134, 136–137, 154; arrangement of sequence 4, 36, 60, 65, 68, 75, 78, 94, 121, 183, 240, 245, 247–248, 254; reconstruction 4, 33, 36, 118, 121, 248; preparation for publication 3, 115, 121, 189–190; transcription and annotation 33, 36, 56, 121–122, 146–147, 151, 162, 183, 191, 245, 255–256; rules 122, 162, 245; SEE ALSO *Daodejing*

Ban Gu 班固 73 fn9; SEE ALSO *Hanshu* 漢書

Baoshan 包山 tombs 18, 21, 31, 35–36, 55, 56–57, 58, 107, 119, 126, 137, 223, 246

"Beifeng, Gufeng 北風 · 谷風"; SEE *Shijing* 詩經

bells 12; SEE ALSO inscriptions

# CITATIONS FROM THE GUODIAN *LAOZI* 老子

References are to Edmund Ryden's edition, above, pp. 195–227

KEY:
RT        Either Wang Bi 王弼 or Heshang Gong 河上公 recension
MWD       Mawangdui
MWD A/B   Mawangdui *Laozi* 老子 , Copies A and B
Page references are the unitalicized numerals.


## Slips Mentioned in Clusters

| | | |
|---|---|---|
| *A 1–20* 36, 137, 154 | | |
| *A 1:1 to 20:28* 36 | | |
| *A 21–23* 36 | | |
| *A 21–24* 137, 154 | | |
| *A 25–32* 137, 154, 155 | | |
| *A 33–39* 137, 154 | | |
| *B 1–8* 152 | | |
| *B 1:1 to 8:23* 157 | | |
| *B 3:8 to 8:23* 139–141 | *MWD* 140 | *RT* 139 |


## A I 1:1 to 2:18 [RT 19/ MWD 63]

| | | |
|---|---|---|
| *A 1:1* 40, 55, 190 | | *RT* 55 |
| *A 1:1–4* 59–60 | *MWD A* 60 | *RT* 59–60 |
| *A 1:1 to 2:18* 34–35, 131–132, 135, 149–151 | *MWD B* 149–151 | *RT* 34–35, 132, 135, 149–151 |
| *A 1:1–24* 160–161 | | *RT* 160–161 |
| *A 1:2* 89, 190 | | |
| *A 1:4* 41 | | |
| *A 1:9–12* 55–56 | | *RT* 55–56 |
| *A 1:11* 92, 98–99 | | |
| *A 1:11–12* 191 | | |
| *A 1:13–16* 36 | *MWD A* 36 | *RT* 36 |
| *A 1:15–18* 57–58 | | *RT* 57–58 |
| *A 1:16* 93 | | |
| *A 1:17* 55 | | *RT* 55 |
| *A 1:17–20* 236, 249 | | |
| *A 1:17–24* 60–61, 66–67, 236–237 | *MWD A/B* 60–61, 66–67 | *RT* 60–61, 66–67 |
| *A 1:25 to 2:4* 37 | | *RT* 37 |
| *A 1:25 to 2:10* 67–68 | *MWD A/B* 67–68 | |
| *A 2* 60 | | |
| *A 2:3* 98–99 | | |
| *A 2:5* 100 | | |
| *A 2:5 to 2:18* 37 | *MWD A* 37 | |
| *A 2:7* 101 | | |
| *A 2:11–14* 59 | | *RT* 59 |

Received Text *Laozi* 老子 Chapters Mentioned

CPSIA information can be obtained
at www.ICGtesting.com
Printed in the USA
BVOW03s1802121017
497478BV00001B/29/P